MAJOR & MRS H

Battlefield Guid

MARKET-GAF

Leopoldsburg-Eindhoven-Nijmegen-Arnhem-Oosterbeek

For Diana

Front cover: The Nijmegen Bridge with German 3.7cm anti-tank gun

Airborne Museum, The Hartenstein, Oosterbeek

MAJOR & MRS HOLT'S
Battlefield Guide to

MARKET-GARDEN

Leopoldsburg-Eindhoven-Nijmegen-Arnhem-Oosterbeek

Tonie and Valmai Holt

Leo Cooper

By the same authors:

Picture Postcards of the Golden Age: A Collector's Guide
Till the Boys Come Home: the Picture Postcards of the First World War
The Best of Fragments from France by Capt Bruce Bairnsfather
In Search of the Better 'Ole: The Life, Works and Collectables of
Bruce Bairnsfather. Revised edition, 2001
Picture Postcard Artists: Landscapes, Animals and Characters
Stanley Gibbons Postcard Catalogue: 1980, 1981, 1982, 1984, 1985, 1987
Germany Awake! The Rise of National Socialism illustrated by
Contemporary Postcards
I'll Be Seeing You: the Picture Postcards of World War II
Holts' Battlefield Guidebooks: Normandy-Overlord/Market-Garden/Somme/Ypres
Battlefields of the First World War: A Traveller's Guide
Visitor's Guide: the Normandy Landing Beaches
Major & Mrs Holt's Concise Battlefield Guide to the Ypres Salient
Major & Mrs Holt's Battle Maps: The Somme/The Ypres Salient/
Normandy/Gallipoli
Major & Mrs Holt's Battlefield Guide to the Somme + Battle Map
Major & Mrs Holt's Battlefield Guide to the Ypres Salient + Battle Map
Major & Mrs Holt's Battlefield Guide to the Normandy Landing Beaches + Battle Map
Major & Mrs Holt's Battlefield Guide to Gallipoli + Battle Map
Violets From Oversea: 25 Poets of the First World War
Reprinted as 'Poets of the Great War'
My Boy Jack: The Search for Kipling's Only Son

First published in 2001 by LEO COOPER an imprint of Pen & Sword Books Ltd
47 Church Street, Barnsley, South Yorkshire, S70 2AS

A CIP catalogue record for this book is available from the British Library

ISBN 0 85052 785-6

CONTENTS

PICTURE ACKNOWLEDGEMENTS.

Our thanks to the following for supplying us with pictures and giving us permission to reproduce them:
Alan Denman p272; Alan Hartley p234; Aldershot Airborne Museum p42;
Berry de Reus/Hartenstein Museum p2/3; Bob Vranken p54 (Limbosch);
CWGC p63 (b&w); Den Dungen Market Garden Comité p64, p70 *Bas Reliefs*;
Eindhoven Lights Festival Committee p39; G. H. Fonteyn p67;
Frans Ammerlaan p186 Nos 3/3a, p187 Nos 4b/4c, p 242 (façade); Hartenstein Airborne Museum p215 No3;
Jan Brouwer p186 No 2, 187 No 5, 191 (SLI/RDG);
Overloon National Oorlogs Museum p82 (exterior/tank);
Quinta Buma Fotografie p278 (Marchers); *The Times* p8/p21

ABBREVIATIONS/VOCABULARY

Abbreviations and acronyms used for military units are listed below. Many of these are printed in full at intervals throughout the text to aid clarity. Others are explained where they occur.

AA	Anti-Aircraft	Mil	Military
AB	Airborne	MM	Military Medal
ACC	Army Catering Corps	MOW	Military Order of William
Acfn	Aircraftsman	Nav	Navigator
AGRE	Army Group Royal Engineers	OP	Observation Point
AL	Air Landing	PIR	Parachute Infantry Regiment
BR	British	Pz	German Panzer units
Can	Canadian	RA	Royal Artillery
CCS	Casualty Clearing Station	RAMC	Royal Army Medical Corps
Coll	Collective	RAP	Regimental Aid Post
Coy	Company	RASC	Royal Army Service Corps
CWGC	Commonwealth War Graves	RC	Roman Catholic
	Commission	RCIC	Royal Canadian Infantry Corps
DZ	Dropping Zone	RDG	Royal Dragoon Guards
DCLI	Duke of Cornwall's Light Infantry	RE	Royal Engineers
DFC	Distinguished Flying Cross	REME	Royal Electrical and Mechanical
DFM	Distinguished Flying Medal		Engineers
DLI	Durham Light Infantry	RHA	Royal Horse Artillery
HCR	Household Cavalry Regiment	RIR	Royal Irish Rifles
HLI	Highland Light Infantry	RNF	Royal Northumberland Fusiliers
Int	Intelligence	R Sigs	Royal Signals
IPC	Independent Parachute Company	RV	Rendezvous
KORR	King's Own Royal Regiment	RUR	Royal Ulster Rifles
KOSB	King's Own Scottish Borderers	RWF	Royal Welch Fusiliers
KOYLI	King's Own Yorkshire Light	SA	Sturm Abteilung
	Infantry	SP	Self-propelling gun
KRRC	King's Royal Rifle Corps	Sp Mem	Special Memorial
KSLI	King's Shropshire Light Infantry	SWB	South Wales Borderers
Lt	Light	VVV	Dutch Tourist Authority
LZ	Landing Zone	Wksp	Workshop
MiD	Mentioned in Despatches	WO	Warrant Officer
Middx	Middlesex		

INTRODUCTION

This is a book which is primarily about Operation MARKET-GARDEN: the reasons for it, the plans for it, how they were put into practice, how the Operation evolved and the reasons why it failed in its major aims. It sets out to show the modern visitor where these momentous events took place and what there is to see there.

However, much of that same ground on which the triumphs and disasters of MARKET-GARDEN were played out was also the scene of earlier and later campaigns. Before the 17 September 1944 start of Operation MARKET-GARDEN there was the 1940 invasion of Holland by the Germans, gallant defence by the Dutch, acts of resistance during the Occupation, sites of German reprisal and the air war. When the men of Arnhem had been evacuated over the Rhine there were the winter of 1944/45 battles in The Island, followed by the thrusts into Germany from the Groesbeek area, of Operation VERITABLE in February 1945, leading up to the RHINE CROSSING in March. Memorials to these battles often adjoin those to MARKET-GARDEN and in several of the military cemeteries on the Itineraries in this book casualties from each year of the war lie buried close to each other.

It would, therefore, be invidious to be blinkered about only including MARKET-GARDEN information along the routes. A man who died for his country and for liberty in 1940 or in 1945 deserves as much homage as a man of September 1944. The same concept applies to memorials to a Regiment's gallantry. Therefore, while MARKET-GARDEN is the main theme, items of historical interest in earlier and later campaigns that are along the main Itineraries are described in brief as they occur and some of them are described in Extra Visits.

So much has been written about this Operation, so many post-mortems and dissections, so many wise conclusions made by armchair historians in later years. To use modern terminology, so much spin has been put on the events, especially at contentious points such as the Nijmegen Bridge where American accounts often seem to bear little relation to British ones. Some regimental histories naturally wish to show their men in the most favourable light and are economical with the truth regarding the contributions of others. The personal memories of veterans can inevitably be enhanced or diluted by what they have subsequently read or discussed.

One may therefore be justified in asking two pertinent questions: 'Why another book about MARKET-GARDEN' and 'What was the true story of MARKET-GARDEN and the reasons for its ultimate failure?'

The first answer is that this book covers the entire Corridor in detail. No other guide book does. Very few 'history' books do. We started studying MARKET-GARDEN in 1978 when we were preparing our first battlefield tour to the area. In the last nearly quarter of a century we have been amassing information, in large part from veterans who accompanied us on the ground (many of whose memories we taped) or who corresponded with us, and from local people who either lived through the battles or who have made in-depth studies of what happened in their area in September-October 1944. Over the past two years we have intensified our research, revisiting Belgium and the Netherlands many times and have formed a view that offers answers to the second question, though we will often ask the reader to decide. We have certainly uncovered much new information, some of it highly controversial, and are convinced that the principal keys to the success or failure of the Operation were the actions around the Nijmegen Road Bridge.

Ultimately, at this distance in time, we have been forced to accept that there will be some questions which will remain forever unanswered and therein lies the reason for the continuing fascination of the campaign.

Tonie and Valmai Holt,
Sandwich, 2001

Remarkable photograph showing Irish Guards Tanks under attack just north of Joe's Bridge at the very start of OPERATION MARKET   Courtesy of The Times

How To Use This Guide

History Of The Battles/Personal Stories

This book is designed to guide the visitor around the salient features, memorials, museums and cemeteries, landing and dropping zones of the MARKET-GARDEN battlefield, and to provide sufficient information about those places to allow an elemental understanding of what happened where and when.

Prior To Your Visit/Timing It

Before setting out on a visit, read this section thoroughly and mark up the recommended maps with the routes that you intend to follow.

A better understanding of the conduct of MARKET-GARDEN and why it took place can be obtained by knowing the background to the operation. Therefore the traveller is advised to read the Historical Summary below before setting out on the tour.

For current information about travelling in the Netherlands see the **Tourist Information Section** below.

Choosing Your Routes

If You Wish to Visit a Particular Place

Use the index at the back of the book to locate what you wish to visit. If it is a particular grave, find the location from the Commonwealth War Graves Commission/American Battle Monuments Commission (see below) before you set out.

If You Wish to Tour the Entire Corridor and Arnhem Battlefield

Itineraries One to Four are laid out so as to start at the beginning of The Corridor and follow it right up to The Island. Itinerary Five covers the Arnhem-Oosterbeek Battlefields and ends back over the Rhine in Driel.

If Time is Limited

The best-known American actions are covered in Itineraries Two, Three and Four, the British in One , Four and Five. The Polish participation is covered in Itinerary Five.

The Itineraries/Kilometres-Miles Covered/duration/RWC/OP/Maps

The five Itineraries need not be taken in any particular sequence, nor travelled in the directions given in this book, though it will ease navigation if they are.

The composition of the Itineraries is based upon what the authors, in many years of conducting interested groups around the area, have found to be the places that most people have asked to see.

An historical account covering each Itinerary can be found in the Historical Summary section below which should be read before, or concurrently with, setting out. The area covered by each Itinerary is detailed in the Contents list above.

Details of the routes are given at the beginning of each timed and measured Itinerary. Beginning and end points are given. The times stated do not include stops for refreshments. In the heading for each stop is a running kilometre/mileage total, a suggested length of stay, a reference to the Holts' Battle Map which accompanies this book and an indication [R/WC] if there are refreshment or toilet facilities. 'OP' indicates an Observation Point from which features of the battlefield may be seen.

Travel instructions are indented and written in italics to make them stand out clearly. Extra Visits and Personal Memories have a shaded background so that they, too, stand out from the main routes.

It is absolutely essential to set your kilometre/mileage trip to zero before starting and to make constant reference to it. It is our experience that car odometers can vary considerably. Also the total mileage can be affected by factors like the number of times you overtake, exactly where you are able to turn round, etc. Therefore the given mileage may not tally precisely with your own but should nevertheless give you a useful guideline. Distances in the headings are given in miles as well as kilometres because the trip meters on British cars still operate in miles. Distances within the text are sometimes given in kilometres as local signposts use those measures.

EXTRA VISITS

In addition to the Itineraries, Extra Visits are described to sites of particular interest which lie near to the recommended routes. They are boxed and shaded so that they stand out clearly from the main route. Estimates of the round trip mileage and duration are given. Other points of additional interest are occasionally indicated thus: [**N.B.** By taking such and such a road the following may be visited.]

MAPS

This guide book has been designed to be used with the accompanying *Major & Mrs Holt's Battle Map of MARKET-GARDEN* and the words 'Map–' in the heading indicate the map reference for the location. Frequent use of this map will also assist you in orientating, give a clear indication of the distances involved in possible walks and show points of interest which are not included in the Itineraries or Extra Visits.

Also recommended is Michelin Map 211: Nederland/Pays-Bas, 1:200,000, which covers all the Itineraries in the book. Those wanting highly detailed maps may wish to purchase the 1:25,000 *Topografische Kaart van Nederland* maps, which are similar in format to Ordnance Survey maps, available in local VVVs, where detailed Falk town plans are also available.

TELEPHONING TO THE NETHERLANDS

The International code for the Netherlands is 00 31. This is indicated in all phone numbers as '+'.

HISTORICAL SUMMARY

Strech out thine arme no farther
then they sleve wyll retche
Proverb (Coverdale 1541)

This Historical Summary is intended to provide the reader with an outline of the events and arguments which led up to the start of Operation MARKET-GARDEN and with a précis of what actually happened, so that the greater detail which is presented in the text of the itineraries can be placed in perspective. Frequent reference both to the in-text maps and to the Holts' Map which accompanies this volume will aid understanding. **The Plan in Outline** is presented first, followed by **An Overall Summary of What Happened** so that readers can be familiar with the shape of the campaign before diving deeper into it.

An explanation of what actually happened over the 10 days of the Operation is greatly complicated by the fact that distinct and different actions took place simultaneously at locations separated by 60 miles (100 kilometres) or more. Therefore, with the aim of allowing the reader to obtain a clear picture of what happened where, we give a composite formation by formation description of **What Happened on 17 September**, the first day of the Operation, but describe subsequent and more detailed events in the itineraries on the spot where they took place. The **HISTORICAL SUMMARY** is thus divided into the following sections –

THE PLAN IN OUTLINE
AN OVERALL SUMMARY OF WHAT HAPPENED 17 - 25 SEPTEMBER
REASONS WHY OPERATION MARKET-GARDEN WAS LAUNCHED
  All over by Christmas?
  In at the kill – Patton or Montgomery?
  A Broad or a Narrow Front?
  The Field-Marshal and the V2
REASONS WHY OPERATION MARKET-GARDEN FAILED
  Inexperienced Commanders
  Absentee Management
  Failure to fly sufficient airborne forces in on 17 September
  Delay at the very beginning at Joe's Bridge
  Not enough urgency by the British armour – 'Success is a heady wine'
  Failure at Son

American confusion at Nijmegen
Drop zones too far from the Arnhem Bridge
Failure of the British radios at Arnhem
But what about the Germans?
Intelligence, the SS and King Kong
THE PLAN IN MORE DETAIL
XXX Corps (British)
101st Airborne Division (US) (The Screaming Eagles)
82nd Airborne Division (US) (The All Americans)
1st Airborne Division (Brit) (The Red Berets)
WHAT HAPPENED ON 17 SEPTEMBER
XXX Corps
101st Airborne Division
82nd Airborne Division
1st Airborne Division

THE PLAN IN OUTLINE

The Military Aim

To establish a 21st Army Group bridgehead across the River Rhine at Arnhem.

The Method

Arnhem lay at the end of a main road (The Corridor) leading from XXX Corps' forward positions at Joe's Bridge in Belgium, through 100 kms of enemy-held Holland. The road crossed bridges over five significant river obstacles.

The method was to capture all the bridges by dropping airborne forces on or around them (OPERATION MARKET) and then to drive ground troops at speed up the road and over the bridges using an armoured column reinforced by artillery and air support (OPERATION GARDEN).

The Tasks

Airborne Forces– First Allied Airborne Army

101st (US) AB Division (The Screaming Eagles). Commanded by Major-General Maxwell D. Taylor. Tasked to drop between Veghel and Eindhoven and to open, and keep open, the XXX Corps Corridor over the Wilhelmina Canal at Son and the Zuid Willemsvaart Canal at Veghel, as well as crossings over the smaller rivers Dommel and Aa.
82nd (US) AB Division (The All Americans). Commanded by Brigadier-General James M. Gavin. Tasked to drop between Grave and Groesbeek, to take the bridges over the River Maas at Grave and the Waal at Nijmegen, and to dominate the high ground, known as the Groesbeek Heights, between Nijmegen and the German border.
1st (BR) AB Division (The Red Berets). Commanded by Major-General R.E. Urquhart with General Stanislaw Sosabowski's First Polish Independent Parachute Brigade Group under his command. Tasked to capture the bridges at Arnhem and to establish a bridgehead across the Rhine.

Ground Troops

XXX Corps. Commanded by Lieutenant-General Brian G. Horrocks. Tasked to advance at maximum speed northwards along The Corridor and to establish positions on the high ground north of Arnhem.

AN OVERALL SUMMARY OF WHAT HAPPENED 17-25 SEPTEMBER 1944

On Sunday 17 September 1944 in Operation MARKET, an Allied airborne army consisting of the American 82nd and 101st Airborne Divisions, and the British 1st Airborne Division, dropped behind enemy lines in Holland intending to capture the bridges over five significant rivers.

On the ground, in Operation GARDEN, the British XXX Corps had the simultaneous task of driving rapidly up a single road into enemy territory and across those bridges to their objective 60 miles (100 kms) away – the town of Arnhem.

The operation had been mounted at the instigation of Field-Marshal Montgomery in a bid to outflank the defences of the Siegfried Line and then, by driving south into the Ruhr, finish the war by Christmas 1944 (Sketch Maps 1 & 2).

The operation failed. The ground forces did not get across the Arnhem bridge. The men of the British 1st Airborne Division were forced into two small areas – one around the northern end of the Arnhem road bridge (Sketch Map 6) that was their target and another that came to be called The Cauldron (whose shrinking boundary was called The Perimeter) (Sketch Map 5) around the Hartenstein Hotel in Oosterbeek. The Germans called it the *Hexenkessel* – the witches' cauldron. Despite an astonishing display of determination and stubborn resistance, they were surrounded and defeated before XXX Corps could reach them. Of the 10,000 or so men who had landed around Arnhem by parachute or glider less than a quarter returned.

Much mutual criticism followed. The Americans accused XXX Corps of being too slow. In his memoirs General Ridgway said

> [The] stand at Arnhem was a monument to British valor, but a monument too to human weakness, to the failure to strike hard and boldly.

The British claimed that Eisenhower, the Supreme Commander, did not give them the administrative support that they needed to enable the operation to succeed. The British Army blamed the Air Forces for not dropping enough men on the first day of the operation... wireless sets did not work... air photos were ignored... the Germans captured the operational plans... the British tanks did not like to fight at night... the Americans took too long to capture the Nijmegen bridge... excuses and accusations were legion... and so was the bravery of those who fought, American, Belgian, British, Dutch, Polish, and German.

REASONS FOR LAUNCHING OPERATION MARKET-GARDEN

There are many interlocking reasons why MARKET-GARDEN took place. The most fascinating and all-pervasive aspect of what was one of the Second World War's most daring

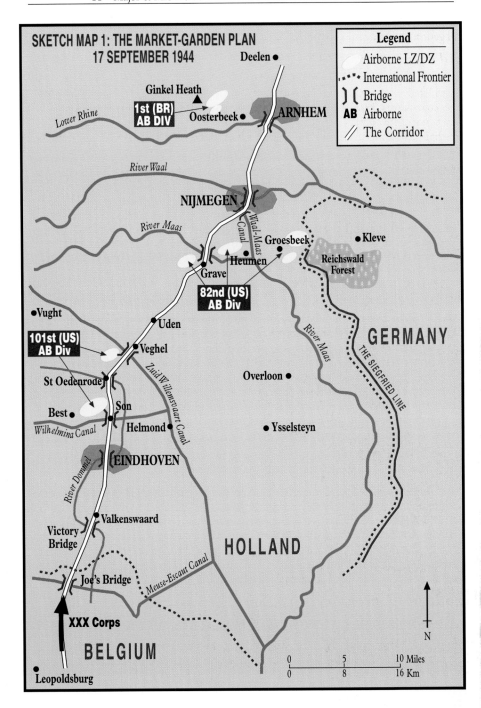

SKETCH MAP 1: THE MARKET-GARDEN PLAN
17 SEPTEMBER 1944

Legend

- Airborne LZ/DZ
- International Frontier
- Bridge
- **AB** Airborne
- // The Corridor

Deelen

Ginkel Heath

Lower Rhine

1st (BR) AB DIV

Oosterbeek

ARNHEM

River Waal

NIJMEGEN

River Maas

Waal-Maas Canal

Groesbeek

Kleve

Grave

Heumen

Reichswald Forest

82nd (US) AB Div

Vught

Uden

River Maas

GERMANY

101st (US) AB Div

Veghel

THE SIEGFRIED LINE

St Oedenrode

Zuid Willemsvaart Canal

Overloon

Best

Son

Helmond

Ysselsteyn

Wilhelmina Canal

EINDHOVEN

River Dommel

Valkenswaard

HOLLAND

Victory Bridge

Joe's Bridge

Meuse-Escaut Canal

N

XXX Corps

BELGIUM

0   5   10 Miles
0   8   16 Km

Leopoldsburg

and innovative operations is that it was promoted by the most careful and conservative of all generals – Montgomery. Why did he do it? Some possible reasons are discussed below.

All over by Christmas?

Following the success of the airborne landings on 6 June further airborne operations were considered as early as 13 June in an attempt to widen the Normandy bridgehead. The first was code-named WILD OATS and was a drop behind German lines south-west of Caen, but it was not carried out for a number of reasons, including concern over the German flak that might be encountered. Next, a drop code-named BENEFICIARY envisaged the capture of St Malo and, once again, concern about German flak was one of the reasons why the drop was never made. By the end of July two more drops had been considered but cancelled.

On 25 July the US 1st Army began an assault that broke through at St Lô and then on 1 August Lieutenant-General George Patton's 3rd Army smashed out via Avranches and began an armoured drive that covered 100 miles in a week, reaching le Mans on 8 August (see Sketch Map 2). That same day, following active prompting by General George C. Marshall, U.S. Chief of Staff in Washington, who had been impressed by the activities of Brigadier Orde Wingate in Burma, the 1st Allied Airborne Army was formed under US Lieutenant-General Louis H. Brereton.

Once again an airborne operation was planned, this time not in an effort to aid a breakout, but as a complement to the advancing US ground forces. This plan, code-named

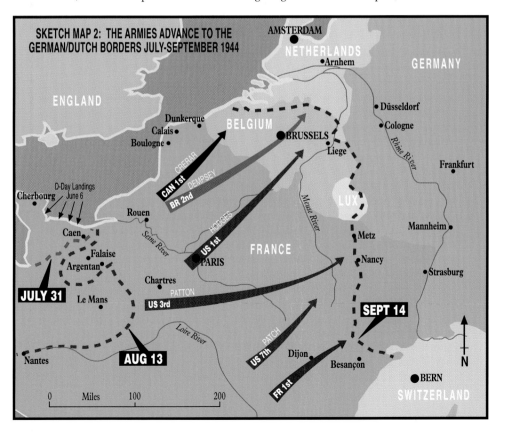

SKETCH MAP 2: THE ARMIES ADVANCE TO THE GERMAN/DUTCH BORDERS JULY-SEPTEMBER 1944

TRANSFIGURE, was completed by 13 August and cancelled five days later as Patton's rapid progress made it unnecessary.

Montgomery's British 21st Army Group break-out from Normandy began more slowly on 30 July and was confirmed by the defeat of the Germans at Falaise by British, Canadian and American forces on 19 August. Thereafter the British advance accelerated. On 3 September they captured Brussels and the next day Antwerp, the culmination of a striking advance of over 250 miles in five days by the 11th and Guards Armoured Divisions. During this period airborne operations LINNET and LINNET II were conceived and cancelled, but the intent to use the Allied Airborne Army was firmly entrenched in the minds of the Allied Commanders. The U.S. chiefs in particular wanted to see what the airborne force could do. Just about everyone on the Allied side had the 'victory virus'. So dramatic had been the achievements from the middle of August to the first week of September – and the Russians had reached Yugoslavia destroying 12 German divisions in the process – that it looked like a repeat of the German collapse of 1918. Anything now seemed possible.

Thus, by the beginning of September 1944, the British had liberated Brussels and the Americans and the French Paris, and the Allied armies were sweeping across Europe towards Germany. Commanders, British and American, felt that the Germans were effectively defeated and that the war could end quickly, maybe even by Christmas: too quickly, perhaps, to make use of the Airborne Army (for whom new shoulder patches had been made) unless something was planned very quickly - and then there was the question of who would be in the military limelight at the war's end, Montgomery or someone else?

In at the Kill - Patton or Montgomery?

Since October 1942 and his victory at El Alamein Montgomery had never lost a battle. That fact and his skilled use of the media kept him in the public eye and high on the popularity list both in Britain and America. His direct criticisms of the failure of the American troops at Kasserine in February 1943 brought him into conflict with General George Patton and in the invasion of Sicily Patton challenged Montgomery's 8th Army to beat his own 7th Army in a race to complete the capture of The Island. Patton won.

The personal rivalry between the two men was firmly established, but when Patton was sidelined for slapping a shell-shocked private soldier in the face after accusing him of being a coward, it looked as if the contest was over. Patton, however, was too good a general to leave on the shelf and he was nominated to command the shadow army in England that was part of the deception plan prior to the Normandy landings. On 1 August 1944, he was back in action in Normandy with his 3rd Army and led the remarkable American drive across France in direct contrast to the stalemate on the British front around Caen for which Montgomery was being criticised. Now Patton was getting the popular headlines – not Montgomery – and it looked as if the war might soon be over. How might Montgomery regain the limelight and beat Patton into Berlin?

It may seem simplistic to attribute major historical events to the personal ambitions of individuals, but it is not so. Too often it is assumed that the commanders of armies or the leaders of countries are not influenced by the same desires as ordinary mortals – for recognition, promotion, success and public acclaim. They are, and in spades. To aggravate matters in the Montgomery versus Patton rivalry there was the 'Broad Front' and 'Narrow Front' controversy.

A Broad or a Narrow Front?

As the Allied armies advanced towards Germany so their supply lines became longer and longer. All materiel was still coming onto the continent via Normandy and, despite the efforts of the Red Ball Express, an almost continuous line of lorries stretching the near 500 miles from the beaches, it was becoming increasingly difficult to provide the leading formations with the supplies that they needed – in particular petrol. Such were the shortages that the fighting generals argued with each other over who should get what. What was really needed if the momentum of the advances was to be sustained was a port in the north – Antwerp.

Eisenhower also had the challenge of deciding upon the best way to end the war now that the German border was in sight. His favoured policy was that of an advance on a broad front, but without Antwerp and with the shortage of supplies the real situation on the ground boiled down to that of two main thrusts – one by Patton in the area of Metz and one by Montgomery nearing the Dutch border. Montgomery argued that there should be a single rapier-like thrust in the north under his command (Bradley told Patton that he thought it would be a 'butter-knife thrust'), while Patton naturally wanted to maintain his momentum in the south (in his diary on 17 September he noted, 'To hell with Monty. I must get so involved that they can't stop me') and both knew that there were not enough supplies for each to have their own way. Therefore each pleaded his own case to the Supreme Commander. Montgomery, the Land Forces Commander since D-Day, was the senior ranking officer and used that position in getting access to Eisenhower, but he was soon to lose that job to the American, something that he did not relish and for which he would need to be compensated. Perhaps he could be allowed to have his airborne operation but not his single all-out thrust.

In America President Franklin D. Roosevelt was coming up to be elected for a record fourth term and now that for the first time American forces in Europe outnumbered those of Britain, Eisenhower was under political pressure to see that they were well to the fore and in the news. In fact if he had decided to go for the single thrust that Montgomery advocated it would have probably been led by the stronger force – the Americans – but that would have upset the delicate balance of Allied co-operation and so that option was out. In Britain, too, it was clear that party politics, suspended for the duration of the war, were going to return in the near future and politicians, whose personal ambitions had been sublimated in the National Government, began to make moves. One of those moves could have prompted Operation MARKET-GARDEN and all because of a hole in the ground in Chiswick.

The Field-Marshal and the V2

On 1 September 1944, Eisenhower assumed command of the Allied ground forces in Europe, replacing Montgomery who, presumably as compensation, was promoted to Field-Marshal. It did not placate him. Instead he renewed his efforts to persuade the Supreme Commander to divert all supplies to him in order to make his 'rapier-like thrust' in the north and then a new urgency suddenly materialised – a German secret weapon appeared.

London had thought itself safe from the air once the Blitz was over but on 15 June 1944, the attack on London by the V1 flying bombs began in earnest with over 200 being launched in the first 24 hours. However, by September 1944 the V1 menace seemed to be over since the rapidly advancing Allied Armies had put London out of its range. Provided that the armies continued to advance at their recent speed even the rocket weapon that intelligence had reported would not be able to reach London. Duncan Sandys, who had been appointed by his father-in-law Churchill a year earlier to co-ordinate intelligence information on the V1 and V2, decided to tell the nation that at last its capital city was safe. Why do that? Well, it could be a way for an aspiring politician to make sure of his public image, in anticipation of the approaching peace and imminent re-emergence of party politics. On Thursday 7 September he held a press conference announcing the end of 'the battle of London' and on the next day newspaper headlines, accompanied by pictures of Duncan Sandys, declared that the city was at last safe. That evening mysterious explosions occurred in Chiswick and near Epping. Sandys knew that the first V2s had arrived but the public did not and if they found out the real reason for the explosions his image would be less than a happy one.

What could be done to rescue the situation? Perhaps if the V2 launching sites could be over-run in the next few days it might be possible to prevent a major bombardment or even keep the existence of the weapon secret long enough for the Chiswick explosion not to have a negative effect on Sandys' standing. (In fact a Secrecy Order was placed upon the news so that it would not leak out to the public) The rockets had come from an area in Holland between the Hague and Wassenaar, roughly 100kms west of Arnhem. A message from the Chiefs of Staff certainly went to Field-Marshal Montgomery almost immediately, whether prompted by Sandys or not, asking what could be done about the Dutch V2 launching sites. Within 48 hours Montgomery had Eisenhower's approval for a new airborne operation designed to cross the Rhine and to debouch into the areas from which the V2s were being launched. It was called MARKET-GARDEN and it took the place of yet another cancelled plan – COMET. The Allied Airborne Army had seven days in which to get ready.

REASONS WHY OPERATION MARKET-GARDEN FAILED

It is rarely possible to find a single reason why a complicated military operation failed. Generally there is a mix of reasons and there is certainly a mix for MARKET-GARDEN, although we do propose later what we feel was the major factor.

Hindsight, of course, allows one to highlight factors that were not visible to those involved (e.g. the strength of the German resistance) – a matter of not being able to see the wood for the trees – and it is easy to pontificate from an armchair.

Nevertheless, where planning or performance seems inadequate, it is important to say so in order to seek an understanding of why events unfolded as they did.

Inexperienced Commanders

The overall responsibility for the operation was that of the American Lieutenant-General Brereton and his appointment of the British Lieutenant-General 'Boy' Browning to plan and command it was a mistake. Browning, though the 'father' of the British airborne forces, had no airborne combat experience. On 17 September he flew in his whole Corps HQ, taking thirty-eight precious gliders away from the combat troops, yet exerted no significant pressure on the conduct of operations. What is more, the bulk of the airborne forces involved was American and, in Major-General Ridgway, Brereton had available an experienced and aggressive airborne general with recent and successful action in Normandy. He would have kept a firmer and more driving hand on the tiller. In his biography of Ridgway Jonathan M. Sofer tells of a rivalry between the two men in which Browning, 'who hoped to get command of all Allied airborne forces (for OVERLORD) had virtually accused Ridgway of cowardice for taking a boat into Sicily instead of jumping himself'.

Major-General Urquhart, chosen to command the British 1st Airborne Division at Arnhem, also had no airborne experience and accepted his orders to land his men too far from the target. Had he been a true airborne general it is likely that he would have refused to agree 'to the point of resignation' and the dropping plan might have been changed in order to put troops down nearer the bridge. This might have allowed larger numbers of airborne troops to get to the Arnhem bridge quicker and thus be able to hold onto it until XXX Corps turned up. General John Frost, who had led the airborne stand at the Arnhem Bridge, had some firm views about this, made in an exclusive interview with the authors, more of which is quoted later as appropriate.

A PERSONAL OPINION
By Major-General John Frost

This is a very difficult thing because you've got to balance the airborne experience with battle experience and there was nobody in the airborne at the time among the senior ranks who had any battle experience at all. General Lathbury had had only one battle – in Sicily – which had been a pretty abysmal failure anyhow and that was all... It was an airborne division and meant to go with quite a different sort of technique than the ordinary infantry.

Major-General John Frost with Tonie Holt, 1982

Dutch caricature of Lieutenant-General Sir Miles Dempsey

Absentee Management

The ground forces involved were part of the British 2nd Army commanded by Lieutenant-General Miles Dempsey whose three Corps were to be part of the Operation. XXX Corps was to drive straight up The Corridor road, V111 Corps was to cover the right flank and X11 Corps the left. As the fighting progressed the efforts of XXX Corps were frequently diverted from their main task of reaching the bridge at Arnhem by the need to react to flank attacks on The Corridor. Both Field-Marshal Montgomery, the 21st Army Group Commander, and General Dempsey seemed detached from what was going on. General Frost had a view on this.

A PERSONAL OPINION
By Major-General John Frost
When you read the Official History you see how very little is said about activity on the part of the Army Commander. This is General Dempsey.... There is one mention of General Dempsey coming up and he obviously did not meet General Gavin. But if you talk to General Horrocks and say 'How often did you see Dempsey during this battle?' he says, 'I never saw him once – until he had to go back to get orders to withdraw the Division.'

The American Official History does show a picture of General Dempsey and General Gavin conferring but does not say where or when, while General Horrocks said that from the afternoon of 19 September he and General Browning took all the major decisions together.

Failure to fly sufficient forces in on 17 September

If two missions had been flown on the first day it is likely that the airborne forces would have had sufficient strength to take both ends of the Arnhem bridge that day and, despite delays in The Corridor to the south, have held on until XXX Corps arrived. Because he felt that two missions in a day would tire the aircrews, involve night flying and prevent adequate servicing of the aircraft, Brereton ruled that there should be only one, thus forcing the airborne operation to take place over at least three days. Inexplicably Browning accepted this. Ridgway would not have done so. In fact Clay Blair in his book *Ridgway's Paratroopers* gives a detailed analysis of how two trips could have been flown on the first day and points out that it was done for the DRAGOON Operation (the Landings in France in August). If the first lift had left England at 0500 hours it would have returned to base at about 1100 hours. There could then have been a three-hour interval for servicing and rest followed by the second departure at 1400 hours, returning at 1900 hours. It would still have been light when the planes arrived over Holland at about 1630 hours and, while it would have been dark when they returned to England, the airfields could have been illuminated.

General Frost was vehement on this point.

A PERSONAL OPINION
By Major-General John Frost
That of course jeopardized the whole operation because once the first lift had been landed and while there were people still dropping and guarding dropping zones that

A Personal Opinion continued

was a fair indication that more people were coming in. I have never been convinced that it wasn't possible to drop two lifts in the day. After all it's a comparatively short hop from airfields in the east and south of England to Holland and back. It's only a matter of an hour's flying time each way and to my mind it's nonsense to think that we couldn't have emplaned in the dark and taken off at first light and those aircraft would all have been back in England by midday at the very latest. There was plenty of time then to have taken the second lift and then drop them and come back. When taxed with this the American Airborne commander Brereton says that his men weren't skilled enough to fly by night. But nobody had to fly by night. There were quite enough hours of daylight. That to my mind was a very great mistake.... I know that Hollingshurst, one of the senior Air Marshals in the RAF, was very keen to do two in a day. It's such a silly little hop really when you think what was being done in Burma by the same sort of pilots. The run across to Holland and back was chicken feed.

If there had been two missions on 17 September then at two of the most critical places on The Corridor, i.e. Arnhem and Nijmegen, there would have been sufficient forces for the bridges to be captured quickly. At Nijmegen that could have meant that when XXX Corps arrived at around midday on 19 September the Guards could have crossed the bridge a day and a half earlier than they actually did and with obvious results.

Delay at the very beginning at Joe's Bridge

Little attention has been given to the effects of the delay in the Guards' advance caused by the loss of eight or nine tanks not much more than 20 minutes after starting out at 1435 hours on 17 September. As is discussed later on, there is a real possibility that some, if not all, of the tanks were casualties not from German fire but from the 'friendly fire' of RAF Typhoons, a fatal hiccup that is 'overlooked' in conventional histories. However, the Guards had a very limited objective for the day which was to get to Valkenswaard, only 12 kms up the road, which they did just before darkness. If they had not lost so many tanks early on they might have reached Valkenswaard mid-afternoon and decided to go straight on to Eindhoven, thus liberating it a day earlier. However, the Americans had not captured the bridge at Son intact so that would still have needed repair, but it could have been crossed at least half a day earlier.

2nd Bn, Irish Guards Tanks and 3rd Bn Infantry at the Belgian-Dutch Border, 17 September 1944. Note the concrete Corridor road

Not enough urgency by the British armour – 'Success is a heady wine'.

The blanket criticism given by many American commanders that XXX Corps was too slow ('they stopped for tea' is a constant mantra in American accounts) is difficult to refute. (Some Australian historians make exactly the same accusation for the delay in the British exploitation of the landings at Suvla Bay in 1915.) Despite the heinous problems introduced by the one narrow road and the poor weather which limited air support, there are particular times when, given the urgency of the operation, the Guards' spearhead seemed to be marking time. Even at the very beginning, setting an objective only 12 kms away on the first day, when there were 100 to go and seemingly two days in which to do it, could not have impressed sufficient urgency on the leading troops. General Ridgway tells how on 20 September he came upon British troops stalled on The Corridor around Son, apparently confronted by German forces, and how, after waiting for 40 minutes and seeing no activity, he got into his jeep and drove all the way to Nijmegen. Then perhaps the most difficult of all delays to understand is that in not continuing the advance to Arnhem after crossing the bridge at Nijmegen. The first Grenadier tanks crossed the bridge at about 1830 hours on 20 September, but the advance was not continued until 1100 hours the following day, some 6 hours after all effective action by John Frost's men at the Arnhem bridge had been overcome. It is interesting to speculate whether, had it been the Irish Guards tanks that had made the first crossing, their natural ebullience would have led them to continue. Speaking long after the war, General Horrocks implied a responsibility for the slowness of the advance. Previous startling progress across France and Belgium, the possibility that the war might be over by Christmas and that the Germans appeared to be beaten, bred an overconfidence that all would go to plan almost without trying. 'Success', he said, 'is a heady wine.'

Failure at Son

The failure of the 101st AB Division to take the Son bridge intact on 17 September held up the advance of XXX Corps, whose forward elements had reached the area around 1900 hours on 18 September. It was eleven hours before the advance could continue. If the bridge had been taken intact, then, even if the armour had stopped overnight to rest and refuel, the effective delay would have been smaller.

American confusion at Nijmegen

The Guards reached Nijmegen at around 1200 hours on 19 September. Browning had emphasised that taking the high ground at Groesbeek was Gavin's first priority, not the bridge. John Frost disagreed.

A PERSONAL OPINION
By Major-General John Frost

It is in fact a gentle slope and it's always nice to be a little bit higher than your enemy and as such it does perfectly control the exits from Germany through the rather wooded territory there but what happens on those Groesbeek Heights had absolutely no effect or no influence on what happened at the Nijmegen Bridge. The vital thing here was the bridge. It didn't matter how much you went and sat on the Groesbeek Heights, which were only about 300 or 400 feet high anyhow, if you haven't got the Nijmegen Bridge, and no German sitting on top of those heights can hurt anybody who's trying to take the Nijmegen Bridge. It's an irrelevant factor in my view.

Gavin, however, told Colonel Lindquist, commanding the 508th PIR, to send a force to the bridge immediately after landing. This was not done (the matter is discussed later). If an American force had gone directly to the bridge they would have taken it and the Guards could have rolled on towards Arnhem on the afternoon of 19 September, some 36 hours earlier than they actually did and while Frost still held the northern end of the Arnhem bridge (effective resistance there finished around 0500 hours on 21 September). If there is ONE reason for the failure of Operation MARKET-GARDEN then in our view it is that the capture of the bridge here was not given absolute priority. The delay allowed the Germans to move strong forces south of the bridge and to prevent its capture for 3 days. No other delay throughout the Operation exceeded 24 hours.

Drop zones too far from the Arnhem Bridge

The major asset of an airborne assault is that of surprise. By having the drop zones so far (the furthest almost 8 miles away and even the nearest some 5 miles away) from their target, the bridge at Arnhem, the 1st AB Division were denied that asset. It was not difficult for the Germans to work out where the British were heading and to concentrate their forces to stop them. The reasons given for the selection of the zones ranged from the condition of the ground to the concentration of enemy anti-aircraft fire in the area. Originally it was intended to drop the Polish forces just south of the bridge itself, but the ground was later considered to be unsuitable. An interesting question is, 'If it was deemed possible to drop the Polish forces just south of the Arnhem bridge why couldn't the 1st AB have been dropped there?' Some cynics have suggested that because the 'Poland' that the Polish forces had been formed to liberate no longer existed (the Russians had taken it over) the Poles were likely to become an embarrassment to Britain after the war. Therefore by sending them into an area supposedly well covered by anti-aircraft fire, casualties would be high and the scale of the problem reduced. If this sounds far-fetched, readers would do well to remember what the British did to the Cossacks, as detailed in Nicholas Bethell's the *Last Secret*.

While the British are criticised for accepting drop zones too far from their target it is not often pointed out that the 82nd Airborne Division dropped at least 7kms (almost 5 miles) from the Nijmegen bridge. Of course there was concern about the high ground, the built-up area and the possible threat of a German attack from the Reichswald Forest, but it is fair to ask why gliders had not been used to make a *coup de main* attack on at least one of the bridges, bearing in mind the success of John Howard's attack at Pegasus Bridge on 6 June. John Frost has his own answer..

A PERSONAL OPINION
By Major-General John Frost

It would certainly have been possible to have dropped a small body of parachutists on the south bank of the river and it certainly should have been possible to have landed a small number of gliders on the road in Arnhem itself to take the north end. After all, if the Germans could do this in 1940 at Eben Emael it's nonsense to say that we couldn't have attempted to do the same thing in 1944 with all the advantages and things that we had by this time. So there you have a mistake to start with – a *coup de main* should have been done

In his *Memoirs* Field-Marshal Montgomery wrote,

> The airborne forces were dropped too far away from the vital objective – the bridge... .
> I take the blame for this mistake... I should have ordered... that at least one complete
> Parachute Brigade was dropped quite close to the bridge so that it could have been
> captured in a matter of minutes.

Failure of the British radios at Arnhem

Control on a modern battlefield depends upon the radio. General Urquhart lost practical
control of his Division almost immediately after landing because his tactical radios did not
work. He could talk neither forward to his battalion commanders nor back to XXX Corps.
Thus he lost the ability to react to changing conditions. However, each of his battalions had
clear orders and one, the 2nd Battalion, did get to The Bridge on the first day. Therefore the
only likely tactical result of the radio failure was that Urquhart was unable quickly to divert
1st and 3rd Battalions to reinforce Frost at The Bridge. We discuss possible reasons for the
failure of the radios at the visit to Ginkelse Heide.

But what about the Germans?

In the SHAEF weekly intelligence summary No 26 for the week ending 16 September 1944,
was the note that two SS Panzer Divisions might be refitting near Arnhem, but the tone and
attitude of the overall summary was that the Germans did not have enough forces to hold the
West Wall (the Siegfried Line). Thus, the optimistic view that the Germans were effectively
beaten was re-inforced, a case of hearing what you want to hear. In a similar situation on 1
July 1916, the British Army suffered the greatest one-day loss of men in its history because the
Generals in charge wished to believe that the preliminary artillery barrage would destroy the
German barbed wire (it did not). Their subordinates were too frightened to oppose the
culture of absolute belief. Here in 1944 such acquiesence to a leader's view is perhaps
understandable, bearing in mind the advances of the previous weeks and so possible enemy
reaction was virtually ignored. He was, the culture proposed, already defeated.

In the film *A Bridge Too Far* the most telling illustration of the failure of the higher
commanders to take account of German resistance in their planning, is the performance by
Gene Hackman as Major-General Stanislaw Sosabowski protesting at a briefing conference
for MARKET-GARDEN. Captain Jan Jozef Lorys was one of the General's staff officers and
he told the authors the background to the real incident. The General, he said, was

> a good man to work with, very straightforward... we had air photos twice a day and
> we saw changes, improvements to German defences around Nijmegen and Arnhem.
> The General would bring this up at various conferences... this was not very well looked
> at. At a certain conference he jumped and shouted, 'The Germans! The Germans!' It did
> not look to us that they were beaten completely, they were retreating but they were
> getting ready to fight.

Sosabowski was of course proved to be correct, not an outcome that endeared him to the
British military establishment. Additionally of course there was the unforseen but telling
coincidence that the two German officers primarily responsible for the defence of Holland -
General Student and Field-Marshal Model - happened to be located where they could react
quickly and effectively.

Field-Marshal Montgomery later (*Memoirs*) admitted that,

> The 2nd SS Panzer Corps was refitting in the Arnhem area, having limped up there after its mauling in Normandy. We knew it was there. But we were wrong in supposing that it could not fight effectively.

Intelligence, the SS and King Kong

There was a two-way movement of clandestine activity from Britain to Europe – escapees, generally of Jewish refugees or RAF men shot down, who were coming back and agents going in, under the aegis of organisations like SOE (the Special Operations Executive). An SOE operation in Holland, code-named NORTH POLE, was penetrated by the Germans who operated it themselves between 1942 and 1944 capturing over sixty Dutch agents. Two of the agents escaped via a resistance group named the 'Dutch-Paris Line'. Associated with this line for a time was a smaller line run by a Dutch agent called Christiaan Lindemans sometimes known as 'King Kong' (qv) who is said to have warned General Student that an airborne operation in Holland was likely, though this has since been disproved. Student denied that he had ever met him. Dutch-Paris had over 150 of its members arrested (forty did not survive) and suspicion fell upon Lindemans. Apart from the fact that the instigators of MARKET-GARDEN did not wish to hear any news that might prevent the operation taking place, it was inevitable after NORTH POLE that the British mistrusted reports coming from the Dutch underground - including the one that two SS Panzer Divisions had appeared in the area of the forthcoming operation. There are many variations of the story that General Browning deliberately tore up aerial photographs that showed the presence of enemy tanks. These photos had been taken at the insistence of Major Brian Urquhart (no relation to the General) Browning's Intelligence Officer. In his entertaining autobiography, *A Life in Peace and War*, he wrote,

> The information coming in from various sources, including the Dutch Resistance, and the mounting evidence that the German Army routed in Normandy was re-forming itself...[made me]... increasingly anxious. I was also worried by the state of mind of General Browning and my brother officers... the MARKET-GARDEN operation was constantly referred to as 'the party'.

Brian Urquhart noticed comments in a 21st Army Group Intelligence Summary that elements of the 9th and 10th SS Panzer Divisions were refitting in the Arnhem area - something confirmed by Dutch Resistance.

> When I informed General Browning and Colonel Walch they ... became quite annoyed when I insisted upon the danger... . They said... that I should not worry unduly, that the reports were probably wrong and that in any case the German troops were refitting and not up to much fighting.

Urquhart arranged for RAF Spitfires to take photos near the dropping zones scheduled for 1st Airborne Division.

> The pictures when they arrived confirmed my worst fears. There were German tanks and armoured vehicles parked under the trees within easy range of the 1st Airborne Division's main dropping zone.

Urquhart showed the pictures to Browning only to be ordered to go on sick leave as he was 'suffering from acute nervous strain'. It was clear that 'the party' was not going to be cancelled for any reason but Urquhart does not say what happened to the pictures. None have ever been found. After the war Urquhart became Under Secretary-General of the United Nations, was knighted and lives in New York.

THE PLAN IN MORE DETAIL

XXX Corps - Commanded by Lieutenant-General Brian Horrocks (Sketch Map 1)
The Corps' aim was simple - to advance with maximum speed from the bridgehead across the Meuse-Escaut Canal at Joe's Bridge and, using the bridges captured by the airborne forces, get to **Arnhem**, there to establish itself on the high ground with a view to exploiting beyond to the Zuyder Zee (now called IJsselmeer) and ideally to get to Arnhem within two days. The 5th Guards Armoured Brigade of the Guards Armoured Division was to lead the attack with the Irish Guards Group of infantry and tanks at the front. Thirty minutes before zero hour a heavy concentration of artillery was to be laid upon enemy gun positions and Typhoons of 83rd Group RAF were to give close air support. Because so many earlier planned airborne operations had been cancelled at the last moment, Horrocks did not intend to give the signal for the Guards to advance until he saw the airborne armada overhead and therefore knew for certain that the operation was 'on'.

101st Airborne Division – Commanded by Major-General Maxwell Taylor (Sketch Map 1)
When the Division had dropped in Normandy on 6 June it had suffered many casualties as a result of having been spread over a wide area. General Maxwell Taylor determined not to repeat the experience and planned to concentrate his drop zones. His Division had three Parachute Infantry Regiments - 501st, 502nd and 506th with the following tasks:-
• **The 501st(Colonel Howard R. Johnson)** was to drop on DZ A near **Veghel** and to take the road and rail bridges over the Aa River and the Zuid Willemsvaart Canal at **Veghel.**
• **The 502nd (Colonel John H. Michaelis)** was to drop on Zone B northwest of **Son** (later to be used for gliders) and to secure the DZ for the gliders, take the road bridge over the Dommel at **St Oedenrode**, be prepared to relieve the 506th at **Son** and help in the move on **Eindhoven.**
• **The 506th (Colonel Robert R. Sink)** was to drop on Zone C beside Zone B (also to be used later for gliders) and to seize the bridge at **Son** over the Wilhelmina Canal and then move south to take Eindhoven and the four road bridges over the Dommel River. A minority task was to take the road and rail bridges at **Best.**
Not only was the Division to take the crossings, it was also to hold the towns and to keep open the 16 miles (25 kms) of The Corridor that passed through them. It was a task that Maxwell Taylor likened to the task of protecting the railways from the Indians in the opening of the West.

82nd Airborne Division - Commanded by Brigadier-General James Gavin ((Sketch Map 3)
The task of the Division was to seize the bridge over the Maas at Grave, to take the high ground in the area of Groesbeek to the east of Nijmegen, to take at least one of the four bridges over the Maas-Waal Canal that guarded the western approach to the city and to take the main road bridge over the Waal that carried The Corridor road through the centre of

Nijmegen (Sketch Map 3). Since the Division was further up The Corridor than the 101st, the ground troops of XXX Corps would take longer to reach it and General Gavin, prompted by Browning, adopted a defensive stance in the Nijmegen area, believing that taking and holding the high ground at Groesbeek as a buffer to German attacks from over the border was essential to, and took priority over, the taking of the main road bridge.

When the Division had jumped in Sicily, Salerno and Normandy, General Gavin had set off in the lead plane. He did the same thing here and had with him Captain Arie D. Bestebreurtje, a Dutch officer, whose role was to liaise with and to obtain information from the Dutch people. Gavin's Division consisted of three Parachute Infantry Regiments – the 504th, the 505th and the 508th and he was promoted to Major-General during the Operation.

• **The 504th (Colonel Ruben H. Tucker)** was to drop both north and south of the nine-span bridge over the River Maas at Grave, to take and hold it, and to head for the smaller bridges over the Maas-Waal Canal at Heumen (Molenhoek), Malden, Hatert and Honinghutje.

• **The 505th (Colonel William E. Ekman)** was to drop south of the town of Groesbeek, move north and take and hold it as well as a glider landing zone south-east of Groesbeek. It was to hold the high ground in the area and assist the 504th in the taking of the bridges at Malden and Heumen.

• **The 508th (Colonel Lindquist)** was to drop on the high ground north of Groesbeek, establish road blocks to the east of Groesbeek/Berg en Dal to stop German attacks from the Reichswald/Wyler area and then to take the Nijmegen road bridge. There is doubt, however, as to when the latter task was given to Lindquist. There were further tasks of helping with the taking of the bridges at Hatert and Honinghutje.

1st Airborne Division – Commanded by Major-General Roy Urquhart (Sketch Map 4)
The primary task of the Division was to seize the railway bridge, the pontoon bridge and the road bridge over the Lower Rhine at Arnhem. Since this was the task deepest into enemy-held territory it was therefore the most dangerous. Originally it had been given to the 101st, but as the British had already spent weeks planning actions in the area for OPERATION COMET (which was cancelled), Lieutenant-General 'Boy' Browning, the Deputy Commander of the 1st Allied Airborne Army, decided that the British Division would have the job instead. Urquhart, although lacking airborne experience, had seen much combat and had proved himself to be a good leader. Despite the current planning climate that proposed that airborne troops should be set down as near as possible to their objectives, Urquhart was forced to choose DZs and LZs between 5 and 8 miles west of the bridge, thus losing the element of surprise. (His reasons are discussed at the stop at Ginkelse Heide in Itinerary 5). When General Gavin heard the plan he said, 'My God, he can't mean it'.

Urquhart's Division consisted of the 1st and 4th Parachute Brigades, each of three battalions, the 1st Airlanding Brigade, again with three battalions, and the Polish Parachute Brigade Group. Because of limited aircraft availability Urquhart decided to land his force over two days with the following first day units and tasks –

• **1st Airlanding Brigade (Brigadier P. H .W. 'Pip' Hicks) (1st Border Regiment, 7th Kings Own Scottish Borderers, and 2nd South Staffords)** - to land on LZ 'S' and to secure it for unloading the first lift and for the arrival of the second lift on 18 September. In addition to set up defensive posts on the main roads west of the LZs.

• **1st Parachute Brigade (Brigadier G. W. Lathbury) (1st, 2nd and 3rd Parachute Battalions)** - to land on DZ 'X' and LZ 'Z' with the task of seizing and holding the bridges at Arnhem. First priority was given to the main road bridge. Battalions followed three different routes, with only one company (of the 1st Battalion) kept back as a divisional reserve, while the Recce Squadron of the Brigade was to attempt a *coup de main* operation using jeeps to capture the bridges.

On the second day the remaining elements of the Division were scheduled to arrive: –

  • **4th Parachute Brigade (Brigadier 'Shan' Hackett) – to** land on DZ 'Y' and LZ 'Z' with the tasks of approaching Arnhem along the Ede road in order to take the high ground north of the town and to secure the drop zones for the later arrival of the 1st Polish Parachute Brigade.

  • **1st Polish Parachute Brigade (Major-General Sosabowski) –** to land on DZ 'K' (south of the Arnhem road bridge) and LZ 'L' (north of the Rhine at Papendal) with the task of crossing the road bridge and occupying the eastern part of Arnhem.

WHAT HAPPENED ON 17 SEPTEMBER

Shortly after 1400 hours all of the airborne forces were on the ground.

XXX Corps

General Horrocks set up his HQ on top of the factory roof just to the east of Joe's Bridge, in full view of the bridge itself. Although he was told by radio that the air armada was on its way, he waited until he saw the planes overhead before he set H-Hour as 1435 hours, but in doing so lost several hours of daylight in which progress might have been made. The leading troop of tanks was commanded by Lieutenant Keith Heathcote of 3rd Squadron, 2nd Battalion Irish Guards, and as he set off the artillery barrage lifted from the German gun positions and formed a moving screen in front of him. The leading tanks had crossed the border into Holland by 1500 hours, but once there were held up by determined enemy resistance, so that it was not until around 1815 hours that the Guards began to move forward again. By darkness the advance had reached only to Valkenswaard, just 8 miles up the 60-mile (100 kms) corridor to Arnhem and, on hearing that the bridge at Son had been blown, Brigadier Gwatkin, the 5th Guards Brigade Commander, decided not to resume the advance until the following morning. It had been a hard day and rather than the low-grade static troops that the Corps had expected to meet, four German infantry battalions, two battalions of the 6th Parachute Regiment and two battalions of the 9th SS Division, had opposed the advance. With twenty-four hours left the Corps still had 52 miles to go to Arnhem.

101st Airborne Division

Four hundred and twenty-eight planes carried the Division into battle. Only three failed to reach a DZ – one pathfinder and two carrying parachutists - but the glider landings an hour later were less fortunate. Seventy gliders took off from England, but only 53 came in without damage. Two failed to leave England, one landed in the Channel, three crashed on the DZ and the rest were scattered. The gliders brought in artillery pieces and observers, plus engineers and 32 jeeps, but it would be seven days before the whole Division was on the ground. In one glider was Walter Cronkite, a reporter for United Press, who would later cover the Nuremberg Trials and become a world-famous television anchor man for CBS.

• *501st PIR. Veghel and Eerde*
When Lieutenant-Colonel Harry Kinnard commanding the 1st Battalion of the 501st PIR landed he discovered that he was near the village of Kameren some three miles north-west of his scheduled DZ. Nevertheless he moved quickly towards Veghel led by some of his men who had taken bicycles and lorries in their eagerness to reach their objectives. The other two battalions had landed on DZ 'A' in good formation and met little opposition. The town was quickly taken, together with the bridges over the Aa and the Zuid Willemsvaart Canal and some 50 German prisoners.

• *502nd PIR. Best and St Oedenrode*
Major-General Maxwell Taylor jumped with the 1st Battalion of the 502nd which was commanded by Lieutenant-Colonel Patrick Cassidy, both of whom had been photographed together in the doorway of their aircraft before taking off from Welford, one of twenty-four airfields in England used for the lift. The battalion dropped two miles south of its planned DZ but Cassidy gathered his men and after an exchange of fire with Germans in the town, in which 20 of the enemy were killed and fifty-eight captured, took St Oedenrode. The town of Best, however, was to prove more difficult.

The initial force that set off for Best was 'H' Company reinforced with machine guns and engineers. The road and rail bridges there were not on the direct line of advance proposed for XXX Corps, but Maxwell Taylor had added them to his tasks in order to provide an alternative route should the main Son road be blocked. Although the bridges would eventually be taken (one blown) it would involve half the Division and a squadron of British tanks, but at the end of 17 September the Germans held both Best and the bridges.

• *506th PIR. Son*
The men of the 506th began landing on DZ 'C' at about 1315 hours and within 45 minutes a two-pronged move through the Zonsche Forest towards the bridge on the main road in Son had begun. The 2nd Battalion advanced directly down the main road towards the bridge engaging in a fire fight with Germans in the houses en route, while the 1st Battalion worked their way in from the right (of the 2nd Battalion). Just as men from the two battalions met within sight of the bridge it was blown. Although Colonel Robert Sink, commanding the 506th, had thought ahead and included a platoon of Engineers in his force, they were only able to improvise a small footbridge, and that, with a captured small rowing boat, was insufficient to enable a strong enough force to cross the canal and to advance upon Eindhoven before dark. That fact, together with a rumour that a German regiment was preparing to defend Eindhoven, persuaded Colonel Sink to abandon the idea of taking the city by 2000 hours (his aim) and to wait for daylight.

82nd Airborne Division

Four hundred and eighty-two planes and fifty gliders carried 7,277 paratroopers and 209 men in gliders. Only one plane and two gliders failed to reach their zones, although many were hit by ack ack fire. One paratrooper was killed when his chute failed to open and another when he was hit by a supply bundle. Seven of those arriving by glider were injured, but there was very little immediate German opposition. The Corps Commander, General Browning, plus a skeleton HQ, landed with the Division in the 505th area while General

Ridgway, its disappointed former commander who had hoped to command the Corps himself, flew overhead in a borrowed B17 to watch the drop.

• **504th PIR.** *Bridges at Grave, Heumen, Malden, Hatert and Honinghutje.*

The Regiment dropped both north and south of the bridge at Grave. One stick of sixteen men commanded by Lieutenant John S. Thompson came down within 700 yards of the southern end of the bridge while the bulk of the force gathered at the northern end. German flak guns offered some opposition but within 3 hours the 504th had taken and secured the bridge. The bridge at Malden was blown by the Germans as the paratroopers charged towards it, but the bridge at Heumen was taken intact in a night attack and later became the main bridge across the Maas-Waal for the advance of XXX Corps on Nijmegen. The 504th with a platoon of the 508th arrived at Hatert to find the bridge destroyed but no attack was made on Honinghutje that day (Sketch Map 3).

• **505th PIR.** *Groesbeek and the High Ground on the German border.*

The drop was entirely successful and one battalion set off for its objective within 20 minutes of hitting the ground. With help from members of the Dutch underground isolated Germans were captured and all-round defensive positions were dug on the high ground around Groesbeek overlooking the routes north from the Reichswald Forest into the Division's area, where a Divisional reserve was established. Patrols sent out after dark made contact with the 504th at the Heumen bridge, penetrated into the Reichswald Forest where it was thought some 1,000 German tanks were in hiding (this proved to be untrue) and were just too late to prevent the destruction of the railway bridge over the Maas River at Mook.

• **508th PIR.** *Hatert, Berg en Dal and the Nijmegen road bridge.*

The orders for the taking of the Nijmegen road bridge were confused. Priority was given to establishing positions on the high ground of the Berg en Dal/Groesbeek ridge and in the area of Hatert to the west to prevent any movement of the Germans south from Nijmegen. The story is examined in more detail in Itinerary Three. While the drop was successful and the high ground secured against what would become ferocious attacks over the coming days, it was some 7 hours before the first co-ordinated attack was made on the road bridge. German SS troops who had only just arrived in Nijmegen repulsed the attack and would continue to hold the bridge for another 3 days - the British would not cross in force until a fourth day passed by which time all effective resistance by 1st AB at the Arnhem bridge was over.

1st Airborne Division

The Division reached its planned LZs and DZs without losing one aircraft to enemy action but thirty-eight of the 358 gliders failed to arrive, mainly because their tow ropes broke. The landing took the Germans by surprise and, in contrast to the Americans, the British put their gliders down before the paratroopers jumped, General Urquhart landing by glider.

• **1st Parachute Brigade - the Arnhem road and rail bridges.**

Because of damage to the gliders on landing the Recce Squadron was unable to unload its jeeps as quickly as planned for the *coup de main* attack on the bridges and not until some time after landing (US sources say 4 hours and British sources say 1 hour) did the parachute battalions set off for Arnhem. 1st and 3rd Parachute Battalions met stiff

opposition from elements of 9th SS Panzer Division under Lieutenant-Colonel Ludwig Spindler and an SS Training Battalion led by Sturmbannführer Sepp Krafft, the Germans establishing blocking lines along Wolfhezerweg and Dreijenseweg (Sketch map 4). Both battalions were still short of the main road bridge when darkness fell. The 2nd Battalion, commanded by Lieutenant-Colonel John Frost, meeting less opposition, reached the northern (Arnhem) end of the road bridge and captured the buildings around it by 2030 hours. Several attempts to reach the southern end of the bridge failed. The element of that battalion that had set out for the rail bridge reached it just as the Germans blew it up and then went on to join the rest of the Battalion at the road bridge the following day.
• **1st Airlanding Brigade - securing the LZs and DZs.**
By 1600 hours the LZs and DZs for the second lift had been secured and a few prisoners taken. While the 1st and 3rd Parachute Battalions battled on their roads into Arnhem and the 2nd Battalion fought at the road bridge, the 1st Airlanding Brigade settled down for a relatively quiet night to guard the LZs and DZs and to await the morrow.

The spirit of the whole Operation is summarised by an exceptional poem, written on the 50th Anniversary by British Arnhem veteran Fred 'Lucky' Luckhurst of 1 Para Squadron RE, who sadly passed away in 1996.

It Was Thus

It was descending on a bright and sunny lunchtime.
It was welcoming smiles and warm handshakes from the Dutch civilians.
It was marching down the leafy lanes
and into the quiet Sunday afternoon streets.
Suddenly it was machine guns. It was stretcher-bearers.
It was machine guns. It was stretcher-bearers.
It was hand grenades and shouts of 'Die you German bastards!'
It was leaping from garden to garden.
It was dodging from doorway to doorway.
It was smashing out of windows and beating out fires.
It was noise. It was night.
It was morning. It was the second lift.
It was more men and more strength, more chances of success.
Days followed night and night followed days
And it was carrying in the wounded and carrying out the dead.
It was frantically waving yellow silk triangles.
It was watching the slaughter of valiant airmen.
It was choking at the sight of much-needed supplies drifting out of reach.
It was cursing. It was praying.
It was the screeching of Panzers and the whirring of the mortar bombs.
It was the mutilated trees and the mutilated men.
It was crapping in the corner of a garage or in the corner of a slit trench.
It was the 'V' sign stuttered out of a Bren gun.
It was the cries of 'Woho Mohamed' and the groans of the badly wounded.
It was the dirt in the mouth and the singing in the ears.
It was the rain-soaked clothing and the blood-soaked earth.
It was the shortage of food and of ammunition, of sleep, of hope.
It was surrender, but it was not a defeat.
It was a brave, brave, brave try.
It was Arnhem, 1944.

'Woho Mohamed' was the battle-cry of the original Red Devils in North Africa in 1942-43. Lieutenant-Colonel R. G. Pine-Coffin, DSO, MC, who commanded the 3rd Battalion in North Africa, described how he first heard it on the day of the Battle of Jebel Mansour. A party of the Battalion, whilst held in reserve, heard an Arab cowherd uttering the cry as one of the cows he was watering from a stream got confused by the cowherd's guttural 'Urrahs' and charged off. The Paras were much impressed by the cry and immediately adopted it as their own. It soon spread to the 1st and 2nd Battalions and was first used as a battle-cry by a company of the 3rd Battalion (probably Dobie's), whilst helping the 2nd Battalion beat off an attack in the Tamera Valley. 'To shout it really correctly,' wrote Pine-Coffin, 'either for stopping cows or killing the enemy, the 'Woho' part should be dragged out as long as possible and the 'Mohamed' clipped very short'.

The cry was often heard during the Battle of Arnhem-Oosterbeek. There are many later variations on the original spelling quoted above.

THE AFTERMATH

After the Battle of Arnhem-Oosterbeek the Germans were left in possession of deserted towns, their citizens all evacuated, many buildings destroyed and still smouldering. Large-scale looting and further wanton destruction took place, the spoils being transported back to Germany in trucks marked 'a gift from Holland'.

For the population of 96,000, evacuated to other parts of western Holland, now came the terrible Hunger Winter. When the Dutch railway workers struck, there were many German reprisals, most significantly the banning of all freight movement from the north and east (where most food was produced) to the west, causing widespread starvation. It is estimated that well over 30,000 civilians died in this period and those that survived existed on tulip bulbs, sugar-beet and the occasional potato. Meanwhile many escapee or wounded Allied men were being hidden, at great risk, by the Dutch Resistance.

PEGASUS I: 22-23 October 1944

The sheltering of these men was co-ordinated by the strong Resistance group based on Ede, where some eighty Airborne men were hidden, forty of them in a sheep-pen, with another 40 in a sheep-pen near Oud Reemst to the east. They maintained a telephone link with Nijmegen through the Provincial electricity station. First Lieutenant-Colonel Dobie, CO of 1 Para Battalion, was sent back over the Rhine to meet General Dempsey, commanding the 2nd British Army, who ordered the 101st US AB Division (then occupying parts of The Island) to give support. Then key members of the Resistance, including Tonny de Nooij (qv) and some of the British soldiers they were protecting, made a recce to the river and chose a crossing site, just west of Renkum. This was agreed by Major Digby Tatham-Warter (qv), who commanded the soldiers, and Dutch leaders of the Ede group. The night of Monday 23 October was chosen, but on Friday the 20th the population of Bennekom was ordered to evacuate within 3 days. The date of the escape was changed to Sunday 22 October and the assembly area was a wood to the northwest of Bennekom (later to be called 'the English Grove'). The evaders, accompanied by local guides and dressed in civilian clothes, travelled by day, mingling with the streams of civilian evacuees. Once assembled they were issued with uniforms and weapons, provided by the Resistance. Their final number was 138, plus ten Dutchmen and two Russians who had escaped from Deelen airport. They set off towards the river at 2130 hours in a light mist, forming a long column, each man holding the man in front. They were guided by Maarten van den Bent.

On the other side of the river routes were prepared by the 2nd Battalion 506th PIR, with jeeps and lorries at the ready to transport them to Nijmegen. A Bofors bombardment had been laid down over the previous nights to confuse the enemy and machine guns and mortars protected the crossing point. With the Americans were some Sappers from XXX Corps to man the twenty-three rowing boats.

The column made its way through the dangerous last lap between Renkum and the Wageningen hill. At 0030 it crossed the Renkum-Wageningen road and then the water meadows to the river bank. Tatham-Warter described how he was then seen and led to Dobie by the extraordinary Canadian maverick, Leo Heaps, whose exploits, as described in his own book, *The Grey Goose of Arnhem*, seem totally incredible. Tatham-Warter wrote,

> He was a very bold and enterprising officer who had, early in the battle of Arnhem, first attached himself to David Dobie's battalion and then somehow purloined a jeep and made his way through alone to the bridge. And now, after a long and exciting escape experience, he had involved himself with the 'Pegasus' operation.

Other senior officers, such as Urquhart, also give credence to some of Heaps's more lurid tales.

By 0200 hours the risky operation, in three crossings, was successfully completed, with the loss of only one of the Russians and the serious injury of Major Tony Hibbert (qv), his legs crushed between two jeeps. Brigadier Lathbury sent a confirmatory message via the BBC: 'Message for Bill, everything is well, all our thanks.' 'Bill' was the resistance leader D. Wildeboer. He and many of his countrymen and women had taken enormous personal risks to ensure the success of this daring operation – the largest escape by Allied soldiers from enemy-occupied territory. The escapees enjoyed a glass of champagne before being de-briefed by Generals Dempsey and Horrocks the following day and then being flown back to the UK.

PEGASUS II: 16-18 November 1944

Encouraged by the success of Pegasus I, and because many men were still being hidden in the area, another escape attempt was planned for 17 November. A crossing point some 2kms further to the east was chosen, with the use of boats with outboard motors with silencers. Unfortunately the telephone link between Ede and Nijmegen was cut on 16 November and communication then depended on difficult radio broadcasts via London. Following the civilian evacuation of October, the Germans had strengthened the area leading to the river and an assembly point had to be chosen much further (some 20kms) away which involved crossing several main roads. The 120 men, consisting mainly of airborne men, plus some RAF, an American, a Frenchman, a Russian and a Dutchman, had to start their hazardous journey early on 16 October. As with Pegasus I, once assembled, they were issued with British uniforms, papers and Dutch guides and divided into two groups. One group was led by Major Hugh Maguire, an Intelligence Officer with 1st AB HQ, who, realising that he was running behind the planned timetable, took a shortcut over a road known to be strongly defended by the Germans. They were spotted and fired upon by the Germans, killing Major John Coke of the KOSB. The group then scattered, only five men reaching the river, too late for the RV. An American in a canoe picked up one wounded man the next day, but the boat was hit and both men drowned. Only seven men of the two groups finally made it over the river. Most of those left behind were taken prisoner, some of the Dutch who had been masquerading as British soldiers were shot by the Germans on 8 March 1945 at Woeste Hoeve near Arnhem, together with 115 other Dutchmen. The final casualty list from this brave but sadly unsuccessful operation has never been ascertained.

The Liberation

Bitter fighting continued throughout the winter in the Nijmegen and Groesbeek areas, where the frontline was taken over in November by the Canadians under General Crerar, and in The Island, where the 506th PIR joined the DCLI in the west. (See Itineraries Three and Four below.) At the end of March 1945 two battalions of the Lincolns took over in The Island and on 3 April two companies crossed the Rhine near the Loo ferry south-east of Arnhem. Gradually the Allies worked their way over the River IJssel towards Arnhem and Ede was liberated by the Canadian Calgary Regiment of the 49th (Polar Bear) West Riding Division on 17 April, which also liberated Arnhem. Many memorials to them exist in the area.

The Reconstruction

When the citizens returned after the Liberation, it is estimated that only 145 houses remained intact. The Sacré Coeur Girls' School on the road to Velp (where a young Audrey Hepburn had lived during the battle, passing messages for the Resistance in her socks) became the centre of municipal administration. There everyone entering the town had to apply for a permit. Separated families and friends were reunited and the number of those who didn't survive became apparent. Imagine the scenes of desolation and chaos that met the orderly Dutch as they entered the outskirts of their forlorn town to find it reduced to rubble. But they set to work with the sort of determination the British showed after the Blitz. The water supply was quickly established and though without gas or electricity, oil or any other fuel, things were almost miraculously cleared and the rebuilding began. So, too, did the mournful task of reburying the dead who lay in many fields and gardens in the area (see Graves Registration below).

The First Memorials

As soon as some measure of normalcy been re-established, the citizens began to think of commemorating their Liberation, their own dead and those of their liberators. The dates of the memorials are included in their description in the following Itineraries, from which it may be seen that some were erected as early as 1945.

The Films/TV/Magazines

Theirs is the Glory. This, the first movie representation of the Operation, was released in September 1946. It mixes actual shots of the battle with re-creation, acted by men and women who actually took part in the real events, and tells the story simply and without judgement. It was directed by Brian Hurst and produced by Castleton Knight, both of whom had experience in wartime feature and propaganda films. It was funded by the Rank

Organisation, the music was composed by Muir Matheson and the novelist Louis Golding worked on the screen play.

About 200 men of the 21st Independent Para Company were flown from their administrative duties in Norway and Denmark to the newly-created Arnhem Film Unit on a mushroom farm at Braintree in Essex, to join a motley crew of RAMC, RASC, Paras, Sappers and Gunners. All were paid £3 per day, with bonuses of £5 for ideas that were used in the script, and they crossed to a still war-torn Arnhem and Oosterbeek on 6 August 1945. Their billets, with Dutch people only newly returned to their homes, or in barracks, were primitive and their duties included clearing locations of unexploded materiel. Around them the Graves Registration Unit was working to find the bodies of their missing comrades, a task many of the men felt compelled to join. Only small areas of the true scenes of the battle (like bits of the Hartenstein, the Tafelberg and the St Elisabeth Hospital and a section of Benedendorpsweg) could be used for the early shots, which required undamaged houses and streets and much was shot in Heveadorp or in England.

One of the leading players was Lieutenant Hugh Ashmore, OC No 3 Platoon, 21st IPC, who gives the briefing at the beginning of the film and who was used in publicity. Major Freddie Gough of the Reconnaissance Squadron played himself, albeit in a role of exaggerated seniority at The Bridge (John Frost is not even mentioned). A much-bandaged Major 'Dickie' Lonsdale re-created his own pep talk in the Old Church, using the door of the church (which is now on display in the Hartenstein Museum) to write his crib. The two war correspondents Alan Wood of the *Daily Express* and the Canadian Stanley Maxted also play themselves and they become the lasting, and very moving, voices of Arnhem. Other enduring scenes are those enacted in the house of Kate ter Horst, who also plays herself, adding to her legend as the Angel of Arnhem.

This 82-minute-long film has a period flavour with its accents and bravura slang of the 1940s services, yet its honesty and the courage it portrays shine through, making it compulsory viewing for any student of the campaign.

Unfortunately the rights to the video have been acquired by Carlton International and it is currently no longer commercially available.

The True Glory. Arnhem had also featured in this filmed account of the War in Europe which was released in August 1945. The commentary was provided by a still-serving RAF cameraman, Richard Attenborough. This is available from *After The Battle* (see below) Videocassette No. 18.

A Bridge Too Far. The best-known MARKET-GARDEN film is based on the war correspondent Cornelius Ryan's extraordinarily detailed book, first published in 1974 and reprinted on the 50th Anniversary of VE Day in 1995. Its title comes from Lieutenant-General 'Boy' Browning's supposed remark to Field-Marshal Montgomery as he briefed him on the operation, 'But sir, I think we might be going a bridge too far,' (though it is now generally accepted that Browning did not actually use the expression). A glance at the long list of servicemen and civilians of all nationalities interviewed by Ryan (from Eisenhower to Maxwell Taylor, from Montgomery to Robert Cain VC, from Kate ter Horst to Jan Voskuil, from Sosabowski to von Rundstedt, Blumentritt and Student) and the detailed bibliography bear witness to the man's extensive research. Purists can point out the odd inaccuracy, but no other book so graphically gives the atmosphere of the entire campaign.

Ryan died of cancer in 1976 and was therefore not able to influence the filming of his book in 1977 by Joseph Levine (producer) and Richard Attenborough (director). Levine planned his biggest production yet with a budget of £15million. Colonel John Waddy served as British joint military adviser and several other senior participating officers were enrolled as such. Jan Voskuil, the acknowledged local authority on the Arnhem battle (father of historian Robert (qv)) and *After the Battle* Editor Winston G. Ramsay, expert on military vehicles, also helped. The cast was a brilliant line-up of international stars. The performance of Edward Fox as the ebullient Horrocks rings particularly true and Paul Maxwell made a convincing Major-General Maxwell Taylor. Michael Caine is less convincing as the Irish Guards officer, Joe Vandeleur. John Frost and Anthony Hopkins, who played him, (as related to the authors by the General) took an instant dislike to each other, which was soon tempered as each recognized the other's professionalism in their own field.

The film begins with authenticity and clarity but unfortunately later degenerates into what is, even to those familiar with the actual events, a confusing patchwork, with some major inaccuracies – especially at the Nijmegen Bridge where the superb actions of Captain Tony Jones (qv) are not even mentioned while Robert Redford appears to take the bridge single-handedly. And yet... it must be remembered that this is a feature film, not a documentary and it does, in many respects, portray the spirit of the Operation – the initial hopes, the obduracy of some of the senior officers, the sheer dogged courage of the men, the delight and support of the civilians, the danger, the disappointment, the dejection.

World at War. This celebrated television series included an episode on Arnhem which also covered the Battle of the Bulge and the Rhine Crossing. It featured General Horrocks who also appeared in a memorable television series on Operation MARKET-GARDEN. Horrocks was a 'natural' on the small screen - enthusiastic but with the ability to explain with clarity this complicated exercise. His performance was obviously keenly studied by Edward Fox.

Magazines. ATB (*After the Battle*) produce several of their superbly researched magazines on the Operation: a Special Edition, Prelude to MARKET GARDEN, THE BATTLE OF ARNHEM and WAR FILM: 'A BRIDGE TOO FAR': No.2 THE BATTLE OF ARNHEM: No. 86 which includes 'The Market Garden Corridor Tour' and No. 96 which includes ARNHEM VC INVESTIGATION (Flight Lieutenant Lord).

Contact: ATB, Church House, Church Street, London E15 3JA. Tel: 020 8534 8833.
E-mail: afterthebattle@mcmail.com
website: www.afterthebattle.mcmail.com

The Fortieth and Fiftieth Anniversaries

These were major and memorable gatherings, with large numbers of veterans and practically all the famous senior officers still fit enough to travel participating. Generous receptions and other events were hosted by the major towns along The Corridor and in Arnhem-Oosterbeek and commemorative medals were struck. After the 40th Anniversary work began on fund-raising for the Groesbeek Liberation Museum, actively supported by General Gavin who was present at the event.

They were also the trigger for many important new monuments to be erected and new books on the Operation to be published. Therefore the dates 1984 and 1994 will be seen throughout this book in the descriptions of memorials. Gatherings have been held on subsequent years, each with a dwindling number of veterans attending, and it is probable that the 60th anniversary in 2004 will be what the Americans so appropriately call 'The Last Hurrah'.

One of the most imaginative commemorative events staged for the 50th Anniversary was the 'MARKET-GARDEN Corridor Tour'. Some 800 historic military vehicles took part in this event which had been planned like a military operation, watched by over a million spectators along the route. Mass para drops were sadly somewhat curtailed by bad weather, but some managed to land at Son and at Ginkel Heath. There was also a fly-past of historic aircraft (including two 'Flying Fortresses' and three Spitfires) some towing gliders. The MARKET element started at Leopoldsburg and worked its way up The Corridor, many veterans joining in for parts of the route. A Torch of Freedom was brought with the column from Bayeux. Veterans of the 504th PIR re-enacted their daring Waal crossing (this time in DUKWs) and Lord Carrington led a group of Sherman tanks across the Nijmegen Bridge. Despite some major delays (which echoed the real thing 50 years earlier) this was a spectacular event which conveyed to the younger generation a tiny flavour of what happened in September 1944. [See *After The Battle* (qv) No 86].

THE MARKET-GARDEN CORRIDOR TODAY

The Profileration and Character of Memorials

Holland is a country rich with municipal sculpture and al fresco ornamentation. Every village, town and city has a goodly number of statues and sculptures on roundabouts, or in their centres, or dotted around housing estates. Many demonstrate the industry or main occupation of the area – either in days gone by or today. So there will be charming figures of clog makers and cowherds, statues of ponies and children, and some fun groups such as the giant skittles in Eindhoven. But many of them are of such an avant garde and symbolic nature as to be totally incomprehensible to the Anglo-Saxon mind. The same applies to some of the monuments to MARKET-GARDEN, and so the first-time reader may well spend some time carefully examining an arrangement of metal or concrete that turns out to have nothing to do with the campaign. Therefore we have illustrated as many of the memorials as we could and have tried to explain their meaning.

Some of them are in a rather sorry state, showing, perhaps, the lack of co-ordinated care such as is provided by the *Souvenir Français* Organisation in France.

Airborne Commemorative Markers

After the war containers, with text, were placed at a number of significant locations around the battlefield. In the late 1960s Officers of 4 Para Brigade (notably General Hackett) replaced them with 7 commemorative wooden posts, surmounted by a brass Pegasus symbol. In the mid-1980s 6 remained.

They were:

1. In front of the Tafelberg
2. At No. 192 Utrechtseweg in what used to be the Pastor's garden
3. On Dreijenseweg, where 156th Para Battalion was stopped
4. By 'The Hollow' on Valkenburglaan
5. By the 'Lonsdale' Church

6. By the entrance to the St Elisabeth Hospital

The wooden posts proved not to be durable and the handsome brass Pegasus badges were easy prey for souvenir hunters. Gradually the wooden posts were replaced by local town councils with concrete ones, with indented Pegasus badges.

Later was added

7. Just before the Nelson Mandela Bridge, marking the nearest point to The
Bridge reached by 1 and 3 Para.

In 1999 was added

8. On the site of the Van Limburg von Stirum School near The Bridge

The Latest Memorials

Perhaps surprisingly, memorials and museums are still being initiated or enlarged. For instance, in 1999 Airborne Commemorative Marker No 8 was erected at the Van Limburg Stirum School (qv) and a new plaque was added to the Frank Doucette Memorial (qv) in Leirop. The following year the Childrens' Monument was erected at Kamp Vught (qv), the Groesbeek National Liberation Memorial (qv) underwent major extension and improvement, the Jacob Groenewoud Plantsoen (qv) in Arnhem was added to, a memorial in the form of a swing (qv) was erected in Nijmegen to those killed in wartime bombing. Several memorials have recently been erected or added to in the Over-Betuwe, the latest being to the crash site of the Dakota in which members of 156th Para were killed near Dodewaard. The house of war artist and sculptor Jac Maris (qv) in Heumen is currently being converted into a museum.

In 1994, after the major events of the 50th anniversary, the Municipality of Renkum decided they would not cooperate in the setting up of any new memorials. Since that date commemorative plaques on seats placed at various points around the battlefield are the only memorials to have been installed.

Keeping the Flame of Remembrance Burning/The Way Forward

Many towns and villages along The Corridor, on The Island and in Arnhem-Oosterbeek have annual commemorative ceremonies and events (see the listing and contacts for current information on page 276). These are normally held either on National Commemoration Day, 4 May or National Liberation Day, 5 May (hence the unveiling of so many monuments on those dates), or on the anniversary of either the battle or the liberation of the particular town.

At present many of these events depend upon organisation by, and participation of, local people who actually remember the events of 1944/45 and the presence of veterans.

Typical are the full programmes in the Nijmegen-Groesbeek and Arnhem-Oosterbeek areas, both largely centred on their main military museums, the National Liberation Museum at Groesbeek (qv) and the Airborne Museum at the Hartenstein (qv). They include wreath-laying ceremonies and services at main memorials and cemeteries, parachute drops (by modern Paras but often with participation of brave - some would say foolhardy - veterans!), tattoos, marches and parades, lunches, dinners and dances, concerts and militaria fairs. To be a spectator of, or participator in, these events is memorable, impressive, moving, sometimes sad, sometimes exciting and great fun.

It must be recognized that 17 September meant very different things to Arnhem-Oosterbeek (the beginning of hope followed by a dreadful battle and nine months of evacuation and starvation before returning to demolished homes) and Eindhoven-Nijmegen (the start of Liberation).

The important question that now arises is, however, what will happen when the last local survivor of the battles and the last veteran of the Operation are no more? One fear is that the acts of remembrance will, in time, die out and those, of so many nationalities, who gave their lives for freedom in the Netherlands will gradually be forgotten.

The question is raised in a country where there is a strong Peace/Anti-War movement, especially among the young. It is also a country with no great military tradition or history of victorious battles honoured. Many feel that commemorative events such as described above 'glorify war', that it is better to forget the past and get on with the future of a united Europe. Happily the flame of remembrance has been passed, still burning strongly, to other young people, like the schoolchildren of the Municipality of Renkum who annually place flowers on every single grave in the CWGC Cemetery and the families who immediately after the war 'adopted' war graves in cemeteries in their commune and have tended them with loving care ever since. Others have become fascinated in the historical aspects of the battles that took place on their soil over half a century ago and they have produced research and publications of an extremely high standard, as is evidenced in the multiplicity of titles in the Hartenstein Airborne Museum book stall.

Also balancing the Dutchman's love of peace is his passion for freedom. It is difficult for those of us who have not endured enemy occupation to understand just what that precious word means. Dutch soil, as defined by the 1940 borders, had not been fought upon until the German invasion of that year since the British invaded Walcheren in 1809. This strong love in part explains the incredibly forgiving and understanding attitude of the Dutch (with very few exceptions) towards the price they had to pay for liberation. They suffered the trauma of battle, their homes were ruined, their possessions lost, their loved ones were killed, maimed, deported or shot, they were forced to evacuate and returned to desolation. Many a GI or Tommy has expressed his wonderment at this phenomenon, at the warm and ongoing welcome that is extended to them when they return to their old battle grounds. As long as one child of 1944 survives, one gets the impression that this will continue. But what then?

The answer seems to have been found in Eindhoven by the 18 September Foundation (qv) under their forward-looking Chairman, Mr. M. Besnard. As well as organising the traditional 18 September Veterans' Welcome and Parade (which, unusually, includes

Illuminated Mississippi River Boat, Eindhoven Light Festival

German participation, including the Ambassador) and ceremony of rekindling the Flame of Freedom brought from Bayeux in Normandy (qv), plus an ecumenical service at St Catherine's Church, their Committee, with the active support of the US Ambassador to the Netherlands, Mrs Schneider, have made it a priority to educate and involve the youth of the city in their annual commemorations. They organise specialised events which are designed to appeal to the younger generation and concentrate on cultural events with the theme of Freedom, Liberty and Peace. They also examine censorship and oppression and attract participation at the highest international level: lecturers have included Ministers of Foreign Affairs, Bishop Desmond Tutu's second-in-command etc. Events include drama and poetry competitions, concerts (both classical and pop), films and street parties and continue for a week over the 18 September period. Another universal attraction at this time is the famous Circuit of Lights Festival (qv). This compares with the Blackpool Illuminations or London's West End Christmas Lights in its spectacular effects, as is appropriate for the City of Lights, the home of Philips.

The event started simply in 1945, with candles in the windows of buildings along the Liberation route. It soon progressed to electric lamps in the streets as well as in the houses. It grew apace until 1969 when it became a 5-yearly event. It had to cease in 1972/73 because of the oil crisis, but in 1983 a small group of youngsters started it up again, having remembered seeing the colourful display from the pillions of their parents' bikes, the traditional way of going round the route. From 1984, when a subsidy was granted from the 18 September Festival Committee, the event grew from strength to strength, with its own committee responsible for wheedling subsidies from local firms like, naturally, Philips, who donate the millions of bulbs, to iron works for the elaborate base of the illuminations, to schools who provide their halls for their 6 weeks of assembly work. Each area of the city has its own group of volunteers responsible for its lights – their design, welding, painting, wiring, mounting, cabling, connection, storage and repair.

There are thirty-six different points along the 'figure of eight' route, which is 22 kms in length. It starts at the station and finishes at the Airborne Monument (qv) and is traditionally followed by local citizens by bicycle. Many of the 600+ illuminations have a September 1944 theme – of tanks, jeeps, aeroplanes, parachutes, Screaming Eagles, Victory 'V's, sometimes with personalities like 'Monty', Churchill and Eisenhower. Others are simply spectacular fun. In 1997 a photographic competition was mounted, the results of which were printed in a colourful book, the proceeds of which went towards the Circuit of Lights.

A similar feeling that it is now up to the younger generation to continue some form of commemoration that is meaningful to them is being expressed by the members of the Lest We Forget Foundation (qv) in Arnhem-Oosterbeek. As the number of veterans they host dropped by half from 1999 to 2000 and some of the veterans found it impossible to march the short distance of the traditional 'Silent March' to The Bridge it has now been discontinued.

Apparent to the worldwide battlefield pilgrim is the lack along the MARKET-GARDEN area of well-defined, mapped and published routes. There are no standardised informative signs for points of interest along them. A good start, however, is being made by the Hartenstein Mueum, which in 2001 organised a walking route from the Museum down to the river and back, with explanatory markers along the way.

Models of excellence for routing and signing can be found in the United States for their

Civil War sites, and in Europe, along the Normandy D-Day Beaches, standard information boards and route literature available at all tourist offices in the area even extend through two separate *Départements* – Calvados and La Manche. Similar clear and easily recognizable signing can be seen on the Somme where some important sites (like trench lines and bunkers) have been carefully preserved and are well-presented and explained to the visitor. Even in Gallipoli, in a remote area of Turkey, the excellently informative and durable bronze markers erected by Australian Ross Bastiaan give the visitor a clear picture of what happened at each historic spot. All these areas, like Ieper in Belgium and, to a perhaps over-commercialized extent, at Waterloo, have recognized the sobering fact that the future and continuance of battlefield pilgrimage lies in the developemnt of 'tourism'. It brings many people to the area, who often visit other attractions, fill hotels, restaurants and museums and bring trade to local shops and businesses. The benefit to battlefield sites is often the upgrading of museums, the creation of adequate car parks and the preservation of historic places. The net result is the guarantee that the events and the sacrifices of local inhabitants and would-be liberators alike – even if in a somewhat diluted form – will be preserved, hopefully for ever more. This surely must be the way forward for the villages, towns and cities along the MARKET-GARDEN Route, but it would take a co-operative and cohesive initiative by all the VVVs and tourist authorities, museums and commemorative organisations in the area.

A sign that attitudes are slowly changing was the unveiling on 8 March 2001 in the small village of Haelen in Limburg in Holland, near the German border, of a unique Joint Monument to all the German and Allied soldiers of WW2. The ceremony was attended by veterans from both sides and was reported by the national press and television.

THE AIRBORNE FORCES MUSEUM ALDERSHOT

As a prelude to a visit to the MARKET-GARDEN Battlefields, a visit to the above museum is rewarding.

At present the Museum (full title Parachute Regiment and Airborne Forces Museum) is in the most appropriate location for it – Browning Barracks – but there are plans to move it in the future, so check the current situation before embarking on a visit.

Browning Barracks, Aldershot, Hants GU11 2BU. Tel: 01252 349619

Open: Mon-Sun 10.00-16.30, last admission 15.45. Entrance Fee payable.

The Museum contains a small book/souvenir shop which has a mail order catalogue. Tel: 01252 310304.

It was opened by Field-Marshal Montgomery on 23 March 1969 and charts the history of Airborne Forces from their inception to the present day. Items include many original photos, personal artefacts and uniforms of Airborne personalities such as John Frost and 'Boy' Browning (who based his on the WW1 Flying Corps uniform) and the original emblem of the Airborne forces – Bellerophon on the winged horse Pegasus, which was chosen by Browning in 1941 and designed in May 1942 by Major Edward Seago as a flash. Among the varied exhibits there are sections devoted to the history of air to ground supply (first used in action at the Houthulst Forest 1-4 October 1918), to the Polish Independent Para Brigade, to the US Airborne of MARKET; there are original paintings, three-dimensional cameos and

Airborne scene, September 1944. Detail of large picture presented to the Museum in 1994 by the artist, Eef Brakel

models, including the Paras at Arnhem and the John Frost Bridge.

An appropriate summary of the MARKET Operation by Dr. John C. Warren of the USAAF Historical Division in 1946 appears in the US Section of the Museum:

When all is said, it is not the monumental size nor the operational intricacies of MARKET which linger longer in the memory. It is the heroism of the men who flew burning, disintegrating planes over their zones as coolly as if on review and gave their lives to get the last trooper out, the last bundle dropped. It is the stubborn courage of the airborne troops who would not surrender though an army came against them. In the sense that both troop carriers and airborne troops did all that men could do, there was, as Gavin said, no failure in MARKET.

THE APPROACH FROM THE CHANNEL PORTS/TUNNEL

The Continental start point might be from the Tunnel, from Calais Ferry Port, from Dunkirk or Ostende. As a guide the timings and distances are given from the centre point – Calais Ferry Terminal. Whichever is the point of entry, the journey is virtually on motorways all the way to the start point for Itinerary One. There are no tolls.

N.B. On the motorways always be aware of at least the next two large towns along the route to ensure that you take the correct exit.

From Calais Ferry Terminus zero the odometer and take the E40/A16 signed to Dunkerque/Bruges. After the Belgian border (58 kms/36.3 miles) take the E40/A18 direction Brugge (Bruges).

At 101 kms/63 miles is the first Petrol/Services Station at Jabbeke.

At Oudenberg and/or coming from Ostende (110 kms/68.5 miles) take the E40/A10 to Gent.

At 142 kms/89miles there is a Petrol/Service Station just after the Gent Ouest exit – a newly refurbished "Milestone". (Expect to pay the equivalent of 25p for the WCs).

Then take the E17/A14 to Antwerp (149 kms/93 miles).

At 203 kms/127 miles is the Tunnel under the Scheldt.

Continue on the Antwerp Ring Road and take the Eindhoven/E34 exit (211 kms/132 miles). Continue on the E34 to Ranst then take the E313/A13 direction Hasselt/Luik and leave it at the Kwaadmechelen Exit No 25 (261 kms/163 miles) towards Leopoldsburg onto the N141.

At 262 kms/164 miles cross the Albert Canal.

Continue through Ham to Oostham. Drive into the town and turn right signed Centrum at the traffic lights. Stop by the church on the left.

To the left of the Church is a memorial garden, in which is

4th/7th Royal Dragoon Guards/12th Battalion KRRC Memorial/Map 1S 1/ 267 kms/167 miles

The handsome black polished granite Memorial was raised in September 2000 at the instigation of local historian Carl Reymen, the town council and local history society in co-operation with the regiments concerned in the battle for Oostham. It bears the legend, 'In proud Memory of the

12th KRRC-4th/7th RDG
Memorial, Oostham

British soldiers who were killed during the Liberation of Oostham', the words 'For Peace and Freedom', an engraved red poppy spray and the words, 'The Creully Club' (qv). The unveiling took place on 16 September in the presence of some 150 MARKET-GARDEN veterans and, unbeknown to many of them, the German tank squadron commander Franz Kopka. A Memorial service is planned to be held here each September.

On 8 September 1944, Guards Armoured Division cleared the bridge over the Albert Canal at Beeringen so that the 4th/7th RDG could cross. In the afternoon B Squadron, together with A Company of the 12th KRRC, swung left through Beverlo towards Oostham. 2nd Troop went straight up the road into the village, 1st and 5th Troops were sent round the flanks.

General Student, who was at nearby Heppen, ordered Franz Kopka of 3rd Squadron Panzerjäger Abteilung to recce Oostham to ascertain the extent of British infiltration. Kopka bypassed the village to the north-east and doubled back to the centre of the village. There he saw a Sherman and fired, missing it 'by the thickness of a Rizla paper'. He then knocked out the first Sherman of 2nd Troop only to be knocked out by Sergeant Wilson in the following tank. The crew got out (one dying later) and the wounded Kopka was evacuated to hospital. He returned to his unit on 17 September in time to command the whole Panzerjäger Abteilung during their attack on Hell's Highway. During this action and on 9 and 10 September Troopers John Hill, age 19, and Stan Moffatt, age 21, of the 4th/7th and Lieutenants Richard Luxmoore (age 21) and Robert Ellis (age 21) of the KRRC were killed. They are commemorated on the Memorial. Trooper K. T. Frampton was shown as being killed in the attack in the Regimental History. He was merely wounded, however, and survived, only to be killed after the war in a motor cycle accident. Troopers Moffatt and Hill are buried in Leopoldsburg CWGC Cemetery [VI.D.6 and 7.] as is Lieutenant Ellis [IV.B.6.]. Lieutenant Luxmoore is buried in Geel CWGC Cemetery [IV.C.6.]

The tank contest continued until it was 2-all and by nightfall the British had taken most of the village, but did not have the strength to keep off the continued enemy attempts at infiltration and had to withdraw.

The next morning A.1. Echelon (of supply lorries) of the RDGs crossed the canal and encountered a suicide squadron of 50 German paratroopers determined to destroy the Beeringen Bridge. After a fierce battle, including much hand-to-hand fighting, the Echelon drove off the enemy, but suffered two killed, 10 taken prisoner.

On 10 September the Regiment came under the Guards Armoured Division and moved towards Leopoldsburg, where they were told a large number of Belgian political prisoners were being held. On 11 September the Belgian Piron Brigade attacked the town and the Germans pulled out. On 14 September the 4th/7th RDG moved into good billets in the married quarters of the military barracks where they 'had the first proper rest, with an opportunity for baths and laundry and entertainment... since we left Normandy [445 miles distant] a month before.' Besides the Memorial are the local WW1 and WW2 Memorials and a mass grave of nine Unknowns.

Return to the traffic lights, turn right and continue to Heppen on the N141.

N.B. In 2001 the Town Council of Heppen was planning to erect a Memorial in the form of a propellor and a plaque with the names of RAF personnel lost in the area during the war.

• Extra Visit to Zonhoven, Site of Field-Marshal Montgomery's HQ (Map 1S/3) Round trip: 42 kms/26 miles. Approximate time: 60 minutes.

Turn right on the N72 through Beverlo to the old coal mining town of Beringen. By-pass the centre, and continue on the A72 over the A2 and immediately after the railway crossing take a left turn at 19 kms/12 miles to Zonhoven Centrum. Continue to the traffic lights, go straight over and at the next roundabout with the N715 (21 kms/12.9 miles) turn left on Houthalenseweg and stop at No. 9 on the left (now a lawyer's office).

On 9 September 1944 Zonhoven was liberated by the Allies and from 12 November 1944 to 7 February 1945, Monty made his headquarters in the house of the village physician, Dr. Armand Peeters. It was called 'Villa Magda' and bears a bronze plaque (just inside the railings on the right of the entrance) commemorating the Field-Marshal's stay and the fact that his cocker spaniel, named 'Rommel', died here. Rommel, who had been Monty's faithful companion from Normandy to Holland, was run over on 18 December 1944 and was buried in the garden of the villa. A white headstone marked the grave but sadly it was stolen.

Monty's HQ at Zonhoven with detail of plaque

Here Monty was visited by General Eisenhower and other American and Canadian senior officers. Dempsey was a frequent visitor. The Field-Marshal in his staff car or jeep was a familiar figure in the village, but the inhabitants kept their important secret well and the whereabouts of the HQ was not even known in nearby villages. Tanks and armoured cars guarded the villa. Every Sunday a large car transported an altar into the church hall and Monty, with his entourage, attended a service in the makeshift Anglican Church.

On 7 January 1945, during the Battle of the Bulge, Montgomery held a press conference here attended by reporters from *The Daily Herald*, *The Manchester Guardian*, *The Times* and from Reuters.

On 7 February a large column formed up outside the villa and the Field-Marshal drove slowly away from Zonhoven, waving to the crowd that gathered to say farewell.

Return to Heppen and rejoin the Approach Route.

Continue through Heppen on the N73 direction Lommel and continue into Leopoldsburg, over the railway line. Follow the one-way system to a large roundabout with a statue of a girl in the centre. Turn left signed Hasselt towards the station. Continue to the T-junction and turn right at the Station and immediately park on the left (274 kms/171 miles).

ITINERARY ONE

LEOPOLDSBURG TO EINDHOVEN

• **Itinerary One** starts at Leopoldsburg in Belgium where General Horrocks gave his famous MARKET-GARDEN briefing, crosses the border into Holland and follows the XXX Corps Corridor to Eindhoven. There it examines the US 101st AB Division's drops and actions.
• **The Route:** Leopoldsburg – Sherman Tank, Site of Cinema Splendid, Belgian Military Cemetery, CWGC Cemetery, Military Museum; Hechtel Sherman Tank Memorial; Lommel - Polish Cemetery, German Cemetery; 'Joe's Bridge' over Schelde-Maas Canal and Memorial; Dutch-Belgian Frontier/Liberation Gate Memorial; Café t'Heertje Memorial; Valkenswaard – CWGC Cemetery, Dommel Bridge, Liberation Memorial; Aalst Liberation Memorial; Eindhoven – Liberation Monument, Bombardment *Bas Relief*, Liberation *Bas Relief*, VVV/Railway Station,
• **Extra Visits** are suggested to the Resistance Cemetery and Memorial, Leopoldsburg Military Barracks; Captain Freddy Limbosch Monument and Grave, Peer; Philips WW2 Memorial; Mierlo CWGC Cemetery; Helmond Liberation and Royal Norfolk Memorials; German Cemetery, Ijsselsteyn; Venray CWGC Cemetery; Lobeek Norfolk Regiment Memorial; Overloon Chapel of the Safe Hide-away, National War & Resistance Museum and CWGC Cemetery.
• **Additional Extra Visits** to Nedersweert CWGC Cemetery and Weert RC Cemetery; Memorials at Zandoerle, Bladel, Netersel, Hoogeloon.
• **Planned duration,** without stops for refreshment or Extra Visits: **6 hours**
• **Total distance: 62 kms/38.8 miles**

• *Leopoldsburg Station. Sherman Tank/ Site of Cinema Splendid/0 kms/0 miles/10 minutes/RWC/Map 9-1/1a/2*

Outside the station is a Sherman tank, No (left) E4151 B1782 40 (G) S, (right) E1231 B1636 LO (G) 2. The caption recounts how on 12 September 1944 Leopoldsburg was liberated by the Piron Brigade

Sherman Tank,
Leopoldsburg Station

(British accounts say that the Belgians 'assisted' the 8th Armoured Brigade to liberate Leopoldsburg on 11 September) and that on 16 September General Horrocks gave his famous briefing (see below) – the beginning of the campaign that came to be known as 'A Bridge Too Far'. The barrel of the main gun points at the site of the Cinema Splendid. On the turret is a Browning machine gun and on the side of the tank is the Guards Armoured Division 'Eye' insignia.

Walk 100 metres down the road past the station to the site of No 49 on the left.
This is currently (2001) an empty gap between the buildings.

On 16 September 1944, the day before MARKET-GARDEN was to begin, Leopoldsburg was 'invaded' by British Military Police who controlled the vehicles that brought in the officers of XXX Corps for their briefing by General Horrocks. He addressed what he described as 'a motley audience' (because of their extraordinary variation in dress – the General himself was wearing a high-necked woollen sweater) at 1100 hours in the Cinema Splendid. Standing in front of an enormous map of Holland and holding a long pointer Horrocks began, 'This is a tale that you will tell your grandchildren and mighty bored they'll be'. He talked for an hour, imbuing his listeners with a sense of excitement and urgency that many of them remembered long afterwards, but not everyone was totally happy with the plan. Armoured commanders were apprehensive about moving tanks along a single narrow road, but a collective aura of adventure and opportunity overtook them all.

The area around the town had been turned into a huge engineer dump in order to support the coming operation. Among the 20,000 or so vehicles of XXX Corps were more than 2,200 engineer and transport lorries carrying the supplies that would be needed if all of the bridges to be captured in the forthcoming airborne operation were blown by the Germans.

Today there is a wide variety of different nationality restaurants within easy walking distance of the station, including many that serve the simple dishes at which the Belgians excel – chicken and chips with mayonnaise and an interesting salad garnish, pepper steak etc.

Return to your car. Continue on the N73 (back into the one-way system) and turn right at the T-junction signed to the CWGC Cemetery. Continue towards the church and turn left and then right following CWGC signs. Straight ahead on Leopold II Laan is

• *Leopoldsburg Belgian Cemetery/1.1 kms/.7 miles/15 minutes/Map 9/3*

The cemetery, which was originally a burial ground for the Germans who died in the nearby Camp Hospital (and who are now reburied in the German Military Cemetery of Kattenbos),

Leopoldsburg Belgian Cemetery

contains 826 burials from WW1 (including 408 Russians). Some of the Belgians also died in the Hospital, others in POW camps in Germany and who were not reclaimed by their families to be buried in their home villages. It was officially established as a military cemetery in the early 1920s.

The WW2 extension (at the back of the cemetery behind the central chapel) contains 418 burials. At the rear are symbolic crosses for the Belgian Resistance workers who were shot at the nearby execution site (qv) and whose bodies have since been removed. There are also members of the Piron Brigade and in the top right-hand corner, a small plot with six Russian graves, one bearing a large Cross of Lorraine. Until the 1950s the cemetery maintenance was assisted by the Red Cross and the Association 'Nos Tombes – Onze Graven' [Our Graves]. It is now exclusively maintained by the Ministry of Internal Affairs – Graves Service (qv).

The Belgian Piron Brigade in Belgium

The Brigade was created on 3 January 1943 at Clacton under Brevet Lieutenant-Colonel Piron and consisted of three Motorised Units (MOTs), an Armoured Squadron, an Artillery Battery and various Support Units.

The Brigade landed at Arromanches on 8 August 1944 and was attached to 6th AB Division. It liberated Deauville on the 22nd, Trouville on the 24th and Honfleur on the 26th.

On 28 August the Brigade was attached to 49th Infantry Division and on 2 September to the Guards Armoured Division. The next day it crossed the border into its native Belgium at Rongy and on the 4th entered Brussels to much joy and acclaim.

On 11 September the Belgian Group left the capital and was attached to 8th Armoured Brigade in the assault on Leopoldsburg, crossing the Albert Canal at Beringen at 1930 hours. At 1700 hours the 1st MOT Unit liberated 900 Political Prisoners at Leo Camp, 2nd MOT Unit moved to the west and 3rd MOT Unit stayed at Beverlo Camp.

Continue on Leopold II Laan to

• Leopoldsburg CWGC Cemetery/1.3 kms/.8 miles/15 minutes/Map 9/4

The cemetery is on the road leading to the military camp that was known as the 'King's Camp'. Of the 800 burials in it, 35 are original burials of casualties from isolated engagements in or near the town. The remainder were either from the military hospital established at Leopoldsburg during the latter part of 1944 or brought in from the surrounding district. There are 638 named UK Army graves (including 1 Special Memorial) and 14 Unknown, 69 UK Air Force and 3 Unknown, 27 Polish Army, 27 Canadian Air Force, 8 Australian Air Force, 1 South African Air Force, 1 Dutch Navy and 3 Dutch Army. Two graves are entirely unidentified.

Unusually, this attractively designed cemetery is not enclosed at the front by a hedge or wall, but by a ditch and rows of trees.

Many of these historic regiments represented here have since been amalgamated or disbanded and cemeteries such as these are among the only places where one can see carved on the headstones their proud regimental or corps badges.

Members of the Canadian, New Zealand and S African Air Forces and the Canadian Forestry Corps are represented.

The ages range from several 18-year-olds to the 45-year-old CSM of 129th Forestry Company, RE, **Robert Johnston Clayton**, 10 December 1944 [Plot III Row C Grave No.5 – III.C.5], 47-year-old **Private Frank Jones** of the Herefordshire Regiment, 20 September 1944 [V.C.5.] and 49-year-old **Sergeant Michael Maloney** of the Pioneer Corps, 18 October 1944 [I.B.5.].

Some entries make reference to a **brother** who also died on service, such as **Private Harold Dawber** of the 4th Lincolns, age 21, 25 September 1944 [V.A.18]. Trooper Ernest Dawber, RAC, 10 August 1940, is buried in Bebington Cemetery, Cheshire.

Corporal John William Harper of the Hallamshire Battalion, the York and Lancaster Regiment, was awarded the **Victoria Cross** when he first led his section, then took command of the platoon when his commander was killed, in an attack on the Dépôt de Mendecité near Antwerp on 29 September 1944. Corporal Harper killed or captured all the enemy holding the position – surrounded by a dyke and an earthen wall. He then led his platoon over 300 yards of open ground under severe mortar and small arms fire, climbed the wall, killed more of the enemy and established his platoon. He was fatally wounded while approaching a ford which crossed the dyke. Harper was 28 years old.

Major Edwin Swales of the SAAF, serving with 582nd Squadron RAF, age 29, won the **DFC** as well as the **Victoria Cross**. On 23 February 1945, as a 'master bomber', Swales took part in the night raid on Pforzheim. Over the target his aircraft was repeatedly attacked and severely damaged, but Swales continued to issue aiming instructions until the objectives were achieved. He managed to bring his plane back over friendly territory and ordered his crew to bale out. Then the plane plunged to earth and the gallant Major was found dead at the controls.

Major David Peel (qv) of the Irish Guards, age 33, killed on 12 September 1944 was awarded the **MC** [VI.C.3]. His father, the Rev. the Hon Maurice Peel, also won the MC and Bar and was Chaplain to the Forces. **Flight-Lieutenant John Pinny** of the 313rd Czech Squadron, RAF, age 24, was awarded the Czechoslovakia MC. He died on 1 February 1945 [I.B.13].

Major Hugh Lister, MC, Welsh Guards, age 43 'B.A. (Cantab.), Clerk in Holy Orders' [IV.A.10.] killed by a German sniper at 'Welsh Corner', was described by a fellow Guardsman as 'a real Christian, never afraid of death' and 'a great loss for the Welsh Guards'.

The aristocracy is represented by **Major Andrew Bonham-Carter** of the RNF [also commemorated on the Hechtel Sherman Tank Memorial (qv)], age 30, died on 11 September 1944, [I.C.8.], son of Air Commodore Ian Bonham-Carter and **Major William Cavendish, Marquess of Hartington**, 5th Coldstream Guards, age 26, MiD, son of the 10th Duke of Devonshire who died on 9 September 1944 [IV.B.13] at Heppen. He had married President John Kennedy's sister Kathleen ('Kit') who was killed in an aircrash on 13 May 1948.

Commemorated on a Memorial in Oostham (qv) where they were killed on 9/10 September 1944 are **Troopers J. Hill** and **S. Moffatt** 4th/7th RDG [IV.C. 6 and 7.], and **Lieutenant R.J.N. Ellis** KRRC [IV.B.6.].

The cemeteries are in the large military area of Leopoldsburg, but the Belgian Army has a very open relationship with the civilian population who may freely move in many parts

Leopoldsburg CWGC Cemetery

of the camp, other than obvious restricted zones. Many of the imposing mansions in the area are occupied by serving and retired generals and several impressive military memorials to earlier campaigns can be seen.

Continue along Leopold II Laan to the next crossroads and turn left on Zegeplaats.

After some 250m the magnificent Statue of Lieutenant General Chazal with a lion at his feet is to be seen on the right. *Bas reliefs* around the monument commemorate the battles of Bruxelles 1830 and Anvers 1859.

Continue on Prince Boudewijnlaan to the main road and turn left.

On the right the splendid Obelisk Memorial to the Mexican Wars is passed.

Continue to the Museum and the VVV on the right.

• *Museum/Leopoldsburg VVV/2.7 kms/1.7 miles/15 minutes/Map 9/5*

This traditional military museum is housed in the old military hospital which in pre-WW2 days was a model of modern military medicine. In 1943/44 the Kriegsmarine was stationed at Camp Beverlo, which was established in the late 19th Century and is to the Belgian Army what Aldershot is to the British. In May 1944 heavy bombing destroyed many of the original buildings. The history of the camp and various Belgian campaigns is demonstrated in the Museum in which there is a small MARKET-GARDEN exhibition. In it is one of the original posts against which many of the people were shot in the nearby forest (qv) and some photos of Leopoldsburg's Liberation by the Piron Brigade. There is also a Royal British Legion Section.

Open: Every weekday from 1300 – 1700 hours (other than public holidays) also the 1st and 3rd Saturday each month. It is closed from Christmas to the end of January. Entrance fee payable. Tel: [00 32] (0) 11 344804.

Many vintage tanks and vehicles may be seen amongst the buildings around it.

Next to the Museum is the **Leopoldsburg Tourist Office**, where a useful detailed map of the town may be obtained. Tel: [0032] (0) 11 402184

N.B. Some 100m down the road towards Leopoldsburg the Police Station is on the right. On the wall is a Plaque to Adjutant Dekeser F. L. J., born in Bierbeek on 11.4.1897, who died for the Fatherland in the German Concentration Camp Van Gross-Rosen on 11.12.1944. Map 9/6 Over the road, in a garden behind the Military Hospital bus stop, is a Patton Tank (M47), acquired by Major John Vanoverbeve, the former Commander of the Garrison, to embellish the garden of his HQ. Map 9/7.

Turn round and continue towards Hechtel.

The Air Club on the right was a pre-war Belgian Recce Airfield. At the water tower behind the airfield many local people were shot by the Germans.

Continue to a white sign to the right (6.7 kms/4.2 miles) to Monument v/d Weerstand (the Resistance Memorial)/Doorgaand E.

• Extra Visit to Limburg Resistance Memorial and Cemetery, Leopoldsburg Military Exercise Ground (Map 1S-4/5) Round trip: 2.2 kms/1.4 miles. Approximate time: 20 minutes

NB: Prior permission to visit this memorial (on weekends and holidays only) in the Hechtel Woods must be obtained from the Security Officer, Kamp Beverlo – Koninklijk Park, B-3970 Leopoldsburg, Tel: [00 32] (0) 11 398785. Secretariat Tel: [00 32] (0) 11 398205, in case there are exercises in progress.

Turn right up the track some .7 miles to a yellow rubbish bin and sign on the left to Dunes des Fusillés.

The information board on the left tells the story of this tragic site, known locally as the 'Secret Cemetery', in 4 languages. Classified regulations issued by the wartime German Military Administration in Brussels bear witness that the Hechtel execution site was started in May 1942. Records were to be kept of all executions that took place here: names, date and place of birth, offence, date of death etc. The cemetery started by the execution site was designated for all those executed in Belgium. Many locals were also shot here. Four execution posts were erected in front of a 'bullet catcher', a wall of stacked logs. Most of the killings took place between 0300 and 0400 hours, the scene illuminated by the headlights of the lorries which had carried the prisoners to their site of death. After being buried in the adjacent burial plot, the graves were marked by a numbered pole.

Monument and RAF Grave, Limburg Resistance Cemetery

A PERSONAL ACCOUNT

From Adjutant Bob Vranken of the Belgian Army.

Before the War my grandfather was a forester in this wood. He, my grandmother and my mother lived in a cottage beyond the execution site, which was enclosed by barbed wire, with a German sniper's tower at each corner. My mother remembers seeing truckloads of people being driven past the cottage into the woods and then hearing screams and the sound of shots. After the liberation my grandfather came to the site where there were still the marks of the studs on the boots of the executioners on the grass, four posts, full of bullet holes, to which the victims were chained, a stretcher stained with blood and a large number of graves. The flimsy coffins were made of crates for carrying straw from the houses of Camp Beverlo. My mother then watched as a doctor who came from Brussels to identify the bodies as they were exhumed set up a table with his surgical instruments and a flask of strong brandy, the fumes of which he had to inhale to take away the dreadful stench. In the third grave to be opened was the body of the doctor's own son, who had worked with the Resistance and disappeared. The poor doctor collapsed and another had to be sent for. She also witnessed a smartly dressed woman alight from an expensive car, kneel by one of the graves and ask for forgiveness. She then returned to the car, powdered her nose, said, 'Well that's done', and drove away. It turns out that she was a collaborator with the Germans and had betrayed her Resistance Worker husband, who was then shot. German deserters were also executed at this place.

Two members of my family – my great-uncle and his brother-in-law - were shot by drunken German soldiers in Hechtel just before the Liberation (qv).

Extra visit continued

The site was visited by Norman Kirby, who was General Montgomery's Intelligence and Security Officer and his Interpreter, on 23 September 1944. He had been sent to the area to recce 'the Chief's' route through Belgium after their stay in Brussels and in a clearing in the middle of a fir plantation near where we had pitched our tents, I stumbled upon an execution firing range. There were four wooden stakes and butts riddled with bullet holes and approximately two hunded graves in an adjoining clearing indicated by posts each bearing a number engraved on a metal tablet.' He recalled being 'brought gruesomely to earth by another reminder of what the war was all about.'

Up till Spring 2001 there was a monument, in the form of a massive rock, on the site where the execution posts stood, with a fine *bas relief* portrait of a Resistance Worker by Louis Dupont after a drawing by Axheles. It is to the memory of Resistance Fighters who fell for Liberty. The Belgian Military then planned to remove the stone to the adjoining plot and re-erect four stakes on the site of the original ones in a project to restore the site to its precise 1944 aspect.

Extra visit continued

To the right is an enclosed area at the side of which are 174 crosses marking the original site of the graves of those who were shot here, although 204 bodies were actually exhumed. They were erected in 1984. Among them is a 'Serg of the RAF' (and it is believed that at least one other RAF airman was shot here), about whom no details are known. A 6-metre high cross was raised on 5 September 1987 by the Limburg Secret Army Veterans. It is known as the Cross of Resistance and to its left is a board with the 698 names of local civilians killed in the war- many of them in the September 1944 period of reprisals - inaugurated by Joseph Bussels, then Burgomaster of Hechtel and author of a book called *The Battle of Hechtel*. A German Padre had kept a list of all those who were shot here, starting in 1942, which made identification easier. Every 4 September there is a ceremony of remembrance at this spot when children place a flower in a container decorated with the colours of the Belgian flag before each symbolic grave.

Turn round, return to the main road, turn right and continue the main itinerary.

Continue towards Hechtel to the crossroads and traffic lights.

N.B. 100m before the crossroads is a small alleyway to the left. Along it is a red brick wall which still shows damage from the Battle of Hechtel. Beyond it is the old distillery where, on the night of 11 September 1944 eleven locals were shot by drunken Germans, including the members of Bob Vranken's family mentioned above.]

• *Extra Visit to the Grave and Monument to Lieutenant Limbosch, Belgian S.A.S., Peer. (Map 1S-9/10)*
Round trip: 19 kms/12 miles. Approximate time: 30 minutes

Continue over the crossroads, direction Peer along Stationsstraat, which becomes Peerderbaan and then Steenweg Wijchmaal to the cemetery on the right.

In the cemetery is the grave of Lieutenant Freddy Limbosch of the Belgian S.A.S. who was killed in Peer on 8 September 1944. Limbosch and his men were dropped during the Liberation of Normandy for OPERATION SHAKESPEARE and again in September 1944 for OPERATION CALIBAN. Their mission was to gather intelligence about enemy movements and to attack wherever possible. They signalled that the enemy was in full retreat and then noticed a concentration of SS troops. Limbosch knew that the advancing Allies should be informed of this concentration as soon as possible. On his way to pass on his news Limbosch was killed.

Turn round, take the second left along Houtestraat, cross over the junction with Elsevaart and then fork right along Limboschstraat. The memorial is in the field on the corner.

The street is named after Lieutenant Limbosch and in it, at the site where he was killed, is his **Monument** in the form of a massive rock with his name and the SAS wings. In spring 2001 Freddy Limbosch's widow still lived in Brussels.

Return to the Hechtel crossroads and rejoin the main itinerary.

Monument to Freddy Limbosch, Peer

Turn left direction Eksel and immediately park on the right. Walk across the road to the tank.

• *Hechtel Memorial Sherman/10 kms/6.1 miles/10 minutes/Map 1S-6/7*

Sherman No (G) E4186 IB1635 LO has been preserved as a memorial to all those who lost their lives during the Battle of Hechtel of 12 September 1944 – 35 citizens, 62 British soldiers and 124 German soldiers. The British soldiers are commemorated on plaques at the base of the tank under their units and formations: X Coy, Scots Guards, 1st and 2nd Battalions Welsh Guards, Irish Guards, Herefordshire Lt Inf, R Northumberland Fusiliers, 151 Field Regt RA TA, Inns of Court Regiment, 3rd Battalion Monmouths, 2nd Battalion Fife & Forfar Yeomanry and the Nederlandse Verkenningsafdeling. The citizens of Hechtel are all named on the other side. By the tank the flags of Belgium and the Union Jack (albeit upside-down) fly proudly.

Sherman Memorial Tank, Hechtel   Memorial to Frans Maes, Hechtel

The leading elements of the Guards Armoured Division had reached this junction on 7 September but were held up for three days by determined German opposition. After reorganising they launched an attack from the south at 1000 hours on 10 September on either side of this crossroads with the objective of taking the bridge over the Groote Barrier up ahead (later to be named Joe's Bridge.). The road north was their main axis of advance (Club Route) and by 1925 hours 2nd HCR were able to see that the bridge was intact but strongly held. The Irish Guards decided to rush the bridge. (See entry for Joe's Bridge below.) Waiting behind Hechtel was the divisional column of some 5,000 vehicles carrying four days' rations and petrol for 250 miles.

Continue to the first turning to the right.

N.B. By turning right here along Ekselsebaan (the N747) and continuing just past house No 42 on the right, is a small black Plaque to Frans Maes, born in Overpelt on 5.9.1916, who was killed here on 31.12.1944. His girlfriend was also shot after they left a New Year's Eve party by a German plane flown by a Belgian collaborator. (Map 1S/8).

Continue through Eksel towards Lommel and turn left towards Kerkhoven on Kiefhoekstraat. At the T-junction with the N746 turn right towards Lommel. Continue to the sign to the right to the German Cemetery. N.B. It is easily missed.

• *German Cemetery, Lommel/24 kms/14.9 miles/20 minutes/Map 1S/11*

This vast park-like cemetery, the largest German WW2 burial ground outside of Germany, contains the graves of 38,962 German soldiers of the '39-45 war and 541 of the '14-'18 war (see Belgian Cemetery above).

In 1945 the American Battle Monuments Commission transferred all German dead found in this area of Belgium and Germany into four provisional graveyards – at Henri-Chapelle, Fosse, Overrepen and Neuville-en-Condroz. At that time Lommel was a temporary American cemetery, but during 1946-7 the Americans ceded it to the Germans. The Belgian authorities then transferred all German soldiers killed in Belgium to Lommel, as well as the First World War burials originally buried in Leopoldsburg. One cross was erected for every two burials, so that nearly 20,000 crosses covered the 16-hectare site. Between 1978-80 the original enamel name-plates were changed to metal ones. They show, when known, the rank, dates of birth and death and grave number. Originally 13,000 of the fallen were unknown. After the German-Belgian War Graves Agreement the Volksbund Deutsche

The endless graves, German Cemetery, Lommel

Kriegsgräberfürsorge (qv) succeeded in identifying 7,000 of them and research work into identifications continues to this day.

The two-winged entrance shelter contains the cemetery registers, postcards, literature and visitors' book and toilets. Ahead of it is a crypt, surmounted by an enormous Calvary, weighing 39 tonnes. At each side of the cross are 3.30-metre-high, 7-tonne basalt sculptures of Mary and John. Inside the crypt is the prone figure of a German soldier, upon whose serene face the light shines through bronze grilles. Around the walls are mosaics. The landscaping was undertaken in the summer months of 1953-1955 by international youth camps from fifteen nations, led by experts from the Volksbund, when 5,000 trees and shrubs were planted – birch, maple, oak, pine and juniper. As the area was originally sandy heath with strong and high weeds and grasses, this was extremely hard work and 15,000 bales of peat and 2,000 cubic metres of forest soil had to be laid before planting could take place.

In front of the rows of 20,000 crosses, which seem to stretch as far as the eye can see, are beds of purple heather. In the centre a tree was planted on the 50th Anniversary of the end of the war in May 1995 as a sign of hope and peace.

Buried here are Wilhelm Schmidt, age 18, Gunther Billing, age 21, and Manfred Pernass, age 23, a team of Colonel Otto Skorzeny's Commandos who had created chaos near Malmédy in the Ardennes by operating in American uniform and changing signposts etc. The three were captured in American uniform and therefore considered as spies. They were shot at 0930 on 23 December 1944 at Henri-Chapelle. They were afterwards buried in a temporary cemetery at Henri-Chapelle and transferred here after the war.

Lommel German Cemetery was the site where, in 1953, the practice of holding International Youth Camps where young people worked on the cemeteries in the spirit of *Reconciliation through the Graves* began. Now some 1,000 children each year, from all parts of Germany, come for a week of education, of visits to schools and to the Polish and British cemeteries in the locality. There are extensive hostel and recreational facilities for them over and adjoining the main entrance building. The current Superintendent of the Youth Programme is the Belgian Frau Lucia Christiaen, whose family home is in Ieper.
Contact: [00 32] (0) 11 554370.

Return to the main road and turn right. At the traffic lights turn right on the N71 direction Hasselt/Neerpelt then left at the crossroads with the N715, signed Lommel. Continue some 200m to the Polish Cemetery on the left.

• *Polish Cemetery, Lommel/32 kms/20.1 miles/15 minutes/Map 1S/12*

This is the largest Polish Cemetery in Belgium, containing 256 white crosses and two Stars of David. It is maintained by the Polish Consulate in Brussels. On the last Sunday of each September a ceremony is held here, in which wreaths and candles are laid in the form of a cross. In the centre of the cemetery is a large Cavalry and, behind it, a memorial to 302nd, 308th and 317th Polish AB units. Polish Battle Honours from both World Wars are listed. Behind the memorial, with doors at each end, is a small museum which contains a Visitors' Book, photos of other Polish campaigns and Cemeteries, and personal memories. The history of the 1st Polish Division in WW2 is charted, including the Liberation of Ypres and its progression through Belgium into Holland.

The key to the museum may be obtained from the Shell/Citroen garage further up the road. THE KEY MUST BE RETURNED AFTER YOUR VISIT. Note that the garage is closed on Sundays.

Continue on the N715 north in the direction of Lommel Barrier to the Bocholt-Herentals Kanal (Schelde-Maas Canal).

To the left of the bridge approach was the café where Captain Hutton came for a quick drink – see below.

Cross the bridge and park in a slip road to the left immediately after the bridge. Walk down the slip road (which was the original road and leads to the site of the original bridge) to the canal bank.

• *Joe's Bridge/Memorial/35 kms/22 miles/15 minutes/Map 1S/14*

This is the spot where MARKET-GARDEN began. The Belgian Army destroyed the original bridge in 1940 and the Germans replaced it with a trestle construction of heavy timbers which in turn, after the operation, was later rebuilt. Here one can sense something of the excitement and anticipation of the men who waited on the afternoon of 17 September 1944 and watched the arrival of the airborne armada that signalled the beginning of one of the most audacious operations of the Second World War.

Under the arch of the bridge, whose Belgian name was De Groote Barrier Bridge, can be seen to the left (east) the factory from whose roof General Horrocks watched XXX Corps open OPERATION GARDEN on 17 September.

On 10 September Allied forces, though advancing north, were still south of the canal. That evening, in fading light, a combined force of Irish Guards infantry, commanded by Lieutenant-Colonel J.O.E. (Joe) Vandeleur (played by Michael Caine in the film *A Bridge Too Far*), and the Irish Guards armour, commanded by his cousin, Lieutenant-Colonel G.A.D. (Giles) Vandeleur, (they were known as 'Colonels Joe and Giles') rushed the bridge. Fire support was provided by tanks concealed in the factory area. After 20 minutes of shooting from the southern ramp of the bridge, Major David Peel led a troop of tanks at speed over it, passing a small lorry on fire halfway up the slope to the bridge and dispersing the remnants of German infantry, who had three 88mm guns on this side, a fourth gun having been destroyed on the southern side. The driver of the leading tank, Lance Corporal Claude Kettleborough, recalling the affair fifty years later, remembered that, 'Fags were to the high port – the rate about four fags per mile.' With the tanks came a troop of 615 Field Sqn, RE, known as 'Joe's Troop' for reasons quite unconnected with Joe Vandeleur. Their job was to make the bridge safe for the tanks by clearing any demolitions. The troop leader, Captain R. D. Hutton, dropped his wire cutters into the canal and had to use his revolver to shoot through the wires of the firing circuit and, having removed the initiators from the charges, went back over the bridge to a café for a drink. Two of his sappers, who had cut the wires to the charges at the ends of the bridge, were awarded the MM. Retaining ownership of Joe's Bridge was not easy in the days leading up to 17 September and, during one German counter-attack, Major Peel was killed. [He is buried in Leopoldsburg CWGC (qv).]

On 17 September a preliminary barrage from six field and three medium artillery regiments, supported by Belgian and Dutch units, was bolstered by a continuous stream of low-flying rocket-firing Typhoons from 83rd Group. The target area of all this firepower was a rectangle stretching from the Dutch border 8kms up The Corridor and 1km either side of

Polish Cemetery Lommel: Memorials and Headstones

Joe's Bridge, the factory and north bank Memorial

it. Everyone was full of confidence. General Horrocks had only one worry, 'The operation was starting on a Sunday.... No operation that I launched on a Sunday in the whole war was completely successful.' It was the same concern that General Sir Ian Hamilton had had about the ill-fated Gallipoli expedition, a campaign that General Urquhart would later call to mind in the evacuation of The Perimeter at Oosterbeek.

As Lieutenant Keith Heathcote in the first tank led off No.3 Squadron of 2nd Irish Guards, they were followed first by No.1 Company of Irish Guards Infantry carried on the tanks of No.1 Squadron and then a squadron of 2nd HCR scout cars, with the barrage rectangle rolling ahead of them. This was the beginning of the 'advance at maximum speed' that General Horrocks had ordered, but later, however, Dutch reports, (documentation issued at the 40th Anniversary of MARKET-GARDEN) say that great delay was caused by Typhoons mistaking the British armour for German and that eight tanks were destroyed by 'shelling by their own Typhoons'. The story that some of the tanks were hit by Typhoons is supported by an account of the 2nd Household Cavalry Regiment (*The Household Cavalry at War* by Roden Orde who commanded the Recce Troop of HCR during the battle) which says that two tanks were hit by Typhoons at around 1530 hours. There is no mention of this in the HCR War Diary, although two armoured cars were reported as being blown up on mines.

There is something of a mystery here since there is general agreement that eight or nine tanks were lost at the beginning of the operation (just over the Dutch border). So who did it? There was certainly German opposition which, as described in the Historical Summary, included Parachute and SS Battalions. These had been organised into an *ad hoc* formation known as 'Division Walther' which was equipped with panzerfaust and 88mm weapons. An Irish Guards' account (*History of the Irish Guards in the Second World War* by Major D. J. L. Fitzgerald) says, 'Nine tanks were knocked out in two minutes', and says that it was due to anti-tank guns concealed in trees at the side of the road (see below). The adjutant of the Irish Guards, Captain Vivian Taylor, travelled in a Humber scout car with the Battalion Tactical HQ which accompanied No. 1 Squadron. One of his tasks was that of liaising with Squadron Leader Max Sutherland and Flight Lieutenant Donald Love, who were the RAF ground-to-air controllers for the Typhoons and who were in a vehicle in the same group (there was also

Liberation Gate Memorial Dutch-Belgian Border

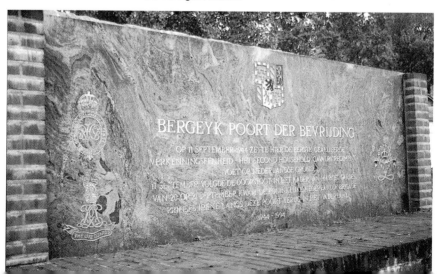

an American sergeant of the 101st with a radio). Taylor is certain that the tanks were hit by German fire. He remembers, 'Two of the things that have remained clearly in my mind were the speed at which the commanding officers (Colonels Joe and Giles) decided what should be done to ensure that our advance should not falter and then how quickly the air controllers brought in the rocket-firing Typhoons.'

Nevertheless, Ian Grant in his *Cameramen at War* casts doubt on the presence of 88mm guns. Film unit jeeps accompanied the leading troops and 'managed to record the "brewed-up" tanks, but were mystified as to the siting of the concealed 88s.' According to their maps they must have been resting on ground that would 'scarcely take the weight of a man.' Inevitably Regimental accounts of actions are often rose-tinted and Fitzgerald's history says, 'The pilots' aim was sure and there were no mistakes'. Whoever shot up the leading tanks – and would it not be dreadful if it had been the Typhoons – caused a significant delay right at the beginning of the ground advance and probably influenced the way that the armour advanced over the coming days, i.e. with natural caution.

On 18 September over 2,000 lbs of explosives were removed from the bridge and the RE signwriter painted the name 'Joe's Bridge' on it, in honour of both the REs and the Irish. General Horrocks later ordered that the name should stand as recognition of Lieutenant-Colonel Joe Vandeleur's leadership. Not to be outdone, once the Nijmegen Bridge had been captured following Sergeant Peter Robinson's brave dash across it (qv), the Grenadiers put up a sign at its northern end saying, 'Grenadier Bridge' and today there is a memorial plaque at the southern end (qv).

On the eastern side of the bridge is a brick **Memorial with a Plaque commemorating the start of GARDEN** in honour of the Irish Guards commanded by Lieutenant J.O.E. Vandeleur 'who captured and held this bridge on 10 September 1944' and their motto *Quis Separabit* – though according to one Irish Guards sergeant the motto is 'When in doubt, lash out'.

Continue to the T-junction with the N174 (38 kms/23.8 miles) and turn left.
Continue to the Dutch-Belgian border. On the right is

• *Liberation Gate Memorial Dutch-Belgian Border/39 kms/24.1 miles/5 minutes/Map 1S/15*

On 11 September 1944 in the struggles before Operation MARKET-GARDEN the leading tank squadron of the Irish Guards took 25 minutes from Joe's Bridge to reach this border, 3kms distant. Readers may be confused by the assertion that the advance on 17 September began at Joe's Bridge, yet here we have Irish Guards well beyond that point six days earlier. Having secured the ground beyond the bridge the armour withdrew south of it before the 17th, leaving it to the infantry to hold, a process known as 'Consolidation'. The first Allied unit to set foot on Dutch soil comprised two armoured cars of the 2nd Household Cavalry (a reconnoissance regiment part of the Guards Armoured Division and known by the Foot Guards as the 'Stable Boys') under Lieutenant Rupert Buchanan-Jardine. Local inhabitants had given him the location of German positions in the area. On 20/21 September the Princess Irene Royal Netherlands Brigade drove through here.

On 11 September 1994 Buchanan-Jardine was again present here at the unveiling of this handsome memorial – but this time as *Sir* Rupert.

In 1944 at about this point there was a Dutch customs house on the left-hand side of the road and hiding in the roof was a Royal Artillery officer named Captain J. F. Cory Dixon of 25/26 Battery 7th Medium Regiment. He was probably the most forward officer in the whole of XXX Corps and his job was to spot the accuracy of the barrage and, if necessary, to adjust it. He had a signaller with him. The opening line of the barrage was about 150 metres north of the memorial. We have earlier proposed a number of reasons for the apparent slowness of the advance of XXX Corps and Cory Dixon suggests another, though at the same time adding to the mystery of the loss of the Irish Guards tanks. He wrote the following to the authors:-

---

A PERSONAL ACCOUNT

By Captain J. F. Cory Dixon

The barrage was perfect; the RAF with Typhoons arrived dead on time (the only time in all my experience that they ever did) BUT the Guards were TWENTY (20) minutes late over the start line which was virtually level with my OP.

The result was that THREE (3) tanks were brewed up on the left of the road and TWO (2) on the right. As this was from an 88 on the right it sounds wrong, but that is what happened. This stopped the advance, and I had wandered forward to see what happened. A short conversation with O/C Vanguard and it was I who ordered the barrage to stop... . It took over FOUR (4) hours to get the barrage restarted on the appropriate start line.

The regimental history of the Irish Guards does not mention any delay in fire support, though it does say that it was at this point that the tanks were hit – 'Infantry in the ditches and anti-tank guns from the wood had struck down the rear of No. 3 and the head of No. 1 Squadron.' It continues that the Typhoons were called in to help and 'in the next hour flew two hundred and thirty sorties – a record in ground support. The tanks, as arranged, fired red smoke at the enemy positions to give the pilots an aiming mark and burnt yellow smoke abundantly and eagerly to mark themselves.'

What is rarely considered is the difficulty that, despite the use of coloured markers, (the tanks had orange panels) pilots have in correctly identifying targets. An examination of the flight logs of the squadrons that took part in the Typhoon support on 17 September produced the following: -

First from 182 Squadron who had attacked gun positions at Arnhem that morning. At 1435 hours a second sortie was flown, led by Wing Commander North-Lewis DFC, 'to attack woods on either side of a road up which our armoured forces were advancing. The area was attacked with H.E.R.P. (High explosive rocket projectiles) with unobserved results.' Thus they might have hit the Irish Guards tanks.

Second is an extract from 247 Squadron's 17 September log that gives an essence of the excitement and difficulty of the pilot's task.

A big day was today. A very big day indeed. At about 1030 the whole Wing was called to Intelligence for a super briefing for a super show... the Winco stressed the importance of ignoring all opposition and pressing home the attack no matter what came up at us... the role of the 'Tiffies' is as airborne armour [an interesting early use of a phrase which is now applied to 'attack' helicopters], to keep the main road open and smash any tanks and guns that can be seen or upon which we can be directed. The whole affair to be carried out at low level regardless of flak. Once again the Wing was told, 'We are prepared to suffer casualties, all attacks must be pressed home regardless of anything... .' Woods and roads were pranged with great gusto and the whole effort was applauded each time by the brown job in the Contact Car... . Little did he know of the narrow escapes our chaps were having, trying to fly in an atmosphere positively charged with mad careering aircraft of all shapes and sizes.

It would appear that hitting the wrong target was a possible and understandable error.
Continue on the N69.
Note that the road along this stretch, with its deep ditches to each side, gives one a realistic impression of the 1944 road. Although Horrocks had ordered that the road should be used for one-way traffic and, therefore, that overtaking was possible with care, the verges would have been important for manoeuvring. A contemporary account tells of a sapper soldier who on seeing a damaged vehicle beside the road put up a sign on the verge saying, 'Danger Mines'. If this is true, that one sign could have slowed the movement of the whole Corps. Part of the ground forces was 130 Brigade of 43rd Division and the Royal Engineers of that Division were so sensitive to the danger of mines that they had produced their own 'Mine Book'. In the front of the book was a quotation from *Proverbs* 4, verses 26 and 27, 'Ponder the path of thy feet and let all thy ways be established. Turn not to the right hand or to the left: remove thy foot from evil'. Thus, although the Division did not leave the area of Hechtel until 20 September, the 'Mine Book' may well indicate the XXX Corps attitude to the threat of mines and it could be that the story of the sign is true and its placing could have followed an incident related by Roden Orde (qv) that took place in this area on 17 September,

> The road was being heavily mortared by the Germans after the Squadron (2nd HCR) had passed the Dutch frontier and there was a jam of tanks, armoured cars, lorries and half-tracks waiting to move forward. Suddenly Corporal-of-Horse Johnson saw a half-track trying to pull across the road onto the grass verge, which was mined. 'Get off that verge!' shouted Johnson in warning, but he was too late. The half-track disintegrated in a violent explosion which must have been caused by a land mine. All the crew except the officer in command, who died of wounds some hours later, were killed instantly.

In fact it was later discovered by the Engineers that the Germans had filled weapon pits with explosive and connected them to pressure pads, a tactic that was unlikely to be used often, but as the Commander Royal Engineers of the Guards Armoured Division, Brigadier C. P. Jones, put it, 'Forward units needed some persuading that the whole of the route would not be mined on this scale.'
Continue towards Valkenswaard to just past the crossing with the road to Bergeijk to the left and Boxtel to the right. Stop at the memorial on the right beside the Café Heertje by the Oude Dorpstraat signed to the right.

• Café 't Heertje' Memorial/44 kms/27.2miles/5 minutes/Map 1S/16

Following the capture of Joe's Bridge on 10 September the next waterway to be crossed was that of the River Dommel, some 3kms ahead of here, which you will cross later. Orders were passed down (it is said they originated with Montgomery himself) for the bridge over the river to be looked at. The job was given the next day to D Squadron of 2nd HCR led by

Lieutenant Buchanan-Jardine (qv). While one car went forward he stopped here, then called the Café Rustoord, at about 1400 hours. Several locals, knowing that the British had taken Joe's Bridge, anticipated their arrival here and celebrated by putting out the Dutch flag, playing patriotic songs and offering the soldiers drinks. Buchanan-Jardine warned them that he was only making a recce and that Liberation had not yet arrived, advising them to take down the flag. Hardly had the scout cars gone back when the Germans arrived and searched the building for evidence of a British presence. Luckily the locals had hidden all the cigarettes and chocolate the soldiers had given to them in their bicycles' panniers, which the Germans forgot to search. However, the owner, Mr van Steenbergen, and his family were turned out of the café which was then vandalized.

Cafe't Heertje Memorial

The distinctive memorial was designed by Ramaz Gozatie and unveiled in 1994. Plaques on the ground recount how 'On this very spot the British Liberators set foot on Dutch soil for the first time' and in 1947 Buchanan-Jardine was awarded the Dutch Bronze Lion.

The plaques are sponsored by the Rabobank of Valkenswaard and Borkel & Schaft.

Continue towards the cemetery on the left surrounded by pine woods. Park in the slip road just before it, keeping well into the side of the road as you walk to the entrance as speeding lorries to the right and massed bicycles to the left can make walking very dangerous.

Valkenswaard CWGC Cemetery in April 1946, daffodils on every grave, and the entrance today

• *Valkenswaard CWGC Cemetery/44 kms/27.5 miles/15 Minutes/ Map 1S/17*

The cemetery, whose capacity was listed as '200 graves' when it was handed over to the Imperial War Graves Commission on 15 June 1946, actually contains 222 graves, almost all of whom fell in the fighting in the woods around Valkenswaard. They are of 214 UK named soldiers and 6 Unknown, plus two RAF. Originally the cemetery was enclosed by a wire fence and each grave was individually shaped and planted with daffodil bulbs. They include several Irish Guards, buried in a row [II.B.], who died on 17 September 1944: **Guardsmen Walter Ackers** (2nd Bn), **Michael Dee** (3rd Bn), **Lance Corporal Michael Delaney** (3rd Bn), **James Johnson** (2nd Bn), **Norman Mallon** (3rd Bn) and **William Moore** (2nd Bn), **Squadron Serjeant Major William Parkes** (2nd Bn), **Guardsmen George Walker** (3rd Bn) and **Thomas Watson** (3rd Bn) and **Lance Sergeant John Watters** (3rd Bn). Also buried here is **Private Herbert Eric Gunther Selig** who, because of his German-sounding name, reversed it. He served, and was buried, under the name of Giles [II.C.15.]. **Major David Davies**, RWF, age 29, 25 September 1944, was the 2nd Baron of Llandinam [I.D.7.].
Continue to the bridge over the Dommel.
The bridge is small and easily missed. It will not be possible to stop on it.

• *Dommel Victory Bridge /47 kms/29.5 miles/Map 1S/18*

Of the twenty Dutch bridges that had to be taken along the MARKET-GARDEN Corridor, this was the first. On 11 September Buchanan-Jardine's leading scout car came within sight of the bridge, which was clearly unharmed, and seeing a German Mark 1V tank standing on it returned to the Café Rustoord. On 17 September it was crossed by the Guards Armoured Division, a feat commemorated by a bronze plaque on the wall to the left which read,

'Victory Bridge Corridor' with the date. In mid-2000 the plaque was, sadly, missing, but its rectangular shape can be discerned on the stonework on the left as one drives over the bridge. It was somewhere in this area that the Irish Guards, having captured a number of 88mm guns, tried to destroy them, but, as their history says, 'only succeeded in firing one into the middle of Group HQ'.

The missing plaque on the Dommel Victory Bridge

Continue into Valkenswaard and turn right on Europalaan at the traffic lights, direction Leende, to the statue on Verzetsplein on the right.

• *Valkenswaard Liberation Memorial/50 kms/30.7 miles/5 minutes/ RWC/Map 1S/19*

The Guards did not reach Valkenswaard, some 13kms from the start line, until the end of the first day. Some authorities claim that it was, in fact, the objective of 17 September. If so, it was hardly compatible with the need to reach Arnhem, 100kms away, in less than 3 days, a task that demanded an average minimum daily progress of 33kms. Another contentious issue is the start time of 1435 hours for the XXX Corps assault, which left only about 4 ½ hours of daylight in which to advance.

Had the MARKET-GARDEN ground-force assault begun at 0600 hours on 17 September there would have been 8½ hours of daylight and the bridge at Son, only 30kms distant, might have been reached that evening, repaired overnight and the subsequent advance made one day earlier. 1 AB Division at Arnhem could have been reached on time and the whole operation might then have succeeded.

The ground force assault was delayed until the airborne force could be seen over Holland – a reasonable precaution since so many earlier operations had been cancelled. It was also considered that a morning assault on the ground might prejudice the secrecy of the airborne offensive.

Nevertheless, Valkenswaard was the first Dutch town to be liberated on the main line of the British advance. Opposition from the beginning of The Corridor had been heavier than expected – particularly from two battalions of 9th SS Division. When, as dusk fell on the 17th, the tanks reached here, they refuelled and stopped overnight, an action that later brought much criticism from the Americans and from the AFPU (Army Film and Photo Unit) men with the force. Ian Grant (qv) says,

> It was dusk before they reached Valkenswaard and the Film Unit prepared themselves for another night run (like those before Brussels and Antwerp) up to Eindhoven and beyond... . From the number of Germans who were now coming in to surrender... there didn't appear to be fearsome opposition. It was, therefore, with great surprise that AFPU were told the armour was going into laager for the night and would proceed again at dawn... . This overnight stop has never been fully accounted for.

In the day's actions the 2nd Battalion had lost nine tanks, eight men killed and several wounded, the 3rd Battalion seven men killed and nineteen wounded. It is interesting to note that the only tank losses were those sustained right at the start of the operation.

At 0600 hours on 18 September the tanks of Major Wignall's C Squadron of the Irish Guards led off along the road towards Eindhoven with armoured cars of 2nd HCR under Lieutenant Tabor 30 minutes ahead of them. Germans with anti-tank guns in concealed positions in the woods delayed the advance and set-piece infantry attacks had to be mounted, introducing more delay. On the flanks armoured cars of 2nd HCR under Lieutenant Palmer scouted ahead on side roads impassable to tanks, circled west around Eindhoven and met 506th PIR north of the city near Woensel (qv) at about 1200 hours, having picked up a few American paratroopers en route. They were welcomed by Brigadier Higgins, the second-in-command of 101st Airborne Division. The main body of XXX Corps, however, would not arrive for another six hours. General Taylor himself told them about the damage to the bridge at Son and asked that the REs be sent up as quickly as possible. 'Phone us', he said, 'the number is Son 224.' Captain Balding of the Household Cavalry passed the message back to the engineers over the wireless giving details of the gap to be bridged.

The Liberation Memorial, designed by Theo Nahmer, was unveiled in 1953. It illustrates the mixed feelings of many Dutch citizens during the occupation – powerless and resigned but nevertheless determined that a better future would come. Liberation was, of course, to come earlier to the people of Brabant in the path of The Corridor.

Turn round and return to the main road.

The **VVV office** is at the Town Hall, Markt 23, Tel: + (0) 49 0292525.

Open: Monday-Friday 0830-1730 hours.

Continue, direction Eindhoven, on the N69 to Aalst/Waalre.

It was here that, later in the day of 18 September, Major Thomas, commanding 14th Field Squadron RE, phoned from a public call box via a German-controlled telephone exchange and got through to the Americans at Son in answer to General Taylor's message.

There was considerable delay to the advance as the Guards approached Aalst, caused both by the presence of a German self-propelled gun and the attempt by the Irish Guards to pass their tanks through the Cavalry armoured cars in order to take on the opposition. The gun turned out to be unmanned.

By the church to the left at the traffic lights turn right (55 kms/34.1 miles) on Brabantialaan, which becomes Sophiastraat, continue over the Dommel and then turn left on Prince Mauritzweg just past the bus stop and second right on Iman van den Boschlaan. The statue is on the left in the small park.

• *Aalst Liberation Memorial/56 kms/34.7 miles/5 minutes/RWC/Map 1S/20*

The dramatic memorial, which depicts three human figures freeing themselves from the straightjacket of German occupation, was designed by Karel Zilstra and was unveiled in September 1994. In this area of Aalst streets are named after Resistance Workers.

Return to the N69 and turn right direction Eindhoven.

About 600m later (200m before the next traffic lights) the road crosses a small stream known as the Tongelreep. As the Guards' leading Shermans and armoured cars reached it, at about 1000 hours on 18 September, they met opposition. There were four 88mm guns, a number of Spandau machine guns and German infantry covering the stream crossing. Immediately a mixed tank and infantry force set out to find a way around to the west (without success) while the main body kept the Germans at the bridge occupied. At midday, Lieutenant Tabor returned to Aalst to report the situation to squadron HQ who 'were found comfortably ensconced with some of them having a haircut in a nearby shop'. Meanwhile a Dutch civilian

Detail Aalst Liberation Memorial

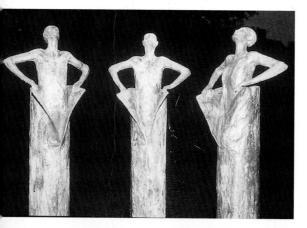

on a bicycle, who said that he came from 'Philips of Eindhoven', had been stopped just short of the bridge by Major Eddie Tyler of the Irish Guards, searched and sent back to Battalion HQ. Sixteen years later at a lunch in London for the finance director of Philips, Major Tyler met that civilian again – he was the finance director. The stalemate at the Tongelreep continued until the late afternoon when the Germans, hearing that Eindhoven had fallen, abandoned their weapons and the

Guards advance, led initially by Tabor on foot, continued. Once under way 2nd HCR motored at top speed up the main road, through Eindhoven and out to the blown bridge at Son where they arrived barely an hour later. Roden Orde (qv) wrote, 'It will be seen that the main burden of the advance along the road to Eindhoven, as far as it concerned the Regiment (2HCR) had been undertaken by four men in two scout cars'.

N.B. At this point by taking the A2/A67/E34 Motorway, direction Eersel, exiting there (Exit 32) and:

(a) following signs to Knegsel and then continuing on Zandoerleseweg to Zandoerle a **German 75mm Anti-tank Gun** (Map 1S/27) may be seen on the village green. It was abandoned by the Germans who were surprised by the rapid advance of the 53rd (Welsh) Division.

(b) taking the N284 to Bladel, on Kroonvensedijk near the Camping Site Tipmast, is a **Memorial Stone to Willem Flipse and Hans Freericks** (Map 1S/22) designed by Fons Roymans. They were shot by the Germans, suspected of being members of the Brabant Resistance Group, PAN – Partizan Action Netherlands - that was actively engaged in sabotage during MARKET-GARDEN and in helping isolated airborne troops at the beginning of the operation. It is thought that they were searching a British troop carrier wearing the blue dungarees and PAN armlet favoured by saboteurs when they were arrested on 20 September. The translated inscription reads, 'Traveller, stay awhile and put your hands together. Remember these [men] with a short prayer. They died for our country.'

(c) by returning to Bladel and continuing through it on the Neterselseweg and shortly after the turning to Het Bosch on the right a **Memorial to the Crews of two C-47 Dakota Glidertugs** (Map 1S/23) may be visited. The low-flying, slow Dakotas, named 'Piccadilly Filly' and 'Clay Pigeon', crashed near the Spiethof Farm on 17 September 1944, brought down by one of the many anti-aircraft guns in the area. Many of the American crews, and several civilians, including three members of the Spiethof family, were killed and are commemorated – civilians on the left and crew members on the right.

(d) by continuing into Netersel centre into Alphons van der Heydenstraat the **Memorial Chapel to the Virgin Mary** (Map 1S/24) may be visited. It commemorates **Fons van der Heyden**, who saved the life of Moses de Lopez, the only surviving crew member of a C-47 shot down near the Bladel Forest. Van der Heyden sheltered de Lopez on his farm which already contained seven other people in hiding. During a German search they were all discovered. Van der Heyden took all the responsibility for the fugitives and was shot on 20 September 1944. In 1947 the survivors erected this chapel in his memory and a street was named after him.

(e) by continuing on De Hoeve, over Westelbeersedijk (the road becomes Kranenberg and then Hoogeind) and then turning left at the T-junction into Hei-eind (Hoogeloon) then roughly half a mile later turning right on Groenstraat, there is a new **'Hiding Place' Memorial** off the road to the left in the shape of a large stone with a plaque beside it (Map 1S/25). It was erected on 21 September 1999 by the Mayor of Hoogeloon, Mr S. P. Grem, and it marks the

Hei-eind 'Hiding Place' Memorial

hiding place of the four survivors of the crew and two of the eighteen paratroopers of the 506th PIR, 101st AB Division when their C47 42-100672, nicknamed 'Clay Pigeon' was shot down on 17 September 1944 (see above). Three tugs also crashed in meadows near Hoogeloon and their gliders had to be cut loose. The survivors of these and some of the other crashes in the area (said to total thirteen) were taken in by the Dutch Resistance, notably by Miss Mary van Hoof and Mr Adriaan Goossens, and the wounded were given medical care by a local doctor and nun. This care was undertaken at the greatest risk as the area was seething with German soldiers. The men, thought to number about sixteen, were then taken to the farms of Karel Smulders, Kees Koolen and Harry Goodkens in Hei-eind and hidden in the woods (together with a German prisoner the group had taken) and supplied with food and drink by over twenty Resistance Workers until liberated on 21 September. Mary van Hoof (who died in 1997 age 88) and Adriaan Goossens were both awarded the Medal of Freedom.

(f) by turning round and continuing into Hoogeloon on Hoofdstraat to Valenslein 1985, a **Memorial Tree with Plaque to RWF Fusilier Eddy** [spelled Eddie on the plaque] Jones (Map**) may be seen. He was killed here on 21 September (his entry in the CWGC records gives his date of death as the 22nd) 1944 during the British advance to widen The Corridor. As his unit was not involved in the Liberation of Hoogeloon, it is a mystery as to how the 19-year-old Fusilier of the 7th Battalion came to be here. He is buried in the CWGC Cemetery at Bergen op Zoom [1.B.8.]. On 5 May 1985, this plaque was unveiled by Eddy Jones's sister.]

Continue along the N69 which becomes Aalsterweg, following the VVV symbols to the junction with Sint Jorislaan to the right and Dr. Schaepmanlaan to the left, signed Stadion.

• Extra Visit to Philips War Memorial (Map 1S/45a) and Stained Glass Windows (Map 10/1) Round trip approximately 5.9 kms/3.7 miles. Approximate time: 25 minutes

N.B. There is a 'strictly no photographs' policy in the Philips Strijp complex where the memorial is sited. However, if you approach the security guard at the barrier and explain the reason for your interest, he may well obtain permission for you to enter and photograph the memorial.

Philips War memorial, Strijp

Turn left and continue following signs to Stadion.

N.B. As the road crosses the River Dommel, to the right is the beautiful and peaceful Gebr. Hornemann Plantsoen Park in which there is a red stone **Memorial to all the Jewish children of Eindhoven who died 1940-1945**. The park is named after two Jewish brothers who were shot by the Germans.

Continue as the road becomes Eden Straat, Mauritsstraat and Vonder Weg to the junction with Mathildelaan. Turn left along Mathildelaan, round the spectacular Philips Stadium, parallel to the railway line on the right, to the Philips Strijp complex at the end of the road.

The memorial, which stands in its own ornamental garden, can be seen straight ahead from the entrance. **Note that**

Extra visit continued

special permission to visit it must be requested at the Guard Room.

Memorial to Philips Workers Who Died in the War. The dramatic memorial by architect Carasso of a prone human figure on a sarcophagus, whose draped shroud falls over the front, was unveiled on 5 May 1950 by Frits Philips in the presence of the families of those commemorated on it. Their names are inscribed on the memorial and they comprise those who died in the strike of May 1943, when the workers protested at Jewish colleagues being co-opted for slave labour and seven of them were killed by the Germans, plus those who died in concentration camps. An annual commemoration, attended by Frits Philips, is still held here on 5 May.

THE PHILIPS FACTORY DURING THE OCCUPATION

In 1939, in anticipation of the outbreak of war, Philips Trusts were set up in the UK and in the USA to safeguard their assets. A complicated plan was formulated to evacuate key personnel and valuable equipment to The Hague. On 9 May a huge convoy and special train were loaded and set off but they ran into the invading Germans and had to make their way back to Eindhoven. The directors, however, arrived at The Hague and all but Frits Philips then sailed from the Hook of Holland to the UK. He remained to negotiate with the Germans who wanted the factory to continue for their war effort – especially for the Luftwaffe. He had to tread the delicate knife-edge between protecting one's own interests and employees (many of them Jewish) and being accused of collaboration, which made for a difficult war for Frits Philips. His story is told in *45 Years with Philips* and in *The History of Philips. Volume 4 Under German Rule.* See also the entry under the Concentration Camp at Vught.

N.B. By continuing along Mathildelaan and turning right under the railway bridge onto Marconi Laan and then left along Groenewoudseweg **Eindhoven Jewish Cemetery** (Map 1S/45) may be visited. The British graves are in the south-eastern part of the cemetery. They are of **Private Z. H. Fischer** of the Palestine Regiment, 15 October 1945; **Gunner Mark Isaaman** of 190 Field Regt, RA, age 31, 17 December 1944 and **Gunner Hyman Shriebman**, Lt AA Regt, RA, age 37, 29 December 1944.

Return along Mathildelaan and continue to the Philips Tower. Turn right along Emmasingel.

On the left, opposite the **Philips Tower**, is another, newly restored, Philips building in which there are two very large multi-panelled stained glass windows **commemorating the Philips Employees sent to the Vught Concentration Camp** (qv) and **to those who were killed in the Allied Bombing raids.**

The Philips Archives are on the left at the end of the road. (Map 10/2)

Continue down Keizersgracht Wal (passing Stadhuis Plein and the Liberation Monument on the left) into P.C. ZN.. Hooftlaan and pick up the main itinerary as Stratumse Dijk joins Hertogstraat by turning left.

Continue straight over as the road becomes Stratumse Dijk. Follow the one-way system signed to Centrum, crossing the Dommel (61 kms/38.2 miles) and continue on Vestdijk to the large roundabout before the station. Turn right along Stationsweg and immediately stop in the parking on the left. Walk to the tourist office, signed VVV, to the left of the station.

• Eindhoven VVV/62 kms/38.8 miles/10 minutes/RWC

The VVV is at Stationsplein 17, 5611 AC Eindhoven.
Tel: + (0) 40 2979115. Fax: + (0) 40 2433135.
E-mail: info@vvveindhoven.nl
Open: Monday 1000-1730; Tuesday-Thursday 0900-1730; Friday 0900-2030 hours. Saturday 1000-1700. Helpful English-speaking staff. Maps/booklets/souvenirs/postcards and tourist literature and information/full reservation service. Information on annual 18 September Liberation commemorations/Circuit of Lights. See Tourist Information below for more information.

N.B. It is highly recommended to pick up a detailed town plan of Eindhoven here.

• Walking Tour to Eindhoven Memorials from the VVV (approximate time: 30-45 minutes).

Cross the road and walk back towards the roundabout. Walk back up Vestdijk, the road up which you drove and cross it as soon as possible, turning right up Nieuwstraat. This leads into Marktstraaat Square and on the building on the facing corner across the square is a memorial.

• Liberation Bas Relief/Map 10/3

Two bronze panels show hands joined by the flames of the torches they hold. They represent

Liberation bas relief

Bombardment bas relief

Liberation Monument with flame

the meeting of American and British troops and the inscription reads,

Liberation of Eindhoven 1944-1994. US 101st Airborne Division General Maxwell D.Taylor. British 30th Corps General Brian Horrocks. Whoever asks for freedom must offer others freedom.

The memorial, designed by Jos Reniers, was unveiled by His Royal Highness Prince Bernhard with an American and a British veteran in September 1994.

Walk to the bottom of the square and turn right to the T-junction with Rechte Straat. Turn left and walk down the street to the junction with Kerkstraat. Turn right and immediately to the right on the wall is the memorial.

• *Bombardment Bas Relief/Map 10/4*

This striking bronze tablet records the German bombardment of 19 September 1944. First the Germans fired bright yellow markers over the newly liberated town and then, with as yet no Allied anti-aircraft guns in the city, about seventy aircraft flew over dropping their bombs. Over 220 inhabitants were killed.

Continue down Kerkstraat to the junction with the main road Keizersgracht. Turn left and walk to the next opening on the left which is Stadhuis Plein.

• *Liberation Monument, Stadhuisplein /Map 10/5*

Eindhoven is linked with Bayeux in Normandy as the first major cities to be liberated in their respective countries and each year on 28 September the 'Freedom Flame' is carried from Bayeux [see *Major & Mrs Holt's Battlefield Guide to the Normandy Landing Beaches*] and rekindled in the special torch holder near the Liberation Monument. The holder bears the legend *Unis par l'Amitié* [United by Friendship] and the coats of arms of Bayeux and Eindhoven. The procession from Bayeux is greeted in Stadhuisplein by local Eindhoven dignitaries and servicemen's associations (including the local Royal British Legion branch) and is organised by the Dutch Society of Friends. A dwindling band of veterans of September 1944 attend each year and take part in other celebratory events organised by the 18 September Festival Foundation (qv), such as the Parade, Cultural Events and the Circuit of Lights (qv).

The handsome Liberation Monument was sculpted by Paul Gregoire. The three figures represent the Soldier, the Resistance Worker and the Civilian. The bird is the Dove of Peace. Around the base in *bas relief* are friezes showing the progression from occupation through oppression to liberation with the words, 'You who stand here remember their death, their great sacrifice, before you go.'

utch welcome to the Liberators, September 1944   'Mad Tuesday'

In September 1944 the 101st AB Division plan had called for Colonel Sink's 506th PIR to cross the Son Bridge over the Wilhelmina Canal and to take Eindhoven by 2000 hours on 17 September. It seems odd that the 506th did not drop at both ends of the Son Bridge in the way that 504th PIR did at Grave (qv). As a result the bridge was blown before they could reach it. Although the 506th PIR eventually got themselves over the canal it was dark before they all crossed and so Colonel Sink, with General Taylor's agreement, decided to wait until morning before going further. At daylight 3rd Para Battalion led the way to Eindhoven with two companies astride The Corridor road accompanied by Dutch civilians wearing white handkerchief armbands and carrying captured German weapons. En route, with help from local civilians and Lieutenant-Colonel Robert L. Strayer's 2nd Battalion, they overcame small pockets of German small arms fire and stiffer resistance from two 88mm guns and mortars in the area of Woensel church, the Germans losing thirteen dead and forty-one as prisoners. Behind the leading companies came General Taylor, who climbed to the top of Vlokhoven Church tower to look over the city. German opposition had ceased. Eindhoven was the first Dutch city to be liberated and civilians appeared with orange armbands and streamers, crowding the streets to welcome the Americans. Even more acceptable were the gifts of schnapps and beer which were thrust upon them. They were in the city centre shortly after midday. Then, as the tanks of the Irish Guards rolled in later in the day, their welcome was just as enthusiastic, but amongst the liberators were Dutch members of the Netherlands Brigade and they had the most riotous welcome of all as described by Ronald Gill and John Groves in their *Club Route in Europe*:-

> Suddenly, riding slowly past the column came a despatch rider. He attracted little attention at first until some Dutch women spotted his shoulder flash – the Netherlands flash! A real Dutch soldier! The British column and the British soldiers were immediately forgotten. The Netherlands representative disappeared from sight under a pile of raving women and the crowd moved off up the street with their soldier still submerged. Dutch men fought for the privilege of wheeling his motor-cycle... . Half an hour later he rolled into view again, full of Bols gin and kissed into a state of blissful coma. With difficulty he mounted his motor-cycle, received a last kiss for luck from everybody and wobbled off up the road. He fell off after ten yards but willing hands helped him on again and finally with three children on his pillion, and bunches of orange flowers tied all over him and his machine, he zig-zagged out of sight.

But it wasn't quite the end of the war for the citizens of Eindhoven. During the night of 19 September some seventy German bombers raided the town, causing 1,000 casualties, killed, wounded or missing.

In the months between the Normandy landings in June and the beginning of September 1944 Allied air attacks on Nazi-occupied Europe had increased. Eindhoven, with its Philips factories and nearby airfield, was often a target. Factory roofs, and even trains, were equipped with AA guns. As the armies of liberation came closer, the Germans and their sympathizers (including the city mayor) began to leave. On 3 September the AA guns were removed and on the following night the Germans blew up their installations at the airfield. There was a curfew from 2000 to 0600 hours and the punishment for violation was death.

Something akin to panic affected the Germans. Using carts, horses, prams, bicycles - any form of transport they could find - they and their collaborators jammed the roads leading east, a flood that reached its peak on 5 September, known as 'Mad Tuesday' (*Dolle Dinsdag*).

The last issue of the German-controlled Eindhoven daily paper, *Dagblad van het Zuider*, was published on 7 September, but then the Germans seemed to recover their balance and the headlong rush to leave stopped.

On Sunday 17 September the roar of aircraft brought out the people of Eindhoven. In the morning they watched the bombers and, in the afternoon, the transports and gliders flying north. At 1700 hours Radio Orange (the Underground radio) gave them the news of the landings and instructions to the PAN (Partisan Action Netherlands) resistance. Hurriedly the Germans blew up the railway installations around the station – then approximately where the VVV is now. It is said that the sound of the Allied assault to the south beyond Valkenswaard prompted a senior German officer to ring his subordinate HQ there during the evening. 'Hold to the last man,' he said, and was greatly encouraged by the positive reply that Valkenswaard would never be surrendered. He did not know that he had been talking to a German-speaking English officer from XXX Corps, who had already taken the town. But on the morning of 18 September the Guards were still stuck in a fight 8kms south of the city and it was 1830 hours before their tanks clattered into Eindhoven.

Inevitably, since the whole operation was eventually deemed to be a failure, there were recriminations and accusations between the British and Americans as to whose fault it was that the men at Arnhem were not reached in time. Indicative of this is the American report that Colonel Strayer radioed to General Taylor shortly after midday from the centre of the city that 'We are in the centre, have occupied the four bridges and there is no resistance', while the history of the 43rd Wessex Division, part of XXX Corps, records that 'the large Dutch town of Eindhoven was found to be strongly held' and 'by early evening the Grenadier Guards group... finally overwhelmed the enemy and gained contact with U.S. troops.'

Return to your car.

• *End of Itinerary One*

OR

Extra Visits to the Mierlo CWGC Cemetery (Map 1S-28); Lierop Frank Doucette Monument; Stiphout 11th Armoured Division Memorial (Map 1S/33); Helmond - Liberation and Royal Norfolk Memorials (Map 1S-34/35); Ysselsteyn German Cemetery (Map 1S/37); Venray CWGC Cemetery (Map 1S-38); Lobeek Norfolk Regiment Memorial (Map 1S-39); Overloon Chapel of the Safe Hide-away (Map 1S/40), Overloon National War & Resistance Museum (Map 1S-41/42) and CWGC Cemetery (Map 1S/43). Round trip: 122 kms/76 miles. Approximate time: 4 hours.

Suggested Additional Visits to Nederweert CWGC Cemetery (Map 1S/30) and Weert RC Cemetery (Map 1S/32).

Approximate extra 45 kms/ 28miles. Approximate extra time: 100 minutes

The somewhat convoluted route out of Eindhoven below is necessary because of the one-way system in the Centre.

Extra visit continued

From the Stationsplein car park near the VVV turn right towards the Philips Tower, past the VVV and right at the traffic lights. Follow signs to Antwerp/Venlo under the tunnel. At the traffic lights turn left past the Holiday Inn and left signed Centrum, again towards the Philips Tower. Pass it on the right on Emmasingel (signed Alle Richtingen) and bear left at the traffic lights and junction on Keizersgracht, continue past the Liberty Monument on the left and turn left on Bilderdijklaan, signed Geldrop.

Continue through Geldrop, direction Helmond. Continue to the green CWGC sign and park after it on the right opposite the cemetery.

Mierlo CWGC Cemetery (10 kms/6.5 miles)

The cemetery was started in the spring of 1945 and burials were concentrated in it from the fighting of September-November 1944 in the surrounding district, mainly to clear the region south and west of the River Maas and, further west, to open up the Scheldt estuary.

It contains 657 named and 7 Unknown burials - 634 UK Army, with 7 Unknown and 13 Air Force, 5 Australian Air Force, 4 Canadian Army and 1 Canadian Air Force.

MiD were **Wing Commander Pilot Maurice Baker**, of 196 Squadron RAF, age 33, 21st February 1945, [VIII.D.13]; **Serjeant Alan Barnes**, 2nd County of London Yeomanry, age 25, 17 November 1944, [V.D.5.]; **Major Frederick Connell**, RASC, age 37, 27 July 1945, [V.D.13.]. **Corporal Albert Davidson** of the 6th Seaforth Highlanders, age 22, 5 November 1944, was awarded the **MM** [V.E.5.]. **Lance Corporal John Jeffreys**, 1st Welsh Guards, age 23, 8 November 1944, captained the Welsh Guards Rugby Football team [VIII.F.3.]. **The Rev Henry Taylor**, Chaplain 4th Class attached 29th Armoured Brigade, age 31, 23 September 1944, was awarded the **MC** [V.B.7.].

Commemorated on a Plaque in Neunen (qv) are Corporal Ralph Stothard, age 28, and Trooper Basil Nicholls, age 21, both of 44th Royal Tanks and killed on 20 September 1944 [II.B.1/2.].

All killed on 3 February 1945 [in VII.A.] and in the RAAF were **Pilot Officer I.C. Osborne**, age 20, 'S.C.E.G.S. Vitae lampada tradunt', **Flight Lieutenant R.Ordell, DFC**, age 24, 'Sydney Grammar School', **P.O. J.G. Killen**, age 24, **Flight Sergeant R. K. Mckaskill**, age 19. On the same date, in the RAF, are **Sergeant C. Scurr**, age 24 and **Flight Sergeant K. K. Reynolds**, age 21.

The father of **Captain Geoffrey Shaw**, R Fus (City of London Regt), attd. 2nd Argyll & Sutherland Highlanders, age 31, 26 September 1944 [IV.A.7.], Lieutenant Max Shaw, also of the City of London Regt, was killed on the Somme on 15 September 1916 and is commemorated on the Thiepval Memorial to the Missing.

Mierlo CWGC Cemetery

Extra visit continued

Continue over two sets of traffic lights and turn right just before the mill, signed Lierop. Turn right again at the roundabout, signed Centrum, and left at the next roundabout, signed Lierop. Continue to the T-junction and turn right on Herselseweg (17.1kms/10.7 miles) and continue under the A67/E34 motorway into Lierop. Turn first on Hogeweg and then first left to Frank Doucettestraat.

The street is named after the 'Amerikaans Vlieger' (American Flyer) 19 September 44. In a small park in the centre of the street is the **Frank Doucette Memorial** (19.2kms/12 miles).

From 1 August–21 September 1944 a camp in the nearby Forest of Lierop at Moorsel was used as a hiding place – often for as many as thirty men at a time. Among them was Frank Doucette, the gunner of an American B-17 bomber which was shot down over Eindhoven on 19 August 1944. Frank joined the Resistance and helped in the acts of sabotage designed to create confusion in the German rearguard. During a battle with the Germans Doucette was killed and a monument was placed on his grave. In 1974 the inhabitants of the street named after him relocated the monument, which tells his story, to this small park in the street. Plaques below the main monument date from 1974 and September 1999.

Frank Doucette Memorial, Lierop

N.B. The Suggested Additional Visits to Nederweert and Weert CWGC Graves may be made from this point.

Leave Leirop on Ten Boomen Laan and join the N266 direction Someren, Nederweert. Continue, with the Zuid-Willemsvaart Canal to the left, into Nederweert to the cemetery on the left.

Nederweert CWGC Cemetery

Nederweert was liberated on 21 September 1944 and the front line remained close by, following the courses of the Zuid-Willemsvaart and Wessem-Nederweert Canals, until 14 November. During that period there were casualties from patrol activity and from daily German shelling of Nederweert as well as from German minefields. After the British crossed the canals and continued towards the Maas, burials continued in this cemetery from the surrounding area.

Of the total of 363 burials there are 13 UK Navy, 290 UK Army, 13 RAF and 1 Unknown; 6 Canadian Army and 31 RCAF, 1 Australian Army and 2 RAAF; 1 New Zealand Army and 3 RNZAF, 1 South African Army and 1 Indian Army.

Buried here is **Private William Foster**, 5th Australian General Hospital, AAMC, age 26, 14 April 1945, [IV.D.4]. He was **MiD**, as was **Lieutenant James Pratt** of 757 Field Coy, RE, age 22, 28 November 1944 [I.B.5.] and **Major Richard Whelan**, RNF, age 38, 31 October 1944 [I.G.9.].

Extra visit continued

Lance Corporal Henry Harden, RAMC attd No 45 RM Commando, age 32, 23 January 1945, was awarded the **Victoria Cross** [IV.E.13]. When four Royal Marines of the troop to which Harden was attached at Brachterbeek were wounded by heavy machine-gun fire whilst attempting to reach some nearby houses, he immediately ran 100 yards over open ground to give them first aid, then carried one on his back to safety. Harden was ordered not to go forward again, and an attempt was made to reach the remaining casualties with the use of tanks. This, and a subsequent attempt under a smoke screen, was unsuccessful and Harden insisted on going out with a volunteer stretcher party and brought one man back. Returning from his third foray with another wounded Marine, Harden was himself killed. Harden's contempt for his personal danger and his cool courage and determination to finish the task 'was an inspiration to his comrades and will never be forgotten by those who saw it' [London Gazette].

Corporal Holden is also commemorated by a plaque on the bridge over the Montforterbeek at Brachterbeek.

Lieutenant-Colonel Charles Holliman, Commanding the 5th Royal Tanks, age 27, 21st January 1945, held the **DSO, the MC and Bar** [III.A.6]. **Trooper Meinhard Ronald Weil** of 23rd Hussars, RAC, age 26, 4 November 1944, served as Winster [I.D.2.].

Continue to the Zuidwillemsvaart Canal. Cross it and follow signs to Weert. 250m to the south is

Weert (Molenpoort) RC Cemetery

In it are 3 RAF graves of 78 Sqn from 23 September 1944.

Return towards Helmond on the N266. Just before the railway on the outskirts of Helmond, turn left, parallel with the railway, and then right on Mierloseweg. Pick up the main Extra Visit itinerary.]

Return to the junction by the windmill with the N614 and turn right direction Helmond. Continue along Geldropseweg, over the Eindhovens Canal, which becomes Hoofdstraat and then Mierloseweg over the railway and over the N270 motorway (29kms/18.1 miles) along Hortsedijk into Stiphout. Turn left at the T-junction and traffic lights signed Gerwen on President Rooseveltlaan which becomes Dorpsstraat. Continue 100m past the church on the left and stop by the Obelisk.

11th Armoured Division Obelisk, Stiphout (31 kms/19.3 miles). Designed by Jef Verhoeven and inaugurated on 20 September 1986 on the occasion of the first reunion of the Normandy Veterans' Association in Holland, the obelisk bears the divisional insignia of a charging bull. It has the legend 'We will remember them. September 1944' and the badges of the 2nd Battalion, Fife and Forfar Yeomanry and the 8th Battalion, Rifle Brigade. The Division's task was to widen The Corridor and make it less vulnerable to German attempts to cut it off.

Turn round and continue straight over the traffic lights, signed 's-Hertogenbosch, to the crossroads with Boerhaavelaan to the right and Jan van Brabantlaan to the left. Turn left and continue as the road becomes Julianalaan, over the N266 and the Zuid Willemsvaart Canal, signed Deurne, onto Oostende to the third set of traffic lights with a small garden beyond and to the right with a small parking area in front of it. This is September 44 Plantsoen. In it is

Extra visit continued

Helmond Liberation Memorial (34 kms/21.5 miles).
This splendid statue of St George and the Dragon, designed by Niel Steenbergen, was inaugurated on the 15th Anniversary of the Liberation of Helmond on 25 September 1944 by 11th Armoured and 3rd Infantry Division of VIII (BR) Corps. It symbolises the triumph of good over evil.

Turn round and return along Oostende and turn left at the first traffic lights, signed Centrum, along Noordende. Continue along the winding road until it becomes Zuidende. After passing Hemelrukse Straat to the left, stop in the parking zone on the right. To the left is Royal Norfolkplein with a small flower garden and in it is

Royal Norfolk Memorial, Helmond (36 kms/22.3 miles).
This brick memorial, designed by Jan van Erp with a raised 'N' and 'R' and a plaque bearing the regimental badge, was donated by the Friends of the Regiment. The figure of Britannia badge was given to the regiment by Queen Anne for its gallantry at the Battle of Almanza in 1707 and the nickname, 'the Holy Boys', is said either to have come from the selling of Bibles for drink in the Peninsula or because the Spaniards mistook Britannia for the Virgin Mary. The memorial was erected in 1984 and commemorates the 40th Anniversary of the Liberation of Helmond by the 1st Battalion on 25 September.

Part of VIII (BR) Corps, the Norfolks were to provide flank cover for Guards Armoured Division in The Corridor. Their progress was slowed by heavy German opposition, especially along the Zuid Willemsvaart by the German 107th Panzer Brigade.

Continue along Zuidende to the junction with the N270 and turn left on Kasteeltraverse, direction Deurne.

[**N.B.** By turning left on Burgemeester Van Houtlaan and immediately left on Molenstraat, one reaches Helmond Protestant Cemetery. There are 3 British graves here : Guardsman Stanley French, 3rd Scots Guards, age 23, 19 November 1944; Craftsman Thomas Hart, REME, age 34, 27 December 1944 and Serjeant Alexander Malcolm, 3rd Scots Guards, age 30, 14 December 1944. (Map 1S/36).]

Continue on the N270 around Deurne to the roundabout and turn right on the N277 signed to Ysselsteyn and right again in the village signed to the German Cemetery [Duitse Militaire Begraafsplaats]. Continue to the cemetery on the left.

German Cemetery, Ysselsteyn (57 kms/35.4 miles).
There is a sign on the entrance for the adjoining *Jeugdont Moetingscentrum* (Youth Meeting Centre). The cemetery is approached by a rhododendron-lined path, at the end of which is the Visitors' Centre. In it can be found details of the men buried here and there are toilets, open during visiting hours. There is also a multi-lingual video presentation about the Kriegsgräberfürsorge and the history of the cemetery. Because of its nearness to Germany, the cemetery receives many thousands of visits from relatives each year. On entering this vast cemetery, the mournful field of over 31,000 granite crosses seems to stretch into infinity. Beneath them, in its 30 hectares, lie 31,502 soldiers of the 1939-45 War and 74 of the 1914-18 War (in a plot immediately to the left as one

11th Armoured Div Obelisk, Stiphout

Helmond: St George and Dragon Liberation Memor
Royal Norfolk Memorial

Ginko Biloba Tree, Ysselsteyn
German Cemetery

Extra visit continued

enters). This huge cultivated plain had to be created from the De Peel moorland. It was reclaimed with very hard work before the 68,000 trees and shrubs could be planted and the 116 plots laid out, mostly with twelve rows of twenty-five graves. The bodies concentrated here were brought in from local civilian burial grounds and from as far afield as Maastricht (including the '14-'18 burials) and the Isle of Ameland. 3,000 soldiers came from Margraten – the fallen of the last month of the war. 1,700 came from the Arnhem battlefield. The first man to be reburied here was Under-Officer Johann Siegel. In the early 1990s the German Focke-Wulf 190 of Edmund Unger was discovered in a forest to the north-east of Eindhoven airport. He was shot down on 5 November 1943 in combat with American Flying Fortresses. He is buried in CA.014.348.

From 1950 the Dutch Graves Organisation started opening the graves of the Unknown and by modern methods was able to identify 7,330 bodies. From 1963 international youth camps, whose motto was *Reconciliation through the Graves*, worked on the landscaping and maintenance of the cemetery. Beginning in May 1976 the original concrete crosses were gradually replaced with natural stone. The work was completed in 1980/1.

Unusually for a German war cemetery in a victorious host country, the generous allocation of land permitted an individual grave for nearly every man buried here. The crosses bear a plastic plaque with a grave allocation number, the soldier's surname, forename and, for the majority, date of death and rank. Through the serried rows leads an 800-metre-long path and in the middle of the cemetery is a circle in the centre of which is a great cross. This is the area where commemorative ceremonies take place. Nearby is a large carillon. On the right of the path is a Gingko Biloba tree, planted as a symbol of hope and freedom (the only type of tree to survive the bombing at Hiroshima) on the 50th Anniversary of the end of the war in May 1995.

Return to the N270 and turn right, direction Venray. Continue to the roundabout, signed to Venray and the CWGC Cemetery, and turn left (65 kms/40.8 miles). Continue to the next roundabout and turn left along Langstraat and at the next crossroads turn left signed Merselo and Uden on Westsingel. Go over the next crossroads and traffic lights, signed Uden and Overloon, continue past a large metal sculpture on the right on the green and turn left on Hoenderstraat, following the green CWGC sign to the cemetery on the left.

Venray CWGC Cemetery (68 kms/42.5 miles).
The 692 burials here date from October 1944 to March 1945. They include 2 RN, 535 UK Army, with 18 Unknown, 2 Canadian and 1 New Zealand. There are 92 RAF with 12 Unknown, 20 RCAF, 4 RAAF, 4 RNZAF, 1 Polish RAF and 1 War Correspondent, **William Rippon**, of the Peterborough Citizen and Adviser, died on 16 March 1945 [VIII.E.6.].

The MC was awarded to **Captain Paul Peppiette**, B.Sc., A.M.I.C.E, A.M.I.Struct.E., RE, age 32, died on 6 March 1945 [I.D.8.].

MiD were **Flight-Lieutenant Bernard Aldhous**, RAF, age 30, 9 March 1945 [VII.C.3.]; **Private Ronald Burgess**, 1st R Norfolks, age 19, 3 February 1945 [II.C.8.]; **Lieutenant**

Extra visit continued

William Cairns, 7th/9th R Scots, age 25, 8 January 1945 [VIII.G.9.] Lance-Corporal Albert Eatough, 1st Lothian & Border Horse, age 30, 27 February 1945 [V.G.12.]; Major Samuel Ginn, 190 Field Regt, RA, age 32, 3 December 1944 [III.E.10.]; Captain Oswald Gray, RF, age 26, 24 March 1945 [V.F.5.]; Major John Kinkaid, RA Attd HQ 6th AB, age 31, 25 March 1945 [VIII.E.3.].

The MM was awarded to Private Albert Harries, 2nd KSLI, 17 October 1944 [II.F.6.]; Serjeant Donald McLeod, 5th Seaforth Highlanders, age 24, 30 March 1945 [IV.B.10.] and Serjeant Joseph Meilleur, 8th Rifle Bde, age 29, 19 October 1944 [III.D.4.].

Lieutenant Michael Becke, 8th KRRC, age 21, 30 November 1944 [V.E.5.] was the son of Major Sir Jack Becke, Kt, CBE. He was a 'Scholar of Oriel College, Oxford; 2nd Class Honours in History' and his brother, Lieutenant John Becke, 12th KRRC, 26 June 1944, is buried in St Manvieu CWGC Cemetery in Normandy.

Lieutenant-Colonel Cecil Millett, OBE, DCLI, age 41, 20 December 1944 [II.B.8.], was Commanding the 2nd KSLI.

Return to Westsingel, turn left and continue following signs to Overloon (turning right at the roundabout and then left) on Overloonseweg. At the bridge over the Loobeek stop on the left, opposite house No. 30.

Royal Norfolk Regiment Memorial (72 kms/44.9 miles).

A small figure of a member of the Regiment surmounts a brick pyramid. Plaques around it are dedicated 'to the men of the 1st Battalion the Royal Norfolk Regiment who suffered and died in the fields around this very place in October 1944. May peace and freedom be their living memorial. This monument was raised by their comrades and friends from Britain and the Netherlands.' It is also dedicated 'to all British, Allied and Dutch soldiers who died to bring liberty to this land to all the innocent victims of war, especially the 300 civilians who were killed in and around Overloon and Venray in 1944. We shall remember them.' The regimental and divisional badges are also on the memorial.

Continue into Overloon. Just before the right turn signed to the museum is a small garden on the left.

Chapel of the Safe Hide-away (74 kms/46.5 miles).

This small chapel, in which is a statue of the Virgin Mary protecting some people, is dedicated to the approximate 2,500 refugees, Jews, Resistance Workers, Allied forces etc, hidden from the Germans, at great personal risk, by the local population of just over 2,000. The flower garden was planted on 15 October 1994.

Immediately after turn right, following signs to the Oorlogs Museum and drive into the large car park.

There are several cafés, souvenir shops and WCs around the park.

Overloon National War & Resistance Museum (75 kms/46.8 miles).

Open daily: June-August 0930-1800; September-May 1000-1700.

Closed December 24, 25, 26 and 31 and 1 January. Facilities for the disabled.

Tel: + (0) 478 641820. E-mail: overloon@oorlogsmuseum.nl

There is a well-stocked book/souvenir stall and refreshment facilities in the Museum. Entrance fee payable.

Extra visit continued

Set in 35 acres of landscaped park, in which there is a variety of interesting exhibits - from a miniature German 'Biber' submarine (of the type used in the Waal at Nijmegen (qv)), to a flail tank, to a German Panther, to a Russian T34, to Sherman, Churchill, Cromwell and Crusader tanks, to statues of Queen Wilhelmina and prisoners in a concentration camp - this important museum contains superb photographs, contemporary ephemera, propaganda, artefacts and materiel of warfare, including a Bailey Bridge and a Wurzburg radar installation like those linked to the Diogenes command Bunker at Arnhem (qv). It charts the September 1944 tank battle at Overloon, describes the hardships of life under the Occupation in Holland and in concentration camps in Holland, Germany and in the Dutch East Indies and the work of the Dutch Resistance. A section is devoted to the Dutch SS under the traitor Seyss Inquart. The original museum was opened on 25 May 1946 by Major-General L.G. Whistler, Commander of 3rd (BR) Infantry Division and a plaque just inside the entrance on the right records the event, after which Princess Juliana was the first official visitor. In this building is a fine bronze *bas relief* by Elizabeth Lucas Harrison, a miniature of the original of which is in the crypt of the RAF Church, St Clement Danes, London, where it was unveiled on 21 June 1981. It is from the Air Forces Escaping Society and depicts an RAF pilot being supported by a Dutch man and girl and is dedicated to 'the countless brave men and women of occupied countries who during WW2 without thought of danger to themselves helped 2,803 air crew of the RAF and Commonwealth Air Forces to escape and return to this country and so continue the struggle for freedom. Many paid with their lives. Many more endured the degradation of concentration camps. Their names are remembered in equal honour with those who were spared lasting tribute and also to serve as an inspiration to future generations.' This bronze was unveiled on 27 September 1989 by Prince Bernhard.

The way out of the main building is through a peaceful chapel. A large new hall houses the larger exhibits such as a Spitfire, a B25 Mitchell III bomber, A V-1 flying bomb, a T-34 and a Sexton tank. Adjoining it is a large cafeteria area with terrace.

A separate 'Cloister' tells the story of the concentration camps and includes many photographs, personal objects and drawings made in captivity. Stark, emaciated, bronze figures stand throughout the exhibit imparting a vivid feeling of the horror of life in the camps.

There is a documentation centre and special educational tours for schoolchildren.

The motto of the museum, whose primary objects are to educate on the obscenity of war and to appeal to one's conscience, is 'War belongs in a museum.'

Drive out of the car park and turn right and right again following green CWGC signs to
Overloon CWGC Cemetery (76 kms/47.2 miles).

Most of the burials here are from the fighting in the area of October-November 1944 in the operation to clear the Germans from the region south and west of the Maas in preparation for the final attack on the Rhineland. So fierce was this battle that the British dubbed it 'A Second Caen' [see *Major & Mrs Holt's Battlefield Guide to Normandy*]. When the British attempt to penetrate to Venlo and Roermond from the north failed due to heavy German

Royal Norfolk Memorial and detail, Lobeek

National War and Resistance Museum, Overloon: Exterior, Spitfire, Air Escaping Society Bas Relief and Sherman V Crab Mk 1 Tank

Extra visit continued

resistance on the Vortum-Mullem-Lactaria defensive line, Field-Marshal Montgomery asked Eisenhower for more reinforcements and was given the 7th US Tank Division. They arrived from the Metz area, confident that they could quickly finish the task, but fell into the often-made mistake of under-estimating the enemy and made few preparations. On 30 September they attacked in five places, thus diluting their strength. The Germans were thrown back a few miles to their defensive line, but the Americans, who suffered heavy losses, did not achieve a breakthrough and were withdrawn from the area on 8 October.

The British then had to pick up the attack again which was assigned to a reinforced 3rd (BR) Division. The divisional commander, General Whistler, concentrated on the road junction in Overloon, as, once the village was captured, it would be possible to advance against Venlo by way of Venray. The Germans, however, had made of Overloon a heavily reinforced stronghold and the General therefore abandoned the idea of a direct assault upon it in favour of a pincer movement. He formed three attack formations, two of which were to carry out the encircling operation to the east and west of the town, and one, called the 'holding group', which was to launch a frontal attack on the Germans to divert their attention. It started on 12 October 1944 with a 75-minute artillery bombardment reinforced by air strikes. At 1215 hours British troops attacked the village and by nightfall the ruins were in their hands.

Of the 279 burials in the cemetery there are 261 UK Army, with 4 Unknown, and 11 RAF with 3 Unknown.

They include **Lieutenant-Colonel Hubert Orr**, DLI, age 34, 25 September 1944, **Commanding the 3rd Monmouths,** who was awarded the DSO [III.E.14.]. **Lieutenant Reginald Longueville**, Coldstream Guards, age 21, 12 October 1944 [III.E.8.] and **Serjeant Edward Rees**, 246 Field Coy, RE, age 24, 14 October 1944 [III.C.14.] were MiD.

The entries in the MARKET-GARDEN Cemetery Registers usually contain the bare facts of Surname, Forename(s), Number, Regiment or Unit, Date of Death, Age, Names of Parents/Wife and Grave Location Numbers. The family of **Private Erwin Max Rivers,** 1st Suffolks, age 30, 25 November 1944, included the facts that Rivers was 'B.Sc., Econ (Hons.); Leverhulme Research Fellowship, London School of Economics. Lecturer on Statistics, Cambridge University' [III.C.7.]. **The brother of Private John Walker**, 1st Bn S Lancs, age 22, 12 October 1944 [IV.B.5.], Trooper Joseph Walker of the 3rd Carabiniers, POW Dragoon Guards, 26 December 1945, is buried in the cemetery at Stockton-on-Tees, the brothers' home town.

Return to Venray and thence via Helmond to Eindhoven on the N270, following Centrum signs to the Station.

Overloon CWGC Cemetery

ITINERARY TWO

EINDHOVEN TO NIJMEGEN

• **Itinerary Two** starts at the VVV Eindhoven and heads north along the XXX Corps Corridor, through the 101st US AB Division DZs to Nijmegen.
• **The Route:** Eindhoven - Woensel CWGC Cemetery; 101st AB Div Memorial; Son – Bridgehead Memorial, New Bridge, Zonhove Screaming Eagle Memorial, Airborne Memorial, Tree to Herbert Pierce, Paulushoeve Parachute and Screaming Eagle Memorials; Best - Joe Mann Airborne Bridge Memorial, Wings of Liberation Museum, Joe Mann Open-air Theatre Memorial; Sint Oedenrode – 101st AB Memorial to Dutch, Castle Henkenshage, Memorial to Troopers Thorogood and Matthews, C47 Propeller; De Koevering Old Mill; Eerde – Local Churchyard, 501st Geronimo Memorial; Veghel – Bridge, Airborne Memorial, Dutch East Indies Memorial; Uden CWGC Cemetery; Grave – Memorials to Dutch Border Battalion, 504th PIR on old Waal Bastion, 2nd Bn (Cider-White) 504th PIR, Civilian Casualties, Burgomaster Louis Ficq, Site of Jewish Synagogue; Grave Bridge - 'E' Coy, 82nd US AB Div/XXX Corps/Princess Irene Royal Brigade; Overasselt Parachute Memorial; Heumen – Jac Maris Plaque, Memorial to Dutch soldiers, site of old lockbridge; Malden; Jonkerbos – Dutch Wargraves Cemetery, CWGC Cemetery; Nijmegen – VVV, Bridge.
• **Extra Visits** are suggested to Soeterbeek Bridge, Nuenen Liberation Memorial and 44th R Tanks and 506th PIR Benches; Best 15th Scottish Division Memorial; Schijndel - Mother Hen Monument, 51st Highland Div Memorial; St Michielsgestel - Memorial to civilians shot, Liberation Memorial; Vught - National Monument Concentration Camp, Fusillés Memorial, 51st Highland Div Room, Student's HQ; Den Dungen Silent Wings Memorial; Heeswijk-Dinther Liberation Chapel, Landings Monument; Typhoon Room, Volkel Airbase; Airstrip B-82; Heumen – Jac Maris House; Nijmegen - Memorial to Resistance Workers, Public Garden, Herman Oolbekkinkstraat, Rustoord Cemetery, Plaque at Jewish Cemetery.
• **Planned duration**, without stops for refreshment or Extra Visits: 7 hours 30 minutes.
• **Total distance:** 115.5 kms/72.1 miles

N.B. Note that from early 2001 major road works were started to create ring roads from south of Son to north of Veghel which could well result in delays and diversions around the suggested routes below and which may require some imaginative interpretation of the directions. The resulting new roads will, however, eventually take a great deal of congestion off several important roads in this Itinerary.

• VVV Eindhoven/0 kms/0 miles/RWC

Drive under the railway line through the Vestdijk Tunnel, turn right following signs to Nijmegen/Helmond/Tilburg and turn left following the same directions just past the large yellow skittles onto John F. Kennedylaan. Exit, after the traffic lights, on Europalaan/Orpheuslaan(1.9 kms/1.2 miles) and turn left onto the bridge over the dual carriageway. Continue to the first road to the left and turn onto Baffinlaan. Continue to the cemetery on the right.

• Eindhoven (Woensel) General Cemetery/2.7 kms/1.7 miles/20 minutes/Map 1S/4b

At the entrance to the cemetery is an old brown CWGC sign and a Dutch Wargraves sign. The CWGC plots are approached by the main avenue of the cemetery, three plots (EE, KK and RR) lying to the north of it and two (JJB and JJ) to the south, near the Old Tower, the remains of a 15th Century Church that stood here until 1800. The Cross of Sacrifice and the Register Box are in Plot RR in a pleasing alignment on a large lawn.

There is a total of 687 burials in the five plots, 138 of which are UK Army, 4 Dutch Army, 1 Polish and one non-war grave. There are 426 named RAF and 6 Unknown, 49 named RCAF and I Unknown, 38 RAAF, 9 NZAF, 1 South African, 12 named Polish Airmen and 1 Unknown. Some of the aircrews are buried in joint graves.

MiD were **Flight Sergeant Reginald Bazley**, RAF, age 37, 1 January 1945 [KK.251]; **Flight Sergeant (Pilot) Norman Bowering**, RAF, age 26, 4 July 1941 [JJ.28]; **Sergeant Ian Craig**, RAF, age 32, 2 February 1943 [JJB.12]; **Flight Sergeant (Pilot) Herbert Hannay**, RAF, age 21, 12 June 1941 [JJ.12]; **Sergeant Cyril Humble**, RAF, age 20, 12 June 1941 [JJ. 13-14]; **Sergeant William Lapsley**, RAF, age 20, 4 July 1941 [JJ.26]; **Flight Lieutenant Peter Raw**, RAF, 21 March 1944 [KK.14] and **Pilot Officer Derick Shearburn**, RAF, age 22, 22 September 1944 [KK.207].

Awarded the **DFM** were **Flight Sergeant Reginald Bailey**, RAF, age 22, 22 June 1944 [KK.77]; **Pilot Officer William Coates**, RAF, age 20, 25 March 1944 [KK.28-31]; **W.Op Alexander Finlayson**, RAAF, age 29, 31 August 1943 [EE.108]; **Flight Sergeant Harold Houldsworth**, RAF, age 20, 22 June 1944 [KK.92]; **WO David Kelly**, RAF, 22 June 1944 [KK.81]; **Sergeant Ronald Lilleywhite**, RAF, age 20, 22 February 1943 [JJB. 6] and **Flight Sergeant Charles Taylor**, RAF, age 20, 22 June 1944 [KK.78.].

Awarded the **DFC** were **Flight Lieutenant (Naval) Norman Cornell**, RAF, died on 22 June 1944 [KK.80] and **Flight Lieutenant Gerard Johnson**, RAF, age 23, died on 8 February 1945, who has a **Bar to his DFC** [RR.26]; **Flight Lieutenant Wilmot Lowes**, RAF, age 24, 1 February 1945 [RR.14]; **Flying Officer (Naval/Radar) Ronald Mallett**, RAF, 29 June 1944 [KK.99]; **Flight Lieutenant Colin Penfold**, RNZAF, age 27, 23 April 1944 [KK.44]; **Flight Lieutenant John Siebert**, RAF, age 23, 28 March 1941 [FF.4]; **Flight Lieutenant (Naval) John Stewart**, RAF, age 33, 23 May 1944 [KK.57] and **Flight Lieutenant John Wells**, RAAF, age 21, 22 June 1944 [KK.79].

Amongst the many lads in their late teens or early 20s lies **L.A.C. Reginald Billings**, RAF, age 52, 2 December 1944 [KK. 236]. The father of **Private Israel Averback**, ACC, age 25, 28 September 1944 [KK. Grave 133], Sapper Israel Averback, RE, died of wounds on 7 June 1918 and is buried in Bienvillers Military Cemetery near Arras. **Sergeant Bernard Kipling**, RAF, age 23, died on 10 May 1941 [FF. 8] **lost two brothers** in the war: his twin, Sergeant Guy Kipling, RAF, died 23 June 1943, who is commemorated on the Runnymede Memorial, and

Woensel General Cemetery and Old-style CWGC sign

Corporal Peter Kipling, RASC, died on 22 June 1944, who is buried in Broomfield (St Mary) Churchyard, Essex.

The **father of Sergeant Basil Collins**, RAF, age 28, died on 26 July 1942 [JJ.87], Private Harry Collins of the Ox and Bucks, was killed in Belgium on 22 August 1917 and is commemorated on the Tyne Cot Memorial to the Missing.

Lieutenant-Colonel John Symons Commanding 72 Medium Regt, RA [KK.178] age 40, 26 October 1944, was the son of Brigadier-General Adolphe Symons, CMG.

WO Donald Miller BSc, age 24, 16 February 1945, served with the Dutch Sqdn [RR.33].

Sergeant Oldrich Havlik [JJ.48] and **Sergeant Pauel Varjan** [JJ.50], both served in the Czech Sqdn RAF, 14 April 1942. **Sergeant Josef Talab** served in the Czech Sqdn, 14 April 1942 [JJ.49].

Pilot Officer Noel Millidge, RAF, age 28, 27 August 1942, was a Scholar of the Guildhall School of Music and played in the BBC Empire Orchestra, the Buxton Municipal Orchestra and the National Opera Co. Orchestra [JJ.115].

Return to Europalaan and turn right, recross the bridge and then turn left back onto John F. Kennedylaan and continue northwards, passing a petrol station, to the Winston Churchilllaan/Sterrenlaan Exit.

Vlokhoven Church, from whose tower General Taylor watched the advance on Eindhoven on the morning of 18 September, is over to the left, about halfway between where you rejoined John F. Kennedy Laan and the Winston Churchilllaan exit.

- **Extra Visit to Soeterbeek Bridge; Nuenen Liberation Monument, 44th R Tanks and 101st AB Benches, Plaque to Corporal Stothard and Trooper Nicholls. (Maps S1-48/49/50/51**
  Round trip: 9.1 kms/5.7miles. Approximate time: 25 minutes

Exit, turn right along Sterrenlaan and continue to the third turning on the left, signed Nederwetten. Turn left at the traffic lights and immediately fork right on Soeterbeekseweg. Cross the bridge over the River Dommel and stop immediately on the left.

Willem Hikspoorsbrug, Soeterbeek (1.8 kms/1.1 miles). On the bridge is a sign, erected in 1984, which, translated, reads, 'God spared us without thought at this weak bridge,

Willem - Hikspoorsbrug

ter herinnering aan 19 september 1944

God spaarde ons ongedacht
Door deze zwakke brug
Haar zwakheid was haar kracht
Hier moest de vijand terug

21 september 1984

William Hikspoors Bridge over the Soeterbeek with Plaque

Extra visit continued

whose weakness was its strength. Here the enemy had to withdraw.' It relates to an incident on 19 September 1944 when 107th Panzer Brigade, which had been diverted from the Russian front, had arrived at Venlo railway station that morning and, via Nuenen and Nederwetten, had by evening reached the Dommel here, intending to attack The Corridor. As they reached this bridge, Willem Hikspoor, a gardener with Jonkheer Smits van Oyen, who lived near the bridge, managed to persuade Major Freiherr von Maltzan, commanding the force, that the bridge was too weak to carry their tanks. They turned round and made no further attempt to reach Eindhoven. The bridge is now named after the indomitable gardener.

Return to Sterrenlaan and turn left along Europalaan, following signs to Nuenen Centrum. Continue over the roundabout to the 2nd traffic lights, signed Centrum, to the corner of Parkstraat and Europaalan with the memorial on the left corner ahead. Turn left and immediately stop in the Congress Centre car park on the left and walk over the road.

Liberation Monument, Nuenen. (5 kms/3.1 miles). The monument, designed by Martijn Troost and unveiled in September 1994, is in the form of an open sarcophagus, symbolising liberation. On the lid is a *bas relief* of the population celebrating with a flag. Behind is a wall made of bricks from the destroyed Vink family farm, which once stood here. On the wall behind the sarcophagus is a stone plaque with a picture of a tank dedicated to Corporal R. Stothard and Trooper B. Nicholls killed in action on 20.9.44 and buried in Mierlo CWGC (qv). There are also two benches beyond the memorial – one dedicated to the **44th Royal Tank Regiment,** the other to the **101st AB.**

Return to Sterrenlaan and pick up the main itinerary.

Nuenen Liberation Monument and R. Tanks Plaque

Continue along John F. Kennedylaan/N265. Take the next exit to the right signed Airbornelaan. Turn right onto Airbornelaan and 150m later turn left onto De Koppele and immediately park on the right by the school. Walk back towards the bridge. The memorial is on the right.

• 101st AB Division Memorial, Airbornelaan/5.3 kms/3.3 miles /10 minutes/Map 1S/47

On the edge of the small ornamental garden surrounding the memorial is a wooden sign with a dramatic 'Screaming Eagle', commemorating Eindhoven's liberation on 18 September 1944 by 101st AB Division and British 2nd Army. In the garden is a stone monument with a thematic map showing the Wilhelmina Canal, the 502nd and 506th PIR DZs, Son and Eindhoven. Alongside is a torch of freedom and the date '18 September 1944.'

Return to the dual carriageway and turn right along John F. Kennedylaan, direction Son, passing another petrol station. Take the next exit towards Son and Breugel and turn right signed to Son, straight over the roundabout, past another petrol station and continue towards the Son Bridge over the Wilhelmina Canal and at the traffic lights, take the slip road on the right and stop before the bridge.

Son and Breugel. The painter Pieter Breughel the Elder (1525-1569) is presumed to have been born here; there is a memorial to him in Breugel. Further information can be obtained from the Town Hall, Raadhuisplein 4. Tel: + (0) 49 904555.

Walk across the road to the plaque in the small flower garden just before the bridge.

• New Son Bridge/Bridgehead Memorial/9 kms/5.6 miles/10 minutes/ Map 1S/52

British armoured car recce units reached Son around 1700 hours on 18 September to find the bridge blown and men of the US 326th AB Engineers clearing the debris. Two and a half hours later Sappers of 14 Field Squadron arrived, pressed into service some of the German prisoners and began to build the 100ft long Class 40 Bailey Bridge that was to carry the whole of XXX Corps over the Wilhelmina Canal. It was completed at 0615 hours on 19 September and the Guards spearhead crossed immediately, led by Lieutenant Kavanagh's troop of 2nd HCR now under command of the Grenadier Guards Group who had relieved the Irish – but they were now over 30 hours behind General Horrocks's schedule.

This is a major river obstacle and bridging it overnight in under 12 hours was a splendid achievement by the REs. It was an indication of the urgency with which the job was tackled that when an officer asked how things were going one of the Germans asked him to go away because he was slowing up the work! The sequence in which the various units were to be positioned in the column (known as the 'Order of March') as it moved up The Corridor (XXX Corps transport numbered more than 20,000 vehicles) had been carefully thought out, with bridging equipment well towards the front.

Although the 101st had captured the bridge area on 17 September the Germans made a number of counter-attacks on it over the coming days that threatened to cut The Corridor. One of the first and most dangerous was launched by three Panther tanks of 107th Panzer Brigade commanded by Hauptmann Wedemeyer and supported by infantry around 1700 hours on the 19th. They approached to within 200 metres from the east along the southern bank of the canal and one shot from the leading panzer hit a British truck on the bridge and set it on fire, while another hit the bridge itself. Warned by locals of the approach of the tanks the Americans brought up a bazooka, but although they hit the leading Panther there was no apparent damage. General Taylor, who was at the bridge, raced his jeep back to the DZ and brought up a 57mm gun and its crew which, firing from the northern side of the canal, scored two hits, while a GI named Jim 'Slick' Hoenscheidt threw a grenade into the open turret. That finished the affair and the other tanks withdrew with their infantry, leaving six dead and one injured. Two Americans were killed, one of whom, Second Lieutenant James L. Diel, died as he ran towards the Panthers carrying TNT charges. He is buried in the American cemetery at Margraten.

On the south-western corner of the original bridgehead, on the road by the bridge, is a small **marker,** erected by the residents of Kanaalstraat on 17 September 1994 to commemorate **50 years of Freedom.**

The present bridge was completed in 1983 on the site of the old one. It is raised to enable large boats to sail underneath.

Drive over the bridge and park in the slip road to the right. Walk over the road and turn up Debontstraat. Walk to the next turning to the right, Crocusstraat, and turn up it past the large apartment building to the right. Turn right into the car park and left at the corner of the garage block along a small brick path. On the left in a garden is

• *Screaming Eagles Monument, Zonhove, Son/9 kms/5.6 miles/15 minutes/Map 1S/53*

In the gardens of the Zonhove, now a housing development for old people, a sanatorium in 1944, is a memorial in the shape of the Liberation Highway markers that stretch along the route from the Normandy coast. It bears a large Screaming Eagle insignia and commemorates the 2,600 wounded soldiers of the Division who were treated here in a period of four months by the nuns and friars, as well as army medics, after being transported by specially modified jeeps flown in by gliders. The memorial was inaugurated in 1962.

Walk back to your car.

N.B. Alternatively you may reach the memorial by car by continuing to the roundabout and doubling back along the slip road, passing en route, on the right, a circular concrete fountain with the legend '101' around the base in the Raadhuisplein shopping area (Map 1S-54). Briefly come off the slip road as it ends and then immediately turn right on Debontstraat, drive up to Crocusstraat, turn right, park in the car park and follow instructions as for the walking directions. After visiting the memorial, follow Crocusstraat as it turns to the left and then right on Debontstraat, right on Zandstraat to September Plein. Pick up the instructions to the Airborne Memorial below from the second traffic lights.

Continue to the traffic lights in the centre and turn left signed to Best. 150m later turn right at more lights onto Europalaan.

N.B. To the left is 17 September Plein, usually a handy car parking area, but used for the weekly market on Thursday mornings. Off it, along Airborne Straat, is the Town Hall and Library where detailed town plans may be obtained.

Pass the Post Office and then the tennis club to the left and park on the left.
The memorial is in a landscaped area near a large lake with a fountain in it.

10st AB Div Memorial and sign, Airborne Laan

Screaming Eagles Monument, Zonhove

The new Son Bridge in raised position
with the Bridgehead Memorial

• *Son Airborne Memorial/10.2 kms/6.4 miles/10 minutes/Map1S-55/OP*

The memorial is in the form of a US airborne soldier who has just landed, with his parachute still attached and a grenade at the ready in his hand. A bench dedicated to 101st AB Division is beside the memorial. It was designed by Jan Lessen and Jan van Gemert and erected in 1964.

Face the airborne soldier head on.

That is 12 o'clock. The whole of 506th PIR, commanded by Colonel Bob Sink, landed in an open field in bright sunlight 2kms away at 5 o' clock. The bridge at Son is 1km away at 12 o'clock. Two routes forward were chosen, one (2nd Battalion, commanded by Lieutenant-Colonel Robert L. Sayer) behind you to the main road down which you have driven, and continuing past the first traffic lights to the bridge. The other (1st Battalion, commanded by Major James L. LaPrade and accompanied by General Taylor) went through the woods (part of the Zonsche [Sonse] Forest that stretched west from here to Best) to your right down to the canal bank. The canal runs from 3 o'clock to 9 o'clock 1km away. At the canal the battalion was to turn left and to assault the bridge from the flank.

An 88mm gun in the woods and two more close to the canal in buildings west of the main road in the town delayed the American two-pronged attack, each arm thinking that the other had reached the bridge. As a result neither moved with utmost urgency and it was two hours before they reached the canal itself, though A Company of the 1st Battalion took one of the 88's positions with a bayonet charge. As each force moved within 50m of their objective at about 1600 hours it was blown up, showering the Americans with debris. Immediately a small group led by Major LaPrade swam across and stormed the German positions across the canal where a fourth 88mm was positioned, roughly where the small bridgehead memorial is now. It had not fired on the Americans because the other guns had

Airborne Statue, Son

been between itself and its potential targets. Nevertheless, it was not until 0100 hours on 18 September that the whole regiment got over, having built a rope and wood footbridge. They had lost almost 30% of their strength.

The loss of the bridge and the delay in getting the whole regiment across did not stop the Americans advancing on Eindhoven at first light. 'Occupy the center at any price. Do not waste time in fighting the Germans... the rear will take care of them,' ordered Colonel Sink and the GIs headed south.

The Germans, however, continued to try to cut The Corridor and the following day they attacked between Son and Sint Oedenrode, stopping Corridor traffic for three hours, and assaults were also made further north on the 82nd AB Division around Groesbeek. The Sherwood Foresters were sent to help the Americans in the Reichswald area, thus becoming the first British troops to enter Germany. On 22 September the German 6th Para Regiment cut The Corridor between Uden and Veghel, delaying movement for 25 hours and two days later cut it again, although briefly, below Veghel. It has been said that even if XXX Corps had got to Arnhem in time to establish a bridgehead there it would not have improved the outcome of the operation. At the time that the Germans were making their attempts to cut The Corridor they were in the early throes of reorganisation and gaining determination daily. Every now and again they succeeded in cutting The Corridor even if only briefly. Bearing in mind that stubborn fighting went on in The Island (the area between Nijmegen and Arnhem) for over 5 months after MARKET-GARDEN was called off, a XXX Corps bridgehead at Arnhem could have been cut off by resurgent German forces just as 1st AB were, but with even greater casualities.

Continue along Europalaan to the junction with Gentiaanlaan and turn left. Continue to a junction to the right and turn up Australielaan. Turn left at the junction with Azielaan (still on Australielaan) and then immediately left onto Eifellaan through a pleasant, wiggling leafy suburban housing development. In the circle ahead is

• Herbert L. Pierce Memorial Tree/101st AB Seat/12.8 kms/8.00 miles/10 minutes/ Map 1S/56

The plane tree was planted by 101st AB Veteran, Herbert Pierce himself on 27 April 1996. It marks the spot where he landed by parachute on 17 September 1944 on the south-east corner of the 101st DZ C. In 2000 Herbert Pierce was still in contact with friends in the neighbourhood and a regular visitor to the site. The 101st AB seat by the small garden that surrounds the tree was erected by R. J. van den Hoef who lives in No 17 Appenijnenlaan opposite. He is a member of the Son and Breugel 50 Years of Freedom Committee, who produced a marvellous book, highly illustrated with original photographs of *Son and District during the Occupation and the Liberation* (enquire at the Town Hall).

Return past the Airborne Memorial on Europalaan to the N260 and turn right on Boslaan. Continue over the roundabout [watch out for the effect of roadworks] and take the left turn (18.2 kms/11.4 miles) on Hogeberglaan signed to the Rendac Factory. Follow the road round as it becomes Kanaaldijk Noord, past the factory on the right, with the canal to the left, to the flyover of the A2, called Airborne Bridge. Turn right immediately before it on Boslaan Zuid. 100m further on the right is

• Joe Mann Memorial, Airborne Bridge, Best/21.8 kms/13.6 miles/ 10 minutes/Map 1S-57/58/59

Taking the bridge over the canal here was not one of the original tasks given to the 101st. General Maxwell Taylor, thinking that it would be wise to have an alternative route should the Son bridge be blown, sent H Company of the 502nd PIR to take it on 17 September. Unfortunately, elements of the German 15th Army were in the area and the action developed into a major and bloody confrontation involving over 1,000 German troops, American paratroopers and British armoured cars under Lieutenant Palmer of 2nd HCR. The fighting continued until dusk even though the bridge was blown at about 1100 hours on 18 September and in the fighting that day Lieutenant-Colonel Robert G. Cole, commanding the 3rd Battalion of 502nd PIR, who had won the Congressional Medal of Honour in Normandy leading a bayonet charge (see *Holts' Battlefield Guide to Normandy*), was killed. Cole, who was also awarded the *Croix de Guerre*, was never able to wear the Medal and is buried in the American Cemetery at Margraten.

On Wednesday 20 September, hearing that the Germans in the area wished to surrender, the Americans sent forward a party under a Captain carrying a white flag in order to offer terms. They were blindfolded and led to the German major in command who turned down the offer. As they were returned to their own lines their German guides said if it had been their choice they would have surrendered.

This memorial bears a photo of Joe Mann (which has twice been stolen) and the words 'On 19 September 1944, Joe E. Mann an American soldier sacrificed his young life at this spot to save the lives of his comrades.' The detailed story of his sacrifice (qv) is told on a plaque to the right (but see below in the entry for the second Joe Mann memorial). Designed by A. Jacobs, the memorial was unveiled by Joe's sister, Irene Bennett-Mann, in 1984. To the left is a plaque commemorating the 5-8 July 1987 'Best to Berlin Memorial Run'. In the brick path leading to the memorial is the outline of a parachute.

The memorial is lovingly cared for by Dutchman Fritz Lucius of Best, an ex- WW2 Naval man who served in the Far East.

According to local experts, Joe Mann was actually killed some 200m further up the track on the left in a foxhole in what is now the high bank of the motorway. One hundred metres into the woods immediately to the right of Mann's foxhole are the visible remnants (in the shape of well-defined depressions) of a circular defensive position where 78 Americans and 300 Germans were killed or wounded during the action in which Mann lost his life.

• Extra Visit to 15th Scottish Division Memorial, Best (Map1S/60) Round trip: 5.6 kms/3.5 miles. Approximate time: 15 minutes

Turn right under the flyover and then right again to Best, passing Macdonalds on the right and turn left signed Best at the traffic lights and then right signed Centrum. Continue to the roundabout and turn left. Continue on Hoofdstraat to the car park on the left in Boeterhoek Plein. Walk across the road to the park, Koetshuistuin, on the right. Walk across the wooden bridge to the memorial.

From 20 September 1944 the Division fought a fierce battle for Best which lasted for over a month and during which 120 young Scottish soldiers were killed. Liberation finally

Herbert L Pierce Memorial

Tree to the left and 101st AB Seat to the right with detail

American trenches in the Nieuwe Heide with Fritz Lucius

Memorial to Joe Mann MoH, near Airborne Bridge

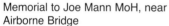

OP 19 SEPT 1944
GAF JOE E MANN
ALS SOLDAAT
OP DEZE PLAATS
ZYN JONGE LEVEN
OM HET LEVEN VAN
ZYN KAMERADEN

Extra visit continued

came on 24 October. The imaginative memorial, designed by Antoinette Briet, was inaugurated on 28 October 1994, is constructed of steel and stone in a 'tartan' pattern. Jumping through the centre are three bronze figures, symbolizing the bringing of freedom.

Return to Kanaldijk Noord and pick up the main itinerary.

51st Highland Div Memorial,Best

Turn round and return the way you have come to the junction with Bestseweg and turn left.

As you drive, the wooded area to your right and left is the Sonse (Zonsche to the Americans) Forest. The action here and around Best proved to be the toughest that 101st AB Division met during 18/19 September. The German forces were part of their 59th Division sent from Tilburg by General Student. The 506th PIR drop zone is 2kms away to your right

Continue to the Museum sign to the right and drive into the parking area.

• *Wings of Liberation Museum, Best/26.2 kms/16.4 miles/40 minutes/ Map 1S/61*

The museum is the brainchild of, comprises the personal collection of, and is partly financed (assisted by The Friends of the Museum Foundation) by the energetic octogenarian Mr Fritz Driessen. Born in 1921 he was arrested in 1941 by the Germans, who released him when they realised he had the contagious complaint, mumps. He then bicycled to France and worked with the Underground in France, Belgium and

Wings of Liberation Museum, Best: Dakota 'Darlin' Dorien' and Dutch Liberation Scene

Holland for three years, mainly building escape lines to Spain for Allied forces. On hearing news of the impending invasion in 1944, Driessen returned to northern France and, after the Breakthrough at Mortain, presented himself to the advancing US Cavalry. From then on until the end of the war Driessen worked in Intelligence with the Americans, through Belgium, Holland (where he was the first Dutchman in US uniform to cross the border of his homeland) and as far as Berlin.

After the war Mr Driessen built up a successful business in steel, sold it and started to collect militaria. His original exhibition was in Veghel, but when the collection outgrew the space he leased this large (12 hectares) tract of land situated on one of the LZs of the 101st AB Division on 17 September 1944. The main building has a traditional chronological exhibition of the course of WW2 in Holland with documents, photographs, artefacts and memorabilia, a multi-lingual audio-visual presentation, a documentation Centre, small souvenir shop and a cafeteria.

The main glory of the museum is, however, in the large themed halls in the grounds. The first one contains a reconstruction of a typical Dutch WW2 scene immediately after the landings, incorporating original 1944 vehicles, equipment and artefacts, which is so vivid and realistic that one feels as if one has stepped back in time. Other halls are dedicated to the 51st (Highland) Division (complete with figures in colourful and authentic uniforms), to Operation BARBAROSSA (containing the T34 and a Katyusha rocket mortar personally donated to Mr Driessen by the Russians), to Aviation (including Link-trainers and flight-simulators and over 300 miniature models of WW2 planes) and a US Mobile Command Post. In the grounds, amongst the many fascinating WW2 vehicles and weapons, is an original Dakota, bought by Mr Driessen as a 75th birthday present to himself. The name 'Darlin' Dorien' on the nose cone is a tribute to his daughter. The museum was opened by Prince Bernhard, a personal friend of the owner, who often pays a visit by helicopter and is then driven around in his own personalized golf caddy car. Mr Driessen has been the instigator of, and contributor to, many of the memorials in the district and his extraordinary museum, manned by enthusiastic volunteers, is well worth a visit. Allow plenty of time!
Open: Mon-Sat 1000-1700. Sun: 1200-1700. Entrance fee payable with concessions for children, Senior Citizens, Veterans. Tel: + (0) 499 329722. Fax: + (0) 499 329930. E-mail: wingslib@tref.nl. Website: wingsofliberation.nl

Continue 0.2kms on Bestseweg to the sign to 'Pavilion Joe Mann' on the left. Immediately turn left through a tall, white asymmetric concrete arch onto Joe Mann Weg. Continue through fir trees to the wooden barrier and park. The monument is to the right beyond the Joe Mann Pavilion Café.

• Joe Mann Memorial, Open-Air Theatre, Best/ 26.9 kms/ 16.8 miles/10 minutes/Map 1S/63/RWC (in summer)

The memorial was erected in the open-air theatre by the people of Best in memory of Private 1st Class Joe E.Mann (qv) of H Coy, 502nd PIR. It was unveiled by Joe Mann's parents on 17 September 1956. On 18 September, the day after the bridge at Son was blown, Lieutenant-Colonel John M. Michaelis, commanding 502nd PIR, led two of his battalions through these woods in an attempt to reinforce the small force that had been sent the previous day to capture the bridge at Best that you visited earlier. At 1100 hours that too was blown and a small group of fifteen soldiers led by Lieutenant Wierzbowski (they were the core of the original force) found themselves isolated and under fierce assault. Pfc Mann and another of the fifteen attacked and put out of action an 88mm gun, but by the evening Mann had been shot four times and his arms had to be strapped to his sides to stem the bleeding from his wounds. In the dawn mist of 19 September the Germans made a grenade attack, one grenade dropping into a foxhole beside Pfc Mann and six others. Mann, shouting 'Grenade!', threw himself onto it, taking the full blast and saving the lives of his comrades. He was posthumously awarded the Medal of Honour, America's highest soldier's award. Mann's action is reminiscent of that of Private 'Billy' McFadzean of the RIR who, on 1 July 1916, the first day of the Battle of the Somme, threw himself on to two grenades from which the pins had fallen out. He was blown to pieces but saved the lives of the men in his crowded trench and was awarded a posthumous VC. Wierzbowski ultimately surrendered the remnants of his force but they were later rescued by GIs of the 502nd and their captors taken prisoner.

The monument was designed by the Nijmegen artist, Ard Bernstein. He chose to represent Mann by a pelican, a symbol of self-sacrifice, derived from the legend of the pelican feeding her young with her own flesh. Four slim pillars support the mother pelican on her nest of young, and *bas relief* figures round the base portray Joe Mann's heroic action.

Return to the main road and turn left towards Best.

Heavy fighting took place in the woods to the right of the road as the Americans progressed from Son to Best. The ditches on either side of the road were used as trenches and for many years after the war cartridge cases were to be found in them.

Continue to the next road to the right, Molenheideweg, and turn up it.

In the woods to the right, the traces of foxholes can still be discerned. Along the first turning to the left, Oude Baan, the Germans built a fake runway.

Continue on the road, which has now become Sonniuswijk, to the farm on the left, No 42/42a.

• Parachute/Screaming Eagle, Paulushoeve, Son/30.9 kms/ 19.3miles/10 minutes /Map 1S/64

N.B. Please remember that this is private property.

The owner of the farm, Wan van Overveld, has erected a metal parachute in the garden and on the house is a Screaming Eagle. The latter was to celebrate the 40th Anniversary of MARKET-GARDEN and was a gift of the Association of Dutch Airborne Friends. The farm was on DZ C (506th PIR) to the south. It was used as an identification point because the name of the farm was written on the roof. An airstrip, LZ W, was then constructed behind the farm from which gliders were taken back to the U.K. The ties between the American liberators and the van Overveld family have remained strong, and, until recently, important commemorative ceremonies were held here.

A PERSONAL MEMORY
By Liza van Overveld, age 14 in 1944.

[Liza, who still lives in a cottage adjoining the farm, remembered going to church with her mother and two-year-old sister on the morning of Sunday 17 September 1944. During the service the priest told them that the church was surrounded by Germans

Joe Mann MoH Pelican Memorial, Open-Air Theatre near Best

The Paulushoeve with Parachute Memorial

A personal memory continued

looking for Dutchmen to dig foxholes for them along the Son Canal. The men all left the church by the back door and were saved. On the nervous journey home, Liza saw the sky fill with aeroplanes, flying low and making a deafening sound, soon augmented by the noise of a heavy bombardment. They managed to get home and the whole family hid in the cellar until they heard loud cries of joy.]

'We ran out of the cellar. Unforgettable! There we were standing eye to eye with our liberators.... Sympathetic men, out of another part of the world, come all the way to us, risking their own lives! And everything that happened in the moments after that was as in a dream. We had to talk with our hands and feet. Unfortunately the language was a big problem. Especially the leaders of the paratroopers were anxious to get information from us about "where to...". They lost their awareness of direction. Most of them had a map and compass but they were on strange territory full of enemies.'

[The family gave the paratroopers milk and whatever help they could. Some of them made their way towards Son and the bridge over the Canal, others to Best. Then came the gliders.]

'It was beautiful to see the gliders land....You could see them opening their front and all of a sudden a jeep drove out of it in full speed into the meadows. They were so quick those Yankees. In the meantime we were smothered with chocolate, cigarettes, chewing gum and even with their own ration packages. We were spoiled and we were more than happy.... What struck us was their extreme politeness. As well as their big love for children.... The first day the lightly wounded men were bound up and attended to in our living room by a doctor or medic. They worked very quickly and efficiently.'

[They were not the only casualties. Many of the farm's cows were killed and their beloved horse 'de Vos' was blinded by the bombardment. And soon refugees from Best, who had lost everything in the fighting and had to run for their lives, made their way to the farm.]

'But the Americans who were with us ... were a very great support for us. They kept cool and by doing so gave us confidence and hope.'

Continue to the junction with the N265.

N.B. At this point, the hamlet of Wolfswinkel is across the other side of the road. It was there that Maxwell Taylor had his HQ on 20 September. That same day General Ridgway, held up south of Son, drove around vehicles of XXX Corps and arrived here. Later in the day he returned to Eindhoven to see Brereton and then went north to Groesbeek to meet Gavin who was in the middle of a desperate struggle and had little time to talk to him. On the left-hand side of the road to the right is Waterhoef Farm, with the name in white on the roof, behind which was a temporary US cemetery (qv) containing 450 graves.

Turn left direction St Oedenrode. Exit at St Oedenrode and then turn left on Sonseweg. At the next junction turn left, back over the N265, and immediately right following signs to St Oedenrode. At the following roundabout turn right on Nijnselseweg. At the next roundabout turn right following signs to Schijndel on Corridor.

• Sint Oedenrode

The town is so-called from the combination of the name of an 8th Century Scottish Princess, Oda, who settled here and 'rode', meaning a small wood. More information can be had from the **VVV**, St Paulusgasthuis, Kerksraat 20.

Open: Mon-Sat: 1 April-1 September. Other months, Tel: + (0) 413 474100.

St Oedenrode was occupied by the Germans until the arrival of the 101st Airborne Division on 17 September, followed two days later by units of the British Army. Together they established a corridor through the village for the passage of troops, during the fighting for which there were both civilian and military casualties. A temporary hospital was set up in the Roman Catholic Girls' School and the twenty-three British soldiers (including 1 Unknown) who died there were buried here.

502nd and 506th PIR dropped to the west of The Corridor between Sint Oedenrode and Son. 502nd PIR dropped nearest St Oedenrode with Lieutenant-Colonel Patrick Cassidy, CO of 1st Battalion, and General Maxwell Taylor, the divisional commander, in one of the leading aircraft. 1st Battalion had the task of taking St Oedenrode. Two German tanks, which could have given opposition, were destroyed by fighter bombers and by nightfall the Americans had overcome slight but determined small arms fire from rear-echelon troops, to capture the town and take fifty-eight prisoners. Fighting continued for more than a week under constant German artillery fire, but, helped for two days by an Irish Guards tank that had been damaged and left behind by the regiment, the Americans cleared the road to Schijndel and never let St Oedenrode be recaptured. The tank commander, Sergeant Paddy

McRory, was recommended by the Americans for the Silver Star. The town issued a handsome scroll of thanks to its liberators in October 1944.

The following monument is then passed on the left but proceed to the next roundabout and double back to it, over the bridge over the Dommel and past the giant yellow clog on the right, so as to be able to pull in on the parking area on the same side of the road.

• Sint Oedenrode Monument to the Dutch from 101st AB Veterans/ 38 kms/23.7 miles/10 minutes/Map 1S/67

The memorial was initiated and funded by the Americans in recognition of the level of resistance in the Brabant and the help that their forces received from the local population in 1944. It was the brainchild of veteran John Seney and was designed by Frans Alkemade, André van Bergeyk and Trudy Peters-Broos. It was unveiled on 21 September 1994 by Lieutenant-General Harry Kinnard who in 1944 commanded the 501st PIR which landed in the wrong place, almost on top of Castle Heeswijk. The inscription is 'Dedicated to the Dutch people in grateful appreciation' and around the monument are scenes of the landings in bronze *bas relief.*

Continue to the roundabout and turn right following signs to Centrum and VVV along Hertog Hendrikstraat to the T-junction in the centre.

The VVV is in the corner on the right at Kerkstraat 20.

Turn left on Kofferen signed Best. Continue to the large glass and concrete building on the right. Turn left, signed 'Kasteel Henkenshage' on Kasteellaan, passing the school on the left, and turn left again. Park outside the Castle.

• Castle Henkenshage/101st AB Plaque/39 kms 24.5 miles/ 10 minutes/Map 1S-68/69

There has been a homestead on this site since 1350. Between 1850 and 1860 the Castle was extensively enlarged and the last private owner, Theodore van Gulick, sold it to the town of Sint Oedenrode. During the war it was used as the distribution centre for food rationing coupons. General Taylor moved his HQ here after 502nd PIR cleared the town of Germans on 17 September 1944.

The Castle is now an up-market restaurant and caterers, specialising in functions and themed dinners. Tel: + (0) 499 375537.

Walk over the drawbridge over the moat that surrounds the castle.

On the right of the entrance is a plaque describing the castle's history including its 1944 links with the 101st AB.

Walk under the tunnel.

On the right is a bronze plaque which reads, 'This vital road junction was liberated by the 502nd PIR on 17 September 1944 with the assistance of the Dutch underground and held against repeated enemy attacks. This plaque is in honour of the Screaming Eagles who gave their lives and as a token of esteem and friendship for the people of the Netherlands. Placed by Comrades of the 101st AB Division Association. 1969'. Below the text is a list of divisional units who took part in the fighting.

That year the 101st AB Division Association presented the town with a small statue of a US paratrooper, which stood in an alcove in the courtyard. Sadly the original was stolen and the Foundation of Eindhoven Airborne Friends presented a new statue during a visit of 101st Veterans. On 17 September 2000 there was no trace of the statue and nobody in the building had any knowledge of it.

Return to the roundabout at the bottom of Corridor, turn left along Corridor, over the next roundabout onto Lindendijk and turn left along Ollandseweg, signed Olland/Boxtel. Continue over the roundabout, past the exit St Oedenrode sign, and past the small turning to Kinderbos on the right. Park outside the house on the left just before the Rijsingen and 'dead end' signs to the left.

Members of the family who live in this house actually witnessed the action described below in which a tank was blown up by German fire at 1600 hours and three wounded soldiers were taken away, leaving the bodies of the two dead soldiers. They maintain contact with relatives of John Thorogood.

Cross the road. The memorial is in an indent in the hedge outside house No. 98.

•Memorial to Troopers Thorogood and Matthews, Sint Oedenrode/43 kms/26.9 miles/10 minutes/Map 1S/70

On 21 September 1944 two British troopers of C Squadron 44th Royal Tank Regiment were killed when their tank was hit by anti-tank shells as they provided infantry support to 502nd PIR. In 1994 this memorial was raised to them on the spot where they were killed. It was designed by Louis Kleyne, the director of the Kienehoef Primary School, and unveiled by George Thorogood, John's brother, in the presence of children of the local school. The Troopers, John Thorogood, age 21, and Stanley Matthews, age 22, are buried side by side in Uden CWGC Cemetery (qv).

Return to the junction with Lindendijk, turn right signed Son & Breugel and continue to the roundabout. Turn left along Eerschotsestraat signed Veghel to the N265. Go straight over to the car park of the C. J. Bever Tuincentrum (Garden Centre) and park. The memorial is in the landscaped area to the right, surrounded with shrubs and plants.

• C-47 Propeller Memorial, Sint Oedenrode/46 kms/ 29 miles/10 minutes/Map 1S/71

The propeller of the C-47 Dakota KG 498, part of 437th Squadron RCAF, is set in a memorial garden. On 21 September 1944 the plane was returning from a supply flight to Oosterbeek when it was shot down by anti-aircraft guns sited near Sint Oedenrode. The entire crew – four Canadians and four British airmen – were killed. The propeller represents all the aircraft that were shot down over North Brabant during MARKET-GARDEN.

Turn right on the N265 and continue direction Veghel to the first major turning left to Koeveringsedijk [1.3 miles]. Turn here and continue to a small turn to the right signed Tennis de Eerde and De Couvering and stop. On the right, with a picnic table on a small grassed area, is

• Remnants of Old Mill, De Koevering/49 kms/30.7 miles/10 minutes/Map 1S/72

Under the roof is a plaque, erected on 18 December 1982, describing the mill and its September 1944 history, when it was completely destroyed in the fighting.

Castle Henkenshage

501st Geronimo Memorial, Eerde with windmill in background

Memorial to the Dutch from 101st AB Veterans, St Oedenrode

Return to the N265, turn left direction Veghel and continue to the traffic lights at the turning to Eerde and turn left on Eerdsebaan. Continue through the centre of the town to the church on the right and stop.

The road runs along the southern boundary of 101st AB DZ A.

• *Graves of 44th Royal Tanks, Eerde Churchyard/53.9 kms/33.7 miles/10 minutes/Map 1S/73*

In the churchyard behind the church, half-way up on the right-hand side, are the well-tended graves of the five 44th Royal Tanks men described on the memorial below who lie side by side.

Continue to the Memorial at the T-junction ahead.

• *501st Geronimo Monument, Old Mill, Eerde/54.2 kms/33.9 miles/ 10 minutes/ Map 1S-74/75*

In the sand dunes of Eerde between Veghel and Schijndel the 501st PIR waged bitter hand-to-hand fighting with the Germans and sustained heavy losses in their efforts to shield The Corridor. In 1981 this exuberant memorial, with the colourful badge of the regiment showing the head of the Apache Geronimo (their battle cry) surmounting a brick base, was unveiled. To the right of the main memorial is a pillar with the names of eleven Americans erected 'To my friends, may they rest in peace' by William and Thelma McMahon in 1989. On the adjoining mill are several plaques. There is a list of names of the dead of the 501st and the story of Sergeant Jacob H.Wingard who at about 11 o'clock on 18 September 1944, was killed in the windmill and is now buried in Margraten US Cemetery (qv). Between the windmill and the nearby house a British Sherman tank was knocked out during the fight on Sunday 24 September 1944. The names of British soldiers of the 44th Royal Tank Regiment,

St Oedenrode; C-47
Propeller / Thorogood and
Matthews Memorial

killed on 24 September, are listed: Trooper Gilbert L. Astin, age 21; Trooper Jasper Jones, age 27; Trooper Frank W. Stacey, age 36; Trooper James E. Hardy, age 30, and Lieutenant Wallace R. Hooper, age 28. They are buried in the churchyard you have just passed.

Every 17 September (or the nearest Sunday) local dignitaries and members of local Remembrance Associations lay flowers at the memorial and deck the mill with WW2-related decorations – dummy parachutes and paratroopers, model aeroplanes, flags etc. Any visiting veteran groups are received with enthusiasm

Return to the N265 OR

• *Long Extra Visits to Schijndel 51st Highland Division Memorial and 'Mother Hen/Bird of Prey' (Map 1S-76/77); St Michielsgestel Liberation Memorial, Memorial to Civilian Victims and RAF Graves (Map 1S-78/79/80; Vught - Student's HQ, 51st Highland Division Room, National Monument (Concentration Camp), Fusilladeplaats Memorial, (Map 11-1/3, 1S-83/82), Den Dungen Silent Wings Memorial (Map 1S/84); Heeswijk Liberation Chapel, Kasteel Heeswijk Landings Monument, (Map1S-85/86)*
Round trip: 64 kms/40.3 miles. Approximate time: 2 hours 45 minutes

Continue to the junction with the N265 (N622) and turn left direction Schijndel. Continue through Wijbosch and at the traffic lights at the first major junction turn left signed St Oedenrode (3.2 kms/2 miles). Continue over the roundabout to the group of statues on the right at the traffic lights. Turn right and stop in the slip road behind the memorial.

51st Highland Division Memorial Statue (5.1 kms/3.2 miles).

To British eyes, this is probably the most beautiful traditional war memorial in Holland. It is a statue of a kilted

51st Highland Div
Memorial Schijndel

Long Extra visit continued

Highlander looking down on a delightful young Dutch girl. The attitude and facial expression of the figures tell all there is to say about Liberation: the happy, trusting face of the girl, the dependable, strong yet gentle face of the soldier. It is reminiscent of the Highlander at the head of Y-Ravine in the Beaumont Hamel Park on the Somme.

The legend on the memorial describes how on 23 October 1944 the 51st Highland Division launched an offensive from this position. By 7 November the enemy were cleared from the 800 square kms south of the River Maas between Schijndel and Gertruidenberg. Its casualties were forty-four officers and fifty-three soldiers. 2,800 of the enemy were taken prisoner.

On the 50th Anniversary of the Operation codenamed COLIN and GUY FAWKES veterans were welcomed back by the Dutch and this statue was unveiled. The base is made of Scottish granite and a panel shows the towns which were liberated, when, and by which Brigade. Above them is the Highland Division emblem and below the Gaelic motto which translates, 'Friends are good on the day of the Battle.' The designer was Alan B. Herriot. Below the memorial is a large 'HD' in green box hedge.

Miniature versions of this group of statues may be seen in the 51st Highland Division Room in Vught (qv) and in the Director's office in the Museum at Best (qv). *Return straight over the roundabout and straight across the traffic lights, direction Schijndel to the next roundabout with the large tulip sculpture, turn left signed Centrum to the crossroads with Hoofdstraat, turn right and then, after the large church on the left, immediately left onto Jan van Amstel Straat. Continue to the St Lidwina Convent grounds on the right. Drive over the small bridge into the grounds and park. Walk to the left round the main building and through the housing complex to the grassed area at the back - Veronica Park. In the park is*

Monument to the Sisters of Love, Lidwina Convent, Schijndel. (10.5 kms/6.6 miles). In September 1944 many of the paratroopers and gliderborne forces who landed or dropped in Brabant were off course and found themselves stranded in enemy territory. In many cases they were hidden and fed by the local citizens, who thus risked their own lives. In the Lidwina Convent, in the midst of the occupying Germans, 27 Americans who landed in the vicinity were sheltered and cared for by the Sisters of Love until October 1944. In 1984 this imaginative and symbolic bronze memorial by Dolf Wang was erected to the Sisters. It depicts a mother hen protecting her chicks from a bird of prey.

Return to the large church and turn left on Boschweg. Continue to the traffic lights and junction with Structuurweg. Turn left direction St Michielsgestel and continue to a left turn signed St Michielsgestel (14.6 kms/9.1 miles). Turn left along Gestelseweg which becomes Schijndelseweg and after passing the town sign take the first turning right on Spijt and immediately left into the slip road. On the right is

Memorial to Sint Michielsgestel's Liberation on 23 October 1944 by the 1st Northants and 7th Black Watch (16.2 kms/10.1 miles), erected in May 1985. There are seats each side of the memorial and a post for hanging wreaths with two Northants Yeomanry plaques (May 1985 and October 1994).

Continue towards St Michielsgestel Centre and turn right into the main square.

Long Extra visit continued

In the square is an interesting ancient tower, some pleasant cafés and restaurants and the **Town Hall** (16.6 kms/10.4 miles), inside which there is a **Display Cabinet** with mementoes of the 51st Highland Division, the US AB Divisions and the Poles, visits of various veterans' groups etc. Market Day is Friday.

Continue to the large church on the right. Stop. In front of the church on its left is **Monument to Citizens of Sint Michielsgestel Shot by the Germans.** This sad memorial was erected in 1984.

Continue just beyond the cemetery on the right and stop (17.3 kms/10.8 miles). There is a CWGC sign at the entrance.

On entering the cemetery, immediately turn to the right corner. There are the **4 graves of an air crew,** all dated 19 September 1944. They are **Flight Sergeant G.S. Breckels**, RCAF, Air Gunner, age 19; **WO S. H. Coeshott**, RAF, Pilot, age 23; **Flight Sergeant S.V. Davis**, RAF, Navigator, age 21, and **Flight Sergeant J.G. Jeffery**, RAF, Air Bomber, age 22.

N.B. To the right past the cemetery is the Beekvliet building. During the war it was a Seminary and the Germans used it as a Transit Camp for Concentration Camps in Germany.

Turn round and return to the square. Turn right at the T-junction signed Vught. *Cross the Dommel.* This is a new bridge, built in 1970.

Turn right direction Vught, continue over the A2 motorway and enter Vught on Haldersebaan, turn left signed Vught-Zuid, on Glorieuxlaan and after about 100m, turn left into the Landgoed Huize Bergen Conference Centre. In September 1944 this was **General Student's HQ** (qv) (22.4 kms/14 miles). He left Berlin on 5 September for Tilburg. On the 14th he moved his HQ here and on 15 September the double agent Lindemanns (King Kong) reputedly came to see him with his latest intelligence report about Allied movements. Although it is always recounted that it was at Vught that the crashed glider containing the Allied plans for MARKET-GARDEN was found, the precise site has not been identified.

Turn round, return along Glorieuxlaan, straight over the traffic lights signed *Vught Centrum and follow the road left along Boxtelseweg.* In the Park Reeburg to the left is a **Memorial Urn to the Women Prisoners of Vught who were killed in Sachsenhausen Concentration Camp.** On the left after the park is the back of Vught Town Hall, looking like a fairytale castle.

Turn first left after the town hall along Leeuwensteinlaan and first left along *Radhuisstraat. Stop by the Town Hall.* To the right of the main entrance is an **'Information Sign'**. Round the corner is the entrance. **51st Highland Room. Vught Town Hall** (23.4 kms/14.6 miles). On the first floor of this picturesque building is a unique room devoted to the 51st Highland Division. Around the walls are photographs of veterans of the Division, many taken during pilgrimages to Vught. There is a glorious stained glass window dedicated to the

Protective Mother Hen
Memorial Schijndel

Sint Michielsgestel Memorials: Liberation by 1st
Northants / 7th Black Watch, and Shot Civilians

Vught: Gen Student's HQ and 51st
Highland Div stained glass window,
Town Hall

Long Extra visit continued

Division, 26 October 1944, a miniature of the Schindel Divisional Memorial, an interesting wooden ceiling incorporating a clock.

Above the main entrance is a fine stained glass window dedicated to the **Red Cross** and by the front door and on the landing on the stairs are Memorials to Belgian Political Prisoners.

N.B. Prior permission to view the Scottish Room must be obtained, as it is a working meeting room and may well be occupied, either by going to the Information Office at the side of the building (see above), which is highly recommended as one can obtain a useful, detailed town plan here, or by telephoning in advance on + (0) 73 6580620.

Turn round and continue along Radhuisstraat, then turn left immediately before St Petrus Church onto Ploegstraat and stop. In the church is a
Stained Glass Window in Memory of the Solidarity of the Women of Kamp Vught (23.8 kms/14.9) by Marius de Leeuw, inaugurated in October 1996.
Continue and turn right on Kloosterstraat following the one-way system. Turn left and then right on Koestraat.

N.B. By going straight on here the Station is reached. In the Station to the left is a plaque, unveiled by Princess Juliana on 23 October 1984, to the 14,000 Jewish men, women and children who were transported to Concentations Camps and near it is a memorial to the Belgian Prisoners of Kamp Vught. Twenty were hanged in the camp in September 1943 (Map 11/5).

Continue to the next junction (24.2 kms/15.1).

N.B. To the right at the end of Taalstraat is Vught Historical Museum. It contains a permanent exhibition on the Concentration Camp, sometimes known as 'Konzentrationslager Herzogenbusch', but better known as Kamp Vught. Open: Sunday, Tuesday and Thursday 1400-1700. Admission free. Tel: + (0) 73 6566764 (Map 11/6).

Turn left on Helvoirtseweg, over the railway to the traffic lights and turn left on the N65, direction Tilburg,. Continue to the traffic lights and turn right signed Cromvoirt/National Monument on Boslaan. The first turn to the right after crossing the railway is signed to
Fusilladeplaats (Mur des Fusillés). The memorial wall is on the site where hundreds of prisoners were brought to be shot by firing squad. It was unveiled by HRH Princess Juliana in 1947 and on it are inscribed the names of the 317 whom it is known for certain were shot here in July, August and September 1944. Many other unknown prisoners were shot here. Behind the wall is the sand hill that the Germans used as a 'safety net' for stray bullets. On 7 May 1995, vandals smeared panels on the memorial with tar. These desecrated panels were removed and now stand, encased, near the symbolic camp gates in the National Monument. The Memorial was restored and reopened in 1966.

Continue with the De Ijzeren Man lake to the left. Turn right into the Camp Vught complex along Lunettenlaan (26.6 kms/16.6 miles). Continue to the black glass command post on the left.

N.B. If you wish to visit the Engineers' Museum, which is in the restricted military area, which includes a training centre for the Dutch Engineering Corps, to the left, you should phone in advance to + (0) 73 6881867 for permission. You must then check in at the

Long Extra visit continued

command post, leave some identification, receive a pass and turn left, using your pass to raise the barrier. Park in the car park to the right and someone will emerge to welcome you.

To reach the Kamp Vught Concentration Camp National Monument, drive straight to the end of Lunettenlaan.

En route the Nieuw Vosseveld Penitentiary is passed on the left and there is also a Moluccan Settlement in the area. Note that the entire area you are driving through was once the Concentration Camp.

Park in the car park beyond the prison and walk to the recreated camp.

Note that there is another path signed to Fusilladeplaats here.

Kamp Vught Concentration Camp National Monument (28.5 kms/17.8 miles). **Open:** 1 April-31 October every day. Tues-Friday 1000-1700. Saturday-Monday 1200-1700. Entrance is free, but there is a charge for guided group tours. Donations may of course be made.

Tel: + (0) 73 6566764. Fax: + (0) 73 6560835.

E-mail: info@nmkampvught.nl Website: www.nmkampvught.nl

The present Monument was completed in 1990 and was opened by Queen Beatrix on 18 April that year on a small part of the vast 1943/4 camp that stretched back as far as Boslaan from which you turned into the complex. It was created as a dreadful reminder of man's inhumanity to man and to make the visitor aware that in many parts of the world oppression, torture and annihilation still exist. It comprises a compound with recreated watch towers near parts of the original fence, within which there is a ditch. As you turn into the entrance there is a Visitors' Centre and toilets to the left. It is highly advisable to pick up the excellent English language guide book here as the explanatory boards that mark each stop on the recommended route are all in Dutch. Ahead is a schematic model of the camp as it was in 1943. The route then takes one through the recreated wash and toilet area, an Information Centre, sleeping quarters and the crematorium, with original ovens – although Vught was not an extermination camp and there were no gas chambers; prisoners were transported to the infamous camps in Germany or Poland to be gassed and Vught was known as 'The Gateway to Hell'. However, Himmler ordered that all prisoners who died in the camp, through whatever cause, should be cremated. There is a replica of the notorious Cell 115, into whose 9-square-metres area, the Camp commandant Grunewald crammed seventy-four women from Barracks 23b on 15 January 1944 when they protested at their barracks leader being locked up. After fourteen indescribable hours, ten women were dead, many others unconscious or out of their mind. Grunewald was later imprisoned for the atrocity.

The area thus preserved or recreated as a reminder of the obscenity of the camp's history is small and very quiet. It vividly imparts its story. As Vught is a National Monument, funds have been allocated to make a large new, modern exhibition. It is doubtful whether it can have a greater impact than this simple memorial. By far the most moving item in the monument area is the new **Children's Memorial**, inaugurated on 4 May 2000. Bronze tablets are inscribed with the names of the unbearable number of 1,269 children, with their ages. 1,800 children were transported from here to

Long Extra visit continued

concentration camps, 1,200 on 6 and 7 June 1943 alone to the extermination camp at Sobibor. Surmounting the tablets are golden Stars of David, and on a ledge at their base are bronze toys – a doll, a top, a truck. Visiting children today place touching tributes to these martyred young people, treasured possessions that they happen to have with them – a necklace, a pen, even prized Pokemon cards.

Kamp Vught in WW2. Building work started on the camp, officially designated Konzentrationslager Herzogenbusch, in 1942. Directly accountable to SS HQ in Berlin, it was the only camp situated outside the borders of the Reich but was laid out exactly like a German concentration camp. Barracks were about 85m long and about 13m wide. With twenty-three watch towers equipped with searchlights and machine guns, the camp was surrounded by a double barbed wire fence and deep ditch. It was used to break Resistance Workers and to house the growing number of Jews that were to be deported to camps in the Reich when transit camps at Amersfoort and Westerbork became too small. Emaciated prisoners from these were used as slave labour to complete this camp in conditions so harsh that hundreds of them died during the first few months. In February 1943 a large number of student hostages were brought to the camp and Philips (qv) workshops or labour yards were set up around the hospital. At one time there were 1,200 Philips workers, many of them Jews. By insisting that these skilled workers were needed for the German war effort, Frits Philips and his managers, many of whom worked in the camp, were able to save many of their Jewish employees from being transported to extermination camps for many months. There were also many acts of sabotage in the workshops. Local opinion about Philips' wartime role was mixed. Some saw Frits Philips as another 'Schindler', others as a collaborator, although there is little doubt that there was no alternative under the Occupation but to work with the Germans as refusal to do so would have brought fearful reprisals, especially to the Jewish workers. As workers from the Eindhoven factory were occasionally allowed in, messages and gifts were smuggled in and out of Vught.

Large numbers of prisoners continued to be brought into the camp, then transported to extermination camps. In May 1944 800 prisoners were transported to Dachau. In June 1944 the last transportation to Auschwitz took place, amongst them the Philips Jewish workers. After this an important conveyor belt was cut in the Philips' workshops and as a result the entire Philips' management were dismissed. As news of the Allied advance through France and Belgium became known, many reprisal executions took place here. On 5/6 September 2,800 men were transported to Sachsenhausen and 650 women to Ravensbruck. The camp was then virtually empty. Part of the camp records were then destroyed and on 13 September the last members of the SS departed. On 22 September the camp was officially handed over to Sister Hulsman of the Red Cross. It was then used by the Allies as a German POW and Collaborators' Camp.

It is estimated that approximately 31,000 prisoners passed through Kamp Vught. No record of the exact number who died exists, but it is known that 15,000 prisoners, of whom 12,000 were Jews, were deported to extermination camps where very few of them survived.

The message that the visitor to the National Monument should understand about the

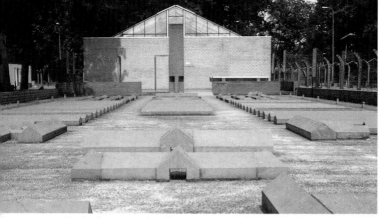

Vught Concentration Camp: recreated layout and personal
tribute on Childrens' Memorial

Long Extra visit continued

terror of the concentration camps is summarized by the words of Friedrich Martin
Niemöller, a U-boat Commander in WW1, who became a Pastor, opposed the attitude
of the Nazi party to the Church, was arrested in 1937 and imprisoned in Sachsenhausen
and then Dachau before being liberated in 1945:

> *When the Nazis came to fetch the Communists*
> *I remained silent*
> *For I was not a Communist.*
> *When they imprisoned the Social Democrats*
> *I remained silent*
> *For I was not a Social Democrat.*
> *When they came to fetch the Catholics*
> *I did not protest*
> *For I was not a Catholic.*
> *When they came to fetch me*
> *There was nobody left to protest.*

After WW2 Martin Niemöller became a controversial pacifist. In 1967 he received the
Lenin Peace Prize and died in 1984.

> *Return to the N65 and turn left direction 's-Hertogenbosch. Continue onto the A2/E25*
> *signed Nijmegen and take Exit 22, 's-Hertogenbosch-Centre signed St Michielsgestel.*

N.B. By exiting here at Junction 24, 's-Hertogenbosch-Center, direction west towards
Vlijmen onto the A59 to Exit No 41 Drunen and then to the centre of Elshout, an
'Underground' Memorial which tells an extraordinary story may be visited. Designed by
P. Powels in 1994 and erected beside the church, it commemorated the Norbertinus
monastery which once stood on the spot and in which thirty-two British and fifteen
American Airborne men were hidden under the eyes of the occupying Germans by the
people of Elshout and Drunen when their gliders were brought down between Loon op
Zand and Drunen. On 21 October the men were transferred to a shelter on the Campina
Heath near Boxtel, where forty-eight Americans were already hiding. On 24 October this
group of hideaways liberated Boxtel, a day before it was reached by the 51st Highland
Division.

Liberation Chapel,
Heeswijk-Dinther with
detail of 101st Para statue

Silent Wings Memorial, Den
Dungen, with designer, Jos
Korsten

Kasteel Heeswijk with
501st PIR Memorial

Long Extra visit continued

Continue and turn left at the traffic lights signed to Den Dungen and left again after the windmill. Continue past the church to the memorial on the right in the car park.

Silent Wings Memorial, Den Dungen (41.4 kms/25.9 miles). This highly original and effective memorial was designed by local teacher Jos Korsten in 1994, with the support of the Den Dungen Market Garden Committee and active member Jacq van Eekelen (author and photographer of the excellent Nord Brabant Memorials book (qv)). It tells the story of the gliders which landed in the middle of enemy territory in September 1944. As at Son, several gliders landed in the wrong location – because they were lost, cut off from their tugs or shot down. The survivors of these stragglers were often sheltered, at great danger, by the local population. Here in Den Dungen the crews of two gliders were cared for for two weeks. The memorial was located here as the triangle Vught – Den Dungen – s'Hertogenbosch was the initial aiming point for all aircraft engaged in MARKET. It was codenamed ELLIS.

A plaque on the post of the memorial tells the story of Glider pilot Dan Griffiths who landed at Den Dungen on 18 September and who was a regular visitor here after the war. In 1990 he was made a Freeman of the town. Den Dungen was twinned with Portishead, Dan's home town, which Jos Korsten and his children often visit. Dan Griffiths died on 9 May 1998, but was involved in the erecting of the memorial before his death. It is a 'living' monument in that the sky is constantly changing through the cut-out shapes of the gliders. It is planned to move it to a more open site in the square, and to make a shiny marble base that will reflect the light.

Continue, crossing the Zuid Willemsvaart Canal (43.5 kms/27.2 miles) and turn right onto the N266 signed Veghel. Turn left signed Heeswijk-Dinther, continue into the village and immediately after crossing the River Aa turn right onto Mgr van Ooorschotstraat following Airborne Monument sign. On the right is

Liberation Chapel, Heeswijk-Dinther (52 kms/32.7 miles). In 1959 US Airborne Veterans raised the money for this Chapel, designed by N. Hansen and M. van Helvert. Within it is a bas relief of the Virgin Mary and a small statuette of a paratrooper and over the entry is the 101st AB's Screaming Eagle. There are plaques to the 501st, 1969, on either side - to Heeswijk to the right and Dinther to the left, both with the date 21 September 1944. Beside the chapel is a 101st AB Memorial Bench.

Turn round and continue into the village centre towards the church. At the T-junction turn left to Berlicum on Hoofdstraat, signed to Kasteel Heeswijk. Continue past the exit Heeswijk sign to the sharp right bend and turn left to the Castle.

Landings Monuments, Kasteel Heeswijk (55 kms/34.6 miles).

This fairy tale castle has origins which date back to the 12th Century. By the 14th Century it was a walled castle and over the years passed from owner to owner. The last family to own it was the Van den Bogaerde van Terbrugge who acquired the castle in 1835 and built up an important armoury collection. Major restoration began in 1950 and the last Baron and Baroness lived in the coach house from 1974 until the Baroness died in 1994. The castle is now owned by a foundation and may be visited.

Across the bridge over the moat to the right is a memorial group erected by J. M.

Long Extra visit continued

Driessen (qv) in 1997. A path leads to an urn, erected on 17 September 1994, on the back of which is the story of Lieutenant-Colonel Francis Sampson, Chaplain to the 101st, who landed on top of another parachutist in the moat. They managed to scramble out, but Father Sampson had to dive in again to recover his Chaplain's equipment. Sampson, who had been captured by the Germans in Normandy but who escaped, went on to become the most senior U.S. Army chaplain, and a great personal friend of Frans Driessen. He died on 28 January 1996.

Beyond the urn is a brick memorial with a plaque which commemorates the landings around the Castle of the 1st Battalion, 501st PIR on 17 September 1944 under Lieutenant-Colonel W.O. Kinnard. They prepared the way for the advancing Allied armies and 'took a heavy yoke of occupation away from this part of the Netherlands'. The Americans were not supposed to land here but were off target. Kinnard left a small detachment here and set off via Heeswijk and Dinther to Veghel where he took the town. When he returned here there was no sign of the forty-eight men that he had left, only bloodstained bandages.

Return through Heeswijk-Dinther to the N266 and turn left signed Veghel.
The area to the right between the village of Dorshout and your next turning was DZ A where the 501st PIR landed (minus Lieutenant-Colonel Kinnard and his men!)
Continue over the railway and immediately turn left into Veghel.
Just before turning the Veghel bridge over the Zuid Willemsvaart Canal can be seen 600m ahead – it is crossed on the main itinerary and was one of the American targets for 17 September).
Continue to the roundabout and go straight over signed Centrum onto Hoogstraat. Turn right onto Colonel Johnsonstraat and stop at the memorial which is where you rejoin the main itinerary. (64 kms/40.3 miles).
The only thing that you have not done by taking the Extra Visit is to drive over the Veghel Bridge.

Turn left towards Veghel.
The area to the left of the road is DZ A where the 2nd and 3rd battalions of the 501st PIR landed.

• Veghel Bridge/58 kms/36.3 miles

This bridge, now modernized, was taken by 501st PIR within one hour of their landing despite one battalion being dropped at Kasteel Heeswijk (see above) almost 5 kms off target. Its commander, Lieutenant-Colonel Harry W. O. Kinnard Jr, ordered a small group to stay and guard the equipment and marched the rest of his men off at high speed to Veghel where they quickly overcame a detachment of Korps Feldt (qv).

Cross the bridge and take the exit signed Veghel. At the next crossroads turn left signed Centrum back under the N265 and continue following signs to Centrum, keeping to the right at the roundabout, into Hoogstraat. Continue to the right turn onto Colonel Johnsonstraat and stop just beyond it. Walk back round the corner to

• Veghel Airborne Memorial/Dutch East Indies Memorial/ 'Klondike'/59 kms/37miles/15 minutes/ Map 1S-89/90/91

The 101st AB Division memorial is in the form of a kangaroo with a baby in her pouch (symbol of the Allied forces leaping over the Dutch rivers) on a huge stone block, which weighs 1,200kgs. It was designed by Neil Steenbergen. Note the small bronze figure of a parachutist on the right of the block which records the fact that the monument was unveiled by HRH Princess Irene of the Netherlands on 17 September 1959. There is also a plaque on the ground commemorating Veghel's liberation on 17 September 1944 by 501st PIR with other units and the intense battle of 22-26 September. Under a stone is an urn containing soil from the fifty States of the U.S.A. Beside the memorial are two benches donated by Friends of the Airborne. Each 17 September, or the nearest Sunday, wreaths are laid and flags are flown at the memorial. Any visiting veterans are royally welcomed and entertained by local Associations for Remembrance.

The primary job given to 101st AB Division had included capturing the bridges and keeping open 25kms of The Corridor north of Eindhoven to just beyond Veghel. The bitter struggle to fulfil their task prompted the paratroopers to christen the road 'Hell's Highway'. General Browning's original plan called for a scattered drop along The Corridor, but General Taylor, remembering the near disaster of the Division's dispersed drop in Normandy, protested. After an appeal to General Dempsey the plan was changed to make drops in two principal areas, one just north of Son, the other immediately south of Veghel [Sketch Map 1]. The capture of Eindhoven was to be a secondary objective. On 17 September, between 1300 and 1330 hours, 6,769 men of 101st AB jumped into Holland, 425 planes out of 428 finding their DZs. One hour later, but less successfully, fifty-three of the seventy gliders that left England arrived. They brought thirty-two jeeps but no artillery,

since General Taylor felt mobility was more important than firepower. As you face the memorial from Colonel Johnsonstraat (named after Colonel Howard R. Johnson, commanding 501st PIR, who was killed during the fighting in 'The Island') the Americans came in both from your left and your rear. They achieved all their objectives within three hours and took fifty German prisoners. The bridges over the River Aa and the Zuid Willemsvaart Canal were reinforced with the help of local people to take the weight of the Allied tanks.

Beyond the monument is a grey stone **Memorial to Veghel Military Members who died in the Dutch East Indies 1943-1949**, erected in 1994. The house opposite bears a large green kangaroo on its front wall.

The large brick building on the corner of Hoogstraat and Colonel Johnsonstraat was

Veghel 101st AB memorial on 17 September with detail of parachutist used as an American HQ when the owner, Doctor Kerssemakers, placed his house at Colonel Johnson's disposal. The word **'Klondike'**, codename for the command post, is incorporated in the ornate wrought iron gates, there is a plaque near the front door and on top of the ornamental façade there is a 'Screaming Eagle'.

N.B. By continuing up the road the Market Square, with many cafés and restaurants, is reached. To the left is Veghel Roman Catholic Churchyard. To the right of the church is the entrance to the churchyard in the far right-hand corner of which is buried Private Allen Middleton, 1/6th Queen's Royal Regt, age 20, 30 September 1944. There is also 1 Unknown British soldier and 1 Unknown Polish Airman. On his grave is a plaque with the name T. Kozontksi, 2 October 1944. The small plot is beautifully tended (Map 1S/92).

Between just below Veghel and Grave, the northern tip of 101st AB area, was a 20kms gap. The only way it could be controlled was by establishing road blocks at top and bottom. This was done, yet hardly 12kms to the west of the 101st DZs around Veghel, in Vught [Sketch Map 1], was the HQ of General Kurt Student (qv), Commander of the German 1st Para Army. Not only did he watch the airborne drops, but by 1500 hours that day he had a copy of the MARKET-GARDEN Operation Order, taken from a crashed American glider. Strangely, although he had commanded the German airborne assault on 'Fortress Holland' in May 1940, the first successful airborne operation in history, General Student did not sense any immediate danger. Once over his surprise, however, he reacted quickly. By an odd twist of fate, the arrival of the airborne forces had been seen by both of the German Generals most fitted to oppose them – Student at Vught and Model at Oosterbeek.

Return to the N265 and turn left towards Uden.

In the German raid on Eindhoven on 19 September eighteen RASC lorries in one convoy loaded with ammunition and small arms were destroyed, the wreckage blocking The Corridor road north. Household Cavalrymen and civilians cleared the road and set the convoy moving again but it was not out of trouble. On entering Uden the lead vehicles took the wrong turning – that to the left to Nistelrode (the N50) which led directly to German lines at Heesch. Realizing the mistake, Major Ward of the Household Cavalry decided that the column must be turned around and the following account is given in *The Household Cavalry at War* by Roden Orde,

> Not only was the cobbled road barely wide enough to take two lines of traffic but from both verges there was a six-foot drop into a ditch ... drivers said that there was not enough room in which to turn without going over the bank. One mistake and we should be confronted with the unpleasant prospect of half the column facing one way and half the other, neither being able to move... . The next few hours were to be an ordeal of bent wings and dented radiators... . [The] Grave bridge...was reached at dawn [20 September].

Continue on the N265 to the junction with the N264.

N.B. By taking the N264 and continuing into the Volkel Military Airbase on Zeelandse Dijk, the Historical Typhoon Room, opened in September 1992, may be visited. Report to the Info Centre in front of the main gate (Map 1S/93).
Please note that the room is only open to the public every first and third Friday of the month between 1400 and 1600 hours and the visit should be booked at least 24 hurs ahead with Vliegbasis Volkel, Zeelandsedijk 10A, Postbus 10150, 5408 ZW Volkel, Netherlands. Tel: + (0) 413 276601. Fax: + (0) 413 276600.

The permanent exhibition is well worth a visit. It contains authentic documents, uniforms, aerial photos, military equipment, various aircraft parts and video footage. It covers the construction of the German Nachtlandeplatz (night-landing airstrip) Volkel and its development into a fully-fledged Luftwaffe airbase. Then on 19 September 1944 a reconnaissance party of two armoured cars of 16th Airfield Construction Group with Guards Armoured reported that the airstrip was much cratered from Allied bombing. Two hundred local civilians (which later increased to 1,000), were then organised to start clearing the debris from it. The speedy progress was halted when two battalions of SS troops with tanks were spotted in the vicinity. They were later attacked by Typhoons from Eindhoven. The fighting was fierce and fluid between Uden and Veghel, with the Allies (including elements of the 101st AB) struggling to keep The Corridor open from frequent attacks by German tanks. Eventually a grass strip was operational on 26 September, and a brick strip on the 28th large enough to accommodate three wings, including Typhoons, Tempests, Spitfires and Mosquitos.]

Continue past the windmill and the rugby ground, direction Nijmegen, to the traffic lights (signed to the N265 to the left) and then turn right to Uden following Centrum and green CWGC signs to the church. Stop by the cemetery on the right.

• Uden CWGC Cemetery/70 kms/43.7 miles/15 minutes/Map 1S/94

Until its liberation in September 1944 Uden was occupied by the Germans and in the early years of the war British and Allied servicemen were buried in the garden of the parish priest, which adjoined the RC Cemetery. Another burial ground was needed in 1943 and the municipality acquired for this purpose the old RC Churchyard, unused since about 1918. The present cemetery is partly enclosed by the high brick wall originally built around the old church (which was burnt down in the 1870s and a new one was built elsewhere in the town) and churchyard. After the war more than 100 graves from the garden of the parish priest, and also a number of isolated graves from various parts of the commune, were moved into this cemetery.

The cemetery now contains a total of 699 Known and 4 Unknown burials, comprising 7 RN, 428 UK Army plus 2 Unknown, 183 RAF, 3 Canadian Army and 50 RCAF, 19 RAAF, 7 RNZAF and 2 Polish. They include the crew of a Halifax of 87 Squadron killed near Bredeweg (qv) when their plane was brought down on 12/13 March 1943: **Flight Sergeant Fred Marean**, RCAF, Pilot, age 23, **Sergeant Harry Bentley**, RAF, age 29, **Sergeant Charley Dyer**, RAF, Flight Engineer, age 32, **Sergeant William McLelland**, RAF, Air Gunner, age 22, **Sergeant Walter Gosnell**, RAFVR, Bomb Aimer, age 19, **Sergeant Bernard Singleton**, RAFVR, and **Sergeant George Benson**, RAFVR. They are buried in Plot 4, Row C, Graves 1-7. Also **Flying Officer John Paape**, RNZAF, age 28, 15 October 1942, [4.B.9.] whose **brother**, Squadron Leader Arthur Paape, RAF, DFC + Bar is buried in Reichswald Forest CWGC Cemetery (qv) and **Troopers John Thorogood** and **Stanley Matthews** of C Squadron 44th Royal Tank Regiment, killed on 21 September 1944 at St Oedenrode and to whom a memorial has been raised (qv). They are buried side by side [1.D.5. and 1.D.4.]. The inscription on the headstone of **Captain Prince Dimitri Galitzine**, 2nd Battalion the Monmouth Regiment, age 26, 26 October 1944, is in Russian [3.D.1.].

The cemetery has voluntarily been looked after with wonderful devotion for more than half a century by the couple who live in the house opposite – Mr & Mrs Ties Verstegen. They greet visiting relatives, invite them into their house for refreshment, correspond with them, place flowers on graves for them and all the time keep a growing dossier on the men buried in the cemetery, which is now in a series of folders with photographs and biographies of many of them. Eventually they were supported by a committee which developed into a Foundation. The Foundation has published an excellently researched, detailed book by A. Verbakel, entitled *Lest They be Forgot* on the history of the Uden War Cemeteries and the men buried in them. Most extraordinary are the accounts of how the Germans, according to the Geneva Convention regulations, undertook the burial of Allied Airmen. Alerted to a crash, they would arrive at the site, search for any survivors, look for any signs of identification and note them, put any bodies into coffins, take them into the old mortuary in Uden and then march in a funeral procession with the coffin to the cemetery. A German Chaplain made an oration over the grave, flowers were placed on it and a salute was fired over it. Local people were co-opted to dig the grave, supply the flowers, the deal coffins and the simple wooden crosses. The municipality bore all the costs. The remains of the wrecked plane or glider were taken to the workshops in the Concentration Camps at Vught (qv) or Amersfoort to be recycled.

Return to the N265, turn right and continue to the roundabout at the junction with the N324.

• *Extra Visit to the Monument to Airstrip B-82 (Map 1N/1) Round trip: 11.2 kms/7 miles. Approximate time: 20 minutes*
Go straight over, signed Nijmegen/Ravenstein. After 2.6 miles turn right signed Overlangel and Neerloon, then right signed Reek, Grave and turn sharp left at the top of the dyke signed (on the back of the sign you can see ahead) to Neerloon. Continue to a farm on the left called the Oude Maas Hoeve and turn right on the small road signed to Keent. Stop at the memorial some 110m on to the right (5.6 kms/3.5 miles).
The Germans constructed an emergency airstrip in the old forelands of the Maas at Keent, which they never used. In September 1944 it was discovered by paratroopers of the 82nd AB, but for one reason or another it did not come into use until 26 September. On that day 209 C-47 Dakotas of 52nd Wing, 9th Troop Carrier Command, landed at Keent with troops and supplies for the Americans and the 2nd British Army. Although marshy and soggy, the airfield continued to be used by fighter squadrons of 2nd Tactical Airforce. The distinctive memorial, showing aeroplanes flying off a spiral spring as if they were circling around the airstrip, was designed by Albert Sanders. To the right of the metal memorial on the ground is an explanatory plaque with a diagram of the layout of the airstrip on this 'Hot spot'. This simple, but inspired, memorial, captures the spirit of the planes that landed on this forlorn, precarious, sodden airstrip.
Return to the roundabout with the N324 and pick up the main itinerary.

Turn right, passing a white windmill on the right, and continue to the third turning to Grave.
Turn right at the traffic lights, passing an old cannon on the left.
Grave is a delightfully picturesque and historical town, whose new developments have been sympathetically designed to blend in with the old.
Turn left on Hoofschestraat and on the left opposite house No. 43 is the courtyard of a new housing complex. On the red brick wall of the old Infirmary is

Cross of Sacrifice, Uden CWGC Cemetery, decorated with floral tributes from local cremation

Spiralling Wings Memorial to Airstrip B-82, Keent

Typical windmill on the N265/N324 roundabout

• *Memorial to the Border Battalions, Grave/87 kms/54.5 miles/5 minutes/ Map 8/1*

A *bas relief* by Jan Kettering shows a soldier of the battalion guarding the town of Grave. It was erected on 31 October 1964 and its caption is 'We went and came back after years'. Grave had been a garrison town for several centuries until the troops left in 1892. In 1938 the Army returned as the Low Countries began to fortify their defences against German military aggression in her desire for *Lebensraum*. In Holland pillboxes were constructed close to the bridges over the major waterways, which were at first occupied by the Military Police. Border Battalions were then formed and mobilized in 1938. Those guarding the Meuse-Waal Canal came under the commanding officer stationed in Grave.

Continue, bearing right on Ruijterstraat to the large brick gateway, the Maasport, at the river bank. Park and walk to the wall to the right of the gateway.

• *504th PIR Memorial, Maasport, Grave/87.5 kms/54.7miles/10 minutes/Map 8/2*

This imaginative memorial, in the form of a parachute canopy draped over the wall of the bastion, was designed by Marcel Joosten and erected on 4 May 1987. It commemorates the airborne landings along the MARKET-GARDEN corridor at 1300 hours GMT on 17 September 1944, in particular the 504th PIR, 82nd AB Division, which landed on both sides of the Grave Bridge. The caption translates, 'From Massachusetts to California young Americans, some of them still kids, came here to give us freedom. All American – we shall never forget them.' The bridge was taken by E Company of the 504th under Lieutenant John S. Thompson (qv) and when they came under fire from Grave town he sent part of his force down to the crossroads south of the bridge to form a road block. D Company of the regiment

Grave Memorials: Dutch Border Battalion. Maasport Parachute and 'Cider-White' Plaque

then came over the bridge and, despite heavy machine-gun and mortar fire, cleared the town.

Turn round and drive back down Hoofschestraat. Turn 1st left and park near the church.

The VVV adjoins the church. Opposite is the old town hall. On 17 September the 400-strong German garrison beat a hasty retreat and, once the remnants had been overcome by D Company, the villagers had a celebration sing-song in the town hall, including the Dutch version of 'Tipperary'. On its wall are:

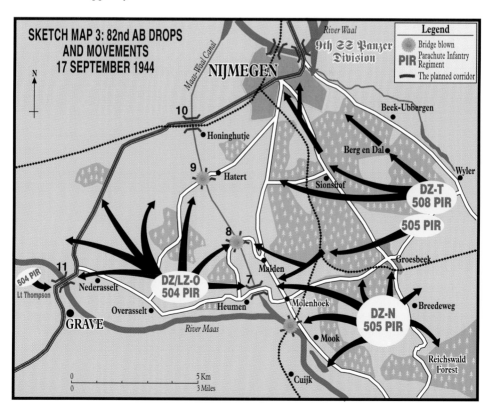

SKETCH MAP 3: 82nd AB DROPS AND MOVEMENTS 17 SEPTEMBER 1944

River Waal
9th SS Panzer Division

N

NIJMEGEN

Maas-Waal Canal

Legend
Bridge blown
PIR Parachute Infantry Regiment
The planned corridor

10

Beek-Ubbergen

Honinghutje

Berg en Dal

9 Hatert

Wyler

Sionshof

DZ-T 508 PIR

505 PIR

8

Groesbeek

Malden

11

Nederasselt

504 PIR
Lt Thompson

DZ/LZ-O 504 PIR

7

Molenhoek

Breedeweg

GRAVE

Overasselt

Heumen

DZ-N 505 PIR

River Maas

Mook

Reichswald Forest

Cuijk

0   5 Km
0   3 Miles

• *Grave Town Hall Memorials/88 kms/54.9 miles/10 minutes/Map 8/3*

1. A plain stone tablet commemorates the more than thirty inhabitants of Grave, Velp and Escharen – soldiers, civilians, including Jews – who died during the five years of war from battle, bombing (at Nuland on 11 May 1940 and in Nijmegen on 22 February 1944) and in concentration camps (e.g. Dachau and Menado). The tablet was erected by F. A. Smits & Zonnen on 4 May 1987.

2. The 'Cider White' (2nd Battalion 504th PIR). The *bas relief* of stylised parachutes and the recumbent figure of a paratrooper, designed by A. Sanders and erected on 4 May 1987, commemorates the fact that, after the Meuse bridge had been captured intact during the afternoon of 17 September 1944, Grave was reached by nightfall. It was taken about midnight. The town hall then became the command post of the battalion, whose radio code was 'cider' and who, as the second battalion of the regiment, had the codename 'white', the first being 'red' and the third being 'blue'.

3. Plaque to Louis Ficq, burgomaster of Grave, who died in Dachau on 9 March 1945. Designed by F.Vervoordeldonk, it was erected in 1946 and recounts how the burgomaster was arrested by the Germans on 3 February 1944 for his public testimony to Queen and Country.

Walk along the street to the junction with the main street and take the small road straight ahead. Turn right at the end. On the wall of the corner building is

• *Plaque on Site of old Grave Synagogue/10 minutes/Map 8/4*

From July 1940 freedom of action of local Jews was restricted and Jewish civil servants and teachers were dismissed. On 5 March 1941 all burgomasters had to give the names of Jewish inhabitants, the first step to their persecution. The plaque, erected on 16 May 1981 by the Amsterdamsche Binnenvaartsocieteit, is on the site of the synagogue, built in 1871 and destroyed during the war. Beside it is an original stone, from which the text was chipped off.

N.B. Grave Roman Catholic Cemetery lies 1km to the south-east of the village, on the south of the road to Gennep. In it are buried 3 British airmen: Sergeant Albert Collyer, RAF, age 25, 12 April 1945; Pilot Officer Patrick Culligan, RAFA, age 21, 26 March 1945 and Flight Lieutenant Oliver Lee, age 34, 2 October 1944.

Return to the N324, turn right and continue towards the Grave Bridge.
There is a well-concealed **bunker** in the bank to the left just before the turning ahead. (Map 6/2).
Turn left down the slip road immediately before the bridge and park.

• *504th PIR Memorial/Bunker/Grave Bridge/89.5 kms /55.8 miles/10 minutes /Map 6-3/4*

This 9-span, 600m long bridge was the most southerly objective of 82nd AB Division and the task of taking it was given to Colonel Reuben H. Tucker's 504th PIR (who were later to make the magnificent assault crossing at Nijmegen). Colonel Tucker decided to drop men at both ends of the bridge as, he said, 'It tended to confuse the enemy' [Sketch Map 3]. At 1305 hours E Company of 2nd Battalion landed in the fields 600m away at 10 o'clock [take the direction towards the van Sasse pumping station down the small road you are parked on as 12 o'clock]; Lieutenant John S. Thompson and sixteen men headed for the blockhouse – they called it a 'flak tower' - at 9 o'clock, barely 100m from you [which you passed before turning off here] wading in water at times up to their necks. It, and the pillbox visible at 1 o'clock in the field below the memorial, had been built by the Dutch in 1936 as part of a defensive line covering major river crossings, but, although the Dutch blew the bridge in 1940, the pillbox and blockhouse were left. The Germans repaired the bridge to its original design and mounted 20mm anti-aircraft guns on the blockhouse. Lieutenant Thompson's men were delighted to find that, as they neared it, the Germans were unable to depress the 20mm weapons sufficiently to fire at them and two quick shots from a bazooka silenced the gun. In the blockhouse they found two Germans dead and one wounded. They cut wires which might be connected to charges (there were 950 kilos of explosives under the bridge) and, using the gun, silenced the pillbox at 1 o'clock. Shortly after, a patrol of the main 504th PIR from the northern side, crossed over to make contact with Thompson's force. The bridge was theirs. Colonel Tucker's regiment claimed that, as they dropped onto the main DZ at 1231 hours on 17 September, they were the first Allied airborne troops to land in Holland. General Gavin was duly informed that 'Bridge 11' had been taken. Before leaving England Gavin had allocated numbers to all of the bridges that he was due to capture and this allowed the Americans to talk about them on the wireless without the Germans realising which bridges they were.

Lieutenant Kavanagh's troop of armoured cars of 2nd HCR reached here at 0820 hours on 19 September, having crossed the Son Bridge at 0615 hours that morning. Recce-ing ahead, they discovered that the main road bridge over the Maas-Waal at Honinghutje on the outskirts of Nijmegen (Bridge 10 - Sketch Map 3) was unusable and therefore the Grenadier Guards (who had taken over the lead position from the Irish), following some miles behind, were diverted through Nederasselt and Overasselt and over the bridge at Heumen (Gavin's number 7); this route became the main axis for XXX Corps. When the Irish arrived later there was a great search for old friends amongst the Americans because the 504th had been under command of the Regiment in Italy. The task of defending the Grave Bridge was later taken over by the Princess Irene Brigade.

The memorial here was designed by Robert Melsen and erected on 18 September 1994. The caption reads,

> On 17 September 1944, during the Second World War, the Maas Bridge at Grave was captured by 'E' Company of the 2nd Battalion, 504th PIR, 82nd US Airborne Division. On 19 September 1944 the first tanks of the XXXth British Army Corps rolled across this bridge. On 21st September 1944 the defence of the southern approach to the Maas Bridge was taken over by the Royal Brigade 'Princess Irene'. This liberation sign has been placed in honour of those who fought for our freedom and gave their lives for our sake. They will live on in our memory forever. 17 September 1944 – 17 September 1994.

On 17 September, or the nearest Sunday, members of local remembrance societies raise flags at the memorial and lay wreaths (normally at 1200 hours) to honour their liberators. The pillbox at 1 o'clock has been carefully restored by the Militaire Traditiekamer, Grave, (a local Military Historical Society) and contains some interesting exhibits – photos, uniforms, weapons and other artefacts. It is only opened on special occasions, but to visit it on other days contact the Secretariat on Tel: + (0) 486 476351.

504th PIR Memorial, Grave, Bridge

Cross the bridge.

The insides of the girders have been painted in graduating colours. Starting at the Grave side (still in North Brabant) the bridge is painted in the white and red colours of the Brabant flag. The spans then gradually merge into the green that symbolises the verdant country of Gelderland – on the far side of the bridge.

Turn right at the traffic lights (you are now following the diversionary route that XXX Corps took) and drive through Nederasselt along Broek Straat and continue towards Overasselt. As the road changes from Broek Straat to Schoonenburg, stop at the memorial complex on the left.

• *Monument to US 325th Glider, 504th PIR and Polish Battalion DZ/LZ, Overasselt/92 kms/57.6 miles/10 minutes/Map 6/5*

The dramatic rusting parachutes, designed by Leo Gerritsen and Henk van Hout, were erected on 17 September 1985. They commemorate the fact that these fields on the left, designated 'O', were used as the DZs and LZs of the US 325th Glider Infantry (23.9.44) and 504th PIR (17.9.44) and later by one battalion of General

325th Glider, 504th PIR and Polish 'Para' Memorial, Overasselt

Sosabowski's 1st Polish Independent Para Brigade (23.9.44) which had been unable to land at Driel two days earlier because of bad weather. Originally the parachutes were to be coloured: red – for the ammunition the paras carried, white – for bandages, blue - for equipment and yellow - for food. On 17 September [Sketch Map 3] the two battalions of Reuben Tucker's 504th that landed here moved east, north and west to their objectives – Bridge 11 at Grave, Bridge 7 at Heumen (the Americans called it the Molenhoek Bridge), Bridge 8 at Malden and Bridge 9 at Hatert. They took 11 and 7, the others were blown up by the Germans.

In 1996 the entrance park with flagpoles and an orientation table were added.

Continue through Overasselt.

During the drive to Heumen the banks of the Maas are to the right. The flat ground to the right of the road from Nederasselt to Heumen is where two battalions of Colonel Tucker's 504th PIR landed. They moved east and north to take bridges over the Maas-Waal Canal and also west to the Grave Bridge [Sketch Map 3].

• *Extra Visit to Jac Maris House (Map 6/13). Round trip: 3.2 kms/2 miles. Approximate time: 5 minutes*

Take the first left up Looisstraat, continue under the motorway to the distinctive white house on the left.

Jac Maris, 'Artist and Resistance Fighter'

Born in Magdeburg in 1900, Jac Maris emigrated with his family to South Africa, returned to Kleve where he was apprenticed to a sculptor and took basic military training with a sports club. Then with memories of soldiers marching off to the First World War he moved with his family to Nijmegen. In 1927 he settled in Heumen, having travelled across Europe, including England, and remained there until his death in 1996.

In the Thirties he served in the air-raid protection service and defied evacuation on the out-break of war to stay in Heumen where he led the resistance group 'Wendel' which stole weapons and identification documents to help those in hiding. He maintained his sculpting work and when his house was raided by the Germans he hid in the base of the statue that he was creating to commemorate the Dutch soldiers killed in May 1940. Just before Liberation he refused to send his men to blow up bridges as he felt the tasks were too dangerous for them, a decision for which he has been criticised.

On Liberation he worked with the Americans and once the Germans had gone he worked for the Ministry of Defence and began his sculpting work again, being commissioned to make many of the memorials in the Nijmegen area visited on the itineraries in this guidebook.

The house, which Maris designed and built, is being established as a museum.

Return to the main Itinerary.

Follow signs under the A73/E31 to Heumen.
Continue into the village on Dorpstraat to the two churches opposite each other. Stop on the right.

• Jac Maris Plaque/97.8 kms/61.1 miles/5 minutes/Map 6/14

On the wall to the left of the entrance of the old Ned Church is a fine *bas relief* sculpture by Jac Maris. Commissioned by the 1st Battalion, the Dutch 26th Infantry Regiment, it was erected on 1 August 1939 when they were billeted in Heumen as a unit of the Border Defence. It commemorates the Battle of Mooker Heath of 1574 and shows the two commanders killed in the battle, Lodewijk and Hendrik of Nassau.

Continue over the crossroads along Boomgard and straight on along Kapt.
Postmalaan towards the banks of the Maas-Waal Canal and park by memorial on the left.

• Memorial to Dutch Soldiers and Site of Old Heuman Lockbridge/ 98.7 kms/ 61.7 miles/10 minutes/Map 6-15/16

As one approaches the lock the memorial to Dutch soldiers is to the left. Designed by Jac Maris and erected in 1947, it commemorates an action of 10 May 1940 when the lockbridge was lowered by sentries of the badly-equipped Dutch border defence for German assault commandos disguised as Dutch Military Policemen and civilians. When they were recognized, a battle ensued for the bridge that continued well into the afternoon of 10 May, during which twenty-four Dutch soldiers were killed. The German objective, however, to capture the bridge quickly and intact, failed. The memorial lists the names of the soldiers of I-26 R.I. who 'died for their fatherland on 10 May 1940'. Its traditional form of a *Pieta* recognizes the sacrifices of mothers in the war.

The picturesque old lockbridge was demolished in 1991. In September 1944 it had turned out to be vital. The Guards were unable to use the main road from Grave to Nijmegen and their alternative route came through Heumen. The German defenders were well entrenched on the small island to the right of the bridge, but, under cover of darkness, a company of 504th PIR commanded by Captain Thomas B. Helgeson over-ran them and took the bridge intact around 1900 hours on 17 September. Shortly afterwards, patrols of 505th PIR arrived from Groesbeek.

Return through Heumen and turn right signed to Malden under the A73/E31 on Luden Laan.
Turn right again on the N271, direction Nijmegen. Continue over the Maas Canal and at the traffic lights turn left signed Malden on the N844.

Malden (103.5 kms/64.8 miles). Even two years after the end of the war 13% of Dutch households and 1.5% of the entire population still lived in temporary accommodation. In 1947 the municipality of Heumen (which includes Malden) incorporated commemorative plaques on houses that were being reconstructed as a symbol of the Netherlands rising once more from the ashes of war.

After the Grenadier Guards reached Nijmegen on 19 September and entered into the contest to take the road bridge, the Irish Group rested here. On the morning of 20 September, in preparation to support the American assault crossing of the river, the Irish moved closer to Nijmegen with one squadron of tanks positioned just to the east of the power station (qv) and another near the factory, having reached their positions with little opposition.

N.B. In Malden churchyard is a Headstone by Jac Maris for W. Thuis. Thuis was a member of Maris's resistance group. He died from injuries received when he was escorting a transportation of German POWs to Belgium. He was buried in the cemetery at Bourg Leopold but on 17 April 1946 his remains were returned to his native town and reburied here with his parents.

Continue through Malden following signs to Nijmegen, to the traffic lights just past a green CWGC sign and turn left signed to Arnhem on Weg door Jonkerbos. Continue to the cemetery, with a carillon tower without any bells at the entrance, on the right. (There is a larger municipal plot on the left.)

• Dutch Wargraves Cemetery, Jonkerbos and Jan van Hoof Grave/109 kms/68.2 miles/10 minutes/Map 6-11/10

In the back right-hand corner is a cemetery of honour, laid out in 1971, beside which flies the Dutch flag, with a plaque to 'The Fallen 1940-1945'. There are forty-eight headstones for victims of the War. The last stone on the right of the back row is that of Resistance Worker **Jan van Hoof** (qv). Beside him lies **C. van Sambeek**, the Company Commander of the Dutch Shock Troops.

Continue 1.1 kms/.7 mile along Weg door Jonkerbos, past the hospital to the right, to the first right turn with a green CWGC sign, signed to de Goffert. Turn here on Oude Mollenhutseweg and continue to the CWGC Cemetery parking area on the right.

• Jonkerbos CWGC Cemetery and Marienbosch Memorial/110.5 kms/69 miles/20 minutes/Map 6-7/8

The cemetery is in a wooded area known as Jonkers Bosch from which it took its name and was created by No. 3 CCS. It contains 1,639 burials, including eighteen soldiers buried in adjoining graves who could not be identified individually. They lie under Special Memorials with the legend 'Buried near this spot'. Two other soldiers under Special Memorials are known to be buried in the cemetery but their graves were subsequently lost. There are 5 RN with 1 Unknown; 970 UK Army with 72 Unknown; 3 Canadian; 5 Belgian; 1 Dutch (and there is a Netherlands War Graves plaque at the cemetery entrance); 2 Polish; 410 RAF with 14 Unknown; 1 RCAF; 34 RAAF; 21 RNAF; 4 Polish Air Force, 1 Soviet Union; 2 entirely unidentified and 9 'Miscellaneous' Unknown from the UK.

A lawn edged with silver birch leads to the elegant colonnaded shelter where the Register and Visitor's Book are housed. Through its arches the Cross of Sacrifice can be seen at the end of the central avenue. Beyond the shelter, to the left, is a stone column which commemorates the men who were removed to this cemetery from one near the Marienbosch Convent in Sophiaweg. It bears a quotation from Rupert Brooke's *The Soldier*, 'There is a corner in [sic] a foreign field That is for ever England' and the inscription, 'To those men of the British and Allied Forces who gave their lives and are buried here. Marienbosch Sept-Oct 1944. Jonkerbosch.' The Marienbosch burial ground was a typical hospital graveyard, with the graves made by medical staff as the men died of their wounds. The graveyard was enclosed by a white wooden fence, the graves marked by white wooden crosses, but with a darker cross for a lone Dutch civilian, Albert van Dam. The left-hand side of the cemetery was for Operation GARDEN period burials for September/October 1944, the right side for

Site of old lockbridge, Heumen

Operation VERITABLE from 8 February 1945. Photos exist of this major cemetery, showing pilgrims visiting the graves (see *Vanished Temp Cemeteries* (qv) by Father Thuring and J. Hey, which also lists the 250 men originally buried there but who are now in Jonkerbos).

The Special Memorials are to the right. The plots are arranged in a pleasing fan shape facing the central Stone of Remembrance, standing as if on parade. Landscaped beds of shrubs, horse chestnut and shaped yew trees add to the beauty of this lovely cemetery

The **MC** was awarded to **Lieutenant Lindsay Baker**, 2/5th Gloucesters, age 21, 3 April 1945 [6.G.8.]; **Major Kenneth Lowe**, 7th Black Watch, age 26, 23 September 1945 [14.C.1.]; **Lieutenant Adrian Slob**, 1st Grenadier Guards, 23 February 1945, from Friesland [18.A.4.] and **Major Sydney Young**, 7th SLI, age 30, 23 September 1944 [I1.F.2.].

The **MM** was awarded to **Lance Serjeant William Pearson**, RE, age 26, 26 November 1944 [Sp Mem 'A'. No 2.] and **Lieutenant Owen Shanks**, 7th Black Watch, age 35, 8 February 1945 [14.G.3.].

The **DFC** was awarded to **WO (Pilot) Mark Azouz**, RAF, age 22, 21 September 1944 [17.G.2.]; **Captain Cecil Ballyn**, RA, attd RAF, age 38, 18 March 1945, who also had a Bar to his DFC [13.E.4.] as did **Flight Lieutenant Leslie Barr**, RAF, age 28, 11 September 1942 [12.D.8]; **Flight Lieutenant Walter Bell**, RAF, age 25, 21 July 1944 [24.I.6.]; **Flying Officer Neville Briant**, RAF, age 24, 5 October 1942 [8.F.4.]; **Squadron Leader Gilbert Campbell**, RAF, 19 November 1944 [20.A.7.]; **Flying Officer (Naval) Douglas Farquhar**, RAAF, age 23, 19 November 1944, whose parents lived in New York State, USA [20.A.8-9.]; **Squadron Leader William Fletcher**, RAF, age 29, 14 February 1943, also had the **DFM** [12.E.2-5]; **Flight Lieutenant (Naval) Norman Fredman**, RAF, age 23, 6 May 1944 [24.E.9.]; **Squadron Leader William Greenslade**, AFC, RAF, 2 October 1942 [20.D.3.]; **Flying Officer Norman Marston**, RAF, age 24, 25 May 1944 [24.J.2-4.]; **Flight Lieutenant Norman Pye**, RAF, 8 April 1945 [17.C.1.]; **Flight**

Tower at entrance to Dutch War Graves Cemetery, Jonkerbos and Jan van Hoof Headstone

Jonkerbos CWGC Cemetery: General view, Memorial to Marienbosch Temp. Cemetery, Personal Tribute.

Lieutenant Thomas Rawlinson, RAF, 25 May 1944 [24.J.6.]; **Squadron Leader Harry Stephens**, RAF, age 32, 6 May 1944 [24.E.8.] had a **brother**, Wing Commander John Stephens, age 25, who also won the DFC. He died on 30 August 1943 and is buried in Friern Barnet Churchyard, Middx; **Squadron Leader Philip Turgel**, RAF, age 22, 26 May 1943 [24.C.8-9.]; **Flight Lieutenant Eric Willcox**, 1 September 1941 [12.G.9.].

The **DFM** was awarded to **Flight Sergeant Frederick Barker**, RAF, age 23, 31 May 1942 [12.H.8.]; **Sergeant Douglas Bebensee**, RCAF, 14 July 1943 [16.E.5.]; **WO (Pilot) Kenneth Breckon**, RAF, age 21, 23 August 1943 [16.B.1-3.]; **Flight Sergeant Francis Hay**, RAF, 30 May 1943 [24.B.8.]; **Sergeant Harry Kay**, RAF, age 28, 14 February 1943 [Coll grave 12.E.2-5.]; **Sergeant Kenneth McKay**, RAF, age 22, 5 October 1942 [8.F.7.]; **Pilot Officer George Miller**, RAF, 14 February 1943 [Coll grave 12.E.2-5.]; **Sergeant Donald Sills**, RAF, age 22, 1 July 1941 [12.G.3-4.]

The **DCM** was awarded to Trooper Frank Craddock, 1st Fife & Forfar Yeomanry, age 27, 8 February 1945 [3.E.4.].

MiD were **Corporal George Binks**, 4th Wilts, age 33, 10 October 1944 [9.G.1.]; **Corporal George Birch**, 1st Leics, age 25, 6 March 1945 [21.B.8.]; **Major William Broome**, 1st Worcesters, age 30, 30 September 1944 [21.E.1.]; **Sub-Lieutenant John Burke**, RNVR, age 22, 15 May 1945 [24.J.9.]; **Lieutenant Norman Clark**, RE, age 25, 6 April 1945 [14.F.5.]; **Flying Officer Robert Davidson**, RAF, age 28, 6 April 1945 [17.C.2.]; **Serjeant Michael Dunne**, 3rd Irish Guards, age 33, 15 February 1945 was **three times mentioned** [22.F.7.]; **Flight Lieutenant**

William Ewart, RAAF, age 25, 2 June 1945 [20.E.3.]; **Flying Officer Ronald Gibbs**, RAF, age 22, 3 February 1945 [8.E.2.]; **Sergeant Ernest Grunsell**, RAF, aged 20, 27 March 1941 [16.C.9.]; **Sub-Lieutenant Peter Hoad**, RN of HMS *Daedalus*, age 22, 27 March 1941 [20.F.9.]; **Major Anthony Hunter**, 6th Royal Scots, **MC, Medal for Distinguished Service in Battle** (USSR), age 32, 20 February 1945 [9.C.2.]; **Sapper Percy Plackett**, RE, age 34, 15 November 1944 [6..G.4.]; **Bombardier George Walsh**, RA, age 42, 26 September 1944 [15.A.5.].

Lieutenant Roger Denys Green, 12th Queen's Westminsters, age 21, 2 April 1945, was awarded the *Croix de Guerre* **with Silver Star** [14.E.2.] **Major Arthur Elveden, Viscount,** 55th Anti-Tank Regt, age 32, 8 February 1945, was the son of Captain Rupert Guinness, CB, CMG, DL, RNVR, 2nd Earl of Iveagh and the Countess of Iveagh, CBE [21.B.7.]. **The brothers** of the following also died on service: **Private Leslie Frost**, 1/4th KOYLI, age 25, 29 December 1944 [15.G.4.], Private Thomas Frost RASC, age 32, 17 February 1942, buried in Wetherby Cemetery; **Pilot Officer George Gascoyne**, DFM, RAF, age 27, 2 June 1942 [20.E.4.], Flight Sergeant John Gascoyne, RAFVR, age 23, 21 February 1945, buried in Reichswald Forest CWGC Cemetery (qv); **Lieutenant Douglas Hutton**, 2nd Argyll & Sutherland Highlanders, age 20, 9 February 1945 [6.E.4.], Private Ronald Hutton, 14th Army Field Wksp, age 19, 23 May 1940, buried in Audruicq Churchyard & Extension, Pas de Calais;. **Private Glyn Samuel**, 1st Dorsets, age 19, 3 October 1944 [4.D.2.], Craftsman Towyn Samuel of 6 Tank Bde Wksp, REME, killed on 24 June 1944 by a flying bomb and buried in Lenham Churchyard, Kent. **The sister of Flying Officer John Wallace,** (Nav) RAF, age 21, 13 May 1943 [24.D.4.], Agnes H. Wallace, Nurse, age 25, died on the SS *City of Benares* (Merchant Navy) on 17 September 1940. She is commemorated on the Tower Hill Merchant Navy Memorial, London.

Guardsman Albert Shaw, 2nd Bn, Grenadier Guards, age 23 [22.A.2.] and **Lance Serjeant William Berry**, age 30 [I.D.2.] were killed in their Humber Scout Car with the Dutch Resistance worker Jan van Hoof (qv) on 19 September. Their headstones record the date of death as 21 September.

A group of 18 members of S Coy, 156 Battalion, 4 Para Brigade were killed on 18 September 1944 when their C-47 Dakota 43-15180 was shot down near Ochten en route to Arnhem. They were half of a machine-gun platoon. The other half were in another plane. **Privates George Brownlow, Arthur Butler, Harold Clayton, John Clayton, Richard Fuller, George Daniel, George Gilliver, Harry Hopwood, Eric Jones, Richard Killingworth, Henry Philpotts, Harold Stanyer, Thomas Stevens, Patrick Taylor, George Tutton** and **Joseph Wilson, Corporal Owen Lilly** and **Sergeant John Kinsleysmith** are buried in Special Memorials 8.A.1-9 and 8.B.1-9. They were originally buried near their aircraft where today there is a memorial (qv).

Captain the Hon Vicary Gibbs (qv), 1st Grenadier Guards, age 23, 20 September 1944, was the son of the 4th Baron Aldenham [22.G.4.]. He was originally buried in the Nebo Seminary grounds (qv), as was **Guardsman Andrew Wardrope**, age 24, 11 February 1945 [22.B.4].

Return to Weg door Jonkerbos and turn right, signed Centrum and Arnhem. Pass the Philips complex on the left, go under the railway bridge and turn right on the N326 towards the centre of Nijmegen on Graafsweg.

On the right is the old Dutch civilian cemetery (112 kms/70 miles) where German casualties of the Nijmegen battle were buried. After the war they were removed to Ysselsteyn.

Drive over the railway bridge and continue to Keizer Karel Plein.

As you drive around the large roundabout area the first exit to the right that you pass is Groesbeekseweg (the road to Groesbeek). It was at that point that A Company of Colonel

Warren's 1st Battalion 508th PIR, making the first American attempt to take the Nijmegen road bridge (about 1km ahead), met German resistance. It was about 2200 hours on 17 September and as the Americans got ready to attack they heard the sound of lorries and men dismounting. When the 508th assault began the SS counter-attack forced the Americans on the defensive and shortly after General Gavin ordered them to withdraw and to reorganise. Nevertheless, Captain Jonathan E. Adams Jr, the company commander, had already led a patrol forward towards the Post Office (qv).

In the centre of the square is an equestrian statue of Charlemagne. Ahead is the handsome Concert and Exhibition Hall, built in 1915 by Oscar Leeuw, with its massive brick façade and classical ornamentation. After Nijmegen's Liberation in September 1944, it was a leave centre for Allied troops and was known as **The Winter Gardens.**
To the left is the RABO Bank building, in the ground floor of which is the

• *Nijmegen VVV/114 kms/71.4 miles*

2 Keizer Karel Plein, NL-6511 NC Nijmegen. Tel: + (0) 24 3297878. Fax: + (0)24 3297879. E-mail: info@vvvnijmegem.nl
On two floors and with helpful, English-speaking staff, the VVV sells tourist maps, souvenirs and has details of local hotels, restaurants, tourist attractions and an attractive range of souvenirs. It is on the site of the former Stork Club, a Canadian Officers' Club.

To the left along Van Schaeck Mathon Singel is Nijmegen's **main railway station** with a **currency exchange booth**.

• *Extra Visits to Memorial to Resistance Workers, Public Garden, Herman Oolbekkinkstraat (Map 6/25), British graves in Nijmegen (Rustoord) Cemetery (Map 6/24) and Plaque to Jewish Casualties, Jewish Cemetery (Map 6/23).*
Round trip: 6.4 kms/4 miles. Approximate time: 20 minutes

Take the Groesbeek turning off Keizer Karel Plein and after 100m fork left to Groesbeek. Continue to the junction with Postweg at the third traffic lights. Turn left and then immediately right on to Herman Oolbekkinkstraat. Continue through the archway at the end of the road and the memorial is immediately to the right (2.1 kms/1.3 miles).
The Memorial, in the form of a pelican, symbol of compassion, commemorates four policemen (three detectives and a photographer), members of the Nijmegen Resistance, who were arrested after the failed assassination attempt on the SD traitor Ederveen. After a trial at Velp they were executed by firing squad in the dune near Overveen on 6 June 1944. The statue, by Ben van Pinxtern, was erected on 12 September 1987.
Return to Postweg and turn right. Continue to
The Rustoord Protestant Cemetery on the right (2.7 kms/1.7 miles). Beside the entrance to this large cemetery is a CWGC sign. The grave of **Private William Currie,** 5th E. Yorks, age 25, 23 September 1944, is in the north-west corner of the cemetery. There are also four 1914-1918 war graves in the south-eastern corner near the entrance.
Continue to the corner of Kwakkenbergweg and the Jewish Cemetery. Drive right past and round it and back onto Postweg. You then stop on the right side of the road.

Memorial to Resistance Workers, Herman Oolbekkinkstraat

Extra visit continued

Plaque to Nijmegen's Jewish Casualties (3.2 kms/2 miles). The cemetery is only open for relatives of the wartime casualties. At the beginning of 1941 there were 527 members of the Jewish Community. Large-scale deportations took place in the autumn of 1942 and by September 1944 it is thought that 501 Jews were deported to Auschwitz and Sobibor, of whom none returned. The plaque, which is to the right on the wall just inside the iron gates (which may well be locked) commemorates those who were not allowed to find their last resting place here.

Return to Keizer Karel Plein and pick up the main Itinerary.

Take Oranje Singel off Keizer Karel Plein signed to Arnhem and continue as the road becomes Sint Canisiussingel towards the Waal.

At the first traffic lights, with the yellow brick building of the Magistrates' Court on the corner to the left, can be seen the tall TV and radio tower that marks the position of the brown brick Post Office (Map 1N/7). The 508th PIR commanded by Colonel Lindquist had a complex role which divided between taking and holding the high ground around Groesbeek and sending a company to take the Nijmegen road bridge. There was confusion concerning Lindquist's exact priorities which we discuss later, but he did send a platoon-size patrol into Nijmegen at around 1830 hours to investigate Dutch intelligence information that only eighteen Germans guarded the southern end of the bridge and, if possible, to capture it. That patrol got lost until the following morning. Gavin, learning that no move had apparently been made on the bridge, told Lindquist 'to delay not a second longer and get to the bridge as quickly as possible'. Although Colonel Shields Warren, commanding the 1st Battalion of the 508th, was ordered to move on the bridge at 1800 hours it was four hours before he could get going with A Company. A supposed member of the Dutch Underground volunteered to lead them to the bridge but en route he disappeared. Warren waited for some time to see if the Dutchman would return. He didn't, so Warren continued and met the Germans at Keizer Karel Plein as described earlier. Warren believed that the bridge could be blown by using control apparatus in the Post Office and at 2200 hours sent Captain Adams, the A Company commander, there with a patrol. The Americans destroyed some equipment, but because of enemy reaction were unable to get out of a shop on the corner of Hezelstraat-Jodenberg until relieved three days later. The Germans, however, would hold the bridge for another three days despite another unsuccessful attempt by the 508th under Gavin's urging to take the bridge on the following morning, the 18th (G Company of Lieutenant-Colonel Louis G. Mendez's 3rd Battalion 508th PIR) and yet another on the afternoon of the 19th by a combined American and Grenadier force (see Itinerary Four, the **Valkhof** entry).

Continue to the large roundabout, Keizer Traianus Plein (115.5 kms/72.1 miles).

• **End of Itinerary Two**

ITINERARY THREE

THE GROESBEEK CIRCUIT

• **Itinerary Three** starts at the Nijmegen Bridge, heads east to Beek via Ooij, climbs to Berg en Dal and Groesbeek, through the American DZs and LZs and General Browning's landing site and returns back to Nijmegen via civilian memorials and CWGC cemeteries.

• **The Route:** Nijmegen Bridge; Ooij Civilian Memorial; Beek – 'Devils in Baggy Pants' Memorial, Civilian Memorial, Lt J. Foley Sign; Berg en Dal Civilian Memorial; Sionshof 508th *Bas Relief*; Groesbeek – Canadian CWGC Cemetery and Memorial to the Missing, 508th PIR DZ T/Operation VERITABLE Start Point, Wylerbaan, National Liberation Museum, Canada-Netherlands Memorial Park, Monument near South Mill, General Gavin/82nd US AB Monument; Breedeweg - Site of General Browning's HQ, Plaques to 505th PIR, St Antonius Church; Klein Amerika - Monument to 505th PIR DZ N/General Gavin's Landing/General Crerar's 1st Canadian Army, German Concrete Bombs; St Jansberg Plaque to Crew of Halifax; Milsbeek – STGT, CWGC Cemetery, Civilian Memorial; Mook – CWGC Cemetery, Monument to Civilian Casualties, RC Churchyard; Site of Allied 1944 Molenhoek Cemetery, Van den Broek Brewery

• **Extra Visits** are suggested to Cuijk – Polish Sculpture to Civilian Casualties, Memorial to Jewish Casualties; Katwijk Monument to Dutch Soldiers, 1940; Linden Churchyard Plaque to C-47 Skytrain/James Martin; Nijmegen – site of 82nd and 101st AB Hospitals.

• **Planned duration,** without stops for refreshment or Extra Visits: 4 hours 30 minutes.

• **Total distance:** 56.8 kms/35.5miles

• *Keizer Traianus Plein, Nijmegen/0kms/0 miles*

From the Nijmegen Bridge take the N325 signed Kleef (Kleve).

This is the important main road into Germany, which is just 10kms away, and control of the road was a priority task of 508th PIR, though it was not achieved until the morning of 18 September. In the heights to the right was a vast Roman fortress, large enough to hold an entire Legion.

Continue, with the rising ground of the Groesbeek Heights to the right, to the left turn signed Ooij and turn left at the traffic lights..

The church visible to the left is at Persingen, the smallest community in Holland.

Continue, turn left into Ooij and stop by the church on the left.

• *Memorial to Ooij Civilians/6.6 kms/4.1 miles/5 minutes/Map 1N/9*

The handsome *bas relief* of St George and the Dragon memorial is built into the church wall. It was erected on 4 May 1989, and the panels flanking St George bear the names of the twenty civilians killed in the cellars of the Scheers' café on 28 September 1944 when a German fighter-bomber dropped two bombs on it after being hit. The other names are of those who lost their lives on the Grebbeberg in 1940, during the bombardment of Nijmegen and after the war by a landmine. New names have recently been added to the panels. There are some Dutch Wargraves in the adjoining cemetery.

Return to the junction with the N325 and go straight over into Beek. Turn right following Doorgaand Verkeer and stop opposite the memorial on the left just before the T-junction.

• *Memorials to the 508th PIR, 82nd US AB Div, Beek Civilians and Lieutenant John Foley/9.9 kms/6.2 miles/10 minutes/Map 6-29/30*

The 'Devils in Baggy Pants' Memorial, designed by H.J. Guse, was erected on 17 September 1981. It commemorates the liberation of Beek by the 508th PIR, known as the 'Red Devils', on 17 September 1944. In C Company of the regiment (American Parachute Infantry Regiments were roughly of the same strength as British Parachute Brigades) was First Sergeant Leonard A. Funk who would return to Pennsylvania as the most decorated American paratrooper of the war. The *bas relief* of a baggy-panted devil descending by parachute originates from an entry in the diary of a German officer who fought against American paratroopers (actually the 504th) at Anzio. It read:

> American parachutists – devils in baggy pants – are less than 100m from my outpost line. I can't sleep at night; they pop up from nowhere and we never know when or how they will strike next. Seems like the black-hearted devils are everywhere.

In 1944 Beek, which sits astride the Nijmegen-Kleve road, had to be taken to gain control of the road. Although the monument records Liberation as 17 September, 508th PIR had so many varied tasks that it did not gain full control of Beek until 21 September, up to when it changed hands several times.

Next to the 508th Memorial is the **local War Memorial** which records the names of forty-two civilians, including Ruth Jakobs, a Jewish lady, killed by a shell after the Liberation in October, whose diary was published in 1999.

Beyond it is a sign to 'Lt. John P. Foley of 'A'Coy, 508th PIR'. On 19 September the company was ordered to take the Duivelsberg, the heights beyond Beek. Foley and his forty-four men were cut off for five days and nights (although he was resupplied with ammunition by American patrols), but held the position until relieved.

Continue to the T-junction and turn left. Continue through the charming village of Beek and then at the VVV in the old electricity company building turn right uphill towards Berg en Dal.

The building on the left at the bottom of the hill is the old customs house. Beek was formerly a border town between Holland and Germany. The hill you are ascending is the Duivelsberg (Devil's Hill). There are still the remains of 1944/45 trenches in the woods here.

At the top turn left signed Groesbeek and Kleef. Turn right at the green CWGC Groesbeek Cemetery sign and continue 50m to the column on the right.

• Memorial Column to Berg en Dal's Liberation and Civilian Casualties/11.8 kms/7.4 miles/5 minutes/Map 6/31

Erected on 5 May 1955, this memorial on the summit of the Duivelsberg is in gratitude to its liberation and to commemorate the fallen of Berg en Dal, 1940-1945. By a curious coincidence, bearing in mind the possible connection between the launch of the V2 rockets on London and the inception of MARKET-GARDEN, SS General Hans Kammler, who was in charge of the V2 programme, had his HQ in the town. Following the 17 September landings he immediately moved out of Holland both his HQ and the 485th Battalion of Group North (near the Hague) which had done the firing. This might therefore be accorded as a partial success for MARKET-GARDEN – though the rockets were back in under two weeks. Heavy fighting took place here and not only were there many casualties but enormous damage to buildings and land. In November 1944 the inhabitants were evacuated and when they returned not one house appeared to be undamaged.

Continue down Clarenbeeksweg, following the road round to the right signed Heiligland Stichting (Holy Land Foundation) and Afrika Museum. Continue past the Afrika Museum on the left then the Holy Land Open Air Museum on the right.

In the grounds of the latter is a **Memorial Chapel to Dr Daniel van Vugt**, (Map 6/28) one of approximately twenty war victims buried in the Holy Land Foundation churchyard. It is occasionally used for commemorations of the fallen and bears plaques to Dr van Vugt, who died in the German concentration camp at Sandbostel on 2 May 1945 because of his work for the Resistance, and tablets to three policemen shot by the Germans on 6 June 1944 at Overveen. The 508th took control of the Foundation grounds.

Continue to the roundabout, go straight over and stop outside the Sionshof Hotel.

• Sionshof Hotel 508th PIR Memorial/Nebo Seminary/15 kms/9.4 miles/10 minutes/Map 6-27/26

By September 1944 the Sionshof had been used for four years by the Germans as an HQ. They also used the Klooster Nebo, the large Catholic Seminary across the road, both of which were taken over by the advancing Allies' War Correspondents and photographers who arrived by glider. Guards Armoured Division Officers moved into the hotel, to be followed by 82nd AB. Here the Dutch liaison officer, Captain Harry Bestebreurtje, made contact between the Allied Forces and the local forces and sent a patrol into Nijmegen to recce the situation near the Waal bridge. Prince Bernhard of the Netherlands lunched here in September 1944. Prior to MARKET-GARDEN the Seminary was used by the staff of a German parachute training school, evacuated from France. It was then used as a combined hospital (treating German POWs until as late as 1946), prisoners' interrogation centre and GHQ. The garden was used as a temporary cemetery. Behind the building an American medium battery pounded German positions in the Reichswald Forest. On the outside wall of the Sionshof is a Memorial *Bas Relief* to 82nd AB Division designed by Ch. Hammes. It depicts a paratrooper of the 82nd AB Division. It was presented by the municipality of Nijmegen to the Sionshof Hotel and unveiled on 17 September 1954 by Major Bestebreurtje. The No. 17 and one of the small parachutes is, sadly, missing. Inside the hotel are more details.

The sensitively written novella, *Five Graves at Nijmegen*, by the Australian correspondent

St George and Dragon Memorial to Ooij's Civilians

'Devils in Baggy Pants' Memorial, Beek

508th PIR Memorial,
Sionshof Hotel

calling himself Eric Baume, described the graves of 'five British Guardsmen, officers and other ranks' in the Nebo grounds. Baume was in the Sionshof during the Operation and talked at length to one of the Franciscan friars, Aurelius Pompen. This conversation was the basis of his book. A sketch accompanied the text which was later shown to have been taken from a photograph. The five white crosses stand around a large ornamental cross and are surrounded by a white wooden fence. Research by Father Thuring (qv) and J. Hey (qv) points to the fact that one of the graves – of which there were actually a total of twenty-three – belongs to a Scots Guardsman Andrew Wardrope who was badly wounded when his tank was brewed up on the Wylerbaan on 8 February 1945. He was brought to the hospital here and died on 11 February. Another identified grave belonged to Captain the Hon Vicary Paul Gibbs (qv), killed at the Valkhof on 20 September 1944. They are both now buried in Jonkerbos CWGC Cemetery [22.B.4. and 22.G.4.].

Turn round, turn right and continue towards Groesbeek. Turn left along Derdebaan signed to the Canadian Cemetery and continue to the left turn to it. Stop in the car park.

• *Groesbeek Canadian CWGC Cemetery/Memorial/19.2 kms/12 miles/20 minutes /Map 6-32/33/OP*

The cemetery is on the highest point for several kilometres and affords an excellent view over the 82nd AB drop and landing areas.

Walk into the cemetery and stand with your back to the Cross of Sacrifice, facing the open fields away from the entrance.

That is 12 o'clock. The Nijmegen road bridge is 7kms away at 7 o'clock, the Arnhem road bridge 19kms away at 9 o'clock. The German Border and Reichswald Forest can be seen 5kms away at 2 o'clock, Groesbeek is 2kms away at 3 o'clock and the Grave Bridge is 13kms away at 5 o'clock [Bridge 11 - see Sketch Map 3]. 82nd AB had two main DZs, one at Grave and one here. 508th PIR came down in the area from your left sweeping round to about 2 o'clock. Between them and the Reichswald 505th PIR commanded by Colonel William E. Ekman dropped, their area curving to the south of Groesbeek. Part of their task was to protect the area for the D+1 follow-up glider landings. Within 60 minutes the paratroopers were moving off to their objectives, some climbing the slope towards you en route to Nijmegen. Patrols were sent into the forest which, rumour had it, concealed German tanks – Gavin's map recorded 'May be pool for refitting Panzer Divs'. The rumour proved to be false. The landings were largely unopposed. One C-47 was hit by flak, too low for the paratroopers to jump. It made a perfect wheels-up landing, on the site of the present cemetery, and the men walked out of the plane.

Originally there were fairly advanced plans to create several small Canadian cemeteries, notably at St Michielsgestel Seminary and in Angerlo RC Cemetery. Finally, however, it was decided to concentrate the Canadian burials here at Groesbeek from a host of small (some with only a handful of graves) burial grounds. The meticulous and laborious work started in August 1945 and continued into the spring of 1946. The cemetery contains 3 RN, 212 UK Army and 10 Unknown, 40 RAF and 3 Unknown, 2,190 Canadian Army and 4 Unknown, 141 RCAF and 3 Unknown, 2 RAAF and 1 NZAF, 3 Belgian, I Dutch, 2 Polish, I Russian and I Yugoslav. The majority lost their lives in the Battle of the Rhineland, when 2nd and 3rd Canadian Divisions and 4th Canadian Armoured Division took part in the drive southwards from Nijmegen to clear the territory between the Maas and the Rhine in February/March 1945.

The VC was awarded to **Sergeant Aubrey Cosens**, RCIC, age 24, 26 February 1945 [VIII.H.2.]. His citation in the *London Gazette* reads,

> In Holland, on the night of 25/26 February, 1945, the 1st Battalion The Queen's Own Rifles of Canada attacked the hamlet of Mooshof. Sergeant Cosens' platoon, with tanks in support, had as their objective enemy strong-points in three farm-buildings. They were twice beaten back and were then fiercely counterattacked. Their casualties were heavy, including the platoon commander killed. Sergeant Cosens assumed command of the few survivors of the platoon, and placed them so as to give covering fire while he crossed open ground to the one remaining tank and directed its fire. After a further counter-attack had been repulsed, Sergeant Cosens ordered the tank to attack the three farm-buildings, the remaining men of his platoon following in close support. He himself entered the three buildings in turn, alone, and killed or captured all the occupants. Immediately afterwards he was shot by a sniper, and died almost instantly. His outstanding gallantry, initiative and determined leadership resulted in the capture of a position which was vital to the success of the future operations of the Brigade.

The MC was awarded to **Lieutenant Donald Ayer**, RCAC, age 32, from Maine, USA, 4 March 1945, [VII.E.3.]; **Captain Harvey Bean**, RCIC, age 23, 14 February 1945 [I.D.5.]; **Major George Skelton**, 3/4th County of London Yeomanry, age 27, 28 February 1945 [VI.F.7.].

The MM and Bar was awarded to **Corporal Stanley Matchwick**, 5th Seaforth Highlanders, age 39, 25 March 1945 [VI.B.12.]. The MM was awarded to **Rifleman Charles Nahwegezhic**, RCIC, age 26, 28 February 1945 [XVI.G.1.]

The DSO was awarded to **Major Samuel McWhirter**, RCA, age 36, 9 February 1945 [I.B.1.]; **Lieutenant-Colonel John Rowley, Commanding the North Shore (New Brunswick) Regt,** age 33, 26 March 1945 [XVII.E.15.]; **Private Harold Schultheis**, RCIC, age 22, 8 March 1945 [IV.F.15.] and **Major Latimer Denison**, Royal Winnipeg Rifles, age 24, 30 March 1945, who also had the *Croix de Guerre* [XX.G.12.]. **Major Willard Parker**, RCIC, age 29, 26 February 1945 also had the *Croix de Guerre* [IX.H.6.]; **Lieutenant-Colonel Ernest Thompson**, RCIC, age 24, 26 February 1945 [IX.B.16.]

The DFC was awarded to **Flight Lieutenant Russell Bouskill**, RCAF, age 28, 2 October 1944 [XV.E.5.] and **Pilot Officer Cecil Hightower**, RCAF, age 32, 26 July 1943 [XVI.B.14.]; **Captain William Reade**, RCAC, age 31, 23 April 1945 [VIII.A.8.]; **Flight Lieutenant William Hodgson**, RAF, age 24, 27 December 1944 [XII.F.6.], who also had the **AFM**; **Squadron Leader William Klersy**, RAF, age 22, 22 May 1945 [XXI.E.15.], who also had the **Bar.**

The DFM was awarded to **Pilot Officer David Crozier**, RCAF, age 28, 13 January 1943 [XV.A.7.]. The MBE was awarded to **Wing Commander John Brown**, 1 September 1944 [VI.G.12.]. The OBE was awarded to **Lieutenant-Colonel Jeff Nicklin**, 1 Can Para, age 30, 24 March 1945 [XXII.C.1.].

MiD were **Lieutenant Francis Arnett**, RCAC, age 29, 25 March 1945 [XV1.C.11.]; **Lance Sergeant Edward Bellows**, 14 Field Sqn, RCE, age 27, 18 May 1945, who also had the *Croix de Guerre avec Etoile de Bronze* [IV.A.13]; **Captain Reginald Boyce**, RCA, age 26, 26 February 1945 [X.C.4.]; **Major Armand Brochu**, RCIC, age 30, 1 March 1945 [VIII.D.14.]; **Captain Geoffrey Gibbs**, 3rd Monmouths, age 29, 30 November 1944 [XII.H.6.]; **Lieutenant-Colonel John Hall, Commanding the 1st Middx,** age 35, 8 February 1945, who also had the *Croix de Guerre* [VI.H.3.]; **Private Harold Schultheis,** RCIC, age 27, 7 February 1945 [IV.F.15.]; **Bombardier Douglas Trumper,** RCA, age 26, 2 March 1945 [XIV.F.13.].

Lieutenant-Colonel Ralph Stockley Commanding the 3rd Monmouths, age 37, 30 November 1944 [XII.H.8.] was the son of Brigadier-General Hugh Stockley, CIE, RE. **The Rev Joseph Dalcourt,** Chaplain 3rd Class of the Canadian Chaplain Service, died on 28 February 1945 [IX.E.14.].

The brothers of the following also fell on service: Private Bruce Wagner, RCIC, age 20, 31 January 1945 [XVI.C.3.], Private Ivan Wagner, RCIC, age 27, 18 July 1944, buried in Bretteville-sur-Laize, Normandy and Private Harry Wagner, RCIC, age 30, 12 August 1944, buried in Bény-sur-Mer, Normandy; **Sergeant Alan Horsfall,** RAF, age 19, 30 August 1940 [XII.H.9-11.], Sergeant David Horsfall, RAF, age 23, 17 May 1943, buried in Bergen General Cemetery; **Trooper Harold Illingworth,** RCAC, age 27, 26 February 1945 [IX.F.1.], Private Charles Illingworth, RCIC, age 22, 4 December 1944, buried in Ravenna CWGC Cemetery, Italy; **Lieutenant Daniel Paré,** age 24, 16 January 1945 [I.D.10.], WOII Viateur Paré, RCIC, age 27, 6 April 1945, buried in Holten Can Cemetery, Holland.

Private Ralph Ash, [XIV.D.9.] and **Private Bruno Boutet** [XXV.A.4.], who were both in the RCIC and died on 2 March 1945, were **17 years old,** as was **Private Herbert Danielson, Black Watch of Canada,** 9 March 1945 [VIII.E.6.] and **Private Barney McGuigan,** RCIC, 26 February 1945 [X.G.6.], while **Trooper John Bartlett,** RCAC, 27 February 1945, was **48 years old** [XXI.G.2.].

There are five members of the **Belanger family,** including brothers **Craftsman Conrad,** RCEME, age 26, died on 2 April 1945 [V.E.9.] and **Private Jean Paul,** RCIC, age 23, died on 24 February 1945 [XI.C.3.]. **Albert Saunderson,** RN, age 20, 9 August 1945 [VI.C.2.], was **'Coder' on HMS** *Odyssey.*

Flying Officer A. F. Hupman, Nav RCAF, and **Flying Officer D Morrison,** RCAF, [both in Coll Grave XV.C.3], **Pilot Officer G. E. Quinn,** RCAF [XX.A.1.], **Pilot Officer C. S. Johnston,** RCAF [XV.C.1.], **Pilot Officer H. Fletcher,** RCAF [XV.C.2.] and **Pilot Officer P. J. McManus,** RCAF [XV.C.4.] are all on **the Lancaster Memorial in Elden** (qv).

In the cemetery stands

The Groesbeek Memorial. Servicemen who fell at Arnhem and who have no known name are recorded on this Memorial.

The Memorial consists of two L-shaped buildings, facing each other across the turfed forecourt between the cemetery entrance and the Stone of Remembrance. The names of the Missing are inscribed on Portland stone panels along the back walls of each structure, with the legend,

> These walls bear the names of the soldiers of the Commonwealth who fell in the advance from the River Seine through the Low Countries and into Germany, but of whom the fortune of war denied a known and honoured grave. 30 August 1944 – 5 May 1945.

On the friezes above the columns is carved the inscription, *'Pro Amicus mortui amicis vivimus'* [We live in the hearts of friends for whom we died] and the names of the great rivers which marked the progress of the campaign: 'Seine, Scheldt, Maas, Rhine, Elbe.'

The names are made up as follows: 951 United Kingdom, 103 Canadian and 2 South African. There are 178 names of the Parachute Regiment, 83 Royal Artillery, 67 Royal Engineers, 47 RASC, 33 Border Regiment, 31 KOSB, 30 Wiltshire Regiment, 24 DCLI, 20 HLI

Groesbeek CWGC Cemetery and Memorial: Personal Tribute, Row of headstones

and 20 S Staffs Regiment, with representatives of 79 other UK Corps and Regiments and 34 Canadian Corps and Regiments.

N.B. There is a separate register for the Memorial, housed in the right hand building.

The VC was awarded to **Lance-Sergeant John Baskeyfield,** 2nd Battalion, S Staffs Regt, 1st AB Division, age 22, 20 September 1944. His citation in the *London Gazette* reads,

> On 20th September, 1944, during the Battle of Arnhem, Lance-Sergeant Baskeyfield was the N.C.O. in charge of a 6-pounder anti-tank gun at Oosterbeek. During the early stages of a heavy enemy attack, the crew commanded by this N.C.O. were responsible for the destruction of two Tiger tanks and at least one self-propelled gun, thanks to his coolness in allowing each tank to come well within 100 yards of his gun before opening fire. Lance-Sergeant Baskeyfield was badly wounded and the remainder of his crew were either killed or severely wounded but he refused to be carried away from his post, and when the attack was renewed he manned his gun alone and fired round after round until his gun was put out of action. His activity was the main factor in keeping the German tanks at bay, and his example and his courage were responsible for keeping together and in action the surviving men in his vicinity. When his gun was knocked out, he crawled to another nearby which was left without a crew, and succeeded in putting out of action another self-propelled gun before being killed. Lance-Sergeant Baskeyfield's supreme gallantry is beyond praise. During the remaining days at Arnhem stories of his valour were a constant inspiration to all ranks.

See also Itinerary 5.

The MC was awarded to **Lieutenant Bertram Horwood,** 12th (AB) Bn, Devonshires, age 21,

6 February 1945 [Panel 3]. **The MM** was awarded to **Corporal Edward Browne**, 2nd R Warwicks, age 26, 30 September 1944 [Panel 3].

MiD were **SQMS George Holderness**, RAC, age 30, 25 September 1944 [Panel 1]; **Lieutenant Leslie Kershaw**, Cheshire Regt, age 27, 12 April 1945 [Panel 3]; **Captain Percy Louis**, RAMC, age 29, 24 September 1944 [Panel 3]; **Captain Francis Smith**, RE, age 46, 16 December 1944 [Panel 2]; **Corporal Richard Verling**, RE, age 27, 22 November 1944 [Panel 2]; **Corporal Albert Wicker**, RE, age 28, 31 March 1945 [Panel 2]; **Major Ernest Ritson**, 156th Para, age 35, 20 September 1944 [Panel 8] was **Twice Mentioned.**

The **DSO** was awarded to **Major Gustave Bieler**, RCIC, 5 September 1944 [Panel 11], who also had the **MBE; Major Francis Suttill**, East Surreys, age 35, 18 March 1945 [Panel 4], who was 'LL.B. (Lond.) Barrister-at-Law'.

The **OBE** was awarded to **Colonel Hilary Barlow** (qv) of the SLI, **Commanding 1 Airlanding Bde, AAC**, 19 September 1944 [Panel 1.]. The **BEM** was awarded to **Lieutenant Stanley Watling**, 156th Para, age 28, 19 September 1944 [Panel 8]. The *Croix de Guerre* was awarded to **Captain Frank Pickersgill**, Can Int Corps, age 29, 14 September 1944 [Panel 11]. The **King's Commendation for Brave Conduct** was awarded to **Serjeant Peter Weisz**, Int Corps, age 24, 1/30 April 1945 [Panel 10].

Private Timothy Bleichroeder of 21st Indep Para Coy, age 22, 25 September 1944 [Panel 9], **served as 'Bleach'**. **Private Herbert Sachs**, The Buffs/10 Commando, age 27, 23 March 1945 [Panel 3], **served as 'Seymour'.** They were two of the approximate 15,000 German Jews serving with the British Army.

The father of Lance-Corporal William Eden, Border Regt, 1 AB Div, age 29, 22 September 1944, [Panel 4], Private John Eden, KORR, age 27, died of wounds from Gallipoli on 24 August 1915 and is buried in Alexandria, Chatby. **The father of Lance-Corporal David Jones**, The Welch Regt, age 30, 24 September 1944 [Panel 5], Private Thomas Jones of the same regiment, was also killed in Gallipoli – at Suvla Bay – on 11 August 1915 and is commemorated on the Helles Memorial. **The father of Private David McKenzie**, 10th Para Bn, AAC, age 23, 20 September 1944 [Panel 9], Gunner Kenneth McKenzie, RA, age 45, was killed in action in London 17 January 1943 and is buried in Dundee Eastern Necropolis. **The father of Lieutenant Robert McLaren**, RA, age 30, 18 September 1944 [Panel 1], Private Peter McLaren, Bedfordshire Regt, age 33, died of wounds in Belgium on 24 October 1917 and is buried in Mendinghem cemetery.

The brothers of the following also fell on service: Gunner Arthur Lock, RA, age 24, 20/21 September 1944 [Panel 2], Gunner Libert Lock, RA, age 27, 16 August 1941, buried in Candlesby, Lincs and Gunner Wilfred Lock, RA, age 30, 16 January 1943, buried in Heliopolis, Egypt; **Driver George Essen**, RASC, 28 April 1945, [Panel 9], Sapper Charles Essen, age 20, 17 June 1940, buried in Pornic War Cemetery, France who was probably a casualty of SS *Lancastria*; **Driver Ernest Page**, RASC, age 46, 2 November 1944 [Panel 9], Driver Charles Henry Page, age 22, 24 February 1945, buried in Jonkerbos CWGC Cemetery [5.F.3.]; **Guardsman John Thornley**, 3rd Irish Guards, age 20, 1 October 1944 [Panel 3], Guardsman Allan Thornley, 3rd Irish Guards, age 19, 7 June 1943, buried in Liverpool (West Derby) Cemetery.

Gunner Cecil Riggs, RA, age 23, **was lost in SS *Samvern*** (London) 18 January 1945 [Panel 2].

Return to Derdebaan crossroads.

The farm on the corner was used by General Horrocks as his HQ at the start of Operation VERITABLE .

Turn left past the cemetery and continue to the junction with Wylerbaan. Stop just before it. Round the corner to the right is

• Memorial to 508th PIR Landings/Operation VERITABLE, Wylerbaan/20.8 kms/13 miles/5 minutes/Map 6/34

Shaped like an airborne canister or the Tinman in the *Wizard of Oz*, this metal memorial records, on the back, the fact that here on 17/18 September 1944 Red Devils of 508th PIR landed with artillery by parachute and glider. 'Devils or Angels, they came to shield the district of Nijmegen. Pilgrim – no matter the name or the colour, shield the vulnerable'. On the front is recorded,

> From this point around 300,000 British and Canadian soldiers set off on Monty's Operation VERITABLE. Pilgrim, strive with whatever it takes to realise your ideals. 16 September 1990.

It was erected by C.Hectors, A. van Grinsen and Father Thuring (qv).

• Extra Visit to Germany to Memorial to Shot Americans, Kranenburg (Map 1N/10) and German Cemetery, Donsbruggen (Map 1N/11)
Round trip approximately 25 kms/15.6 miles). Approximate time: 40 minutes

Turn left on Wylerbaan and continue to Wyler. Turn right and follow directions Kleve and Kranenburg into Germany. Continue into Kranenburg to the small Market Square to the left (5.1 kms/3.2 miles).

To the right is the Roman Catholic Church behind which is a large black **crucifix Tree of Life Memorial** with a table showing a map of the 1944/45 campaigns in the area and a skull and bones at the base.

Continue through the town to just short of a BP petrol station to the left and the Town Hall and VVV to the right. Stop (5.4 kms/3.4 miles).

On the left corner by a lampost is a black **Memorial Bas Relief** with a brick base.

The *bas relief* is flanked by two angels and shows a lily with a chain and the words 'HASS TÖTET LIEBE VERSÖHNT [Hate kills. Love reconciles] 17.9.1944'. The caption below describes how on the day of the Allied Landings two American Parachutist POWs were shot on

German Memorial to shot American Paratroopers, Kranenburg

Extra visit continued
this spot, in cold blood, by an SA man. Their deaths were later investigated by an Allied Military Court.
This is an extremely rare memorial.
Continue to Nutterden.
In front of Nutterden Church to the left is the local War Memorial with the names of the Missing.
Continue to the green sign to 'Kriegsgräberstätte 700m' to the right. (11.3 kms/7.1 miles). Turn here and follow a second sign to the right (at 240m) and turn right at the third (185m) sign to the large car park in front of the cemetery and stop.
Donsbruggen German Cemetery (12.5 kms/7.8 miles). A large signboard describes the 2,381 graves here, 40 of them Unknown, of the February 1945 fighting.
Go up the steps to the stone-enclosed cemetery.
The Register box is to the left of the entrance and ahead is the crypt with the names of the Unknown surrounded by a mass grave. The markers on the graves are flat and are interspersed with symbolic crosses.
Return to your car and back to Wylerbaan to pick up the main Itinerary.

Turn right along Wylerbaan and continue towards Groesbeek.
The row of trees to the left leads to the farmhouse Den Heuvel (Map 6/35), where bitter fighting took place. The road passes through DZ T where 508th PIR and a company of the 505th, dropped. To the left were German trenches and machine-gun nests in January/ February 1945 and on the right can be seen WW2 metal pickets and concrete bombs (qv).
Continue to the National Liberation Museum 1944 on the left and stop in the car park.

• The National Liberation Museum 1944, Groesbeek/ Sherwood Rangers Memorial Sherman/German 75mm Gun/Canada-Netherlands Memorial Park/22.4 kms/14 miles/45 minutes/Map 6-37/37a/38/39/36
Inaugurated on 6 May 1987 by HRH Prince Bernhard of the Netherlands, the museum was funded and realised by enthusiastic American veterans and Dutch volunteers. Built on the spot where General Gavin's 82nd AB landed on 17 September 1944, it has two aims: to keep alive the memory of the crucial events of 1944/45 and to express gratitude to those who gave their lives for the freedom of this part of Holland.
In 2000 the museum underwent a huge renovation and expansion programme, the focal point of which is a vivid diorama, an accurate portrayal of the Waal crossing by the 504th PIR (qv). The authentic-looking uniforms were made for the film *Saving Private Ryan.*
The welcome area has a large mural showing the sky full of dropping parachutes. In the museum visitors live through the period preceding the War, experience the Occupation, celebrate the Liberation and witness the rebuilding of the Netherlands and Europe after the War. The section 'Democracy destroyed' charts the rise of fascism. 'The Occupation' tells the story of the Occupation of the Netherlands and what this meant for the Dutch people. The largest section covers the Liberation – Operation MARKET-GARDEN – and the winter of

Memorial to 508th PIR/
Operation VERITABLE,
Wylerbaan

National Liberation
Museum,
Groesbeek:
General view of
exterior with
German 75mm
gun/Sherman Tank
on Open
Day/Detail of Waal
Crossing Diorama

1944-5 (during which Nijmegen remained a front-line city and 750 civilians were killed), Operations VERITABLE and MANNA and the daily life of the Allied and German soldiers in the Netherlands. The Liberation is also depicted in a recreated decorated street and in many interactive displays, dioramas, models and original film.

Finally there is the Hall of Remembrance, set in a striking building, shaped like a parachute. It contains the Roll of Honour with the names of every single American killed in MARKET. The names of British and Canadians killed in North-West Europe since 6 June 1944 are listed in books along the wall, under their divisional emblem. There are also books with the names of the Polish, Belgian and Dutch casualties.

This impressive museum also has a Film Room, an Education Room, a Documentation Centre and a bookstall and shop. The much-enlarged, smart cafeteria now has a huge panoramic window with views over DZ T and the February 1945 frontline.

Open: Monday-Saturday 1000-1700, Sundays and Public Holidays 1200-1700. Closed on Christmas Day and New Year's Day.

Entrance fee payable, with concessions for groups, children and over-60s.

Tel: + (0) 24 3974404. Fax: + (0) 24 3976694.

In or adjoining the grounds are:

1. A Sherman tank, 'Robin Hood' T152098, presented on 7 May 1988 by the Notts Sherwood Rangers Yeomanry in memory of 208 of their comrades who fell '39-'45. The tank saw action in the Groesbeek area when the Sherwood Rangers worked with the US 508th PIR. At the end of September they moved into the Ooijpolder together and later fought in Operation VERITABLE in the Reichswald Forest and around Kleve.

2. German 75mm Pak 40 L/46 anti-tank gun, seized by Sergeant Mick Savage, Corporal L. S. Maso of the Welsh Guards and Corporal L. S. Britton, RCA, near Horst, just beyond the German border on 8 February 1945, the first day of Operation VERITABLE. This gun had shelled the Groesbeek area every day from September 1944.

From the grounds, follow the path by foot to

3. The Canada-Netherlands Memorial Park.

On 5 May 1998 Princess Margriet of the Netherlands, in the presence of the Dutch Minister of Agriculture and Canadian Veterans, inaugurated this peaceful and reflective memorial to the shattering events of 1944-45. She also planted the tree which is enclosed by railings and bears a memorial plaque. The entire Dutch Royal Family was evacuated in May 1940 - despite an attempt by the Germans to capture them on 10 May - Queen Wilhelmina to London and Princess Juliana and Prince Bernhard to Canada, where Princess Margriet was born.

The Park is designed as a living monument for peaceful contemplation in the form of a wood of Canadian maples and a wild flower meadow enclosed by a hedge of field maple, hawthorn, spindle tree and dog rose, with views towards the Canadian Cemetery over the Drop Zones. The young wood is broken up by terraces (the flagstones of which bear the imprint of Canadian maple leaves) and stone benches.

Turn left out of the museum and continue to the T-junction.

In the car park by the T-junction is a medieval lookout tower housing a restaurant, locally known as The Old Mill. The mill stood there prior to September 1944 when it was hit by artillery and demolished during the winter of 1944-5. The bricks were used to reinforce local roads.

Turn left towards Groesbeek and take the first turning right into the town centre. Continue to the large roundabout beyond which is an old windmill. This is South Mill.

The mill, built in 1817, was used by the underground as a beacon to help escaping airmen. In September 1944 US paratroops used it as an O.P. Today it is still working and can be visited by appointment. Tel: + (0) 24 3971283. Fax: + (0) 24 3977183 (Map 6/41).

Turn left, signed De Horst, and take the 2nd right on Rembrandtsweg and immediately stop by the memorial on the right.

• *Memorial to Groesbeek's Liberators, South Mill/24 kms/15 miles/5 minutes/Map 6/42*

This stylized metal sculpture was erected in 1969 by Joep de Bekker. Its inscription, now missing, read, 'Thanks to our Liberators, 1940-1945'.

In 1940 the inhabitants of villages along the threatened Meuse-Waal Canal were evacuated to Groesbeek. In October 1944, when Groesbeek was itself on the front line, all remaining inhabitants who had not already fled were evacuated.

Return to the roundabout and go straight over signed Mook on Mooksebaan. Continue to the group of small statues on the green on the left just before the right turn up Houtlaan.

• *Groesbeek Evacuation Memorial/24.5 kms/15.3 miles/5 minutes/Map 6/40*

This moving group was sculpted by Greet Norp-Nieuwhof, winner of the competition for an evacuation memorial. Inaugurated in September 1995, it depicts a family – father holding a child by the hand, mother pushing a baby in a pram and the grandfather - all bent forward in anxiety and exhaustion as they leave their home with barely any possessions. The caption translates, 'The Second World War also brought much suffering to the civilians of Groesbeek. In September 1944 they had to flee from the cruelty of war. Here and elsewhere there were many victims. When they came back in the Spring of 1945 all their possessions were destroyed. The tanks and debris of war killed and wounded many people afterwards. The rebuilding of the village under harsh circumstances took many years. The civilians of today commemorate the civilians of yesteryear.'

Return to the roundabout, turn right signed Breedeweg. Continue on Bredeweg past the exit Groesbeek sign to the huge pink modern metal sculpture and turn left, stopping immediately at the information board in the layby just before the memorial group on the right.

• *Memorial to General Gavin and 82nd US AB/25.8 kms/16.1 miles/10 minutes/Map 6/43*

On 5 May 1987 the original star-shaped plaque by Kees Hectors was laid on the ground and the road to the right was named General Gaavinstraat (sic). The inscription is

> Out of gratitude and respect of the population of Groesbeek for the American 82nd Airborne Division, which under command of General James M. Gavin liberated Groesbeek from terror and suppression on 17 September 1944.

On 12 June 1994 walls were added by the Groesbeek Airborne Friends with a plaque bearing the words, 'James M. Gavin, Commanding General US 82nd Airborne Division 'All American'. Mission accomplished. After Action Report. Market Holland Operation, sep-nov [sic] 1944.' This was unveiled by General Gavin's grand-daughter, Mrs. J. E. Gavin, and veterans. On 17 September 1994, the 50th Anniversary, para and glider symbols were added. On 17 September 1997 the monument was 'entrusted to all who believe in peace' in the presence of veterans. The trees in the surrounding garden were planted by individuals and bear their names on plaques.

Return to the pink sculpture, turn left onto Bredeweg and take the next turning left on Koningin Wilhelminaweg. Continue to the memorial on the left at the end of the row of houses.

• Memorial to General Browning's HQ 17.9.44/26.7 kms/16.7 miles/5 minutes/Map 6/44

Erected on 16 September 1990 by C. Hectors, A. van Grinsven and Father Thuring (qv), the inscription reads,

> The British Airborne Corps headquarters under General 'Boy' Browning landed here on 17 Sept 1944 with Horsa gliders as their winged horses. Pilgrim, let love lend you wings when necessary.

The thirty-eight gliders landed in the middle of the battle area at about 1400 hours and the command post, with a staff of 105, complete with radio transmitters and receivers, was operational at 1530 hours. An apocryphal story is that the General walked to the border [about a mile from here - a good walk!], urinated against a tree and said, 'I'm the first British soldier to pee on Germany!'

Return to Bredeweg, turn left and continue to the church on the right and stop.

The area to the right of the road behind the houses is Klein Amerika, DZ N for 505th PIR, which follows next.

Walk to the base of the church tower.

• St Anthony's Church Memorials/27.2 kms/ 17 miles/5 minutes/Map 6/45

On the tower are 6 plaques, sculpted by Niels Steenbergen, funded by the Groesbeek-Nijmegen Airborne Friends and erected on 13 June 1979. They are in memory of soldiers of the 505th PIR killed or missing in action on DZ/LZ N (near Klein Amerika) September-November 1944. One is to Captain Anthony Stefanich, C Coy 505th PIR, who was killed in action on 18.9.44 near Hof Sint Jansberg (qv) when he tried to rescue the crew of a glider that had crashed on enemy-occupied territory while defending the landing Zone. Others commemorated are Guy E. Belcher, Alpheus E. Fowlkes, Kenneth H. Lau and Sonnie J. Rockford, killed along the Tree Row (qv) and Roger F. Coffin, Stanley Creswick, Raymond Dionne, Walter Faranfontoff, Russel O. Eade and J. P. Shelton, killed at Plasmolen, from where attacks on Mook and the lockbridge at Heumen were repulsed. Other soldiers of the Regiment fell near Den Heuvel (qv) where they were stationed from 20 September.

The Pastor of the church, Father Thuring, is an expert on the battle, an author of many authoritative books on the Campaign and a member of the Committee for the Groesbeek National Liberation Museum.

Groesbeek Memorials: South Mill and
Evacuation

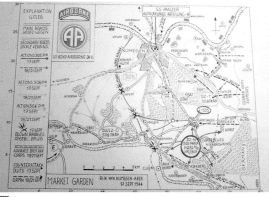

Memorial to Gen Gavin and 82nd AB Div,
Groesbeek with detail of Map

Memorial to Gen Browning's HQ with detail,
Breedeweg

Plaque to Capt Stefanich,
Sint Antonius Church

*Continue round the church on Sint Antoniusweg and as the road bends
sharply left, take the minor road straight on signed Klein Amerika.*
The tree-lined hedge to the left is all that remains of the infamous
Tree Row. In 1944 the line of trees continued right to the forest.
*Just before the farm on the right, bear right along Klein Amerika and
follow this uphill to the double memorial on the right-hand side.*
You are now at the southern end of DZ N.

• *Memorials to the 505th PIR DZ, 17/18.9. 44 and General Crerar's 1st Can Army 1945/29.1 kms/18.2 miles/5 minutes/Map 6-47/46*

The double memorial was erected by C. Hectors, A van Grinsven and Father Thuring on 16
September 1990. The left-hand tablet records that

> With Europe in peril, Paras landed here in their thousands. General James Gavin and
> the All American Division 17 & 18 Sep 1944 Operation Market Garden. Pilgrim, are
> you, like the liberators, ready to lay down your life when your fellows need you.

In the night of the 16th and the morning of the 17th the landings were preceded by massive
bombardments on German air bases, barracks, anti-aircraft artillery and flak positions. At
Klein Amerika, DZ N, 2,291 men of the 505th PIR landed with the HQ of 82nd AB Division.

Memorial to 505th PIR and Gen Crerar's 1st Can Army
with detail, Klein Amerika

Concrete bomb, Klein
Amerika

General James Gavin and his staff landed at about 1315 hours in the field straight ahead at the top of the road. The wood ahead appears triangular in form and was easily recognized from the air. Here Divisional RV was set up after the jump.

The right hand tablet records,

> Here in the winter of 1944/45 tens of thousands of soldiers of Crerar's First Canadian Army held the front line between the Maas and the Waal. Pilgrim, cherish all you hold dear.

The Canadians held what became the front-line here at that time.

The memorials bear some fine pictures of a C-47 Troop Carrier, a Jeep, a GM Ford 3 Ton Lorry and a Carrier.

Continue, following the metalled road round to the right, to the group of houses on the right.
In front of the house, named Klein Amerika, are **German concrete practice bombs** found in the bomb depot at Mooksbaan in the forest to the left when the local evacuees returned in the spring of 1945. (Map 6/48)

Continue to the pink statue on Bredeweg.
You have now effectively made a circuit of DZ N.

Turn right towards the church. Continue past the church and past the turning to Klein Amerika and take the next turning right on the minor road Sint Jansberg. Continue to the green post box of house no 1. Turn left up the track before it.

NB. This is a private house and permission should be requested to photograph the memorial.

• *Plaque to Crew of Halifax, Sint Jansberg/33.6 kms/21 miles/5 minutes/Map 6/49*

Erected on 17 September 1977 by H. van den Hoogen, it commemorates the crew of a Halifax of 87 Squadron killed when their plane was brought down near this spot on 12/13 March 1943. It was one of 23 aircraft brought down during the second air raid of more than 450 bombers on the steel industry town of Essen. From 1941 the Germans took all British and Commonwealth pilots killed in this area to Uden where they were buried, after investigation, in the back garden of the parsonage. After the war more than 100 graves were moved from the garden to the **Uden CWGC Cemetery (qv)**. Listed here are **Flight Sergeant Fred Marean, RCAF, Sergeant Harry Bentley, RAF, Sergeant Charley Dyer, RAF, Sergeant William McLelland, RAF, Sergeant Walter Gosnell, RAFVR, Sergeant Bernard Singleton, RAFVR, and Sergeant George Benson, RAFVR.**

Return to the main road and turn right along Grafwegen. Continue as the road skirts the Reichswald Forest. Its left-hand edge is the German border.
There are bunkers in the Forest dating from 1917 and a narrow gauge railway was made to assist in their construction, built when, on declaration of unrestricted U-boat warfare, Germany, who had no reserves in the area, feared that neutral countries would enter the war. The railway was used by forestry workers in the 20s and 30s and was destroyed during MARKET-GARDEN.

Continue past the playing fields on the right and almost immediately stop just before a sign to 'Zandwinning Tuinen' (sandpit) opposite house No 44. Look in the ditch on the left.

• Royal Pioneer Corps and Other Units 1945 Monument, Milsbeek/37 kms/23.1 miles/5 minutes/Map 1N/4

This rare wartime monument was constructed by Royal Engineers in the area on 2 March 1945. The three stones bear the coats of arms of 2nd British Army (a cross on a shield) the Royal Corps of Pioneers, with the motto 'Labour conquers everything', and 707 Road Construction Company. It was restored by the District Water Board in the spring of 1989. The memorials commemorate Operation VERITABLE which began at 1030 hours on 8 February 1945. Because of the large numbers of vehicles that would be involved and the very wet weather, it was necessary substantially to improve the roads, a task requiring engineers and pioneers. The job was given to 13 AGRE who brought up as much as 600 tons a day of stone from Belgium. This was the area of assault of 51st Highland Division, attacking approximately from your right to your left. They faced a German anti-tank ditch and minefield which roughly ran along the edge of the forest.

Another RE memorial had been erected by 179 Special Field Coy on 23 August 1944 in the Normandy village of Tierceville. It is in the form of a gilded statue of Eros.

Continue into Milsbeek. Turn right on the N271 and immediately right just before the traffic lights towards Milsbeek Centrum. Continue over a series of sleeping policemen to the church and stop. Just past it is a green CWGC sign to the Cemetery to the left. Stop on the left and walk to the cemetery.

• Milsbeek CWGC Cemetery/38.7 kms/24.2 miles/15 minutes/Map 1N/5

This is the smallest CWGC Cemetery in the area. There are 210 burials, all British Army except 1 RM Commando and 1 RAAF. The majority are from February and March 1945 during the advance into Germany during Operation VERITABLE, but some are from September 1944. They include men from the 51st (Highland) Division, the 52nd (Lowland) Division and the 3rd Battalion, Irish Guards.

The MM was awarded to **Driver Charles Cole**, RASC, 22 September 1944 [II.D.12.]; **Serjeant William Dunlop** 1st Gordon Highlanders age 25, 13 February 1945 [II.G.12.] and **Corporal Arthur Townsend**, 5th HLI, age 20, 16 February 1945 [I.A.13.].

Walk towards the T-junction ahead to the memorial on the left corner.

• Milsbeek Civilian Memorial/38.7 kms/24.2 miles/5 minutes/Map 1N/6

The memorial bears the names of twenty-one inhabitants of Milsbeek who were killed during the war – as a consequence of forced labour, in concentration camps and other acts of war.

Return to the N271 and turn right. Continue to Plasmolen.

The village and the hills to the right were the scene of much bitter fighting on 20/21 and 27 September onwards when 325th Glider Infantry Regiment tried to take the Kiekberg Woods but ran into tenacious German defences.

Continue through Plasmolen (where there is a group of attractive restaurants) to Mook.

The village of Mook was taken by parachutists of the 505th PIR (82nd AB Division) on 17 September 1944. On 20 September two of Kurt Student's German combat teams attempted to break into the American lines both here and around Beek and Wyler. General Gavin, who

Plaque to Crew of Halifax,
St Jansberg

1945 Memorials to Royal Pioneer Corps and 707 Road
Construction Coy, Milsbeek

Milsbeek: CWGC Cemetery and Civilian Memorial

had been at the Maas River planning, with Reuben Tucker, the assault crossing scheduled for later that day, rushed from place to place encouraging his troops and while in Mook actually took part in a small arms action against the Germans. Assessing Mook as the greatest danger point, he reinforced Colonel Ekman's 505th with some Coldstream Guards and 300 glider pilots and the position held.

Enter Mook and 300m before the traffic lights turn right, signed to the CWGC Cemetery.
Continue over sleeping policemen to a T-junction. Turn right again following the CWGC sign
and stop immediately on the left.

• Mook CWGC Cemetery/45 kms/28.1 miles/15 minutes/Map 6/21

This is a most beautifully designed cemetery, with a graceful grassed approach and the rows
of graves leading up, past the Cross of Sacrifice, to the shelter at the top of the slope. It
contains 322 burials, mostly from the fighting nearby in September/October 1944 or during
the advance into Germany in February 1945. Casualties in the intervening period were from
artillery and patrol activity. There are 3 RN, 276 named and 11 Unknown UK Army, 3
Canadian and 3 Canadian Unknown, 11 Polish, 6 RAF and 1 Unknown, 4 RCAF, 3 RAAF
and 1 RNZAF.

To walk along the rows of headstones reading the private messages seems particularly
poignant here. For example the grave (which bears no religious emblem) of **Sapper J. C.
Woodhall,** RE, age 22, 17 February 1944, [1.A.16.] reads, 'Into the mosaic of Victory I place
this priceless jewel – my only son.' **Major Edward Andrews,** 1st HLI, age 23, 2 March 1945
[I.B.1.], was awarded the **MC**. The personal inscription on his headstone reads, 'One who
never turned his back but marched breast forward'. **The Welsh inscription** on the grave of
R. Hughes, RWF, age 25, 24 February 1945 [1.B.12.], *Heb un cledd Canu wnawn mewn hedd yn
y nefoedd dawel,* translates 'Without a
sword we shall sing in peace in the
tranquil heaven.'

Lieutenant Anthony Paget, 1st
Ox and Bucks, age 20, 5 March 1945
[I.C.12.], was awarded the **DSO,** the

Mook CWGC Cemetery and
headstones to an Aircrew and
Polish Pte Krzeczowski

Croix de Guerre and was **MiD**. He was the son of General Sir Bernard Paget, KCB, DSO, MC. **Private Jon Adams**, 4th KOSB, age 19, 18 February 1945 [II.C.15.], was awarded the **DCM**. **Lieutenant-Colonel George Dickson, Commanding the 7th RWF**, age 30, 6 March 1945, [1.C.14.] was awarded the **DSO**.

The **twin brother** of **Private Percival Ayres**, 7th Hants, age 21, 28 March 1945 [II.B.3.], Private Wilfred Ayres, 1st Hants, age 20, 6 June 1944, is buried in Bayeux Cemetery. **The brother of Serjeant Arthur Dudley**, 2nd KSLI, age 35, 7 October 1944 [I.E.10.], Acfn George Dudley, age 20, 19 August 1940, is buried in Chelmarsh (St Peter) Churchyard, Salop.

Private Leonard Osborne, 2nd R Warwicks, 5 March 1945, was only 17 [I.C.11.]. Buried together in 4.C. and all bearing the same date, 28 August 1942, is the aircrew **Mitchell and Peirce, Berrelt and Dobson** (in 2 joint graves) and between them **Lowrie**. Next to them is the Polish headstone of **Strzelec (Private) Mieczyslaw Krzeczowski**, 24 September 1944, who was killed in Oosterbeek and for some reason buried here with the inscription 'T. Cjczyzno'. This name could not be traced in Polish records but in 1988 Jan Lorys, one of Sosabowski's Staff Captains and a leading light in the Polish ex-Service community in London, explained that this meant 'For You My country'. With the help of his service number Krzeczkowski was finally identified and the headstone changed.

As in many of the Allied war cemeteries, individual graves here were 'adopted' by local people when the temporary crosses were changed to the standard headstone.

Walk over the road to the local cemetery and descend towards the right-hand wall of the cemetery. On the second row from the bottom is

• *Memorial to Mook Civilians killed on 19-20.9.44/45 kms/28.1 miles/10 minutes/Map 6/22*

In the fierce fighting around Mook in September 1944 the town hall, parsonage, schools and many other buildings were destroyed and eight inhabitants were killed. Five were hit by shellbursts in the shelters where they hid, three were hit when they tried to rescue livestock from their burning homes. By the evening of 20 September almost all the inhabitants had fled, only to return to their damaged village in April 1945. The memorial lists their names and bears the words of the poet, L. de Bourbon, which translate:

> *Victims of man's idle struggle*
> *No more blossom did their eyes see on earth*
> *But for the party God preserved for them*
> *Flowers will be in bloom perpetually.*

The road at the bottom of the cemetery is called General Gavinstraat.

Turn round and drive straight down to the traffic lights on the N271. Go straight over the road and park near the church and the VVV.

• *Mook-en-Middelaar Roman Catholic Churchyard/45.4 kms/28.4 miles/5 minutes/Map 6/20*

On the south of the church is the grave of Private Eric Holmes, 1st Suffolks, age 19, 8 October 1944.

Turn left along the N271 towards Nijmegen and continue under the railway.

The railway line goes over the Maas to the left. On 17 September 505th PIR, moving up from DZ N, reached the bridge only to find that the Germans had blown it.
Continue to Molenhoek.
On the right is the Van der Valk Motel de Molenhoek with excellent food. Tel: + (0) 24 3580155.
Just before the Motel turn left on the small road Molenstraat and stop by the memorial on the right by house No. 10.

• Site of Allied Wartime Cemetery, Van den Broek Brewery/47.7 kms /29.8 miles/5 minutes/Map 6/17

From 20 September 1944 the Allies buried their dead behind the nearby former brewery. The monument, unveiled on 17 September 1984 in the presence of General Gavin with prayers by the Rev George B. Wood, who parachuted into Groesbeek on 17 September as a divisional chaplain, commemorates 637 'gallant soldiers and airmen of the United States and British armed forces in the fall and winter of 1944 they gave their lives to liberate the Netherlands of Nazi tyranny'. In fact there were 836 burials here. All Saints' Day was celebrated here on 2 November 1944 in the cemetery which was closed four years later. A full description of this major cemetery, with the names of all originally buried here, and the circumstances of their death when known, can be found in *Vanished (Temp) Cemeteries* (qv) by Father Thuring and J. Hey. The Americans were repatriated or reburied in Margraten US Cemetery (qv) and the forty-one British and Commonwealth soldiers were reburied in Mook CWGC Cemetery (qv). The members of C Coy 307th AB Engineers originally buried here were killed rowing paratroopers across the Waal.

Memorial to site of Temp. Cemetery, Van den Broek Brewery, Molenhoek

Return to the N271 and turn left towards Nijmegen. Continue to the junction with the N844 signed to Nijmegen to the right.

• Extra Visits to Statue to Cuijk Civilians (Map 1N/2) and Jewish Memorial (Map 1N/3); Katwijk Dutch Soldiers Memorial (Map 6-18/19) and Memorial to James Martin and Crew of crashed C-47, Linden (Map 6/6).
Round trip approximately 26.4 kms/16.5 miles. Approximate time: 60 minutes

Take the N271 bridge over the Maas-Waal Canal and turn right onto the A73/E31 motorway direction Venlo. Take the first exit (No 4) to Cuijk, signed 2kms to the left on the N321. Continue to the roundabout. Turn right signed Vianen and then immediately

Extra visit continued

left signed to Cuijk on a cyclists' sign. Cross the railway line (8.8 kms/5.5 miles) and immediately turn right on Parallelweg. Continue to the Station on the right and park.

Opposite the station is a **Statue of the Good Samaritan** (9.1 kms/5.7 miles) sculpted by an anonymous Polish artist. It was presented to the town by the Association of Dutch present and former Shock Troopers to commemorate the inhabitants of Cuijk killed in the war. The statue has an interesting history. It was made from a piece of stone from the Berlin Reichstag and was originally destined as a gift for Pope Pius XII. The Russians would not open their zone border and, with the help of the Dutch director of the Charity Mission in Berlin, the statue found its way here and was erected on 28 July 1956. A pillar standing by the sculpture bears a plaque commemorating the Shock Troopers of Cuijk fallen 1946-1996. In 2000 there appeared to be something missing from the top of the pillar.

Continue, bearing left following the one-way system on Veldweg, Fraterstraat to the T-junction at Grotestraat. The VVV is then signed to the left. Turn right and immediately left on the short road Maasveld to the road which runs along the Maas. Turn left towards the large church and stop just before it.

Against the wall of the former synagogue on the left is the **Memorial to the Jewish Inhabitants of Cuijk** (10.1kms/6.3 miles) - twenty in number at the outbreak of war. Seven of them went underground, but the others were deported – the last four leaving on 9 April 1943 for the concentration camp at Vught (qv). All died in camps at Auschwitz, Sobibor or Vught. The memorial lists thirteen victims, with the camps in which they died. All were of the Cohen or Andriesse families. The memorial, by E. Hermans and erected on 2 May 1985, asks us to Remember and reflect on those who 'were taken away from us because they were Jews'.

Turn right under the bridge and left along the banks of the Maas signed Mook. Follow signs, turning right, into Katwijk. Turn right at the Y fork and drive to the banks of the Maas.

The Monument to 24 Dutch Soldiers on the right (13 kms/8.1 miles) is a 7-metre high sandstone obelisk, designed by A. M. van Breugel and erected on 17 July 1947. The soldiers were killed defending

Cuijk: Memorials to Civilians and old Jewish Synagogue

Extra visit continued

the sector of the 'Meuse Line' from Katwijk to the railway bridge near Gennep. Captain B. Hueting, who was commander of the company that was billeted in Cuijk in 1940, was one of the instigators of the monument. The inscription, which lists all the 24 – 1 Captain, 5 Sergeants, 9 Corporals and 9 soldiers, reads,

> From the citizens of Cuijk and surrounding districts, 2nd Battalion - 26 R.I. and P.T. Corps - to their comrades who fell on May 10th 1940 doing their duty in the unequal fight against the German conqueror.

The border region of the Netherlands had been mobilized on the Italian invasion of Albania on 10 April 1939. Full mobilization took place on 29 August 1939.

The railway bridge visible to the left is the Molenhoek Bridge, blown by the Germans on 17 September.

Turn round and go first right on Mariagaarde.

On the Mariagaarde churchyard to the right is a **Dutch Wargraves** sign. It relates to the graves of three Corporals of the 2nd Battalion, 26th Infantry Regiment in the cemetery.

Continue under the railway and over the water following signs to Linden past the Achtkant Stelling Mill on the right. Turn left, go straight over the next junction and under the A73 motorway. Continue to the church in Linden. Park and enter the churchyard.

Inside the wall to the left is a **plaque to the crew of a C-47** (16.5 kms/10.3 miles). The caption reads, 'Pray for the souls of James Martin and his comrades, fallen in this place on September 17th 1944.' Nobody now knows who erected this touching memorial.

On that day twelve series of forty-five C-47 Skytrains passed over carrying paratroopers to Groesbeek. Some of the slower planes were hit from positions on the Meuse-Waal Canal and the railway bridge near Mook. They all continued to fly in formation towards their DZs. One of the planes hit was being flown by James Martin. Nevertheless he managed to drop all his paratroops but one near the Wylerbaan (qv) and the plane crashed here. The five members of the crew were killed and Martin received a posthumous Flying Cross for his brave action. He is buried in Jefferson Barracks, St Louis, Missouri in common grave 84/153-155.

Turn round, return under the motorway and at the 1st junction turn right to Cuijk and Nijmegen.

On the left is the handily situated Van der Valk Hotel de Cuijk with café and restaurant. Tel: + (0) 485 335123.

Enter the A73 motorway direction Nijmegen. Take the first Exit (No 3) to Malden on the N271 and rejoin the main Itinerary (26.4 kms/16.5 miles).

Plaque to James Martin, Linden Churchyard

Do not continue on the N271 but turn right and continue through Malden on Rijksweg then St Annastraat. Continue to the next traffic lights.

• Extra Visits to the Hospitals of the 82nd (Map 6/12) and 101st AB Division (Map 6/9). Round trip approximately 4.5 kms/3.1 miles. Approximate time: 10 minutes.

Turn right at the second traffic lights onto Houtlaan and continue some 300m to the massive monastery building on the left.

This is the Berchmanianum, used in September 1944 as the **82nd AB Divisional Hospital.** Today it is a Retirement Home and a prior appointment must be made to visit it. Tel: + (0) 24 3838485. Fax: + (0) 24 3558712.

Continue to the roundabout, turn left and take the 1st street to the left after the tall multi-story building (Erasmuslaan) and follow it until it rejoins Annastraat. Turn right and continue to the 6th traffic light and turn left on Groenestraat. Turn left at the traffic lights on Dobbelmannweg. There is a big church on the left.

The vestry behind the church and the school on the left are all that remain of the buildings used as the **101st AB Hospital** from late September 1944 and during their period on The Island when 2,765 casualties were treated. The Hospital was plainly marked as such but on 29 October the Germans bombed it, killing three Medics and wounding six.

Continue to the traffic lights at the crossroads with Hatertseweg and turn left.

Continue to the junction with St Annastraat and pick up the main itinerary.

Continue to Keizer Karel Plein. Take the 1st exit to Centrum on Oranjesingel back to Keizer Traianus Plein, Nijmegen (57 kms/35.5 miles).

• End of Itinerary Three

2 bikes, 4 passengers

Cycles at Eindhoven Station

ITINERARY FOUR

NIJMEGEN CENTRE AND THE ISLAND

• **Itinerary Four** starts at the Valkhof, visits central Nijmegen's WW2 memorials, crosses the Waal road bridge and follows XXX Corps through The Island. It ends at Heteren.

• **The Route:** [Ideally, as driving in this busy city centre is difficult, much of the city route is better done on foot and, apart from the Waal Crossing OP, on a quiet Sunday.] Swing Memorial, City Hall Plaques, The Valkhof, Belvedere, Hunner Park, Jan van Hoof Statue, Jan van Hoof *Bas Relief*, German 3.7cm anti-tank gun, Grenadier Guards Plaque, Canadian Maple Tree Grove, Jewish Memorial, Civilian Memorial St Steven's Church, Memorial to Dutch Soldiers, Plein 1944, Belgian POWs Plaque, Waal Crossing Point, Jan van Hoof Execution Site, Titus Brandsma Memorials.

The Island: Lent - Memorial to Nuns of St Joseph Home Convent; Symbolic Tree Memorial, 'Robinson Tunnel'; Fort Hof van Holland; Memorial to 504th PIR River Crossing; Elst – Railway Workers Plaque, SLI/Worcesters/RDG Memorial, Executed Hostages, First Civilian Killed; Heteren – Allied Wargraves, The Island Museum, 101st US AB Division Memorial.

• **Extra Visits are suggested to:**

Memorials in the East of The Island: Bemmel – Jac Maris Liberation Monument, Family Costermans Plaque; Chapel of Remembrance, Haalderen Liberation Monument; Gendt Civilian Victims/Liberation Memorial; Doornenberg Phoenix Civilian Victims Memorial; Angeren - Memorial to Leijser Family, Memorial to Piet Kaak and Herman Scholten; Huissen - Civilian Mass Grave, Relief Operation to Civilians Plaque, Evacuation/Liberation *Bas Relief.*

Memorials in the West of The Island: Slijk-Ewijk – 101st AB Plaque, Allied Graves; Zetten – Liberation Monument, Plaques to Dutch Railway Worker and POW in Java; Dodewaard Memorial to the Fallen, Memorial to Crashed Dakota with Members of 156 Para MG Platoon and Pilot; Opheusden - Memorial to Piron Brigade, 101st AB Plaque; Kesteren Resistance Worker Column; Randwijk Memorial to the Fallen.

• **Planned duration,** without stops for refreshments or Extra Visits: 4 hours

• **Total distance:** 33 kms/20.6 miles

• *The Valkhof, Nijmegen/0 kilometres/0 miles/ RWC/OP/Map ***

Swing memorial to
Schoolchildren

Jan van Hoof Statue and Canadian
Plaque

Jan van Hoof bas relief, road
bridge

Grenadier Guards Plaque

Canadian Maple Trees

• *Main Walking tour of Nijmegen (approximate time: 75 minutes)*

Park in the underground Kelfkensbos car park at the Valkhof
This is an extremely clean and secure (by TV cameras) car park. Parking is Monday-Saturday 0800-0400. Sunday 1200-0400. There is an hourly charge, maximum 3 hours. By the exit are WCs, with a charge of 50cts.

Exit by the sign Uitgang [exit] Voerweg Kassa and up the escalator into the large open square

Jac Maris Statue to
Dutch WW2
Servicemen

Plaque to Belgian
POWs

Jewish Memorial

(which on Monday and Saturday mornings is a bustling market).
Turn left and walk towards along Kelfkensbos to the junction to Waalkade to the right. Cross
over the road and walk along Burchstraat towards the historic City Hall. Just before it turn left
on the upper level of the smart new shopping centre in Marikenstraat. Continue to the clearing
on the right.

• Swing Memorial to Accidental Victims of 22 February 1944 Bombing (Map 7/9)/City Hall Plaques (Map 7/8)

The memorial, surrounded by iron railings, was unveiled in 2000 in the presence of families
of the 762 victims, of whom 24 were children and 8 were Sisters of the Society of JMJ [Jesus,
Mary & Joseph] who were in the Infants' School on the Raadhuishof, who were killed in the
Allied raid. In particular memory of these children the memorial is in the form of a swing,
De Schommel, designed by Henk Visch.

Return to Burchstraat, turn left, continue past the medieval building of the City Hall and
immediately turn into the gate of the next building on the left.

In the gateway is a **Plaque to the Nijmegen citizens killed in Indonesia** 1945-1949. and
Plaques from MARKET-GARDEN Veterans Club and Operation VERITABLE Veterans.

Return towards the car park exit and walk towards the Valkhof Museum.

The Valkhof Museum of Art and Archaeology, which opened in June 1999, shows Roman

The Nijmegen road bridge, September 1944

art and artefacts with a Knights of St John section and art exhibitions.
Open Tuesday-Friday 1000-1700 hours, Saturday, Sunday, public holidays 1200-1700 hours. Includes café and shop. Tel: + (0) 24 360 8805.

Turn left through the ornamental wrought iron gates and over the small bridge.
This crosses the 15th Century original town walls, part of the second line of fortifications around the town, remnants of which can still be seen.

Walk into the wooded knoll.

• *Valkhof*

Here on Nijmegen's most historic site the Romans founded Oppidum Batavorum (city of the Batavians) and at the end of the 8th Century Charlemagne built a palace here. Later Roman Emperors expanded the fortress which Emperor Frederick Barbarossa refined in 1155. It was demolished in 1796. The ruins which may still be seen here are of the 16-sided St Nicolaas Chapel, which originated in 1030, and the 1155 St Maarten Chapel.

Walk to the viewing platform and face across the river.
The Waal Road Bridge dates from 1936. Before that all traffic had to cross the river by chain ferry (a Nijmegen invention) which was attached to a cable fixed upstream and which swayed to and fro as it crossed the river.

Of all the bridges over the major rivers which were the targets of the airborne forces, only the Nijmegen Bridge remained wholly under German control at the end of D-Day. Its capture had been the responsibility of 82nd AB Division, but General Browning's orders to General Gavin were that his first task was to seize and hold the Groesbeek Heights. There is no doubt that had the Americans gone for the bridge in force immediately after landing they would have taken it. But could they have held it against German counter-attacks mounted from Nijmegen and the Reichswald Forest until the Guards, delayed below Eindhoven, arrived?

Face the obvious church spire at Lent. That is at 12 o'clock. At 1 o'clock is the Nimegen road bridge. At 3 o'clock the road runs under the bridge and on the left of the viaduct arch is the Guards' Plaque (not visible from here). At 4 o'clock is the Belvedere Tower and just beyond it a grassed area called 'Hunner Park'. Two kms beyond and slightly to the right of it, but not visible, the Groesbeek Heights (covered by Itinerary Three) begin. From here the German border, marked by the western edge of the dense Reichswald Forest, is only 12kms away, beyond the tower. To General Browning it seemed possible that strong German forces were hidden in the Reichswald. Unless he controlled the Groesbeek Heights the Germans could attack his flank and cut off any paratroopers at the bridge. Thus his orders were: first the heights, then the bridge. General Gavin did not agree. With his airborne experience he felt that the key was to capture the bridge. Therefore, before 82nd AB left England, he ordered Colonel Lindquist, commanding 508th PIR, to send one of his battalions directly to the bridge after landing. That is what General 'Slim Jim' Gavin remembers. Colonel Lindquist retrospectively disagreed, saying that he was told to take an objective in the town. Curiously, the records of interviews which were carried out at the time with men who took part in order to settle the matter cannot be found in US Army files. It was not until evening that Gavin realised that no attempt had been made to take the bridge and he told Lindquist 'to delay not a second longer and get to the bridge as quickly as possible'. In all it was to be some 8 hours after landing before any significant attempt to take the bridge began and, by that time, the quick-reacting Field-Marshal Model had sent troops of 9th and 10th SS Pz Division into Nijmegen. The force around the bridge and Hunner Park was later estimated to have been increased from eighteen men at the time the Americans landed to over 400 SS troops, with an 88mm gun where the Jan van Hoof Resistance Memorial in Keizer Traianus Plein now stands, and five 47mm weapons around Hunner Park. There can be little doubt that had Gavin's orders been followed, the bridge – or at least its southern end - would have been taken that day.

The 508th PIR had dropped between Groesbeek and Berg en Dal, some 7 kms east from here beyond the Belvedere, and so their assault came in from that direction (see the Holts' Map.) The main body got no further than Keizer Karel Plein reaching it around 2200 hours just as the 9th and 10th SS Pz forces arrived at the southern end of the bridge. One platoon of the 508th did get to the Post Office building (qv). The next attack, again by 508th PIR, began at 0715 hours on 18 September and en route through the streets the Americans were showered with fruit and flowers by Dutch civilians. The attack was stopped by the SS at Hunner Park. Generals Gavin and Browning plotted another attempt for the afternoon of 18 September, but Browning called it off because he considered that holding the high ground around Groesbeek was more important. One may feel that he was wrong and that General Gavin's instincts were right, but, on the afternoon of 18 September the Guards, who were supposed to cross Nijmegen Bridge, were still south of Eindhoven, more than 40kms away, and there was no news from Arnhem. That night the Germans, using petrol cans and grenades, set fire to hundreds of houses in the bridge area, thus it was not until the afternoon of the following day, the 19th, that the next attempt to take the road bridge was made.

The Grenadier Guards Group (i.e. tanks and infantry) arrived in the area of the Sionshof (qv) around midday on 19 September having crossed the bridge at Heumen. General Horrocks had set up his XXX Corps HQ in the schoolhouse in Malden (see Holts' Map) and Browning had pressurized Gavin that 'the Nijmegen bridge must be taken today. At the latest tomorrow.' Horrocks, Gavin and General Alan Adair, commanding the Guards

Armoured Division, held an immediate conference whose outcome is clouded in differing British and American interpretations – as is the story of much of the fighting in and around Nijmegen where the authors, in reading national accounts of what happened, often wondered if they were talking about the same battle. In essence it was decided that a three-pronged attack would be made using British tanks and American paratroopers. One column was to take the road bridge, one the railway bridge and the third the Post Office in Nijmegen centre. The Dutch liaison officer insisted that the apparatus for blowing up the road bridge was there, although the 508th had destroyed some apparatus there on the 17th, but, as they had been cut off by the Germans, that information cannot have got through to the Grenadiers. The first, main bridge, column, consisting of a company and a squadron of Grenadiers plus most of the 2nd Battalion of Colonel Vandervoort's 2nd Battalion of the 505th PIR and supported by Typhoons, moved off at 1530 hours up Nijmeegsebaan (the road leading north from the Sionshof) onto Groesbeekseweg. Then, led by Dutch guides, they went via smaller roads north-east to the edge of Keizer Traianus Plein where the Belvoir Hotel now stands (in 1944 the area was known as the Keizer Lodewijk roundabout) leaving them barely 300m from the bridge. The Germans opened fire with two self-propelled guns and several anti-tank guns plus infantry small arms fire. The leading tank was knocked out and two more damaged, killing the troop leader Lieutenant J. A. Moller who is buried in Jonkerbos CWGC [22.F.1.]. The Grenadiers and Americans took to the buildings and, under cover of small arms fire, attempted to outflank the German defenders, but as night fell they had made no more progress.

The second column, of Grenadiers plus D Company of the 2nd Battalion of the 505th which was heading for the railway bridge led by Captain J. Neville, were stopped short of their objective by a Panther tank and ended up isolated amongst German infantry and burning buildings to the west of the railway bridge. It would be 48 hours before they were reunited with the main force.

The third column, heading for the Post Office and led by Major G. Thorne, was made up from two platoons of infantry and one troop of tanks from the Grenadiers plus a platoon of US paratroopers plucked off the road by General Gavin. They, unlike the other two columns, made it to their objective which was unoccupied. Thorne occupied the building and, apart from a foray towards the road bridge, which was repulsed, remained there overnight.

Thus up to this point four unsuccessful attempts had been made to take the road bridge. Firstly the lost American 508th platoon-strength patrol of 17 September, secondly the 508th company-strength attack that evening that had reached the Post Office, thirdly the 508th company-strength attack at 0745 on 18 September that got within striking distance of Keizer Traianus Plein and fourthly the combined Grenadier and US attacks of the afternoon of 19 September.

Once more 24 hours passed before the next assault, but this time, however, it succeeded. Colonel Reuben Tucker's 504th PIR made their magnificent assault across the river at 1500 hours on Wednesday 20 September. This assault is described below, but the Guards too were to face some of the fiercest fighting of the campaign over the next few hours. The Grenadiers, whose aim was to take the bridge, came up with a plan to surprise the Germans. They reasoned that the defenders would not expect an attack to come from the city centre. At 0830 hours (on the 20th) the Grenadiers began to fight their way through the maze of small streets to the west of the Valkhof. At 1530, now in their assault positions, they launched a three-pronged attack – one company (the King's) to take the Valkhof, another to take Hunner Park and elements of US PIRs on the far right to take the ground beyond the Keizer Traianus Plein roundabout. The Valkhof defenders were taken completely by surprise and two platoons of Grenadiers climbed into the position before the Germans knew that an attack had begun. Five minutes of hand-to-hand fighting left the Valkhof in Grenadier hands, though Captain The Hon Vicary Paul Gibbs ((qv), the 23-year-old company commander, was killed. He is now buried in Jonkerbos CWGC Cemetery, [22.G.4.] having first been buried at the Nebo Seminary at the Sionshof ((qv). Now overlooking the bridge defences, they began to fire upon the Germans dug in along the river bank while in the centre, with tank support and using smoke and phosphorus grenades, the Grenadier force was able to send a patrol down onto the bridge. It was clear. Sadly the patrol commander, Lieutenant Peter Michael Benson Greenall, was killed by a German rushing over the bridge in a side-car. He is buried next to Vicary Gibbs [22.G.3.] in Jonkerbos but his date of death is recorded as 21 September. At last, after four days of trying, the southern end of the Nijmegen road bridge had been taken.

Now it was time to get across. The Red Berets at Arnhem had been isolated for three days, one day longer than they were supposed to hold on. Would it not seem vital, if the operation were to succeed, to press on immediately once the bridge was taken? Apparently not, because after crossing the bridge the Grenadiers would wait until the following morning, the 21st, before going on. As the Americans frequently claimed about the British, 'They had stopped for tea'. Had they?

Walk back over the small bridge, turn left and follow the path by the corner of the museum round to the platform below the tower.

• Belvedere OP

The original Belvedere, forming part of the old city walls, was built in the 15th Century. Today it is a restaurant. Tel: + (0) 24 322 6861. Lunch by appointment. Dinner daily from 1800 hours.

Ahead is the Nijmegen road bridge over the Waal, built in 1936. To the left of its span the spire of Lent Church can be seen over the river. To its right, on the horizon, the Arnhem TV Tower at Den Brink can be seen on a clear day.

Sergeant Peter Robinson and his troop of Grenadiers crossed this bridge around 1830 hours on Wednesday 20 September, just 10 hours before the tenacious survivors of 2 Para were finally forced off the bridge at Arnhem. The Arnhem bridge is on the horizon (not visible) in the area just to the right of the Den Brink Tower. Looking at the panorama ahead, one can speculate what would have happened if the Grenadiers had kept going, once over the bridge ahead, as Colonel Tucker had wanted them to do. Would they have reached Arnhem, or would the Regiment have been wiped out and the bridge lost? The argument can never be resolved. What is certain is that the Americans and British who fought to take the bridge exhibited extraordinary courage. Sergeant Robinson, peering out of the top of his Firefly (Sherman tank), led his troop 40ms onto the bridge and was hit. His radio failed, so he changed tanks and continued. Under a hail of grenades and small arms fire from German soldiers firing from the bridge girders, he and his Troop Sergeant slewed past a barrier pole and a barricade, shooting up a German 88mm gun which was placed by the northern approach, and continued north to The Tunnel (qv). In a way the Grenadiers' attack on the bridge, though successful, may have been a mistake, because it was made on the assumption that the Americans held the northern end. They did not.

Return towards the museum and turn left under the bridge and then right into the park, heading for the roundabout. At the edge is

• *Hunner Park Time Capsule/Map 7/13*

This is in a raised, circular area, surrounded by a small brick wall. It contains a 'Time Capsule' with information on Operation MARKET-GARDEN which was sealed in September 1974. It will not be opened until September 2044.

The great roundabout area ahead is called Keizer Traianus Plein. In September 1944 this square was the scene of very heavy hand-to-hand fighting with bayonet and even spade and many were killed here. On the far side is a statue of the Emperor Trajan who granted Nijmegen official market rights in c104AD, thus making Noviomagus the first township on Dutch soil. In the centre of the roundabout, crossed to after descending the steps from the Time Capsule and carefully watching traffic from the left, is

• *Jan van Hoof/Resistance Statue/Maple Tree/Map 7/14*

In 1944 Jan van Hoof (qv) was a student and member of the Dutch Secret Service. He gathered much precise information about the Waal bridges and the explosives planted beneath them. He became Nijmegen's best-known resistance worker, credited with the saving of the Nijmegen road bridge, yet was the object of some controversy. The story is that van Hoof was sent into Nijmegen with the 82nd AB Division and was said to have defused the demolition charges on the bridge by penetrating the German lines to cross the bridge to the detonators on the Lent side. A local committee was set up in 1949 to investigate the verity of the action. It was satisfied that he did actually cut some cables and Jan van Hoof was awarded Holland's highest award for gallantry, the Military Order of William. His citation claims that he alone carried out 'the task of disabling the means of detonation with danger to his own life'. After the war the citizens of Nijmegen raised money to erect a monument, not only to van Hoof, who was shot by the Germans on 19 September (qv), but to all those who were killed during Nijmegen's liberation. The bronze standard bearer statue that Marius van Beek designed was erected here on 17 September 1954. Annual commemorations take place here.

Beside the statue is a Canadian Maple Leaf Tree, planted on 5 May 1995, 50 years after the Liberation of the Netherlands by Canadian troops 'and a new tulip was named 'Canadian Veteran' as a symbol of friendship between Holland and Canada'.

Walk across the series of pedestrian crossings controlled by traffic lights to the footpath (and beware, it is also a cycle path) on the right hand side of the bridge, turn left and walk along the bridge to the circular indentation at the far end of the bridge span.

• *Bas relief by Jac Maris to Jan van Hoof/Map 1N/8*

One of the first Dutch memorials to be erected after the war and sculpted by Jac Maris (qv) its inscription reads, 'To Jan van Hoof: his comrades. September 18th 1945. Nijmegen war veterans.' It depicts van Hoof de-activating the explosives on the bridge on 18 September 1944.

Return to Hunner Park, walk back up the steps and follow the path down towards the river skirting the base of the Belvedere.
On the left is passed, on a raised platform,

• German Gun /Map 7/12

This German 50mm anti-tank Panzerabwehr Kanone 38 is a relic of the fierce fighting for the Waal road bridge. From 17 September successive attacks on Hunner Park were repulsed by the Germans. About 1530 hours on 20 September the Valkhof and Hunner Park were attacked from three sides by Grenadiers and US paratroopers and at about 1800 hours the park, riddled with trenches, protected by an anti-tank wall and with anti-tank guns, and the bridge, were in Allied hands (see account above).

Below the gun is the Nijmegen Coat of Arms which in season is a beautiful floral display. *Continue to the river bank.*
To the left is the Railway Bridge. In 1983 the current single-span bridge replaced the three-span bridge built in 1878. Beyond it the chimneys of the factory and then the power station can be seen. Note the power cables crossing the river. It was at this point that the Waal crossing was made by 504th PIR (qv).

As the Grenadiers crossed the road bridge to your right **Captain A. (Tony) G. C. Jones, RE**, followed in his Humber scout car immediately behind the four tanks. His task was to defuse demolition charges. He told his own story of what happened just as the last tanks went through the road block.

A PERSONAL ACCOUNT
Captain A.G.C. Jones
    I was on the second span from the northern end of the bridge. I got out of my car and told the [wireless] operator to take over the Bren gun. The first thing I saw as I got out of the car was about half a dozen wires on the footway at the side of the bridge. These I cut. I walked up to the road block and saw about ten Tellermines 35 in a slit trench near it. These were obviously designed to close the block. I removed the igniters and threw them in the river.
    I then ordered my driver to turn the car round and walked back over the bridge until I came to a set of charges lying on the footpath at each side of the bridge just to the north of the second pier from the north end of the bridge. These had been designed to cut the concrete roadway but had never been placed in position and were quite safe.

Jones then collected seven German prisoners who appeared from behind various arches and took them back and reported that the bridge was clear. The rest of his troop was sent forward under Lieutenant Vivian and he returned to the northern end of the bridge where, with Vivian, he went down into the bridge piers. They found TNT packed in green painted boxes labelled with serial numbers relating to those painted on the girders. These were fitted with electric detonators and were connected to one of the wires that Jones had cut earlier. They removed them and went on to check the rest of the bridge. As they finished they met American soldiers who had just killed an SS officer who had shot at them from the bridge arch, an action wrongly shown in the film *A Bridge Too Far* as having happened before the Grenadiers crossed the bridge. Jones and Vivian ended up with a total of eighty-one prisoners.

It is inexplicable that Captain Jones did not receive the Victoria Cross for his acts of supreme bravery. In his book, *Corps Commander*, Sir Brian Horrocks, when talking of the Americans who had made the river crossing (he mistakenly identified them as men of the 505th – they were actually 504th) and Peter Robinson and his men who made the dramatic crossing of the road bridge, wrote of Tony Jones, 'Perhaps the bravest of all these very brave men was Lieut. Jones a young Sapper officer.'

Eight days later, on 28 September, twelve German frogmen blew a 20m hole in the road bridge and destroyed one of the piers of the railway bridge. The swimmers, pushing six floating naval mines, had entered the river 11 kms upstream from Nijmegen. Only eight survived. The road bridge was repaired and reopened within 48 hours.

Walk to the left of the arch under the bridge. On the wall is

• Memorial Plaque to the Grenadier Guards/Map 7/10

The bronze plaque with the badge of the Guards Armoured Division, erected on 18 September 1994, the 50th Anniversary, and unveiled by Lord Carrington (qv), commemorates the capture of the road bridge by the Grenadier Guards. The tunnel is called Grenadier Guards Viaduct.

Walk back across the road and continue uphill with the Nijmegen Coat of Arms to the left. Bordering the flower garden is a grove of trees.

• Canadian Maple Trees/Map 7/11

A bronze plaque, in the vegetation in the centre of the double line of trees, records that 'These forty [now reduced to just over thirty trees] Sugar Maple trees are presented on behalf of the Province of Ontario, Canada, to the City of Nijmegen by the "We Do Remember" National Committee on the occasion of the thirty-fifth Anniversary of V.E. Day [7 May]. 1945-1980.' After the area was taken in September 1944 the Canadians remained in Nijmegen and this 'living monument' of the national symbol of Canada commemorates their stay and Victory in Europe.

Return to your car, exit from the car park, setting your odometer to '0'. Follow the one-way system round the Keizer Traianus Roundabout signed Waalkade and Casino and return past the Museum and open square. Turn right and drive down to the Waalkade, the road running along the Waal, and turn left towards the railway bridge past the Casino. Continue over the small roundabout and park as soon as possible in the spaces on the left (1.3 kms/.8 miles).

• Short Walking Tour of Nijmegen (approximate time: 20 minutes)

Walk to the left and up Priemstraat to the small square at the end of Nonnenstraat. The square has a plaque to 'Kitty de Wijzeplaats 1920-1942 Killed in Auschwitz.' Here is the old Jewish Synagogue, built in 1756. In 1814 Henriette, the daughter of the then Cantor, Isaac Presburg, married the father of Karl Marx, founder of 'Marxism'. Another daughter, Sophie, married Leon Philips in 1820. Their son was one of the founders of the Philips light bulb factory in Eindhoven in 1891. Next to the synagogue building is the former Jewish School built in 1873. In the centre of the square is

• Jewish Memorial/Map 7/5

Designed by Paul de Swaaf, this sculpture of a mourning lady looking towards the old Jewish Schul, was unveiled in 1995. The figure stands beneath a tree and is surrounded by railings in which there are Stars of David. Within the railings is a plaque which reads, 'Kom vanavond met verhalen hoe de oorlog is verdwenen en herhaal ze duizend malen alle malen zal ik wenen.' These are lines by the Dutch poet, Leo Roman, which translate, 'Tonight come with stories of how the war has faded away and repeat them a thousand times. I will weep every time.'

Walk up the Noorderkerktrappen steps to Saint Steven's Church and round the wall to the left. At the base of the tower is

• Monument to Civilian Victims/Map 7/6

Designed by Mari Andriessom and erected on 17 September 1979, the winged figure commemorates all the citizens of Nijmegen killed between 1940 and 1945. Around 400 people died in the first years of the war, then the American bombing of Nijmegen of 22 February 1944 resulted in about 750 casualties. Another 750 or so were killed during the period when Nijmegen was a front line town from September 1944-March 1945.

The townspeople requested a National Monument (an officially designated memorial) to remember their dead. From October 1945 until into the Sixties one Central Committee and eleven Provincial Committees vetted all designs submitted as National Monuments. Their aim was to prevent a spate of well-intentioned but 'unworthy' memorials being erected. This memorial was rejected, as was the plan to erect a Commemorative Cross on Hatertseweg and a memorial for fallen sportsmen in the Goffert Stadium.

Walk to the right down Ganzenheuvel and continue on Houtstraat into Plein 1944. The memorial is in the far right hand corner of the Square.

• Statue to Dutch WW2 Servicemen/Map 7/7

Designed by Jac Maris (qv), this monument of a soldier kneeling beside his wounded comrade commemorates Dutch forces killed during WW2 - an estimated 2,300 soldiers (killed in the German attacks of May 1940) and 2,900 sailors who served with the Royal Navy. It was erected on 5 May 1951 when the name of the square was changed from Koning Hendrikplein to Plein 1944, in memory of the Liberation of Nijmegen. After other requests for a National Monument for Nijmegen had been turned down (see above), this was the one that was finally approved. Maris described it thus,

In the trench I am protecting my comrade. He has been shot down. I am ready to fire. I'll stay here until someone comes to his aid. Solidarity! If you want to protect your comrade who has fallen, and you cannot take care of him, you hold him, but you also crouch down for anything that may come.

Return to your car and continue past the area where the road widens into a square.
This is the site of the Old Harbour, once contained within the town walls. It was filled in

when the walls were demolished in 1874 to make room for expansion. It was at this stage that the wide boulevards fanning out from the hub of Keizer Karel Plein were laid out.
Continue to within about 300m of the railway bridge and park on the right opposite a plaque on the wall to the left.

• Plaque to Belgian POWs, Waalkade/1.6 kms/1 mile/5 minutes/ Map 7/2

The inscription on the plaque reads,

> In May-June 1940 the citizens of Nijmegen spontaneously rendered assistance to tens of thousands of Belgian prisoners of war on their way to Nazi camps in cramped Rhine barges.

It was erected on 16 May 1992 by the National Belgian Federation of ex-Prisoners of War.

Between 30 May and 5 June ninety barges, packed with a quarter of a million Belgian POWs, were moored at the Waal quay. The road bridge had been blown up on 10 May and was lying in the water, blocking their way to the camps in Germany. Citizens from the surrounding districts of Nijmegen provided the starving prisoners with bread, water, milk and medical care. This, one of the first acts of resistance in newly-occupied Holland, was quickly forbidden.

Follow the road round the Veemarkt and turn right under the railway bridge and at the traffic lights right again following signs to Weurt/Noord Kanaal-haven. Continue to the right turn Winselingseweg opposite playing fields. Turn with the power station building on the left and continue to the end of the road with the v.d. Stadt building and the Noviant Chemicals security gate ahead. Stop. Leave your car.

N.B. To reach the wonderful OP at the edge of the river overlooking the crossing point it is necessary to apply to the security officer and hope that he speaks English and will open the gate for you! The resultant view is well worth the effort. Note that the gate is not manned on a Sunday when only a limited view of the crossing point and Lent church are visible from behind it.

• Waal Crossing Point/4.3 kms/2.7 miles/10 minutes/Map 1N/8a/OP

The crossing took place to the left, immediately below the power line cables. With the pylons on the far bank at 12 o'clock, the Fort Hof Van Holland is at 1 o'clock, Lent Church is at 2 o'clock and the railway and road bridges beyond it are at 3 o'clock.

The task of crossing the Waal here was given to Major Julian A. Cook's 3rd Battalion, 504th PIR. The attack was delayed while they waited for British assault boats to arrive. The weather, which had grounded most of the tactical air support in previous days, lifted sufficiently for rocket-firing Typhoons to pound German positions on the north bank at 1430 hours. As they were low on fuel they could not wait for the crossing to be launched and returned to their base in Brussels. Fifteen minutes before H-Hour, twelve guns of 376th Para Field Artillery Battalion and 153rd Field Regiment, RA bombarded the far bank. At 1500 hours the Americans pushed off from the banks in front of you, the current swinging the small boats to the left. The Germans opened fire from the dyke with machine guns and 20mm cannon from Fort Van Holland, following the furiously paddling Americans onto the far bank below the power lines. Away to the right heavy enfilade fire from the railway bridge caught the boats. Later, more than thirty machine guns were found on the bridge. Despite supporting fire from tanks of the 2nd Battalion Irish Guards, which were strung side by side along the bank from here towards the bridge, as well as mortars of the 504th, only thirteen (some reports say ten) boats were fit to return to pick up the second wave. The surface of the river, as one paratrooper remembered it, was packed with machine-gun fire like 'a school of mackerel on the feed'. Six times the crossing was made between H-Hour and 1900 hours. The American losses are detailed at their Memorial below. An extremely detailed, almost minute by minute, account of the crossing is to be found in WAALCROSSING by Father Thuring, Frank van den Bergh, L. Zwaaf and J. Thuring, published by the Groesbeek National Liberation Museum in 1991.

The 504th PIR assault against murderous machine-gun fire was described by General Horrocks, who watched both them and Peter Robinson's crossing from the roof of the power station, as 'the best attack that I ever saw carried out in the whole war'. He wanted to award British medals to them and during the war the men of the 82nd were to win six MCs, eleven MMs, two DSOs and twenty-three DCMs. Also watching from the ninth floor of the power station were General Browning, Lieutenant-Colonel Giles Vandeleur and his adjutant Captain J. V. Taylor, who remembered not just the 'calmness and courage shown by men of the 504 Combat Team' but also 'the muzzle flashes of the German guns from somewhere in the area of Elst and the shells landing among the attacking troops and the tanks'.

Captain T. Moffatt Burriss was a wartime soldier who had served with the 82nd in Sicily and at Anzio before dropping into Holland. After the war he became a successful businessman then a politician, serving in the South Carolina House of Representatives for 15 years. In 1999, in response to requests from his children to tell them about his war, he wrote *Strike and Hold*, an account of his experiences. The narratives here [and later] are based upon his book and upon conversations with him, and cover the period from the time when the Americans were briefed by General Horrocks to make the highly dangerous daylight assault crossing of the river to his arrival on the opposite bank.

A PERSONAL ACCOUNT
By Captain T. Moffatt Burriss, 504th PIR

The British general asked, 'What do you think? Can you do it?'

Colonel Tucker asked him, 'If we take the bridge, what assurance do we have that your troops will get to Arnhem immediately?'

General Horrocks replied, 'My tanks will be lined up in full force at the bridge ready to go hell bent for Arnhem. Nothing will stop them.' All of us took this as a solemn pledge...

The British were to supply us with assault boats – paddleboats rather than motorboats – and they promised to deliver them by 1100.... We watched 1100 come and go, then 1200, then 1300. The British paratroopers at Arnhem were running out of time....When we saw the boats we were stunned. They were flimsy, collapsible canvas boats that looked as if they wouldn't make it across a swimming pool...'OK men' Major Cook said, 'use your rifle butts as paddles.' It was like a Laurel and Hardy movie, only with real lives at stake – hundreds of lives. We would be crossing the river in clumsy flat-bottomed boats propelled by makeshift paddles while the Germans were firing at us with virtually every weapon at their disposal.

Personal account continued

We heard the drone of tanks (Irish Guards) and saw them swing into place right behind us. Then they opened fire on the enemy positions across the river. As soon as we launched the first boats, mine among them, chaos reigned... several boats were swept downstream before everyone could scramble onboard... two or three boats capsized...others were stuck in the muddy embankment. German shells began landing nearby. Finally, God only knows how, we got everybody on boats and started paddling across the river. When we were a third of the way across, the river suddenly exploded. As the Krauts unleashed their full firepower the surface of the water looked like it was in the middle of a sudden rainstorm, the sky actually hailing bullets... men began to slump forward in their boats. Some screamed, but most went silently... one, two then three boats sustained direct hits from mortar shells and disintegrated in a burst of flame, with bodies cast in all directions... I was sitting on the stern of the boat next to the engineer... 'Captain', he said, 'take the rudder. I've been hit.' Just as I reached for the rudder he leaned forward and caught a 20mm high-explosive shell through his head... . As I watched his body float downstream I could see the red blood streaming from what was left of his head... .

We landed and piled ashore.... . 'OK men,' I shouted, 'Lets go. Straight ahead for the dyke.' The [German] machine gunners shifted their fire from the boats to the charging ground troops...men began to drop on both sides of me... several of us... reached the front side of the dyke and were now safe from the machine guns on the back side... . 'Use your grenades', I yelled... . The earth underneath us trembled with the almost simultaneous explosions. Then there was a moment of silence in front, followed by the screams of wounded Krauts. All along the line, other German gunners stood up ready to surrender. But it was too late.

Our men, in a frenzy over the wholesale slaughter of their buddies, continued to fire until every German on the dyke lay dead or dying.

The Americans rallied into small groups and then, with grenade and bayonet, took the dyke and the Fort

Return to the railway tunnel and drive under it to J. Ivens Plein. Drive along the side of the square into Parkweg ahead and as the road turns right park on the left as soon as possible. Walk back to the near corner of the square. Flat in the ground is a plaque to

• Site of Jan van Hoof Execution/5.9 kms/3.7 miles/5 minutes/Map 7/1

On 19 September Jan van Hoof appeared at the Sionshof Hotel with sketches of the German

fortifications in the vicinity of the Waal Bridge. At first he refused to guide a reconnaissance vehicle into Nijmegen, but later that same afternoon agreed to conduct a Humber scout car of the Grenadier Guards through the centre of the town from the Post Office towards the rail bridge. As the vehicle entered the Nieuwe Markt it was hit by a

Site of Jan van Hoof
execution, J. Ivens Plein

Titus Brandsma:
Memorial and mosiac
detail on Chapel

Lent: Huize St Josef
with Plaque to
Sisters of Divine
Providence and
Symbolic tree

German gun and caught fire. Lance-Serjeant William T. Berry RE and Grenadier Guardsman Albert Shaw were shot and almost immediately died of their wounds. They were buried in a field grave and reburied in Jonkerbos CWGC Cemetery (qv) but with the wrong date of 21 September 1944. Van Hoof survived the attack but was picked up by the Germans, tortured and shot at this spot.

The stone was laid on 19 September 1945. This, with the *bas relief* to van Hoof (qv) on the Nijmegen Bridge, was the first Dutch memorial to be erected.

The square also contains a large sculpture to the movie-maker Joris Ivens, who was born in Nijmegen.

Return to your car and continue along Parkweg.

On the right is the Kronenburger Park, laid out in the 'English style' in 1880 and unique in Holland for its 150 varieties of trees and deer park.

Continue to the open parking space on Kroonstraat on the left. Stop.

Here is

• **Memorial to Titus Brandsma** (6.2 kms/3.9 miles) designed by P. Dijkema and Frans Verhaak. As an adviser to the Roman Catholic

Association of Journalists and a Professor at the University, Brandsma opposed German propaganda. He died in Dachau on 26 July 1942. The dramatic, tall white memorial represents the machine guns mounted on high posts at the edge of the concentration camp and the Chapel behind is shaped like a camp block. Above its door is a mosaic of the Virgin Mary and Baby Jesus and the name TITUS BRANDSMA around it. In 2000 plans to develop the area, which had resulted in the boarding up of the Chapel, were dropped, but it has yet to be renovated.

Turn left on Doddendaal and then right on Regulierstraat which becomes V. Berchen and continue to the traffic lights. Turn left along Nassausingel following signs to Arnhem to Keizer Karel Plein, go round the roundabout and return to Keizer Traianus Plein. Follow signs to Arnhem and drive over the bridge.

You are now in the area known by the Allies in 1944/45 as 'The Island' and by the locals as Manneneiland [Men's Island] because of the large number of men hidden in the area during the Occupation and particularly during the battles that raged from September 1944 through the following months. Its correct current local name is the **Over-Betuwe**. The Island was largely flooded in December 1944 when all the inhabitants had been evacuated.

Pass the Lent-West exit.

300m past this exit sign is a bunker on the right. This was built by the Dutch prior to WW2.

There is a story that on 17 September the German officer responsible for blowing up the bridge was in the bunker and that he remained undiscovered for some days. Much argument revolves around why the Germans did not blow the bridge once they learned of the airborne landing: they probably wished to keep it intact to use in a counter-attack.

Take the next exit signed Lent.

N.B. The whole aspect of the river bank round Lent will alter drastically when radical changes planned to the course of the Waal and new housing developments are effected. In March 2001 250 live shells were found on one building site alone.

Turn right signed Bemmel and first right on Schoolstraat. Continue to the large Huize St Jozef building on the right. Park and walk to the entrance. To the left of the door is

• *Plaque to the Sisters of Divine Providence, Lent/10.6 kms /6.6 miles/5 minutes/Map 1N/13*

When the inhabitants of The Island were evacuated in September 1944, the only remaining civilians in what was the Convent (then an Allied HQ) were ten Dutch and German nuns. The doors were open 24 hours a day to straggling refugees and the wounded. The nuns provided temporary shelter, tended the wounded and sometimes cooked for as many as 500 people. The bronze plaque, inaugurated on 24 November 1947, bears the image of the Good Samaritan.

Turn round, return to the junction and turn right along Laauwickstraat and then 1st left at the junction with Lentseveld and stop by the school.

• *Symbolic Tree Memorial, Lent/10.7 kms/6.7 miles/5 minutes/Map 1N/14*

Erected on 20 September 1969, this stylized tree by Jan Schoenmakers bears the inscription, 'From the stump a new tree grew. In remembrance of 1944.' It consists of a dead black branch shaped like a bridge, symbolizing the dark war years.

- **Extra Visit to Memorials in the East of The Island: Bemmel - Jac Maris Liberation Monument, Family Costermans Plaque, Chapel of Remembrance; Haalderen Liberation Monument; Gendt Civilian Victims/Liberation Memorial; Doornenberg Phoenix Civilian Victims Memorial; Angeren - Memorial to Leijser Family, Memorial to Piet Kaak and Herman Scholten; Huissen - Civilian Mass Grave, Relief Operation to Civilians Plaque, Evacuation/Liberation Bas Relief.**

Round trip: 13.3 kilometres/8.3 miles. Approximate time: 75 minutes.

Continue along Laauwickstraat direction Bemmel and follow the winding road into Bemmel.

Bemmel. From 21-25 September 1944 the area to the west of the main Lent-Elst road was the scene of bitter fighting between the British tanks and the strong German opposition centred around Oosterhout. The Allied breakout occurred on the 24th when Wessen was taken and contact was made with the Welsh Guards who had been attempting to push through to Bemmel since the 22nd. That evening 69th Infantry Brigade arrived to reinforce them and the tanks, together with the 5th E Yorks, finally took Bemmel when the Germans abandoned it. A brigade thrust was then made which pushed the Germans back to the line Halderen-Baal-Rijkersworerd.

After a heavy German shelling attack on 29 September the inhabitants of Bemmel were mostly evacuated (only a few men remaining) to Ressen, Valburg and Ewijk. On 15 November the evacuation was completed.

Turn right on Loostraat towards Centrum and right at the traffic lights signed VVV/Gemeentehuis. Turn right signed VVV along Kinkelenburglaan.

In the park in front of it is a dramatic bronze **Liberation Statue by Jac Maris** (qv) (Map 1N/15) (4 kms/2.5 miles) depicting a man rising from the debris of a destroyed town and crying, 'Why me?' It was erected on 4 May 1957.

Turn round, return to Dorpstraat, turn right and turn first left on Leemkuilselaan. Continue to the end of the road and follow it as it bears left and stop by the first house on the right, No 1 (4.3 kms/2.7 miles).

N.B. Remember that this is a private house.

On the wall by the steps to the cellar to the left of the front door is a **Plaque to the six members of the Costermans Family** (Map 1N/16). The inscription reads,

As a token of respect and gratitude offered to Mr & Mrs Costermans-Jansen by the families who stayed here from 21 September-15 November 1944, the frightening period of Bemmel's liberation.

Over thirty people, including thirteen children, were sheltered by the family in the cellar of the farmhouse De Leemkuil.

Plaque to Costermans Family, No 1
Leemskuilselaan, Bemmel

Jac Maris Liberation Memorial, Bemmel

Chapel of Our Lady of the Flowering
Betuwe with sign

Haalderen
Liberation

Gendt Liberation Doornenburg War Victims Huissen War Victims

Extra visit continued

Return to Dorpstraat. Turn right and then left to the junction of Loostraat and Henckenrathweg.

Note from this point the small blue, white and black signs to the Chapel of Our Lady. These will guide you all the way.

Go straight over signed Elst. Continue as the road turns right, then continue on de Plats as the road bends right. Leave Bemmel, go over the A15.

Note that the new high speed railway to Arnhem is now under construction and may cause considerable disruption to the route.

Continue on de Vergert and turn to the left on Heuvelsestraat. Continue past the farm on the right to the path to the Chapel on the left, No 5. (7.8 kms/4.9 miles)

Memorial Chapel to St Mary of the Flowering Betuwe (Map 1N/17) erected in 1946 on the site of the heavy fighting of September-October 1944. On 1 October there was a fierce battle between the 7th Green Howards and the 10th SS Panzer Division who attacked this high point (it is called a 'hill' and is a few feet above the surrounding plain). The Germans had little protection from heavy Allied bombing, the water level being too high for them to dig in and they retreated to a new defensive line beyond the River Linge.

The Chapel has been lovingly tended by the Janssen family - by Kurt who came daily to change the flowers until his death in 1991, and then by his neice Grada. The display of flowers and plants is beautiful. Inside are several photos, a tribute by Grada to her uncle and a poem by an English veteran praising her faithfulness.

Turn round and at the junction turn left on Vergert to the junction. Continue straight on on Heuvelsestraat to the T-junction with the N839 and turn right on van Elkweg. Go straight on at the traffic lights signed Bemmel. Continue into Haalderen and stop just past the church on Van de Mondeweg (11.5 kms/7.2 miles).

Extra visit continued

Haalderen. The inhabitants were evacuated, with only the barest of possessions, to Brabant and to Belgium. The battle for the town was bitter, but on 6 October, when a German attack on Elst and Driel failed, the 50th (Northumbrian) Division took the town. **The Liberation Monument** (Map 1N/18) by Paula van Kilsdonk, erected on 4 May 1985, is of an open brickwork design. Its inscription reads, 'War, never to be forgotten, never to be repeated. WWII.'

Continue to the traffic lights, turn right and continue into Gendt, through the square to the T-junction. Turn right on Nijmegsestraat, past a large anchor on the left and take the next left on Pastor Pelgromlaan. Stop opposite the Town Hall. The memorial is on the left (15.7 kms/9.8 miles).

Gendt remained in German hands until April 1945, one of three German bridgeheads remaining on the left bank of the Rhine after the fighting of 7 October. On 13 October the inhabitants were evacuated by the Germans on the Pannerden ferry.

The Liberation Monument (Map 1N/19) by Ed van Teeseling, erected on 4 November 1950, is a tile picture of French Euville limestone, framed by bricks. It depicts a woman (symbolising the Liberation) and a child (symbolising the future). The inscription reads, 'From our fractures a finer nation is growing.'

Return to the roundabout, go straight over and at the junction go right. Leave Gendt and go right. Continue into Doornenburg on to Pannerdenseweg and continue to the church on the left. The memorial is then on the right (19.4 kms/12.1 miles).

Doornenburg. Like Gendt, this village remained in German hands until April 1945. It was liberated on the 2nd – Easter Monday. From 2 October the town was repeatedly hit by Allied bombing attacks, the late Medieval Castle being particularly badly damaged, and on 12 October the Germans evacuated the population to the Liemers (the area across the Pannerdens Canal). They blew up the Roman Catholic Church and the **Memorial to Civilian Victims** (Map 1N/20) is on the site of the altar. Designed by Van Donsel, it was erected on 4 May 1958. It is in the form of a Phoenix rising from the ashes on top of a bronze sphere mounted on concrete pillars. The names of the victims are inscribed, the youngest 1 year old, the oldest 84, with several from the same family. Next to it is the church's altar stone bearing the inscription, 'In memory of the victims of the 1940-1945 War'.

Turn round, then left and right on Duisterestraat. Leave Doornenburg and continue to the T-junction. Turn right signed Angeren. At the junction turn left signed Arnhem on Lodderoeksestraat. Enter Angeren on Jan Hoosterstraat and at the junction turn right on Kerkstraat. Continue to the church (25.1 kms/15.7 miles).

On the wall of **Angeren** Roman Catholic Church is a **Bronze Tablet to Piet Kaak**, killed in action at the Grebbeberg in May 1940, and **Herman Scholten** (Map 1N/21), killed in action in Java in August 1949. It bears a cross (symbolising suffering, struggle and victory) and a helmet (symbol of the soldiers who paid the supreme sacrifice for their country) and was presented to the parishioners in 1950 by the Old Soldiers' Association.

In the churchyard is a **Memorial to the Leijser Family** (Map 1N/22) who were all killed in their farmhouse on the Paddepoel Dyke, hit by bombs during the 5 October 1944 Allied bombing raid. Evacuees sheltering with them were also killed. The names

Extra visit continued

of all 27 victims are inscribed on a marble tablet surmounted by a wooden cross.
Turn round, return to the junction right and continue on Iepenstraat towards Huissen.
At the crossroads and traffic lights turn right signed Huissen and at the roundabout go
straight over. Turn right to Centrum.
Huissen was hit by an Allied air raid on Sunday 17 September 1944, during which
twenty-three civilians were killed. Their names are inscribed on the low sandstone wall
of the **Civilian Victims' Mass Grave** in the RC churchyard. Above the grave, made on
2 November 1947, is a memorial cross designed by Wim Harzing. It depicts Christ and
an impression of the air raids. (Map 1N/23).

On 1 October the Germans launched a strong counter-attack from Elden and Huissen
on Allied-held Elst. At that time there were about 10,000 people living in the area - 6,000
locals and 4,000 evacuees. On 2 October there was another heavy Allied air raid, which
killed ninety-eight civilians. Their names are also on the memorial wall. After this, many
of the surviving inhabitants fled to safer shelter – many to the Veluwe (the region to the
north of Arnhem).
Continue past the church on the left to the T-junction and turn left on Nazareth to the
Market Square and stop (29.4 kms/18.4 miles).
On the wall of the **Town Hall is a Bronze Memorial Plaque** (Map 1N/24) embossed with
the coat of arms of Huissen. Erected on 5 May 1985 it records the assistance given by their
fellow citizens to those in need after the battles of 17 September-23 October 1944.

High on the wall of No. 1 Tempelierenstraat is a *Bas Relief* **Memorial Tablet** (Map
1N/25). Erected in July 1948 it shows men in travelling cloaks, symbolising the evacuations
of October '44-May '45, the gable of a house in Langestraat and a flying eagle with a broken
swastika in its talons (symbolising the Liberation and the fall of Nazi Germany).
Return to Lent on the N839 via Bergerden and Bemmel and theA325. Pick up the main
Itinerary (13.3 kms/8.3 miles).

Turn round, continue back along Laauwikstraat, cross over the A52 and turn left following
signs to Elst to the railway tunnel.

• Robinson Tunnel/11.8 kms/7.4 miles/Map 1N/26

The bridge is much the same as it was in 1944 although it has been refaced. On the evening
of 20 September 1944 many of the inhabitants of Lent sheltered in this railway tunnel as
fighting raged around them. Three of them were killed by a German SS soldier.

Taking the direction as the road continues after the railway bridge towards Elst as 12
o'clock, the 504th crossing was made below the power station, 1,500m away at 8 o'clock.

It was to this exact spot that Sergeant Peter 'Robbo' Robinson brought his own and one
other Grenadier Guards' tank, having dashed across the Nijmegen road bridge with four
tanks at around 1830 hours on Wednesday 20 September. What happened next and why the
tanks did not then press on to The Bridge at Arnhem is a story upon which British and
American participants do not agree. Essentially the British say that the Americans did not
appreciate the difficulties and, typified by Captain T. Moffatt Burriss of the 504th (see

account of the river crossing above), the Americans say that the British "stopped for tea". Examples of each of their versions of what happened now follow: -

The American version.

Burriss, having landed on the north bank collected about 10 men and made his way to the northern end of the main road bridge.

A PERSONAL ACCOUNT
By Captain T. Moffatt Burriss.

It was beginning to get dark. As we looked at the south end of the bridge we saw silhouettes of tanks heading across it in our direction....Two tanks passed within feet of us. They were British. When the third one arrived we swarmed all over it.... 'You guys are the most beautiful sight I've seen in months,' I said. 'Let's go on to Arnhem and save the paratroopers there.' We could hear firing in the vicinity of the two lead tanks [then] the lead British tank was knocked out by a German 88. The remaining four tanks backed up to the north end of the bridge. That's when the British tank crews brought out their teapots. I was furious. I charged to the front of the tank line where I found the British commander Capt. Peter Carrington [later British Foreign Secretary and then Secretary General of NATO] of the Grenadier Guards. 'Why are you stopping?' I asked him. 'I can't proceed,' he said crisply. 'That gun will knock out my tanks.' ... 'We'll go with you. We can knock out that gun.' ... 'I can't go without orders,' he said [see Peter Robinson's account concerning the Grenadiers' attitude over the need for orders below.] 'OK', I said, 'I'm giving you orders.'

He was a British captain. I was an American captain. He wasn't about to recognise my authority.... 'You mean to tell me you're going to sit here on your ass while your own British paratroopers are being cut to shreds – and all because of one gun?' He shook his head. 'I can't go without orders.' I looked him straight in the eye. 'You yellow-bellied son of a bitch. I've just sacrificed half of my company in the face of a dozen guns and you won't move because of one gun.'

Then I cocked my tommy gun, put it up to his head and said, 'You get this tank moving or I'll blow your damn head off.' With that he ducked into his tank and locked the hatch. I couldn't get to him.

Burriss then goes on to relate how both Major Cook and Colonel Tucker had similar arguments with Captain Carrington, but to no effect. Apart from the lack of orders to advance, among other reasons given later for not moving on, were the lack of Grenadier infantry, the shortage of ammunition (their tanks were rationed to about eight rounds each), the absence of air support and the coming darkness. When asked by the authors if he would actually have shot at Carrington, Burriss hesitated long enough for the question to be changed to 'Would you have fired near him?' The answer, given over 50 years after the event was, 'Probably, given the way that I felt at the time.' In his book, though, Burriss admits,

'We were probably too hard on Carrington.... He was the senior British officer at the battle site, but the man in command of British tanks was General Horrocks. I'm convinced that Horrocks told Carrington to stay exactly where he was, thereby dooming not only the rescue mission but also the entire operation to end the war.'

Personalities of the Nijmegen Road Bridge: Lord Carrington, the British Ambassador, Bill Croft, Peter Robinson with Valmai Holt, City Hall Nijmegen on the 40th Anniversary

Lieutenant T. Moffatt Burriss in doorway of a C-47, June 1944

We asked T. Moffatt Burriss if he had ever met Lord Carrington. He had not - they narrowly missed each other at the Nijmegen Bridge at the 50th anniversary - but he believed that he knew what Burriss had written about him.

In April 2001 the authors wrote to Lord Carrington (created a Life Peer in 1999 after a long and distinguished political career) inviting him to put his side of the story. 'What an extraordinary story', he commented of Burriss's account.

'Is it really very likely that, having captured the bridge and having met up with our American friends, one of them starts waving a gun at me? In any event, we were all under orders to hold the bridgehead until more troops had crossed. There is, of course, no truth in the story.'

Major-General Tony Jones at the authors' 40th Wedding Anniversary, 1998

The British version

Sergeant Peter Robinson, Regimental Number 2613912, was the troop commander with four tanks in his troop. His own tank was a Firefly (a Sherman with a 17-pounder gun – the others had 75mm guns). His troop was the lead troop of the regiment. His squadron 2i/c was Lord Carrington – known in the regiment as the "Short Peer". In civilian life Robinson was a fisherman and during his later years accompanied many official and other tours back to the battlefield. The following account was given to the authors on the 40th Annniversary.

A PERSONAL ACCOUNT
By Sergeant Peter Robinson

It isn't fair to have one regiment in the lead all the time... you all took it in turns to lead.... The Irish Guards started off leading first of all... probably Number 1 Squadron and then somebody else and then it comes to the individual Troops. Somebody's got to be in front there and of course you take that in turn as well and that was where I came unlucky.... The bridge wasn't taken, which was our objective. We reached the far end of the bridge and immediately there was a road block.... So the troop sergeant covered me through and then I got the other side and covered the rest of the troop through.... We were still being engaged, there was a gun in front of the church [Lent] three or four hundred yards in front of us.... We knocked him out... we got down the road to the railway bridge...we cruised round there very steady.... We were being engaged all the time.... Just as I got round the corner and turned right I saw these helmets duck in a ditch and run... and gave them a burst of machine gun.... I suddenly realised they were Americans.... They had already thrown a gammon grenade at me [confirmed in Burriss's book] so dust and dirt and smoke was flying everywhere.... They jumped out of the ditch... they kissed the tank, they kissed the gun because they'd lost a lot of men, they had had a very bad crossing.

Well my orders were to collect the Colonel [American] who was in a house a little way back and the first thing he said to me, 'I have to surrender. I can't carry on. I've lost nearly all my men. I haven't got many left.'

Well I said,

I'm sorry. My orders are to hold this bridge to the last man and the last round. I've only got two tanks but if you'd like to give me ground support for a little while until we get some more orders then we can do it.' He said he couldn't do it, so I said that he had better come back to my wireless and talk to General Horrocks – because before I started on the job I had freedom of the air. Everybody was off the air except myself because they wanted a running commentary about what was going on. So he came over and had a pow wow with Horrocks. The Colonel said, 'Oh very well,' and I told him where I wanted the men but of course you can't consolidate a Yank ['Consolidation' in the British army is the process of adopting defensive positions after the capture of an objective and it involves soldiers staying at their posts] and they hadn't been there ten minutes before they were on their way again.

Lord Carrington joined us [at the railway tunnel] about two or three hours after because he had been sitting on the north end of the bridge protecting that. He came over after a Lieutenant Jones (qv) debugged the bridge. We stopped there until about 4 o'clock the following afternoon. The Irish Guards went through us and they came and fetched me back on a scout car to our Headquarters.... There was an 'O' Group there with all the Generals who wanted to know what had happened.... They taped recordings... in those days the recordings were done on records.... They sent them off with a DR [Despatch Rider] and the DR was never seen any more.

Inevitably there is some confusion about how many of the four tanks that originally crossed the bridge spent the night in the area of the tunnel. Some accounts describe at least one tank being shot up and set on fire and the crew being taken prisoner. Carrington's tank then joined Robinson. Robinson says there were four tanks at the tunnel overnight and he is likely to be the most reliable source. He certainly remembers that he, the crews and Lord Carrington whiled the night away with a bottle of whisky. Confusion abounds over the Nijmegen bridge battle – General Horrocks in his book *Corps Commander* records that the crossing was done by the 505th and that the bridge was taken on the 21st and the US Official History map shows the capture as the 23rd. Neither is correct; the crossing was done by the 504th and the date was the 20th. When the authors pressed him for reasons why he did not drive on after reaching the railway bridge, Peter Robinson echoed Lord Carrington's reply to T. Moffatt Burriss –

> When the American said that he had to surrender I told him that I couldn't – I hadn't had any orders to surrender – and I hadn't any orders to go any further. If you tell a Guardsman to jump he jumps, if you don't he won't.

A few months later Peter Robinson was personally awarded the DCM by Field-Marshal Montgomery.

Perhaps now it should be asked why orders to advance were not given. To uncover an answer it is important to understand the culture of a disciplined fighting force such as the Guards Armoured Division. Tanks and infantry fight together, particularly in close country such as that in this area. In a regiment of three battalions one battalion might be equipped with tanks while the others remain as infantry. The infantry provide close protection for the tanks and the tank crews and the foot soldiers learn to co-operate with each other, all members of the same regiment with the same command radio network and the same Commanding Officer. The Irish Guards tanks would work with Irish Guards infantry, the Grenadiers with Grenadiers, each developing their own special fighting techniques. When Peter Robinson's tanks crossed the Nijmegen bridge they had no infantry support, their infantry were still holding the recently captured ground at the Valkhof and Hunner Park. Although Burriss's Americans offered to provide support, it was not a practical proposition. They were unused to each others' methods of working and their radios were not compatible. Also it was time for the Irish Guards to take over. Peter Robinson has explained above how it was necessary to alternate the leading formation. It was getting dark and they were short of ammunition; thus it was a situation in which to order an advance could lead to the loss of many tanks, vehicles which were difficult to replace and were needed elsewhere to protect The Corridor. The decision to wait until the following day is understandable, particularly when taking into account just what it was like to be in a tank, a condition now described by Sergeant Bill Croft who, until a few days before, had commanded Peter Robinson's troop.

A PERSONAL MEMORY

By Sergeant Bill Croft
It may interest you to know something of a troop leader's tasks. There are 101 things to do. He has to guide his tank, make full use of the ground, give orders to the other

A personal memory continued

tank commanders, keep in touch with his infantry, scan the landscape for the enemy, direct his gunner onto targets, judge the range, position his other tanks, pass messages back to his squadron leader over the air and at the same time be on the alert for all unexpected situations. He must also be an accomplished map-reader. The Sherman, an American tank, was a very reliable one. Weight approx. 30 tons, speed around 28mph, powered by a Chrysler engine which had 5 banks of 6 cylinders, a crew of five: tank commander, gunner, wireless op, who was also the gun-loader - a 75mm or a 17-pounder which we called a Firefly – the driver and co-driver. The co-driver operated a Browning MG. The tank commander could also have a Browning mounted on the turret. The turret could be rotated 360°, clock or anti-clockwise, operated by the gunner. This was the only advantage that we held over the Tiger or Panther of the Germans. Their traverse was manual operation, relatively slow.

In addition a commander must be able to rely upon his orders being carried out while subordinate commanders are aware that if they attempt to exceed their orders they may interfere with plans they know nothing of. Thus, in the absence of an order to advance from a Corps Commander who was in radio contact, a subordinate commander would wait. Why, then, were no orders to advance given? General Horrocks, reviewing the situation some years later, said, 'On the evening of the 20th we had both bridges and I would have been a very happy man but for three things – One, I had had no word from 1st British Airborne Division. Two, German resistance was getting stronger. Three, I was beginning to look over my shoulder at the lifeline to the rear.'

It was not until 1100 hours the following morning, almost 20 hours after the Grenadiers secured the Nijmegen Bridge, that tanks of the 2nd Battalion Irish Guards began to move through the Grenadiers and over the bridge from the south side in an attempt to continue the advance to Arnhem. During the night and the early morning the 504th commander, Colonel Reuben Tucker, had fumed in anger and frustration at what he saw as British slowness. Yet there were problems of which he was not aware: the road ahead was elevated and exposed, and the Germans were counter-attacking The Corridor south of Nijmegen. Nevertheless it is difficult to equate the actions of Guards Armoured Division on the night and morning of 20-21 September with the earlier instructions of their Corps Commander, General Horrocks, 'to keep going like hell'. Oddly, the fault may be that of Horrocks himself. Although the initial briefing that he had given at Leopoldsburg had been a vintage performance he did not maintain the pressure on his XXX Corps commanders to keep driving forward. It has been suggested that he was ill. Additionally Montgomery did not – uncharacteristically – keep pressure on Horrocks. It was as if he regretted the rashness with which he had entered into MARKET-GARDEN and now distanced himself from it. Thus, with the two immediate senior commanders appearing somewhat disinterested in what was going on, impetus was lost. Geoffrey Powell in his excellent *The Devil's Birthday* says that even Lieutenant-Colonel Joe Vandeleur who led the Irish Guards wondered why his orders to advance had taken so long to arrive and remembered 'a general lack of urgency'.

By the time that the Irish did advance the Germans had been able to prepare defensive

Fort Hof van Holland: the way in and the interior

Memorial to the 504th Waal Crossing showing power lines and the names of the casualties

positions along The Corridor and the 2nd Battalion quickly lost three tanks in the leading troop. In a following tank was Guardsman Roger Keyes. His Sherman was ordered to get off the embanked road and to take cover and then,

> Eventually we were ordered to carry on forward and we knew that our tank would be hit before long and it was. The noise was what I imagine it would be like to be inside Big Ben when it struck, the tank immediately went on fire [as Shermans usually did when they were hit – the Germans called them 'Tommy-cookers].'

Even with hindsight it does not sound as if it was a moment for a mad rush forward and later efforts by the Welsh Guards, 43rd Division and a Brigade of 50th Division did not succeed.

There is yet another fascinating conundrum associated with the bridge area. Barely 200m east of the bridge is today's A325 dual carriageway. In September 1944 it existed in the form of a hard base of sand – known as the 'sand road'– and ran from here to the Arnhem road bridge, bypassing the town of Elst which was to prove such a stumbling block to the XXX Corps advance. If the Grenadiers had taken that road... ? The sand road was certainly navigable by tanks as the Germans used it from Arnhem later in the month to bring Tiger tanks south, but it seems that there was a German sign here warning of mines, though none were there on 20 September.

Drive under the tunnel and immediately turn left down the small Zalige Straat.

NB. There is a weight restriction on this dyke road.

Continue to the turning on the right by a house and stop. Walk along the track and turn over the drawbridge into the Fort.

NB. The fort is private property. Permission to enter/photograph it should be obtained from the residents. It is also a nature reserve and access is therefore restricted.

• *Fort Hof van Holland/12.5 kms/7.8 miles/10 minutes/Map 1N/27*

The wooden drawbridge leads over a 20m-wide moat. This small square fort is one of a number of border fortifications built by the Dutch before the turn of the century. In some contemporary accounts of the 1944 fighting it is wrongly named as the 'Lent Fort'. The Germans had mounted 20mm cannon on and around the walls. The Americans charged from the river with fixed bayonets, with instructions to bypass the fort, but Company H of 504th PIR, led by Sergeant Leroy Richmond, decided to silence the cannons. Some men swam the moat, others went over the bridge and through the tunnel into the centre of the fort. The defenders had withdrawn into the central building with its narrow slot-shaped windows. The paratroopers poked their weapons through the slots and the Germans surrendered. The Americans then moved on towards the Robinson Tunnel.

Walk back to your car. Continue towards the Waal and turn right following the narrow road on the top of the newly reinforced dyke.

In 2000 extensive reinforcement work was undertaken on this stretch of the dyke when a great deal of unexploded material was uncovered. When the work is completed it will offer a short route to Oosterhout.

Continue to the memorial on the left, just before the power cables.

• *Memorial to the Waal Crossing of 504th PIR/13.1 kms/ 8.2 miles/10 minutes/Map 1N/28*

This commemorates the crossing, just before 1500 hours on 20 September, of the 504th PIR in twenty-six canvas boats with plywood bottoms under dangerously heavy fire. Five more crossings were made (see account above). The approximate route taken by the boats is that of the power cables.

The striking Memorial by Marius van Beek and Professor Dr F. J. A. Huygen was unveiled on 18 September 1984 by General Gavin by walking through a covering veil between the pillars. On the ground in front of it is a tablet bearing the names of the 48 men who gave their lives in this superb act of heroism and determination. They were from the 3rd Battalion 504th PIR, plus elements of 307th AB Eng Battalion, 376th FAB HQ Battery and the Regiment's HQ and, later 1st Battalion and some men of 2nd Battalion of the 504th. The Memorial has been adopted by the W. I. Rijnders School and is on the site of the initial bridgehead.

Beyond the Memorial, on the road to Oosterhout, on 21 September, Private John R. Towle, a 'bazooka man' of the 504th PIR, rushed beyond his company's outposts to intercept a German attack supported by two tanks and a half-track. He managed to break up the attack before he was mortally wounded by enemy mortar fire. Private Towle was posthumously awarded the **Medal of Honour** (Map 1N/29).

Turn round and return to the main road and turn left towards Elst, passing a vast new housing development on the left. Continue to the junction with Oosterhout signed to the left.

• *Extra Visits to Memorials in the West of The Island: Slijk-Ewijk – 101st AB Memorial, Allied Graves; Dodewaard - Memorial to the Fallen, Memorial to Crashed Dakota; Kesteren Resistance Worker Column; Opheusden - 101st AB Plaque, Memorials to Piron Brigade and Civilians, 101st 1st Aid Post, Major Horton Plaque; Randwijk Memorial to the Fallen; Zetten – Liberation Monument, Plaques to Dutch Railway Worker and POW in Java. Round trip: 56 kilometres/35 miles. Approximate time: 2 hours*

Turn left signed Oosterhout and then right, following Doorgaand Verkeer. Leave Oosterhout and turn left at the T-junction signed Slijk-Ewijk. After 150m stop on the left by the Dorpshuis Beatrix (4 kms/2.5 miles).

On the wall is a **Plaque with the Screaming Eagle** insignia (Map 1N/30) which bears the legend, 'In October-November 1944 the US 101st AB Division fought on the 'Island" for our liberty.' Divisional HQ was situated at Slijk-Ewijk [known to the Yanks as 'Slicky-Wicky'].

Continue along the road to the local cemetery on the right with a CWGC sign.

At the end of a long gravel path the **CWGC graves** (Map 1N/31) are at the back. They are of **Signalman R. Waddington, R. Sigs, 9 October 1944**, and **Captain R.V. Marchand, RA, 8 October 1944**.

Continue to the dyke and turn right.

The dyke road, in British military accounts often referred to as the 'Bund,' has come in from Lent. On 22 September, taking advantage of cover from the thick fog, in an attempt to bypass the German opposition along The Corridor, a force made up from elements of 2nd HCR, 4th/7th RDG, 7th SLI, 5th DCLI and 8th Middlesex motored along the Bund at speed from here to Slijk-Ewijk. They drove up the road past the cemetery en route to Valburg where they overcame opposition by Hans-Peter Knaust's battalion of veterans and Hitler Youth at the de Hucht (qv) crossroads and 'Dashed for Driel'.

Note that the dykes, which were first built by monks in the 14th Century, are

Memorials in the West of The Island:
1. 101st AB Div HQ, Slijk-Ewijk

2. Dodewaard Memorial to the Fallen

3. Ochten C-47 Memorial and 3a. Detail

Op het terrein achter deze gedenknaald stortte op 18 september 1944 een Dakota neer.
Daarbij kwamen alle inzittenden, zes Amerikaanse bemanningsleden en achttien
Engelse parachutisten, om het leven. Op weg naar de droppingszones ten westen van
Arnhem werden zij met nog een aantal andere vliegtuigen het slachtoffer van het in de
uiterwaarden van Ochten opgestelde Duitse luchtafweergeschut.

Bemanning, behorende tot het Amerikaanse 314e Troop Carrier Command:

J.W. Bobo	X. C. Connett	L.A. Ottoway
G.A. Collier	H. G. Honeysett	H. Pluemer

Para's, behorende tot het Engelse 156 e Parachute Battalion:

G.T. Brownlow	G.H. Gilliver	H.J. Philpotts
A. Butler	H. Hopwood	H. Stanyer
H. Clayton	E. E. Johns	Th. Stevens
J.F. Clayton	R. Killingworth	P. Taylor
R. Fuller	J.C. Kinsley-Smith	G. Tutton
D.L. George	O. Lilly	J. Wilson

4. Opheusden: a. Detail of Piron Brigade Memorial, Town Hall b. American Aid Post Monument c. Maj Horton Plaque

5. Zetten Liberation Memorial

Extra visit continued

constructed in a zigzag shape, which better withstands the force of the water.

Continue on Waaldijk under the A50 and into Dodewaard past a small church to the right to Pluimenburgsestraat and turn right. Continue to the memorial on the left just short of the main square (15 kms/9.4 miles).

Dodewaard Memorial to the Fallen (Map 1N/32). The yellow brick memorial bears a red brick column broken by a black triangle. Designed by G. van Dorland and inaugurated on 2 May 1990 it represents pre-War freedom broken by the occupation and evacuation and rising again through resistance and liberation to recovery. It commemorates twelve citizens of Dodewaard killed in the area, three citizens who died in the former Dutch East Indies and the Allied Liberators - 'those whom we lost during and after World War II owing to acts of war. The enemy was defeated as a result of your sacrifice.'

Extra visit continued

Units of the 101st AB were involved in bitter fighting against strong German opposition in the area which continued until mid-April 1945. Dodewaard was finally cleared by the Piron Brigade (qv).

Continue to the junction before the square and turn right signed Opheusden.
Continue towards the A15 and turn left just before it signed Ochten. Continue on Bonegraafseweg to the memorial on the right (19 kms/11.9 miles).

The handsome black and red marble obelisk **Memorial is to the occupants of C-47 Dakota 43-15180** (Map 1N/33) that was hit by German flak from anti-aircraft guns sited on the river foreland of Ochten. It crashed, carrying half of the 156th Para Battalion MG platoon and its crew, on 18 September 1944 - one of 10 planes brought down in the vicinity. It was erected in 2000 by the Adriaan van Westreemen Stichting and unveiled on 3 May in the presence of the brothers of Privates Thomas Stevens and Henry Philpotts, both among those named on the bronze plaque, which carries a handsome outline of a Dakota. The casualties were originally buried at the crash site by villagers, including the sole Para to survive the crash who was sheltered in a nearby house but who died the next day. Wooden crosses were put on the graves but they were washed away in the winter flooding. The American crew - S/Sgt J. Bobo, T/Sgt G. Collier, S/Sgt X.C. Connett, 2nd Lt H.G. Honeysett and Captain L. Ottaway were reburied in the US Military Cemetery at Neuville-en-Condroz, Belgium. Captain H. Pleumer was buried in New Jersey. The eighteen British Paras could not be individually identified after the war and were reburied in Jonkerbos CWGC Cemetery (qv) in Plot 8, rows A/1,2,3,4,5,6,7,8,9 and B/1,2,3,4,5,6,7,8,9 with the inscription 'Buried near this spot.'

Turn next right on Lage Kampseweg, over the A15, over the crossing with Varakker and turn left on Parallelweg into Kesteren. Keep to the left of the railway line on Broekdijk to the junction with Ommestraat. Turn right and continue on Hoofdstraat to the junction with Schenkhofstraat. Turn left on Nedereindsestraat to the churchyard (25 kms/15.7 miles).

Kesteren Churchyard Monument to Johannes van Zanten (Map 1N/34). The broken column, symbol of a life cut off, is to the resistance worker who was betrayed by a Dutch Military Policeman and arrested in Utrecht in September 1944. He was shot in the William III Barracks in Apeldoorn on 2 December 1944 and was posthumously awarded the Knightship of the Order of the Bronze Lion. The column, which bears van Zanten's likeness in *bas relief*, was erected on 3 July 1945.

N.B. By returning to the junction with Hoofdstaat and turning left and first right onto Boveneindsestraat to Hazenhof there is a Plaque to sixteen men of 10th Para and one American of the USAAF, hidden here when their plane crashed in De Maten. (Map 1N/35)

Return to Parallelweg and continue direction Opheusden. Turn left, cross over the railway and enter Opheusden. Continue past the church and turn left and then right into the square in front of the Town Hall on Burgemeester Lodderstraat (29.4 kms/18.4 miles).

Opheusden Memorials (Map 1N/38-39). In early October 1944 the 101st AB took over positions between Opheusden and Elst from the 43rd Wessex Division (who had reached here on 23 September, but progressed no further north). They stayed on The Island until 29 November. The Dodewaard-Opheusden front was allocated to the 506th PIR who

Extra visit continued

were involved in heavy fighting with German units which, supported by tanks, crossed the Rhine and advanced from Kesteren on Allied positions. For the 101st 'Opheusden was by all odds the largest single battle of The Island campaign' [*Rendezvous with Destiny*, the Divison's History]. Opposing them was the German 363rd Volksgrenadier Division. After ten days of bitter struggle and heavy casualties (eleven officers and ninety-one men on 6 October alone) the History would be able to report that by 15 October

> The 363rd had been virtually wiped out. Giving up all hope of a breakthrough on The Island the Germans fell back 2,400 yards. Both sides settled down to patrolling the no-man's land thus created.

In the Town Hall is a white marble **Plaque with a splendid Screaming Eagle** 'In remembrance of the 101st Airborne Division U.S.A. Sept-Dec 1944'. It was erected on 20 September 1979. Outside the Town Hall are **Memorials to the 101st** with a bronze Screaming Eagle, **to all Opheusden civilians killed in the war** (both inaugurated in 1990) **and to the Belgian Piron Brigade** (qv) whose 3rd Battalion liberated Opheusden on 18 April 1945. The latter was designed by H. J. van Brenk and was inaugurated on 8 May 1976. The brick monument bears a grey granite tablet commemorating the Brigade. The tile bearing the Brigade's colourful badge was presented by Belgian veterans.

Continue to the junction with Patrijsstraat and turn right. At the junction with Smachtkamp turn left and continue to the end of the road. Just before the railway line on the left (30.6 kms/19.1 miles) is

A small **Memorial to the Americans** of the 101st AB (Map 1N/40) who died in the first aid post on the site. Here a 17-year-old Dutch volunteer, Leo Jeucken, who had attached himself to the Americans, was also killed. The memorial, erected on 17 September 1999, is in the form of a 'V' with the names of the six casualties on a plaque.

Return and take the third right on Fazanstraat. Continue to the T-junction and turn right on Dalwagenseweg. Continue to the bridge over the River Linge (31.8 kms/19.9 miles).

On the left railing of the bridge, just short of the railway station, is a brass **Plaque to Major Oliver M. Horton and the soldiers of the 101st AB** (Map 1N/41) who were killed in the Battle of Opheusden, October 1944, erected on 22 September 1944 by the US 101st AB Division. It bears a Screaming Eagle. Horton, leading Coy H, the 3rd Battalion, 506th PIR, was hit by artillery at 1000 hours on 5 October. He was awarded the Silver Star.

Turn round and return on Dalwagenseweg to Tolsestraat. Turn right and continue on De Hel as it bends left to join Randwijkerserijndijk. Turn right into Randwijk to the Ned Herv Church, opposite is (40 kms/24.8 miles)

Randwijk Memorial to the Fallen (Map 1N/42). Inaugurated on 4 May 1987 by the Leden Oranje-Comité, the brick memorial bears a plaque 'To the memory of all those who gave their lives for our freedom'. Randwijk was liberated by a Recconnaissance Unit of the Gloucesters, but as heavy fighting continued, the population had to be evacuated. The town was retaken by the Germans in December 1944.

Take the N836 signed to Zetten and immediately after crossing the River Linge turn right on Heldringstraat. Continue through the town to the junction on the left with Kerkstraat.

Extra visit continued

Stop where you can. The memorial is on the right on Wilhelminaplein (43 kms/26.9 miles). The impressive **Liberation Monument** (Map 1N/43), designed by G. Berns, was inaugurated on 24 September 1984. It takes the form of a symbolic dugout representing the many civilians and military who are buried in the area – the negative aspect - and then, rising from the slit trench, is the positive – a shining 'V' made of stainless steel which represents the Liberation. The inscription is on a black granite tablet and on five tiles are the coats of arms of Great Britain, the United States, Belgium, Canada and Holland. The monument has been adopted by the Rev. van Lingen School. Note that 'V' stands for Victory but also for *Vrijdom* (Freedom) in Dutch.

Leave Zetten on the N836, passing the station on the right.

N.B. On the wall of the Station is a Plaque to Railway Worker Wilhelmus Antionius Thijssen who died during the raid which destroyed Nijmegen station on 22 February 1944 and where he was attending a course. Designed by H. G. J. Schelling it was erected on 22 November 1948. (Map 1N/45)

Join the A15 direction Elst. Continue over the Valburg junction and take the exit to Elst. Rejoin the main itinerary just after it crosses the A15 (56 kms/35 miles).

Plaque to 'The Incredible Patrol'

Continue over the A15 into Elst. Continue over the traffic lights to the next traffic lights.

To the right is Elst Station where there is a **bronze tablet to commemorate the railway workers of Elst who lost their lives during the war:** Willem Zwijnen was killed by shrapnel on 23 September 1944 at his home along Visstee and Cornelius Mientjes was killed along the Arnhem-Elst railway line on 30 September 1944 (Map 1N/46).

Turn left signed Centrum, keeping to the left of the charming statue group with a horse (there is an annual horse fair in Elst) and continue on Dorpstraat to the Gemeente (Town Hall) on the left and stop just past it.

• **'Incredible Patrol' Plaque.** In the Town Hall, is the plaque which used to be in Heteren Town Hall. The tiled plaque tells the story of Hugo Sims, Peter Frank, William Canfield, Frederick Becker, Robert Nicolai and Roland Wilbur of 501st PIR who, on the night of 29 October 1944, crossed the Rhine at Heteren in rubber dinghies. They landed to the east of Renkum, slipped behind the enemy lines, reached the Ede-Arnhem highway, hid throughout the following day and that night captured thirty-two enemy officers and men. They returned with their prisoners across the Rhine.

On the right, in front of a small ornamental fountain and park, is

•Memorial to the 7th SLI, 1st Worcs and 4th/7th RDG, Elst/21.4 kms/13.4 miles /5 minutes/Map 1N/48/RWC

The memorial, designed by Marina van der Kooi, was erected on 17 September 1984. The inscription reads, 'On September 25th 1944 Elst was liberated by 7th Somerset Light Infantry

Memorial to 7th SLI and 4th/7th RDG, Elst

Regiment, 1st Worcestershire Regiment, 4th/7th RDGs. The SLI liberated Oosterhout (qv) on 22 September, but their progress towards Arnhem was stopped by German tanks near Elst. On the 24th the Somersets and Worcesters managed to fight their way into the outskirts of Elst. About 100 inhabitants sheltered from the battle in the cold store of the nearby auction rooms. A small-scale tank battle then ensued in the town centre, the Germans finally succumbing to the Allies' superior numbers. By the evening of the 25th Elst was liberated.

On 22 September the 4th/7th RDG and the 5th DCLI had attempted to bypass Elst to the west. As their column of tanks moved forward two German tanks came out of a side road and, assuming that the column was one of theirs, joined in. They were dispatched by a member of the DCLI using a PIAT. That evening, however, there was another sad incidence of friendly fire, or 'blue on blue'. As darkness fell the leading tank saw an armoured car ahead and knocked it out. It turned out to be from 2nd HCR.

Walk to the memorial behind in the right hand corner of the garden.

The Island Museum, Heteren

Grave of Hendrik van der Horst, 17 September 1944

Heteren Screaming Eagle Memorial

• *Memorial to Executed Hostages, Elst/21.4 kms/13.4 miles/5 minutes/Map 1N/49/RWC*

Designed by Th. Jeukens, the memorial was erected on 25 October 1946. It commemorates the three hostages (of seven actually taken), executed by a unit of the Sicherheitsdienst near this spot on the night of 13-14 September 1944. W. L. van Dijk, G. de Koning and A.M.M. Puthaar (two headmasters and a Council employee) were killed by firing squad. That night part of the Arnhem-Nijmegen railway line at De Laar, south of Elst, was blown up and the arrests and the burning of farms were subsequently made. The acts were partly to encourage the 500 workers required to dig anti-tank ditches at Zevenaar. It has never actually been proved that the citizens who were executed took part in the sabotage. The memorial also remembers all the other citizens of Elst who were 'killed by acts of violence of the occupying forces'.

Continue through Elst on Valburgseweg to the Algemene Cemetery (begraafplaats) on the right.

•*Grave of 1st Citizen of Elst Killed on 17.9.44./21.9 kms/ 13.7 miles/10 minutes/Map 1N/50*

Hendrik van der Horst, verger of the Dutch Reformed Church, climbed to the top gallery of the bell tower with some friends to watch the action in Oosterbeek. From the tower Mr van der Horst and the small group with him had been able to see the gliders landing. He was killed by a bullet from a German sniper who suspected him of being an observer for the Allies. The memorial headstone was presented to his relatives on 17 September 1946 by members of the church. The grave is to the right of the stone chapel. It bears a quotation from Job, 'And then the Lord answered Job out of the whirlwind.'

Turn left immediately, signed Heteren, and right at the roundabout and continue to the next small staggered crossroads at De Hucht.

It was here at **De Hucht Crossroads** (Map 1N/51) on the evening of 22 September that the tail end of the 5th DCLI group making its way towards Driel met five Tiger tanks head on and took refuge in the ditch. Major Parker of A Company, who had successfully charged a couple of Tigers in Normandy, guessing that the tanks would return to Elst later, decided to lay a trap at the crossroads. Men with PIATs were placed around the area and No.75 mines were strung across the roads. When the tanks returned they were preceded by two despatch riders who blew up on the mines. The first tank was hit by six PIAT bombs and blew up, the second received similar treatment and the third tried to back out. Parker's men pulled a line of mines behind it and finished it off with a PIAT. The remaining two tried to reverse at speed and fell over into the ditch when CSM Philp dropped a grenade into the turret of each. In a tight-knit regimental community there can be little doubt that Philp would have known CSM Adams (qv) who was killed two days later and buried in Driel.

Continue and turn right onto Logtestraat.

On the right a large old farmhouse complex is passed (25.3 kms/15.8 miles). Called **Landgoed Schoonderlogt** (Map 1N/52) it was occupied by the family Mom during the War. It was used by the Hampshires as their HQ as they moved up through The Island in September and then on 5 October by the 2nd Battalion, 101st AB under Major Richard Winters, DSC. A photo exists of the Major standing under the archway into the farm. Five hundred or so of his men were camping in the farm's orchards. In 1982 the 101st AB presented the Mom Family with a certificate creating them 'Honorary Members' of the

Division. Forty or so civilians from Elst also sought refuge here until everyone was evacuated towards Nijmegen when the Germans blew the dykes on 2 December (qv).

Turn left on Achterstraat, under the A50 to the junction with the N837 in Heteren.
The CWGC Plot is a hedge-enclosed area on the left.

• Heteren General Cemetery Allied Wargraves/30.7 kms/19.2 miles/10 minutes/Map 2/9

In the large grassed area is a long row of CWGC headstones. They are to 1 Unknown Airman, 3 British soldiers, 10 RAF, 5 RCAF and 3 RAAF, killed on 18, 20, 21, 23 and 25 September 1944.

Turn right, signed Driel. Continue to the last turn left before the T-junction at the sign to Museum 40-45 on O. L. Vrouwestraat to No. 36 on the right past the Italian restaurant.
It has regimental insignia on the fence.

• Museum 'The Island'/31.8 kms/19.9 miles/ 20 minutes/Map 2/8

This private museum was created 'in homage to all who bravely fought for the liberation of the Betuwe'. It is owned by Marcel ten Bohmer who found the diary his father started on his 16th birthday as Operation MARKET-GARDEN began to rage around him. That diary inspired Marcel to start this collection which for the past fourteen years has been his passion. As he found items – weapons, uniforms, ephemera etc – Marcel painstakingly researched the provenance of those items and has, in many fascinating cases, been able to trace and often meet their owners. The exhibitions are all immaculately preserved and displayed, including the jeep once used by the local fire brigade and the many different nationality uniforms with their personal histories.

It is opened by appointment. Tel: + (0) 26 472 22 85. Admission is free. Over the 4 May Liberation Day and September MARKET-GARDEN anniversaries, the Museum is open all the time and is especially popular with veterans.

Return to the main road, turn left and right at the T-junction onto the dyke.
Continue under the motorway to the memorial immediately on the right.

• Heteren Screaming Eagle Memorial/33 kms/20.6 miles/5 minutes/ Map 2/10

Erected on 27 September 1982, the brick memorial with a splendid Screaming Eagle badge and flanked by two wooden benches, bears the inscription, 'The Americans of the 101st Airborne Division fought here for our liberty. Oct-Nov 1944.' On either side are seats with the 101st AB insignia. The memorial is on the site of an old Dutch searchlight base, built in 1939.

After 1 (BR) AB Division withdrew from Arnhem-Oosterbeek, fierce fighting continued on The Island until the Spring of 1945. On 2 October 101st US AB Division were moved north, past 82nd US AB, to relieve 43rd (BR) Division. The first Americans to arrive here were 501st PIR on 4 October. In the following month General Taylor was slightly wounded while inspecting 101st AB positions along the river bank. The Americans were involved in fierce fighting with German units entrenched in nearby brick factories. In defending the ground they gained over 300 men of the Division were lost.

• End of Itinerary Four

ITINERARY FIVE

OOSTERBEEK – ARNHEM – DRIEL

This Itinerary, covering the area of the objective of the entire MARKET-GARDEN OPERATION, is the most complicated and the longest, yet is probably the most fascinating of all.

It is certainly the most difficult to describe to the reader with simple clarity to satisfy all interests and requirements. For instance, does the visitor wish (a) to retrace the main routes followed by the different Para formations towards Arnhem, or (b) to visit the main focal points of the battlefield, such as the Ginkel Heath DZ, the Hartenstein Museum, the CWGC Cemetery, the Escape Route and the John Frost Bridge or (c) to visit all the memorials and monuments on the battlefield or (d) does he or she wish to drive the most direct route from the furthest DZ to the objective of The Bridge to ascertain for his/herself just how far from the objective the Paras were dropped and gliders landed?

After much debate and consideration of how much time the visitor might have in the area and what his/her priorities might be, we have decided to make choice (b) our main Itinerary. This can be accomplished in a full day of touring. Choices (a) and (d) can be undertaken by carefully following the accompanying Major & Mrs Holt's Battle Map, where the three 1st AB routes are clearly marked. The scale will give you the distances. Choice (c) is covered by clearly explained Extra Visits which are detailed below, which cover the majority of the memorials. Any not covered are marked on the Map. Of course anyone having a particular interest in a specific site who is not sure where it is covered should consult the Index.

• **The Main Itinerary, Five,** starts at Heteren, looks at the DZs and LZs at Ginkelse Heide, passes through the middle of the area where the three parachute battalions and the 1st Airlanding Recce Squadron came down on the first day and began their move on Arnhem, follows part of the Middle Route and the last half of the Lower Route, covers the fighting in The Cauldron at Oosterbeek and the withdrawal across the river, moves on to Arnhem and the John Frost Bridge, and finishes at Driel.

• **The Route:** Heteren; Ede Cougar Tank; Ginkelse Heide LZs and Memorials; Wolfheze 1st AB Memorial Seat; The Kussin Crossroads; Hartenstein Airborne Museum; Airborne Monument; Quatre Bras 21st Independent Para Coy Memorial; VVV Oosterbeek; Airborne Commemorative Marker No 2; the Schoonoord; The Tafelberg; Airborne Commemorative Marker No 1; 21st Independent Para Coy Memorial Vase; No 8 Stationsweg; Airborne Commemorative Marker No 3; Arnhem-Oosterbeek CWGC Cemetery, Flowers in the Wind Memorial; Oosterbeek Local Cemetery; Air Despatch Memorial; Old ('Lonsdale') Church and

Memorials; Ter Horst House; Site of Baskeyfield's VC; Airborne Commemorative Marker No 7; Arnhem Walking Tour - Sword in Provincial House, 'Devil's House' Stained Glass Window, Eusebius Church Memorials and Viewpoint, Man Against Power Statue, Bakkerstraat Plaque to Shot Civilians, Frost's HQ Plaque, Jacob Groenewoud Memorial Garden, 25-Pounder Gun and Polish Memorial, Airborne Commemorative Marker No 8, Airborne Plein Memorials, John Frost Bridge Memorials; Windmill generator OP; RE Memorial; Driel-Heveadorp Ferry; Driel Polish Memorials, 5th DCLI Plaque; 7th Bn Hants Memorial.

• **Extra Visits are suggested to:** The Surrender Room, Wageningen; Hackett's Hideaway, Ede: Papendal Sports Centre Plaque; Leeren Doedel and Preserved Foxholes; The Culvert, Johannahoeve; 3rd Para Memorial Seat, Wolfheze; Klein Amerika; Heelsum AB Memorial & Seat; Renkum RC Cemetery; Westerbouwing Viewpoint & Dorset Plaques; Wolfheze Psychiatric Institution Cemetery and Memorials; Airborne Commemorative Marker No 4, The Hollow; 1st Border Positions on The Perimeter; 'Airborne House' Plaque; Dutch Women at War Memorial OP; Plaque Old German SD HQ; September 1944 Memorial; 14 Zwarteweg; Old St Elisabeth Hospital, Airborne Commemorative Marker No 6; Arnhem Evacuation Memorial; Moscowa Jewish Cemetery and CWGC Plot; Cross to 19 Civilians; Dakota Crash Site; Air Warfare Museum Deelen Airport; German Command Bunker; Arnhem 1940-45 Museum; Elden - Original 1940s Roadway, Civilians Memorial Column, Plaque on St Lucas Church, Lancaster Bomber Memorial; Groenewoud Plaque to J. McNee and J. Hyde.

• **Planned duration,** without stops for refreshment or Extra Visits: 5 hours 30 minutes
• **Total distance:** 59.8 kms/37.4 miles

• *Heteren: Entry Point at Junction No 18 with A50/0 kms/0 miles*

From Heteren take the A50 over the Neder Rijn. Take the first exit, No 19, on the N225 left towards Wageningen. Continue past the large Parenco factory complex on the left and then the turning to the Zetten ferry. Enter Wageningen and continue to the next traffic lights.

• *Extra Visit to the Surrender Room, Hotel de Wereld, Wageningen (Map 1N/53). Round trip: 1.9 kms/1.2 miles. Approximate time: 15 minutes.*

Go straight across on Ritzema Bosweg and continue to Bevrijdingsstraat. Turn left to 5 Mei Plein.

The building is on the right. Now an Education Centre, (Tel: + (0) 317 484413 e-mail: sander.essers@sg.osa.wau.nl) the old Hotel de Wereld was the scene of the German Capitulation to the Dutch. To the right of the entrance is a Commemorative Plaque recording that 'In this building on 5 May 1945 Lieutenant-General Charles Foulkes, CB, CBE DSO, the General Officer commanding 1 Canadian Corps accepted the unconditional surrender of 25th German Army from Col General Johannes Blaskowitz.' In actual fact the

Hotel de Wereld Wageningen

Extra visit continued

papers were handed over on the 5th but not signed until the 6th. Terms of the Instrument for the Surrender included the clearing of the canals 'of obstruction, mines etc' and the assistance 'in the arrangements for feeding the Dutch civilian population'.

The beginning of the end had started in March when Queen Wilhelmina, 'dressed in a long woollen coat with a piece of old fur around her throat' and looking 'like a stout Dutch country lady out for a stroll' [Alden Hatch], as depicted in the statue of her in the grounds of the Overloon Museum (qv), made her first visit to the liberated provinces of her country, crossing the Dutch border near Ede. On 17 April Prince Bernhard moved his HQ to the Palace of Het Loo in Apeldoorn, which had been used by the Germans as a military hospital, actually living in his own nearby house, Spelderholt. On his return, loyal locals returned precious furniture and even the Prince's personal clothes and jewellery, which they had taken and hidden for safekeeping for the five years of German occupation. His main preoccupation in the days leading up to the formal surrender was to get food into his starving country and to make sure that his troops would not wreak unlawful vengeance on the many German troops roaming the country. On 4 May the Prince heard the news of the German surrender to Montgomery at Luneburg Heath, which was to become effective at 0800 hours on 5 May. He met with General Foulkes who told him that the Dutch forces were forbidden to bear arms for at least three days - a difficult message for Bernhard to deliver to his Resistance Workers. He was anxious that Holland should not lapse into anarchy and at his staff's celebration party warned, 'We have won the war, but we still have to win the peace.'

The next day he met with the General Foulkes, General Blaskowitz, British and American commanders and Dutch Resistance leaders around a trestle table in the Hotel de Wereld. Bernhard, who refused to speak German during the ceremony, recorded that Blaskowitz, 'a gentleman of the old school', had had a row with Hitler and resigned. Hitler recalled him to command the collapsing German force in Holland at the very end. The Russians later accused him of war crimes and he committed suicide. Bernhard stipulated to Blaskowitz that he would only accept the surrender if all the SS men were disarmed and imprisoned. Blazkowitz maintained that he did not have the power to do so. Bernhard had good reason to fear the fanatical roaming SS men who felt they had nothing more to lose. In fact twelve of his own friends were killed by SS after the surrender. Bernhard was particularly at risk because of his German extraction, which caused the Germans to regard him as a traitor. During a fact-finding tour of his newly liberated country immediately after the Surrender, Bernhard took the precaution of wearing a disguise - a beret and a khaki shirt and a 'ridiculous false moustache' [Hatch].

On entering the building the canteen, with some photos of Wageningen during the war, is straight ahead. The Capitulation Room, to the right, is beautifully panelled with stained glass windows but as it may well be in use for a meeting it is wise to telephone ahead if you wish to visit it other than during the three weeks from 5 May each year when the original furniture is replaced and an exhibition is mounted.

In the 5 May Square is a striking **National Liberation Memorial** by H. Richters. *Return to the traffic lights and rejoin the main itinerary.*

Turn right on Diedenweg direction Ede/Bennekom. Continue and take the right turn to Bennekom (10.9 kms/6.8 miles). Continue to a roundabout and follow signs to Centrum. Continue through Bennekom, follow Ede signs under the motorway and enter Ede. Go under the railway following Apeldoorn signs and continue past the church tower on the left to the turning to Molenstraat to the left (18.4 kms/11.5 miles).

Extra Visit to Hackett's Hideaway, 5 Torenstraat, Ede (Map 1N/55). Round trip: .6 kms/.4 miles. Approximate time: 10 minutes

Turn left on Molenstraat. Continue to the Square on the left and park. By the Prénatal shop at No 2 on the corner is the tiny Torenstraat. Walk up it to the Onder de Toren Wine Merchants adjoining the Balkan Yugoslav Restaurant. This is the site of No. 5.

After escaping from the St Elisabeth Hospital (see below) Brigadier Hackett was brought to Ede by Resistance worker 'Piet van Arnhem'. After stopping briefly at the house of Tonny de Nooij in Brouwerstraat (which is the road along which you are parked) where he met Brigadier Lathbury, who had also been rescued from the hospital by Piet, Hackett was taken to No 5 Torenstraat. First his severe stomach wound was treated by a Dutch doctor who wondered at the skill of Lipmann Kessel (qv), Surgeon to 16th Para Field Ambulance. Then he was gently nursed back to health and strength by the kindly owners (also members of the de Nooij family) who risked grave danger for harbouring him and who Hackett came to love and admire. It was not until 29 January that he was deemed fit enough to leave and was escorted to a safe house in Maarn near Doorn. There to his surprise he was reunited with Lipmann and other Airborne colleagues. Lipmann tidied up Hackett's wound before they were all moved along the next hazardous leg of their escape route - by rickety canoe through the Merwede River, through the maze of swampy channels to the River Waal. Finally Hackett arrived at HQ 21st Army Group where Monty gave him a slap-up dinner with oysters and wine. On 7 February he arrived back at Northolt and arranged for the BBC to broadcast to his Dutch friends the coded message, 'The Grey Goose has gone'. General Sir John Hackett's experiences are described in detail in his book, *I Was a Stranger*, Chatto & Windus 1978. The title comes from St Matthew Chapter 25 Verse 35, 'I was a stranger and ye took me in.'

Continue to the junction with the N224, turn right direction Arnhem and continue to the roundabout.
On the right is the Pannenkoekenhuis de Langenberg. Tel: + (0) 318 610485.
Turn right and immediately left into the slip road.

• Cougar No 13 Tank/20.3 kms/12.7 miles/5 minutes/Map 1N/56

This Canadian tank took part in the liberation of Ede by the Canadian Calgary Regiment of the 49th (Polar Bear) West Riding Division on 17 April 1945. It was restored on 10 March 1980 by the 8th Canadian Hussars, Princess Louise's Maintenance Troop. A plaque

Cougar Tank No 13, Ede

acknowledges all the sponsors of the restoration who include the MoD, various local Rotary Clubs, schools, builders and banks.

Continue on the N224, passing Military Barracks and training areas to the right.

At 22.4 kms/14 miles a Memorial can be seen in the heath to the left. This is to **Belgian Refugees** of the First World War who had a camp on this site (Map 2/1).

Continue to the Café on the left.

The Zuid Ginkel Café, Tel: + (0) 318 653972 is a favourite haunt of veterans and over the period of the Anniversary is always very busy. 133rd Para Field Ambulance set up a DS here on 18 September as the medical orderlies scoured the burning heath for wounded.

Turn right opposite the café onto the unmade road and follow a sandy track to the sheep barn. Park.

The sheep barn was standing in 1944.

• *Ginkelse Heide and Airborne Memorials/23.7 kms /14.8 miles/15 minutes/Map 2-2/3*

The Memorial, in the form of a pillar with the insignia of the KOSB, a Pegasus and the Airborne Badge, is surmounted by a symbolic Dove of Peace. It was designed by Mrs M. M. Heuff van Oven, erected by the people of Ede and unveiled by General Urquhart on 19 September 1960. Below the Memorial is a quotation from Isaiah 40.31, 'They shall mount up with wings as eagles.' There is a large stone with the inscription in white 'Luchtlanding 17-18 September 1944' [actually the area was not used on 17 September]. 'Luchtlanding' can mean both parachute and glider landings – 'Drop' Zones were for parachutists and 'Landing' Zones for gliders.

Weather permitting, there is a commemorative drop and short service of commemoration here, normally at 1100 hours, on the nearest Saturday to the 17 September Anniversary. In 2000 there was still a sprinkling of veteran parachutists in the drop, some even dropping solo, others in tandem with their modern Para counterparts. It is a thrilling sight, and very well attended both by loyal locals and visiting veterans, families and other interested groups and individuals from the UK. If you wish to see the drop it is advisable to arrive early or you may have to park a long way from the heath. To stand here alone, however, on the quiet heath, covered in parts by heather, with only the images retained from familiar photographs and film scenes in the mind, is an extraordinarily evocative experience.

Ginkel Heath DZ Y

Airborne Memorial and detail, Ginkel Heath

Ginkelse Heide was Drop Zone Y, the furthest from The Bridge of all the DZs. General Urquhart would have preferred to have put his troops down on top of the Arnhem Bridges in order to capitalize on the primary advantage given by the use of airborne forces – that of surprise. However, Air Force commanders said that German anti-aircraft defences in the area were so concentrated that it was not possible to fly tugs and transports close to the bridges. It was also claimed that the polder (low-lying reclaimed land) immediately to the south of the road bridge, the only nearby non-built-up area, was too marshy either to land or drop upon. (This was later found to be untrue and the reader should look back to the entry on the soggy Airstrip B-82 on the polder at Keent near Grave, where 209 C-47 Dakotas landed on one day.) The General, not an Airborne man, and who in hindsight may be considered as having 'drawn the short straw' in being given this command, was persuaded, and chose assault zones some 10kms away from his objective.

There were not enough planes to drop the 82nd AB, 101st AB and 1st AB at the same time on the same day. Airlift priority had been given to the American AB since their targets were closest to XXX Corps' start point and had to be captured first. Also Air Force authorities said that essential maintenance, shortness of daylight hours and crew fatigue would make two sorties a day impossible. Some para soldiers wondered whose side the Air Force was on. Therefore, with only one sortie a day, the aircraft allocated to General Urquhart would take three days to deliver his whole division - one 'lift' per day: hardly conducive to surprising the enemy.

This heath was a drop zone for the second lift, scheduled for 1000 hours on 18 September, consisting of 4 Para Brigade (10th, 11th and 156th Para Battalions) plus those British parts of the Division that had not landed elsewhere the day before. Often overlooked are the Supporting Arms and Services that back up the infantry elements of fighting forces, thus, as part of the 'Brigade Group', were also 2nd Anti-tank Battery RA, 4th Para Squadron RE, 133rd Para Field Ambulance RAMC and personnel from 3rd and 13th Light Aid Detachments REME. No forces landed here on 17 September but it was secured for the next day's activities by the 7th KOSB (from 1st Airlanding Brigade which had landed on LZ S which you will shortly pass). Bad weather in England delayed the drop and the first troops did not begin to arrive until 1500 hours. 11th Para Battalion was sent immediately to the Arnhem area, eventually joining up with the South Staffords in the assault past Zwarteweg (qv) where General Urquhart was holed up. The remainder of the Brigade prepared to move towards Arnhem late in the afternoon of the 18th. They all ended up manning The Perimeter.

Return to the main road, turn right and continue on the N224 over the A12, direction Arnhem/Wolfheze. Continue to the traffic lights and the junction with the N783 signed to Wolfheze.

The road to the right, the N783 Wolfhezerweg, leads past LZ S (see the Holts' Map). The road that you are now driving along was the Upper Route, code-named LEOPARD. On the 17th there were German armoured vehicles in the woods to your left ahead and German infantry on the right. Lieutenant-Colonel Dobie's 1st Para Battalion, whose task was to take the high ground behind Arnhem, came up Wolfhezerweg from the area of Wolfheze railway station intending to use the Upper Route, but, despite fierce fighting, were unable to get any further. Hearing that Colonel Frost was at the bridge and needing help, Dobie decided to forget his allocated objective and that evening headed for the bridge.

• *Extra Visits to Papendal Sports Centre Memorial Plaque (Map 2/23)/ the Leeren Doedel (Map 2/24)/Traces of Foxholes and Slit trenches (Map 2/25)*
Round trip: 7.8 kms/4.9 miles. Approximate time: 30 minutes

Continue on the N224, under the A50.

The A12 was under construction in 1944 and was known as the 'Hares" Path – the road to Germany, along which the Dutch presumed the Germans would flee like hares! It was only finished in 1968/69.

Take the first right at the traffic lights, following signs to the National Sports Centre. Drive into the entrance and park outside the main reception building.

The National Sports Centre, Tel: + (0) 26 4821853 has extensive sporting and training facilities, including an 18-hole golf course, three hotels and three restaurants.

Walk into the main building. Turn to the left inside the door and walk to the end of the corridor.

On the wall to the right is the **Plaque** which reads, 'From 17-27 September 1944 this area was involved in the Battle of Arnhem. Lest We Forget.' The area immediately south of here was LZ L where the Polish Parachute Brigade was planned to arrive in gliders on 19 September. The parachute element of the Brigade was intended to land on DZ K south of the Arnhem road bridge that same day. But poor visibility in England prevented the parachute force, which included General Sosabowski, from taking off. The airlanding element, however, did arrive here on the 19th to be met with savage anti-aircraft fire. Figures vary as to the number of Polish gliders that landed - thirty-four according to General Sosabowski (cf his memoirs, *Freely I Served*), twenty-eight according to the respected author Martin Middlebrook (*Arnhem 1944, The Airborne Battle*) - illustrating the dangers of being dogmatic about precise details when relating military history. The Poles, with jeeps, trailers and six-pounder guns, drove south fast,

Extra visit continued

probably following much the same route as the main itinerary until they reported to Airborne Headquarters at the Hartenstein Hotel.

Return to the traffic lights.

On the corner on the right at 505 Amsterdamseweg is the good value Van der Valk **Hotel West End** with typical Dutch food. Tel: + (0) 26 4821614

Turn right. You are now on the Upper Route. Continue along Amsterdamseweg to the Leeren Doedel restaurant on the right. Park.

During the battle the **Leeren Doedel**, now the **Pinoccio Pizzeria** Tel: + (0)26 3332344, was at the top end of a German blocking line that ran south astride Dreijenseweg to Utrechtseweg (Sketch Map 4). It began forming on Sunday afternoon under the command of SS Lieutenant-Colonel Spindler, who collected together various small groups of the 9th SS. After withdrawing from the Wolfheze area on the night of the 17th Krafft's force also established themselves here under Spindler, forming the top hinge of the line. Krafft's rapid reactions on the first day had stopped 3rd Para and forced 1st Para to divert, now Spindler's force would prevent any further reinforcement of 2nd Para at The Bridge. The next evening the KOSB were held up, having moved up from the Johannahoeve farm area, and on the third day (Tuesday 19 September) the advance of 10th Battalion and an attack by 156th Battalion of 4th Parachute Brigade were unable to cross the line. The effect of Spindler's force was to turn 1st AB south into the conflict around the St Elisabeth Hospital and thence back into The Perimeter. This crossroads is effectively the closest 1st AB got to Arnhem along the Upper Route. The building was the HQ of Kampfgruppe Spindler.

On the wall of the terrace extension is a **Plaque** which translates, 'Destroyed 26 September 1944 [it was actually the 21st].' The destruction was mainly by RAF Typhoons. The restaurant had been built to a high standard in 1939 and its destruction also caused the death of the owner. The building was full of the dead and wounded. Understandably his son felt very bitter about the Allied intervention, with its tragic consequences for his family. Rebuilding began by KL van Toor on 20 July 1955.

From the car park walk down Dreijenseweg to the junction with Sportlaan.

In the woods to the right can be found traces of September 1944 foxholes and slit trenches where desperate hand-to-hand fighting took place.

N.B. These are historic remnants of the battle and should not under any circumstances be climbed into or walked upon. That they still remain is some sort of miracle and they should be preserved for future generations. It is to be hoped that they will soon be protected so that the military historian can see them without damaging them.

Return to your car, turn round and return to the traffic lights and pick up the main itinerary as it turns right and you turn left.

Turn right and continue towards Wolfheze.

On the right, as the wooded area stops, was LZ S for 1st Airlanding Brigade. It was here that the 1st Border Regiment, the 7th KOSB and the 2nd South Staffords landed, together with a platoon of 9th Field Company RE and 181st Airlanding Field Ambulance. Their prime function was to protect the landing zones for the second lift and to establish road blocks on the access roads from the west. They were not involved in the first day's push into Arnhem. Roughly in the middle of LZ S is the area of Reijerskamp Farm where **Flight Lieutenant David Lord VC** (qv) crashed in his Dakota KG374. The machine had flown to Arnhem on 18 September, successfully releasing his Horsa, despite heavy flak. On 19 September it was flying a supply drop mission. Some 7 miles from the target the plane was hit, but Lord decided to carry on with his mission. When he was forced to give the order to bale out, the one survivor, Harry King (qv), was thrown clear of the plane. The other crew members, Pilot Officer Richard Medhurst (son of Air Vice-Marshal Charles Medhurst) and Flying Officer Alec Ballantyne (the wireless operator), plus the four Air Despatchers, who were described as 'magnificent' - Corporal Philip Nixon (qv), Driver Len Harper (qv), Driver James Ricketts (qv) and Driver Arthur Rowbotham (qv) - were all killed. (See Arnhem-Oosterbeek CWGC Cemetery entry.)

To the left the radio and television tower at Den Brink is visible. It is on high ground from which the Germans fired on the 2nd Battalion as it made its way to The Bridge.

To the right is Duitsekampweg (30.9 kms/19.3 miles), so called because there was a WW1 Camp for German internees here 1917-1919 - Holland was then a neutral country. On 17 September probably the first Dressing Station was set up in Nos 8, 9 and 11 along this road by 181st Airlanding Field Ambulance where casualties from the landings were quickly treated. A fierce battle soon raged around the temporary medical facility and on the 18th they moved across the railway line to the mental hospital (qv). On the 19th there were so many casualties that the Schoonoord (qv) and Vreewijk Hotel in Oosterbeek and the Paasberg School were also taken over.

Continue towards the railway.

- ***Extra Visit to The Culvert (Map 2/13).***
Round trip: 1.3 kms/.8 miles. Approximate time: 15 minutes

Just before the railway, turn left along Johannahoeveweg. After some 200m as the road turns left to Sara Mansveltweg continue straight ahead on the unmade track.

N.B. In the winter this narrow road becomes very muddy and is only safely negotiable with 4-wheel drive. It may be safer to leave one's vehicle here and continue on foot.

Continue, pass the sign to the Johannahoeve Estate, to the track to the right leading through a culvert.

The Culvert under the Railway. On 17 September part of Major Freddie Gough's Recce Squadron and a troop of REs came up this track as far as the culvert. Their *coup de main* task was to motor by the shortest route possible to The Bridge to remove any demolition charges and to hold it until reinforced. After a successful rendezvous after landing on LZ Z, (see the Holt's Map – you can drive through LZ Z on an Extra Visit) 23-year old Lieutenant Peter Bucknall's two jeeps of C Troop were to lead the dash to The Bridge. As his own jeep (which contained their wireless) had not arrived, Bucknall roared off in the direction of Wolfheze in what should have been the second jeep, followed a few minutes later by his own jeep.

When the latter crossed the railway line at Wolfheze and turned along this track they came under fire from the railway embankment. Lance-Sergeant Thomas McGregor was

Extra visit continued

killed and most of the other passengers were wounded. They continued a desperate shooting match with the Germans until, finally waving a white cloth, they were taken prisoner. Later that day Bucknall's jeep was discovered, the occupants all having been shot in the back and scorched by flame-thrower. The remainder of C Troop, led by their OC, Captain John Hay, were beaten back by the strength of the Krafft (qv) battalion's blocking line which straddled the railway line and extended to beyond the Hotel Wolfheze (qv). The 'Recce' Squadron made no further attempts to continue the dash for The Bridge despite the fact that, contrary to many early reports that none of their jeeps had arrived, they had several vehicles available. Most of C Troop's dead from the unhappy engagement were buried in the field next to No. 9 Duitsekampweg, near the dressing station that had been set up there.

The Culvert, Wolfheze

Lieutenant Bucknall, Troopers Ronald Brumwell, William Edmond, Edward Gorringe (originally listed as missing until identified in 1987), Leslie Goulding and Lance Sergeant McGregor were re-interred together in the Arnhem-Oosterbeek CWGC Cemetery [16.B. 5, 6, 7, 8, 9 and 10.].

The culvert was constructed for water drainage purposes, not intended as a roadway, but on 19 September it was used as such by much of the 4th Para Brigade transport because the railway crossing at Wolfheze was under German control. Major E.J.M. Perkins who commanded 4 Para Squadron RE recalled that, 'By this time many of the jeeps were carrying stretcher cases and there was only just sufficient headroom to allow such vehicles to pass through at a very slow speed.'

Try walking through the culvert - it is very atmospheric.

Turn round and start back towards the junction.

According to Middlebrook, there was a small line of trees here which on 18 September Captain Lionel Queripel (qv), the 2i/c of A Company, 10th Para Battalion, was tasked to hold. After battling to hold on all night, the position was overwhelmed the next morning, Queripel sending his remaining men off whilst he, although badly wounded, hung on, armed with his pistol and a few grenades. He was never seen alive again and is buried in the Arnhem-Oosterbeek CWGC Cemetery [5.D.8.]. Captain Queripel was awarded a posthumous VC (qv) for his outstanding gallantry. Other witnesses place his scene of gallantry nearer the Leeren Doedel (qv). Sadly all witnesses are now dead.

Return to the junction with Wolfhezerweg and turn left, picking up the main itinerary.

It was in the Wolfheze railway area that David Dobie's 1st Para Battalion, en route from their drop zone, met elements of Gough's Recce Squadron who told them that there were German armoured vehicles ahead. Dobie had arrived here having taken the small road that runs alongside and south of the railway from DZ X and intended to cross the railway and continue along the track that is the subject of the Extra Visit above. Having heard that news, he decided to head north, back up the road down which you have driven, and hence met, and was stopped by, the Germans at the junction with the Upper Route.

Cross the railway line.

To the right, after roughly 0.6 miles (1 km), the railway runs between LZ S in the north and DZ X and LZ Z in the south (see the Holt's' Map). Major-General Urquhart landed on Z on the first day and immediately set about trying to co-ordinate the battle.

One of the most important factors in the achievement of success on the battlefield is that of communication, the ability to control one's forces to meet changing circumstances. During the Arnhem part of MARKET-GARDEN radio communications were very poor. It was due to this failure of the radios that General Urquhart went searching for the scattered parts of his command. Lewis Golden, who was adjutant of the 1st Airborne Signals Regiment who fought with the Division, believes (see his memoirs, *Echoes from Arnhem*) that the General himself may have precipitated the circumstances that led to his inability to communicate by radio with his brigadiers. The radio system by which units communicate is called a 'net', each net operating on a different frequency. One designed for command purposes, such as this, is a 'Command Net'. When Urquhart landed he was told that the jeeps of the Recce Squadron commanded by Major Freddy Gough had not arrived (this was not true - see above) and that therefore it would not be possible to carry out the *coup de main* attack on The Bridge. He then set off in his jeep to visit 1st Parachute Brigade and told his radio operator to contact Gough so that they could devise another plan. However, Gough's radio was not working on the same frequency (net) as that of the General. In order to try to find Gough's frequency the operator had to detune from the Command Net and search the airwaves, thus making it impossible for the General to communicate with his HQ. The mistakes in the use of the radios were compounded as the days went on, including the expectation that they would work from moving vehicles which, generally, they would not. Many different reasons have been advanced for the failure of the radios, from lack of preparation by the signallers themselves, to the use of the wrong crystals and wrong frequencies. Three things peculiar to the area of operations were probably to blame – the number of trees, the dampness of the ground and the presence of ferrous materials in the sandy soil which affected the ranges over which the radios could operate. However, there can be little doubt that in the same way that the presence of German armour was ignored by the High Command when deciding to go ahead with MARKET-GARDEN, the inadequacy of the radios was also known beforehand. Some weeks before, Captain Bill Marquand, who commanded 1st Para Brigade Signal Section, had carried out an exercise at Grimsby to test the Brigade signals equipment and, according to Lewis Golden, 'it proved inadequate'. There were also other reasons:-

A PERSONAL OPINION
By Major-General John Frost

There may be a time when because of postponements the batteries begin to run down. If that takes place you start off with a set which isn't working 100%. As the aircraft comes into land, be it a glider or you come in by parachute, the set takes a pretty hefty bang which very often is enough to put the thing out of tune. So you've got quite a lot of difficulties before you even start an airborne operation.

To the left is **Wolfheze Station.** After the battle, and as a result of the railway strike (qv), the Germans put personnel on all local trains, stopping the transportation of food from east to west. A purpose-built railway line led from here to the airfield at Deelen and the Diogenes Command Bunker (qv).

Next to the station is the **Restaurant Het Wolvenbosch.** Tel: + (0) 26 4821202, a favourite meeting place for many years of the KOSB when they returned to Arnhem.

• *Extra Visits to 3rd Para Battalion Memorial Seat, Klein Amerika (Map 2/5)/Heelsum Airborne Memorial & Seat (Map2-6/7)/ Westerbouwing Viewpoint & Dorset Plaques (Map*2-27/28)/ Section of 2nd Para Battalion Route.*
Trip from Wolfheze to Utrechtseweg: 12.5 kms/7.8 miles.
Approximate time: 45 minutes

N.B. This Extra Visit rejoins the main itinerary at the Koude Herberg Crossroads, omitting the next two main stops.

Immediately turn right along Parallelweg, running beside the railway line. Take the first small road to the left, immediately after the Van Beeck Calkoen School direction Boshoeve (.8 kms/.5 miles).

This road marks the extreme north-eastern edge of LZ Z. N.B. It can be extremely muddy and slippery.

Continue on this small track past the Psychiatric Institute on the left.

Eighty-five civilians were killed in the bombing of the Wolfheze area during one morning alone. The heavy bombing had been approved by Urquhart because it was thought that there were Germans in the Asylum which was very close to LZ Z. The bombing was done by the Americans who had asked for a personal assurance from the General that it was what he wanted. Perhaps they were mindful of the controversy that had followed the bombing of the Abbey at Monte Cassino in February 1944. It was here that white-clothed patients from the asylum were seen wandering by Urquhart just after landing on 17 September – 'They were all smiles and full of greetings and some just stared... . They looked none the worse for their experience and did not interfere,' he wrote in his memoirs.

Continue to the first T-junction and turn left, continuing past the Boshoeve Farm on the bend.

You are now travelling through the area where Lieutenant-Colonel Dobie's 1st Para Battalion came down on 17 September. They then moved off (back the way that you came) to the Wolfheze railway crossing.

Continue to the Renkumsheide Farm and turn left (2.6 kms/1.6 miles) passing Jonkershoeve on the right.

You have DZ X and LZ X on your right and LZ Z on your left.

Continue to the Klein Amerikaweg junction and park by the tree on the right (3.4 kms/2.1 miles).

On the left is a house on the site of the farm that was there in 1944. The area was known

Extra visit continued

as Klein Amerika because of the modern US farming methods that were pioneered here. This area was the RV of Lieutenant-Colonel Fitch's 3rd Battalion. Lieutenant-Colonel Frost's 2nd Battalion had their rendezvous at the southern edge of LZ Z by the Hotel Klein Zwitzerland (qv). Each battalion moved off eastwards towards the Middle (TIGER) and Lower (LION) Routes respectively.

Walk up the path ahead to the bench.

3rd Para Battalion Memorial Seat/OP

The idea of veteran Len Wright, the seat was presented by the Battalion, in memory of their fallen comrades, to the inhabitants of Renkum, in gratitude for their courage and undaunted support during the Battle of Arnhem, September 1944. Sadly, in July 2000 the English plaque was missing.

With one's back to the bench, take the path as 12 o'clock. At 3 o'clock the Den Brink radio and TV tower can be seen. To a first approximation that is the direction in which the 2nd and 3rd Battalions headed.

Return to the car. Follow the road to the right signed to Klein Amerika and continue into Renkum, passing Airborne Weg to the right. Turn left at the crossroads onto Bennekomseweg into Heelsum and continue to the memorial to the right at the 'P' for parking sign.

The small road opposite leads to Klein Zwitzerland where the 2nd Battalion had its RV and the Battalion moved down this way to the Lower Route. The itinerary from here follows the route taken by the Battalion to Oosterbeek.

Heelsum Airborne Memorial and Seat (5.4 kms/3.4 miles)

Erected by local inhabitants in 1945, this highly imaginative memorial, surmounted by a winged Pegasus and made up of battlefield remnants, was moved from its first site nearby when the motorway was built and turned round so that it could be seen from the new road. Sadly many of its original components – parachute containers, shell cases, helmets etc - have been stolen and have been replaced with substitutes. In 1994 it was restored and new plaques and explanatory diagrams were added. A modified 6-pounder gun still forms part of the memorial. The inscription reads, 'Heelsum. In this place landed 1st AB Division on 17 September 1944 at 1 o'clock.' The time referred to is the local Dutch time which was one hour behind the time used by the landing forces.

Heelsum Airborne Memorial

Beside the memorial is a **Seat donated to the Rotary Club of Oosterbeek** on their 40th Anniversary by the Rotary Club of Downham Market and Shanklin, IoW (twinned with Oosterbeek) on 14 September 1991.

N.B. By turning right through 180° to go along Utrechtseweg direction Renkum, continuing through Heelsum and into Renkum and then turning right just past the garage on the right into Groeneweg (1.9 kms/1.2 miles), **Renkum RC Cemetery** may be visited. The

Extra visit continued

cemetery is then on the right. There is a CWGC sign by the gate. It contains, amongst others, the grave of **Serjeant James Gibbons**, 156th Para, age 25, 20 September 1944 (4.2 kms/2.6 miles round trip).

From the Memorial turn right and left under the motorway signed Arnhem, first right at the T-junction onto Doorthwerthsestraat and then left.

On the left are the typical small wire fences which in September 1944 badly hampered the heavily laden AB troops. You are now driving along Frost's exact route.

Continue on Roggekamp, signed Oosterbeek/Arnhem, to the crossroads, continue following Doorgaand Verkeer signs under the motorway and bear left, still on Roggecamp.

Frost probably met his first opposition here. There was some fighting among the trees and German prisoners were taken en route to Doorwerth, which in 1944 only contained some twenty-five houses.

Continue on W. A. Scholtenlaan through the new housing development to the crossroads with Italiaanseweg. Continue.

To the right is the village of Heveadorp which, as it contained the only houses in the area untouched by the battle, was used at the beginning of the film *Theirs is the Glory*.

Continue to the T-junction and turn right on Oude Oosterbeekseweg. Continue to the next T-junction and turn right on Van der Molenallee towards Westerbouwing and immediately right into the Restaurant car park.

Westerbouwing Restaurant/Dorsets Plaque/Seat (10.9 kms/6.8 miles) RWC/OP. Tel: + (0) 26 3332019. Closed during the week in the winter, it makes an ideal venue for a lunch break on the battlefield tour. There is a small scenic chairlift which may or may not be working. Note the tall tower which is visible from the Royal Engineers Memorial on the south bank and provides an excellent reference point. The terrace has a marvellous view over the river and as far as Nijmegen on a clear day. Two major attempts were made to get reinforcements across the river, one by the Poles into The Perimeter on the night of the 22nd and one to here by the 4th Dorsets on the night of the 24th. Oddly, Horrocks had that morning made the decision to evacuate 1st Airborne so it is valid to ask why the Dorsets were sent across. In his 43rd *Wessex Division at War*, Major-General H. Essame (then commanding 214th Infantry Brigade) wrote, 'It was

Plaque to 4th/5th Dorsets, Westerbouwing

Extra visit continued

considered essential to get a firmer grip on the far side in order to enable them to be withdrawn.' It sounds bafflingly similar to Sir Douglas Haig's logic for the carnage of the Passchendaele offensive, 'to be in a better positon to start the new year.'

Even if the 'firmer grip' made military sense, the choice of Westerbouwing as a destination must be questioned. The Germans had been in and around here for at least two days. Essame continues,

> The site selected for the crossing was the ferry at the western end of The Perimeter.... It was overlooked by the enemy on the high ground on the far side [essentially where you now are]... incessant mortar and machine gun fire made movement in daylight... between Driel and the river bank impossible.

The attack, therefore, was scheduled for 2200 hours, with a planned simultaneous crossing by the Poles into The Perimeter. The transport bringing up some of the assault boats took a wrong turning and drove into enemy lines at Elst and two more lorries slid off the road leaving insufficient boats for both crossings. Accordingly the Poles' crossing was cancelled. The Dorsets had to carry their boats some 600 yards down to the river while under mortar and machine-gun fire and did not set off until 0100 hours, a time of strong current. One boat was hit by mortar fire and others swept away by the current, but eventually elements of four rifle companies landed below the Westerbouwing heights under fire and were plunged into close-quarter fighting. They fought their way up the slope in front of you, led by their Commanding Officer Lieutenant-Colonel G. Tilly in a bayonet charge, though in the end his party had to surrender. A small group did get through to the Hartenstein but the night's enterprise cost the battalion thirteen officers and two hundred men.

On the exterior wall of the restaurant is a **Plaque to the Dorsets** to commemorate the actions of the 4th and 5th Battalions (the 5th provided fire support for the crossing) between 24-26 September 1944. Up a small path is a **Commemorative Seat to the Dorsets** and the British flag flies above it.

On 16 September 1994, as part of the 50th Anniversary, the Dorset Regiment made a commemorative crossing in four boats.

Turn left out of the car park and right at the T-junction signed to the Hartenstein Museum into Oosterbeek.

Immediately to the left in the woods, in one of the ironies of war, a British soldier's body was found after the war with seven spoons, perhaps from the restaurant, in his pocket.

Take the first left signed Wolfheze/Airborne Museum. Continue to the junction with Utrechtseweg on Van Brosselenweg.

N.B. The Kussin Crossroads (see below) is some 650m to the left.

Turn right to rejoin the main itinerary on Utrechtseweg following signs to Oosterbeek.

Continue 100m to the memorial on the right and stop.

• 1st (BR) AB Memorial Seat/31.2 kms/19.5 miles/5 minutes/Map 2/16

The semicircular brick structure includes a wooden seat and in the centre is a plaque, bearing the Pegasus insignia with the inscription, in English and Dutch,

In memory of the units of the 1st British Airborne Division and of the 1st Polish Independent Para Brigade which landed in the vicinity on 17, 18 and 19 September 1944. From here they advanced in the direction of Arnhem to seize the road bridge as part of Operation MARKET-GARDEN. This Battle of Arnhem lasted from 17-26 September 1944.

• Extra Visit to Wolfheze Psychiatric Institute Cemetery/Memorials (Map 2-14/15). Round trip: 1.9 kms/1.2 miles. Approximate time: 15 minutes

Take the road called Plein 1t/m6, and at the T-junction turn left into the grounds of the Gelderse Roos Psychiatric Institution.

There has been much recent modernization of the Institute where patients live in pleasant, open-policy accommodation, but there are still some original 1944 buildings in existence. It is on the north-east corner of LZ Z.

Continue to the large notice board opposite the Church and continue following signs to Mortuarium and Begraafplaats. The cemetery is behind the Mortuarium.

This dates from c1900 and is still open for burials. In it is an impressive **Memorial to the staff and mental patients** who 'fell during the birth of Liberation' (mainly during the bombing). Their names, including the Hendriks father and son, are inscribed around the edge of the memorial. There are also headstones to Jan Schiedam and Geurt Answik, shot by the Germans in the grounds on 19 September 1944.

Return to the AB Seat following Uitgang signs and pick up the main itinerary.

Continue on Wolfhezerweg, the N783, over the motorway.
Some of the trees along the road at the exits to houses bear white bands which are reminiscent of those used during the blackout to help navigation. The tops of iron railings in the area were also painted white. The HQ of SS Pz Grenadier Depot and Reserve Battalion 16 under *Sturmbannführer* Sepp Krafft was in the old Hotel Wolfheze, now the modern Bilderberg Hotel Wolfheze (Tel: + (0) 26 3337852), whose entrance is passed on the left (32.6 kms/20.4 miles). When the landings began the unit was carrying out exercises in the woods and Krafft immediately sent one company towards the landing zones and placed another in defensive positions around here. The first company reached LZ Z and after brief bursts of machine-gun fire fell back here. Krafft rapidly decided that the Arnhem road bridge was the target and used his troops to form a blocking line on the east of, and parallel to, the road along which you are driving, stretching from Utrechtseweg almost to Wolfheze station. He sent one platoon into the woods just north of the station and it was this force that halted 1st Recce Squadron on its drive into Arnhem. While issuing his orders Krafft was visited by General Kussin, the town commander of Arnhem, who promised reinforcements and set off back to Arnhem down this road, although advised by Krafft not to do so. It was a fatal mistake as you will see. Heavy fighting continued until dark, Krafft's rapid reactions playing a major part in preventing 1st and 3rd Para from reaching Arnhem. That evening Krafft withdrew to join up with the forces at Dreijenseweg (Sketch Map 4). In October 1944,

1st (BR) AB Memorial
Seat and detail,
Wolfheze

Wolfheze Psychiatric Institue Memorial and
Graves in Cemetery

SKETCH MAP 4: 17 SEPTEMBER 1944 - THE
ADVANCE OF 1st (BR) AB DIVISION AND
THE MAIN GERMAN BLOCKING LINES

LZS

Upper Route -LEOPARD

Wolfheze

1st Bn DOBIE

Leeren
Daedel

Johannahoeve

Amsterdamseweg

DZX

(In the evening Krafft
joined Spindler)

LZX   LZZ

Dreijenseweg

SS Trg Bn
Krafft

9th SS
Pz Group
Spindler

0   1 Mile

Wolfhezerweg

1.6 Km

3rd Bn FITCH

Koude Herberg
Café

St Elisabeth
Hospital

ARNHEM

Middle Route -TIGER

Kussin killed

Utrechtseweg

Hartenstein
Hotel

Lower Route - LION

Heelsum

OOSTERBEEK

2nd Bn FROST

Benedendorpsweg

Site of Pontoon
Bridge

Old Church

Westerbouwing

The John
Frost Bridge

Bridge blown

after the fighting was over, Krafft completed his war diary and sent a copy to Heinrich
Himmler on his birthday who replied, 'My Dear Krafft, Sincere thanks for your birthday
wishes. Heil Hitler! Congratulations on the Arnhem operation. Sincere greetings to you and
your men.' The diary is a model of military writing that any graduate of an army staff
college would be proud of and showed respect for the conduct and resistance of the British
troops, yet it also displayed Krafft's inability to understand the British sense of humour. He
reported, 'Inscriptions on the gliders are interesting: 'We are the Al Capone Gang: Up with
the reds: Up with the frauleins' skirts.' How far this is connected with the political

convictions of the troops themselves or whether it is due to Bolshevist or American influences is not known.'
Continue to the T-junction with the N225.

• The Kussin Crossroads/33.3 kms/20.8 miles/Map 2/18

It was here that General Kussin (speeding down the way you have just come) after his meeting with Krafft bumped into a leading platoon of 3rd Para led by Captain Jimmy Cleminson that was coming up from the right along the Middle Route. Kussin's driver, Max Koester, stopped and tried to reverse, but everyone in the car was then killed. [The famous photograph of the dead General in his car was used in the film *Theirs is the Glory* (qv).] Although usually referred to as a 'crossroads', this is more accurately described as a T-junction and will soon become a roundabout.
Turn left
To the left is the entrance to the 4-star **Hotel de Bilderberg** Tel: + (0) 26 3649849.
Continue on Utrechtseweg to the roundabout (34.2 kms/21.4miles).
Known as the **Koude Herberg Crossroads** in September 1944 because of the inn of the same name that stood on the left corner with Valkenburglaan, this was at the western extremity of The Perimeter. Late on 19 September 17 and 18 Platoons of C Company of the 1st Borders occupied the area. They were supported by 6-pounder guns named after the 1915 Gallipoli Campaign - 'Hellespont' and 'Scimitar Hill' - and suffered repeated attacks. As the battle moved to the junction with Van Lennepweg, Sergeants Lewis, Smith and Walker of the Army Film Unit filmed another gun - 'Gallipoli' - knocking out a German self-propelled gun. It was among the few seconds of original film to survive. During the filming the most famous still picture of the Arnhem Battle - of Private Ron ('Ginger') Tierney firing a mortar - was taken. Veterans returning in 1946 found the original mortar tube. When they returned in 1993 the mortar pit was still discernable at the edge of the woodland to the south of Van Lennepweg, the next turning to the right.

• Extra Visit to Airborne Commemorative Marker No 4, The Hollow (Map 3/1)
Round trip: 1 km/.6 miles. Approximate time: 10 minutes.

Turn left up Valkenburglaan to the riding stables on the right. At the edge of the road opposite is
Airborne Commemorative Marker No 4
Some 200 yards to the north is the area where the dwindling 4th Brigade was surrounded, under heavy enemy fire. Brigadier Shan Hackett just managed to roar out of the inferno in a clearing with a wounded man in his jeep as flames from a burning jeep engulfed the area. That wounded man was Lieutenant-Colonel Derick Heathcoat Amory, who went on to become Chancellor of the Exchequer and Viscount Amory. Desperate hand-to-hand fighting ensued and Lieutenant-Colonel Sir Richard des Voeux, CO of 156th Battalion, Major Ritson, his 2i/c, and the Brigade Major Dawson were all

Airborne
Commemorative
Marker No 4

Extra visit continued

killed shortly before this battle [they are buried in the Oosterbeek CWGC Cemetery]. Hackett decided to press on southwards and called to Major Geoffrey Powell [later to become an accomplished author, including *The Devil's Birthday*, an excellent account of the Operation] to gather his men together. They made for the hollow behind this pillar, cleared it of the Germans who held it and formed a defensive perimeter around it. It was held by some 150 men of 156th Battalion with only the ammunition they carried and no food or water. They saw off repeated attacks until annihilation stared them in the face. At 1700 hours Hackett called the remaining officers and NCOs together at the lip of the hollow and outlined his simple plan: to break out suddenly under smoke grenades and covering fire, leaving the wounded behind.

The wild rush of filthy, bloodied men, many carrying German weapons, burst into the orderly positions of A Coy of the Borders within The Perimeter where they received some well-earned food, water and sleep. The Brigadier then reported to Divisional HQ in the Hartenstein.

Return to Utrechtseweg and rejoin the main itinerary.

Continue along Utrechtseweg to the right turn to Hoofdlaan.

• Extra Visit to 1st Border Positions on The Perimeter
Round trip: 1 km/.6 miles. Approximate time: 10 minutes.

Turn right on Hoofdlaan, with the park below the Hartenstein to the left and turn next right on Van Lennepweg. Continue to the bend in the road with a path to the left and stop.

In this area C company of the 1st Borders established their RAP and held off repeated German attacks from their arrival late on 19 September, when they set up their HQ in House No 3 Van Lennepweg, until the night of 25th/26th. In 1993 the bodies of Privates Ernest Ager and Douglas Lowery (both listed in the Battalion Roll of Honour as killed on 24 September) were found here in a slit trench in a garden. In 1997 the body of Corporal Froud (listed as killed on 21 September) was also found nearby. All three were reburied in the Arnhem-Oosterbeek Cemetery (qv). There were also many German cartridges (the Regimental diary records that 'at times we fired more German ammo than British'), phosphorus bombs and British spoons. Alan Green in his book *1st Battalion The Border Regiment - ARNHEM 1944* adds a postscript which records that setting out for the Operation the Battalion had a strength of forty-one Officers and 754 Other Ranks. When the Roll was called in Nijmegen on 26 September nine Officers and 241 Other Ranks answered their names. Green maintains that 'the proportion of those killed and wounded was higher in the 1st Battalion, the Border Regiment, than in any other Battalion in the Division.'

Return to the junction

Hoofdlaan to the right winds down to Benedendorpsweg.

Return to Utrechtseweg, turn right and rejoin the main Itinerary.

Continue to the Hartenstein Museum on the right. Drive past the museum and turn right following signs into the car park. Walk to the museum.

On the right is the attractive **Brasserie Kleyn Hartensteyn.** Tel: + (0) 26 3342121 with typical Dutch food. In September 1944 this was the coach house of the Hartenstein estate (after the war it became the Fire Station) and the building was used to collect the wounded before the evacuation to Apeldoorn.

Continue towards the museum. On the left is

• Memorial to the People of Gelderland/Map 3/5

The inscription on this handsome memorial, erected by airborne veterans, which bears the Pegasus insignia and Gelderland coat of arms, reads,

> 50 years ago British and Polish Airborne soldiers fought here against overwhelming odds to open the way into Germany and bring the war to an early end. Instead we brought death and destruction for which you have never blamed us. This stone marks our admiration for your great courage, remembering especially the women who tended our wounded. In the long winter that followed your families risked death by hiding Allied soldiers and airmen while members of the Resistance helped many to safety.
>
> You took us then into your homes as fugitives and friends. We took you forever into our hearts. This strong bond will continue long after we are all gone.
>
> 1944 September 1994.'

It beautifully summarizes the special relationship which still exists between veterans and the local populace. Let us hope that it will continue through forthcoming generations.

Continue to the Museum entrance.

En route are anti-tank guns from the battle and a Sherman Tank used during the Liberation of Arnhem in April 1945. To the left are pleasant gardens, beyond which is the site of the tennis court. In here some 200 German POWs were penned and given tools to dig themselves in for protection from their own fire. In this area the Public Relations Unit also sheltered, including the Canadian BBC correspondent Stanley Maxted, who came to be regarded as the Voice of Arnhem, and Alan Wood of the *Daily Express*. They sent their immortal reports to be relayed by the BBC and printed in the national papers, letting the world know about the heroic stand at Arnhem-Oosterbeek. The Film Unit and photographers also operated from here.

• Hartenstein Airborne Museum, Oosterbeek/35.4 kms/22.1 miles/1 hour RWC/Map 3/4

This museum is undoubtedly at the heart of the conflict universally known as the Arnhem Battle, but which in reality is the Battle of Oosterbeek. For veterans, faithfully returning to the area year after year, it is, with the Cemetery, the focal point of their pilgrimage and many have donated documents, photographs, personal accounts and artefacts to enhance what has become a unique collection.

The Hartenstein, meaning 'Deer Place', was often wrongly spelt as 'Hartestein' on Dutch 1930s maps and in contemporary accounts (much as 'Pointe du Hoc' in Normandy was repeatedly called 'Pointe du Hoe' on contemporary maps). It is often seen as 'Hartestein' during the film *Theirs is the Glory* (qv). Indeed there is still a small sign towards the car park and tennis courts that says 'Hartestein'. Until 1942, when requisitioned by the Germans, it had been an elegant hotel. They abandoned it, still in excellent condition, in the panic of the news of the first landings on 17 September.

Here at the top centre of The Perimeter was the Divisional Headquarters of General Urquhart, Commander of the 1st Airborne Division. It was set up on a 'temporary' basis on Monday 18 September when it became clear that the planned HQ in the barracks in Arnhem would not be reached. A temporary Maintenance Area was also set up in the park and by late that evening Lieutenant Randall, the MO of HQ RA, had set up an RAP. Soon the cellar

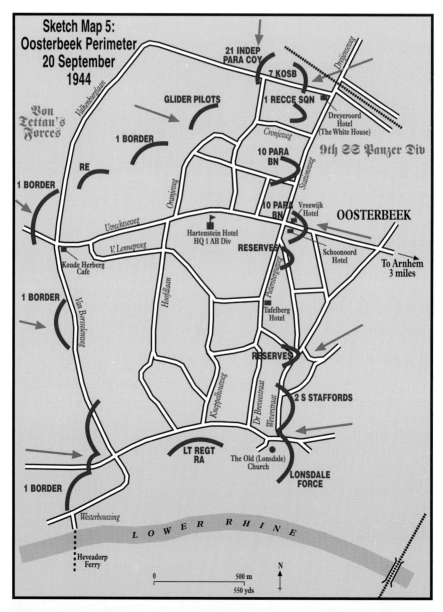

Sketch Map 5:
Oosterbeek Perimeter
20 September
1944

Hartenstein Airborne Museum: 1. People of Gelderland Memorial

2. The entrance

3. Diorama of Gen Urquhart's command post

4. Diorama of 3" mortar foxhole

would be full of the wounded. In the absence of General Urquhart (who had taken off by jeep towards the St Elisabeth Hospital (qv)) command had been taken over by Brigadier 'Pip' Hicks, CO of 1st Airlanding Brigade. He was visited by Brigadier 'Shan' Hackett, CO of 4th Para Brigade, and there was some well-documented dissension between the two brigadiers as to who should assume command. Urquhart returned from his adventures on Tuesday 19 September and in an attempt to get a grip on the situation despatched Colonel Hilary Barlow (often mis-spelt as 'Hilaro' and listed by the CWGC as 'Hilard'), the 2i/c of 1st Airlanding Brigade, to take control of the Arnhem section of the battle that the General had just left. As John Frost put it in *Nearly There*, 'Poor Colonel Hilary Barlow simply disappeared'. News of reverses was pouring in to HQ and by late afternoon of Wednesday 20 September The Perimeter had more or less taken shape around the Hartenstein (Sketch Map 5).

On Sunday 24 September the Germans, in a somewhat pathetic attempt at psychological warfare, wafted broadcasts over the area and the strains of Glenn Miller, appeals to surrender and other taunts were only met by derisory bursts of fire. It was to here that Brigadier Hackett managed to drag himself that evening after being wounded in the stomach and leg at The Crossroads (qv) some 100 yards away. Drowsy with morphine and unaware of the seriousness of his wounds, he was visited by Urquhart, ADMS Colonel Graeme Warrack (qv) and Padre Harlow. He was then taken by jeep to the St Elisabeth hospital as part of the negotiated truce with the Germans (qv).

By the time the fateful decision to go ahead with Operation BERLIN, the Evacuation, had been taken on Monday 25 September, the Hartenstein had again filled with the wounded. In the once beautiful grounds slit trenches full of desperate, weary and hungry men with little ammunition were interspersed with more wounded and the unburied dead. A dreadful stench hung over all. The men had watched the brave but abortive efforts to resupply them by air fail, often ending in the death of the determined aircrews. The shrinking Perimeter was riddled with gaps that could no longer be plugged and metal poured into it from the German guns on all three sides. Yet the men in it held on with a tenacity born of desperation as their comrades fell around them. All hopes of relief by XXX Corps, in whom they had started with so much confidence, faded. It was time to salvage what remained of this gallant band.

Many graphic pictures of the grounds and the Hotel in the successive days of the battle can be seen in the Museum.

The Airborne Museum was originally founded in 1949 and occupied part of Doorwerth Castle. Then the ideal home was found here for the collection and an expanded museum was reopened on 11 May 1978 by General Urquhart. As well as the fascinating exhibits, there is a large model of The Perimeter with a spoken commentary in several languages and, in the basement, lifelike, historically accurate dioramas with sound effects. An impressive new addition is the Colours of the 10th Battalion, Para Regiment. They are housed in a large glass case (which was a challenge to erect) just to the right of the first exhibition hall as one enters the museum. The caption reads,

> This is the final resting place of the Battalion's last Colours, entrusted to the Dutch Community who stood with the Battalion during its darkest, yet finest, hour. These Colours were laid up here on 18 September 1999.

The museum houses important archives and an extremely well-stocked souvenir and bookshop with prices that are internationally attractive (available by mail order as well). There is also a refreshment area and toilets, and the museum is set in attractively landscaped grounds. The knowledgeable staff of the museum are dedicated to preserving the memory of the events of September 1944. There is an active Society of Friends of the Airborne Museum. Battlefield Tours can be arranged for military groups (with their own coach and with prior booking) in four languages. Civilian tours can be arranged with the VVV (qv). A walking tour from the Museum, with explanatory markers, was set up in 2001.

Airborne Museum Hartenstein, Utrechtseweg 232, 6862 AZ Oosterbeek, Netherlands. Tel: (0) 26 3337710. Fax: (0) 26 3391785.

e-mail: info@airbornemuseum.com Website www.airbornemuseum.com.

Open: Weekdays: 1 April – I November 1000-1700. 1 November - 1 April 1100-1700. Sundays and Public Holidays: 1200-1700. Closed Christmas and New Year's Day. Admission fee payable, though Arnhem Veterans are, of course, free of charge.

The Airlift Trust. In February 2001 fundraising began for the worthwhile project of installing facilities for the disabled and the blind in the museum, notably with a state of the art transparent lift column. Donations can be made to Stichting Airlift Oosterbeek. Bank a/c 38.50.66.473/Giro 85.35.432. website: www.airlift.nl.

• *Walking tour from the Museum car park (approximate time: 20 minutes).*

Turn left outside the museum on Utrechtseweg. Almost immediately opposite is

• *Airborne Monument/Map 3/3*

The foundation stone of the monument, designed by Jacob ('Jac') Maris (qv), was laid in September 1945 by General Urquhart and the memorial was unveiled by Queen Wilhelmina in September 1946 but not actually completed until September 1947. It was funded by the inhabitants of Oosterbeek and is known locally as 'the Needle'.

Walk back towards Arnhem to the corner with Stationsweg. In the garden of the large white house is

• *Quatre Bras 21st Independent Parachute Company Memorial/ Map 3/7*

The memorial was unveiled on 21 September 1981. It is dedicated to '21st IPC' and was designed by Saskia Deurvorst of Oosterbeek. The 21st was commanded by Major B. A. B. 'Boy' Wilson who, at the age of 45, was the oldest para in 1st AB Division. The task of Wilson and four officers and 185 men on the first day was to drop 30 minutes ahead of the main force and to mark the three zones, DZ X, LZ Z and LZ S with navigational aids (Eureka beacons and smoke signals) so that they could be readily located. It was done impeccably. As The Perimeter shrank during the battle, they moved into this area.

On the opposite corner of Stationsweg was the Hotel Vreewijk (Map 3/8), also used as a medical facility.

Continue along Utrechtseweg, past the Lunchroom Oosterbeek, Tel: + (0) 26 3390716, which is ideal for a quick lunch snack. Adjoining it is

• *VVV Oosterbeek*

Raadhuisplein 1, 6861 GT Oosterbeek. Tel: + (0) 26 3333172. Here one can obtain local tourist information, town plans, literature about MARKET-GARDEN and book battlefield tours etc.

Cross over the road.

At No.102 (opposite the petrol station) is the welcoming *Baker's Inn* pub. It specialises in UK fare, like ploughman's lunch, and caters for veterans' gatherings with typical English teas. Tel: + (0) 26 3338467.

On the corner of Weverstraat with Utrechtseweg is an original red GPO telephone box, presented on 16 September 1994 by the Arnhem Veterans' Club.

Continue to No 192 Utrechtseweg.

Oosterbeek Walking Tour Memorials: 1. Airborne Monument by Jac Maris with Welcome Arch

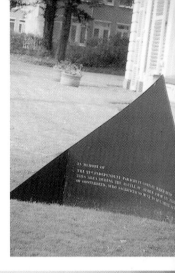

2. 21st Indep Para Coy Mem, Quartre Bras

SEPTEMBER 1944

3. Airborne Commemorative Marker No 2

4. Painting by veteran Reg Curtis in the Schoonoord

5. The Tafelberg

HUIZE
TAFELBERG

6. 21st Indep Para Coy Vase, Paasberg

• *Airborne Commemorative Marker No 2/Map 3/11*

This is sited in what used to be the Pastor's garden. The legend reads, 'In houses and gardens about here 10 Parachute Battalion sorely tried in battle since their parachute landing on Ginkel Heath on 18 September '44, fought to virtual extinction. On 21 September the remnants of the battalion were withdrawn from The Perimeter defence of the division. The battalion had then no officer left and no more than thirty men.'

Walk back towards the Hartenstein. Continue to junction of Utrechtseweg and Stationsweg. This was immortalised by the David Shepherd painting and was known as 'The Crossroads' (or the 'MDS' - Main Dressing Station - Crossroads).

• *The Café Restaurant Schoonoord/RWC/Map 3/10*

Tel: + (0) 26 3390716. This is ideal for a lunch-time snack, but gets very busy during the Anniversary period. It has many pictures of the operation, including an original oil painting by Reg Curtis, a veteran of 1 Para, originally donated to the Hartenstein, but as they had no room it found an appropriate home here where Reg was treated during the battle.

By the late evening of 18 September a dressing station was established here. On 20 September the Schoonoord was captured by the Germans. The ADMS, Colonel Graeme M. Warrack of 1st AB, removed his badges of rank and posed as an orderly. During the night 4th Para Brigade pushed The Perimeter out towards Arnhem and briefly recaptured the Schoonoord, but it was soon retaken by the Germans. The next day it became seriously overcrowded with the wounded and other houses in the area were taken over as dressing stations and RAPs. On 23 September the Schoonoord changed hands yet again and the medical situation had become critical. All casualties were then kept in the RAPs and evacuation to dressing stations ceased. On the 24th Colonel Warrack met with General Bittrich and negotiated a ceasefire so that the wounded could be evacuated through the German lines. He was then permitted to visit Lipmann Kessel (qv) at the St Elisabeth Hospital to warn him to expect several hundred casualties. By the time firing resumed at 1700 hours 250 stretcher cases and 200 walking wounded had been evacuated. The next day Colonel Warrack was informed that XXX Corps would not be arriving and that the withdrawal would take place that night. The more seriously wounded would remain behind with all medical staff - 204 medics and Padres in all. On the 26th, as quiet descended on Oosterbeek, Colonel Warrack met with the Germans and the evacuation of the wounded to Apeldoorn began. His next task was to convert the barracks there into a military hospital and do everthing he could to delay the gruelling onward journey into German POW Camps for his patients. When the majority had left, thoughts of escape were uttermost to the remainder. After being told to get ready to leave, Colonel Warrack hid himself in the 3-feet-high, 12-feet-long and 18-inches-wide roof space of his bedroom, with a Red Cross parcel, some bread, bottles of water, blanket, candles and bucket. He emerged after about a week, slipped away and managed to make contact with the same Resistance group that was looking after Lipmann Kessel and Brigadier Hackett. After many adventures they all finally escaped through the treacherous area of the Biesbosch, where the Waal and Maas merged. For his considerable achievements in the campaign Colonel Warrack received the DSO and the MBE.

Turn left on Pietersbergseweg.
The area beyond the houses to the right was where German prisoners were held in the Hartenstein tennis courts and the direction you are now taking was that of the withdrawal on the night of 25 September.
Continue to walk to

• *The Tafelberg/Airborne Commemorative Marker No1/Map 3-13/14*

In September 1944 the Tafelberg was the HQ of Field-Marshal Walther Model, C-in-C of Heeresgruppe B, who was the German equivalent of Field-Marshal Montgomery. He was at lunch when news of the landings at Wolfheze reached him. Thinking that the airborne soldiers were coming to capture him and his HQ, Model left within minutes and the Tafelberg and the Hartenstein were evacuated. Model reached General Wilhelm Bittrich's HQ (of 2nd SS Panzer Corps) at Doetinchem (20 miles to the east) around 1500 hours, having briefed local commanders en route. Bittrich had already alerted Lieutenant-Colonel Walther Harzer's 9th SS Hohenstaufen Division and Colonel Heinz Harmel's 10th SS Frundsberg Division, and elements of both were moving on Arnhem and its approaches. Model phoned Field-Marshal Gerd von Rundstedt at OB West and was promised immediate reinforcements. By midnight Model had issued orders that directed the German reaction against each of the three Allied divisional areas, the maximum effort being concentrated against Arnhem. The following day von Rundstedt signalled to all units that 'Every town, every village, every bunker is to be defended to the last drop of blood and to the last round.'

This historic building, such a vital part of The Cauldron story, is now at risk. The religious order which occupied it since the war dwindled so significantly that they were forced to wind up and sell the building. It has now been acquired by a builder/developer and local historians/Friends of the Airborne and other organisations are working hard to preserve the distinctive façade and the most memorable features inside. The most emotive area is the section of the stone floor which still bears the bloodstains of the Allied wounded who were brought here for treatment (including Major John Waddy – OC of A Company 156th Para Battalion – who was operated on on the billiard table) and the staircase that was used for the filming of Theirs is the Glory (qv). A dressing station was established here in the evening of 18 September and Captain Michael James of 181st AL Field Ambulance set up an operating facility. By the 21st the Tafelberg was going in and out of German hands, but the medical teams supported by Dutch doctors and nurses continued to treat the wounded until evacuated.

In front of the building is Airborne Commemorative Marker No 1, the original wooden post having been replaced by the new concrete version.
Turn round and turn sharp right along Paasberg. Continue to House No 17.

• *21st Independent Para Coy Memorial/Map 3/12.*

This is in the form of a vase (which always contains fresh flowers) in the garden of the house called 'Monty'. A platoon of 21st Indep Para Coy defended this area in the last four days of the battle. The owner, Han Kardol, was a child of ten years old during the battle and sheltered during it with his family in the cellar.

Return to your car. Return to Utrechtseweg turn right and left at the traffic lights at The Crossroads, following a green CWGC sign along Stationsweg.

No 8 Stationsweg. The 21st Indep Para Coy occupied the houses in Stationsweg nearest to Utrechtseweg on 22 September. In house No 8 was Corporal Rodley, known as 'Max', one of the Company's German Jewish contingent (which was recruited by Major John Lander, the creator of the Unit, in 1942 from refugees from Hitler's Austria, Germany and Czechoslovakia). Some adopted Scottish names and all their papers were made out in their new names. They were intelligent, fervent and had the advantage of being German speakers. Max Rodley dug a slit trench in the garden and made contact with the friendly occupants of the house, the Kremer family. He posed for some photographs for them, with comrades Sergeant Sonny Binnick (who before the war was a professional ballroom dancing champion and after compered *Come Dancing* on BBC TV for many years, and who dropped in rank from Company Sergeant Major to Sergeant in order to join the Company), Sergeant Ben Swallow and Private James ('Paddy') Cameron (who died of their wounds in Apeldoorn and are buried in the Oosterbeek Cemetery [18.C.16. and 4.]), Private McCausland, Private H. Mitchell and Corporal Jeffries. The group photograph is on display in the Hartenstein Museum (qv). That afternoon Rodley was killed in his trench and buried in the garden.

After the battle the house, like many others in the road, was completely battered, with no glass left in the windows. The Kremers, like other families in the area, had to flee, carrying as many possessions as they could in suitcases. Suddenly the father stopped and returned to lock the door! When they returned in May 1945 they found Max Rodley's grave still in their garden, marked by a wooden cross and a helmet.

Rodley had been involved in an incident on 20 September when 21st Independent Para Coy were fighting as infantry in their defence of The Perimeter in which some Germans, who might have been surrendering, were shot. General Urquhart's account (in his book *Arnhem*) of the matter is:

> At some stage, the Germans called on the Independent Company to surrender and Lieutenant H. D. Eastwood, CO of No 1 Platoon, ordered one of his German-speaking troops [Rodley] to reply broadly on the lines that the company was too scared to venture out and that the Germans should send a party to fetch them. Wilson ordered his men to stand by. Nonetheless, he was surprised when about 50 Germans emerged from the wood across the open field. Twelve Brens opened up simultaneously and not a German escaped.

Ron Kent, then a Sergeant with the company, commented in his history of the Parachute Pathfinder Company, *First In!* 'It was certainly not as clear cut as that... they were armed, carried no indication of surrender and did not raise their hands'. He goes on to describe his own version of the event, and remarks, 'The incident was never discussed afterwards – the whole thing was somehow unsatisfactory.'

Note that side roads off Stationsweg are named after Boer War Generals (e.g. Cronje). *Continue towards the railway line.*

Just short of it to the left on the continuation of Stationsweg and standing slightly back off the road is the **Hotel Dreyeroord** (Dreijerood) which contains a great deal of memorabilia of the battle. Tel: + (0) 26 3333169. It was to here on 19 September that Lieutenant-Colonel Payton-Reid of the 7th KOSB led about 270 survivors of his battalion from the fighting below the Leeren Doedel. They called it 'The White House'. At about 1630 hours on the 21st the Germans mounted a strong attack on the hotel and infiltrated into the grounds. The KOSB put up a fierce resistance and inflicted much damage on their attackers, but they suffered heavy casualties and General Urquhart decided to pull them to the west (to Bothaweg and Paul Krugerstraat) to shorten the line that night thus making this stretch of road the eastern edge of The Perimeter (see the Holts' Map).

Cross the railway onto Dreijenseweg.

Immediately to the left is the opposite end of Johannahoeveweg to that taken on the Extra Visit to the Culvert.

Continue past the 'End of Oosterbeek' sign to the marker on the left.

• *Airborne Commemorative Marker No 3/37 kms/23.1 miles/5 minutes/Map 2/26*

The inscription reads:

> 156 Para Bn was stopped here by strong German forces on 19 September having fought their way from Ginkelse Heide. Many were killed and the remainder withdrew to Oosterbeek. This point was the extreme north-east corner of The Perimeter on 21 September.

Turn round and just before the railway turn left along Van Limburg Stirumweg following green CWGC signs to the cemetery car park on the left.

• *Arnhem Oosterbeek CWGC Cemetery/Flowers in the Wind Memorial/ 38.2kms/23.9 miles/30 minutes/ Map 3-21/22*

After considerable debate this site was chosen after the war to bury the casualties from the MARKET-GARDEN operation and later battles. The authors' research at the CWGC archives at Maidenhead have disclosed a much greater input by General Urquhart into the form the cemetery should take than is told in the received story of its conception. In April 1945 Major-General Urquhart, Commander of 1 AB Division, had requested that the Airborne Cemetery should be placed at the Hartenstein Hotel and that it should be called the 1 AB Division Cemetery. In this he was supported by General Gale, the Commander of 1 (BR) AB Corps. 21 Army Group replied that regulations required that the only official name that can be given to a cemetery is that of the nationality of the dead and the place at which it is located. They originally allowed that an 'Extension' could be named after a formation and suggested the name 'Arnhem British Cemetery (1 AB Div Extension)' – the type of phraseology that had been agreed for 6 AB Division Cemetery at Ranville in Normandy. In June Urquhart was informed that Lieutenant-Colonel Stott (Assistant Director, Graves Registration & Enquiry – see below) had chosen this present site, but Urquhart still had some firm ideas of his own. He wanted the cemetery to be primarily for the men of his division, with the only exception being for attached non-airborne troops who fell north of the river. 1 AB men buried in other cemeteries should be moved (even though he accepted that to move men from consecrated ground might be difficult) so that they should all lie together, grouped by Brigades and Divisional Troops, with a separate group for Glider Pilots etc. He also wanted a memorial to be erected in the cemetery – another idea

1. Cross of Sacrifice

2. The Gronert Twins, 17 September

3. 'Flowers in the Wind' Memorial

4. Flt Lt David Lord VC

which was tactfully abandoned.

As one enters the approach to the cemetery, there are benches to the right and left donated by a local hotel. On the right is an **Explanatory Board** in Dutch, English and Polish, with a map, sponsored by the Oosterbeek Rotary. To the left is a brick structure incorporating a seat with a beautiful **Plaque with a gold Pegasus and the flags of Holland, Poland and the UK.** It bears the legend,

Flowers in the Wind

This plaque is dedicated to the children of this region who grace this cemetery every year, paying homage to the men who gave their lives for Liberation.
It was funded by the Arnhem Veterans Club and unveiled on 5 September 1998 by a man and a woman who as children laid flowers on the graves in 1945 and by a boy and girl who laid flowers in 1998. It pays homage to the beautiful annual custom of local children laying flowers on each grave in the cemetery before the Service of Commemoration.

On the left-hand pillar of the entrance gate is a Dutch Wargraves sign.

The cemetery now contains nearly 1,700 Commonwealth burials – 1,314 Army plus 243 Unknown, 77 RAF plus 1 Unknown, and 80 Foreign National graves, the majority of whom are Poles from the 1st Independent Polish Parachute Brigade. The fifty-one Polish graves, the majority of which were re-interred on 29 August 1946 from the churchyard in Driel, are to the left and right as one enters the cemetery. Note that they are all inscribed with the Polish badge, not a religious emblem, as Poland was a Communist country when the headstones were first erected. Many of the Polish were devout Catholics and their veterans and families wished to have a cross inscribed on their headstones. Several requests to the CWGC have so far failed to effect the change. The Polish graves include that of the first Polish officer to be killed in the operation, **Lieutenant Slesicki,** age 37, whom General Sosabowski described as 'a lawyer', who 'abandoned a nice safe job and asked for his old job as a company commander' [34.A.15.]. **Richard Tice**, age 22, was an American, not even of Polish extraction, who volunteered to fight with the Poles because, as he told the General, he 'learned at school that in the American War of Independence, many Poles helped us to win our freedom. I would like to make a small contribution to your struggle.' Tice even learned Polish. Sosabowski was 'deeply touched.' Tice was killed in Driel as a group of Germans approached his patrol. They shouted in English, 'Don't shoot' and Tice thought they were Americans. Lured into the trap the Polish platoon was raked with machine-gun and rifle fire.

There are also 8 Canadian Army (including 1 Unknown), 25 RCAF, 4 Australian and 4 New Zealand Airforce and 3 CWGC employees.

The graves were laid out so that plots IX-XIV were of Ground Forces 'Link-Up', III is Glider Pilots, IV is RAF and the remaining plots, I-XXVI, are of Airborne Forces. After passing the Stone of Remembrance, Plots XXVII-XXXII, which face inwards to the central pathway, are later additions.

[All dates of death in **September** below are in 1944.]

The VC was awarded to **Captain John Grayburn**, 2 Para (formerly Ox & Bucks), age 26, 20 September [13.C.11.]. His citation in the *London Gazette* reads,

Lt Grayburn was a platoon commander of the Parachute Battalion which was dropped on September 17th, 1944, with orders to seize and hold the bridge over the Rhine at Arnhem. He, with his platoon, was to capture the southern end. Lt. Grayburn was wounded in the shoulder almost immediately, but he directed and pressed the assault until casualties became so heavy that he was ordered to withdraw. Later, he successfully organised the occupation of a house vital to the defence of the bridge. Although heavily attacked throughout the next day and night, thanks to Lt. Grayburn's courage, leadership, and skill in disposing his men, the house was held until it was set on fire on September 19th, and had to be evacuated. Lt Grayburn then formed a fighting force of elements of all arms, including the remainder of his company. Although wounded again, this time in the back, he refused to be evacuated. When tank attacks, against which he had no defence, finally forced his retreat on September 20th, he stood up in full view of the enemy, and directed the withdrawal of his men to the main defensive perimeter. He was killed that night. For nearly four days, despite pain and weakness from his wounds, shortage of food and lack of sleep, Lt.Grayburn displayed supreme and unflagging gallantry and determination. Without his inspiring leadership the Arnhem bridge could not have been held for so long.

Captain Grayburn's body was brought in by civilians returning to their ruined homes by the Arnhem bridge in January 1946. He was reburied here on the 24th.

The VC was also awarded to Flight Lieutenant David Lord, DFC, 271 Sqn RAF, age 30, 19 September [IV.B.5.]. His *London Gazette* citation reads,

> On September 19th, 1944, Flt. Lieut. Lord was pilot and Captain of an aircraft detailed to drop supplies to our troops, who were closely surrounded at Arnhem. For accuracy this had to be done at 900 feet. While approaching the target at 1,500 feet the aircraft was severely damaged and set on fire. Flt. Lieut. Lord would have been justified in withdrawing or even in abandoning his aircraft but, knowing that supplies were desperately needed, he continued on his course. Twice going down to 900 feet under very intense fire, he successfully dropped his containers. His task completed he ordered his crew to abandon the aircraft, making no attempt to leave himself. A few seconds later the aircraft fell in flames, only one of the crew surviving. By continuing his mission in a damaged and burning plane, twice descending to 900 feet to ensure accuracy, and finally by remaining at the controls to give his crew a chance of escape, Flt. Lieut. Lord displayed supreme valour and self-sacrifice.'

Lord had spent five years, mostly in India with 31 Squadron, notably supplying Orde Wingate's 'Chindit' force behind enemy lines in Burma for which he was awarded the DFC in July 1943. He moved to No 271 Squadron at Down Ampney in January 1944 and took part in the D-Day Operation in Normandy in June.

The charred bodies of Flight Lieutenant Lord and the crew of his Dakota KG 374 of 271 Sqn were originally buried beside their burnt-out machine. When they were re-interred here, side by side, on 2 August 1945, the surviving crew member, 36-year old navigator Flying Officer Harry King, identified Lord by the DFC and Indian General Service Medal ribbons, Flying Officer Alexander Ballantyne, RAF, age 25 [IV.B.7.], by the fact that he 'always wore his collar and tie on flights' and Flying Officer Richard Medhurst, RAF, age 19 [IV.B.6.] because his tie was in his pocket. It was Medhurst's first operational mission.

The VC was also awarded to **Captain Lionel Queripel** (qv), R Sussex attd 10 Para, age 24, 19 September [5.D.8.]. His *London Gazette* citation reads,

> In Holland on September 19th, 1944, Captain Queripel was acting as company Commander. When advancing on Arnhem, heavy and continuous enemy fire caused his company to split up on both sides of the road and inflicted considerable losses. Repeatedly crossing and re-crossing the road under sustained and accurate fire, Captain Queripel not only immediately re-organised his force, but carried a wounded serjeant to the Regimenal Aid Post, and was himself wounded in the face. Nevertheless he personally led an attack on the strong point blocking their progress and killed the occupants, thereby enabling the advance to continue. Later, Captain Queripel found himself cut off with a small party. Although by then additionally wounded in both arms, he continued to inspire his men to resist until increasing enemy pressure forced him to order their withdrawal. He insisted on remaining behind to cover their retreat with pistol fire and hand grenades, and was not seen again. During nine hours of confused and bitter fighting Captain Queripel unceasingly displayed gallantry of the highest order. [This gallant act is reminiscent of those of Captain Henry Glass who, with two broken legs, remained propped up against the wall of Obourg Station near Mons, and an unknown soldier who stood firing from the roof, covering the withdrawal of their comrades of the 4th Middlesex as the Germans attacked on 23

August 1914.] Captain Queripel's courage, leadership and devotion to duty were magnificent and inspiring.

His body was originally buried in Renkum Communal Cemetery and reburied here on 24 August 1945.

The **MC** was awarded to **Major Charles Bruce Dawson**, R Berks attd 4 Para Bde, age 27, 20 September [6.C.11.]; **Captain Thomas Rose**, 112 Field Regt RA, age 25, 26 September [24.B.16.] and **Captain William Wood**, 124 Field Regt RA, age 29, 25 September [8.B.13.].

The **rare George Medal was awarded to Captain Brian Brownscombe**, RAMC (qv), age 29, shot by SS Oberscharführer Lerche on 24 September 1944 [15.B.10.] at the Arnhem Municipal Hospital, where he was originally interred. Brownscombe won his GM on 30 November 1943.

The **DSO** was awarded to **Wing Commander Peter Davis**, 299 Sqn RAF, age 28, died on 19 September 1944 [4.C.17.], whose brother Pilot Officer Henry Davis, RAF, age 28, died in August 1940, is commemorated on the Runnymede Memorial.

The **DCM** was awarded to **Serjeant Robert Curley**, 1st Hants, age 30, 4 October 1944 [13.A.13.]; **Signalman Donald Stewart**, 1AB Div Sigs, age 21, 24 September [15.B.11.] and **Staff Sergeant Raymond White**, 1st Wing Glider Pilot Regt, age 27, 18 September [16.B.17.].

The **MM** was awarded to **Staff Serjeant Eric Holloway**, 1st Wing, Glider Pilot Regt, age 24, 18 September [3.A.15.]; **Staff Serjeant David Wallace**, 2nd Wing, Glider Pilot Regt, age 24, 24 September [27.B.8.]; **Lance Corporal George White**, R Sigs, age 23, 1 October 1944 [13.A.17.]; **Serjeant Samuel Williams**, 2nd Devons, age 25, 3 October 1944 [9.C.19.] and **Serjeant Donald Wilson**, 3 Para, age 25, 17 September [5.A.13.].

The **DFC** was awarded to **Squadron Leader John Gilliard**, 190 Sqn, RAF, age 24, 19 September [4.B.1.] prior to MARKET-GARDEN, as was the **BEM** awarded to **Lieutenant Stanley Watling**, 156 Para, age 28, 19 September [6.B.19.].

MiD were **Lieutenant Peter Brazier**, 2nd Wing, Glider Pilot Regt, age 22, 23-24 September [21.A.18.]; **Lieutenant Kenneth Gentleman**, Lt AA Anti-Tank Regt, age 22, 1 October 1944 [9.A.2.] (prior to Arnhem); **Lieutenant Robert Glover**, 2 Airlanding Anti-Tank Bty, age 25, 19 September [22.A.8.]; **Flying Officer Clive Graham**, 617 Sqn RAF, age 23, 23 September [4.C.13.] who was the son of Major-General Sir Miles Graham, KBE, CB, MC; **Captain Raymond Hutt**, 74 Fld Regt, RA, age 29, 17 April 1945 [10.A.20.] (prior to Arnhem); **Lance Corporal William Kill**, 1 Para, age 29, 28 September [24.A.5.]; **Lieutenant Ralph Maltby**, RA attd 2nd Wing, Glider Pilot Regt, age 26, 17 September, previously awarded the Russian Order of the Patriotic War, was killed by flak while in his glider on the way to Arnhem [3.C.18.]; **Captain Iain Muir**, 1st Wing, Glider Pilot Regt, age 22, 25 September [3.C.15.]; **Corporal William (Joe) Simpson**, 1 Para Sqn RE, age 29, 20 September [22.B.17.] was also awarded the **US Silver Star. Twice Mentioned** were **Lieutenant-Colonel Sir William R. De B. des Voeux**, 9th Bart, Grenadier Guards, **Commanding 156th Para Regt**, age 32, 20 September [6.A.15.] (prior to Arnhem), **Lance Corporal William Garibaldi**, 10 Para, age 27, 20-21 September [5.D.14.] and **Major Ernest Ritson**, TD, 156th Para, age 35, 20 September [6.D.18.] (prior to Arnhem).

An exception to the general rule that to be buried here one had died during or as a result of the Arnhem-Oosterbeek or Island Battles was one of the sons of Brigadier-General E.S. D'Ewes Coke, CMG, DSO. **Major John Coke**, 7th (AB) KOSB, MiD, age 33, 18 November

1944 [23.B.17] was killed during the unsuccesful Pegasus II attempt (qv) and originally buried in Ede, and **Major Edward Coke**, 6th KOSB, killed near St Oedenrode on 27 September was brought here [21.C.20.] at the request of the family to be near his brother.

Captain Jacobus Groenewoud, Jedburgh Group Claude (qv), age 27, 18 September, is a **Holder of the Order of William 4th Class** [20.B.12.]. The only other headstones to bear the Dutch Lion in the cemetery are of **Private August Bakhuis Roozeboom,** No 2 (Dutch) Troop, No 10 (Inter-Allied) Commando, age 22, one of twelve who landed near Oosterbeek on 17 September who was killed near the Hartenstein, at first buried as an 'Unknown Canadian' and identified in 1996 [1.A.6.] and **S. Swarts,** a 27-year-old Dutch Resistance Worker from Amsterdam. He worked at bringing in the wounded to Doctor van Maanen at the Tafelberg (qv) and was killed on 20 September when his car, No. M51466, was hit by a shell. In July 1945 his widow tried to get his body returned to Amsterdam, but it was reburied here. Later Mrs Swarts decided to let him remain here as he had died as a soldier in the Battle of Arnhem [16.B.18.].

Lieutenant George Austin, RA attd 2nd AB S Staffs, age 24, 24 September, was **Commended for Act of Gallantry** 27 August 1942 [20.C.18.].

The father of **Major Charles Ashworth,** 10th Para, age 35, 20-21 September [15.D.11.], Lieutenant-Colonel Hugh Stirling Ashworth was killed in action in Egypt on 26 March 1917 while commanding the 4th R Sussex Regt. The father of **Captain Nigel Beaumont-Thomas,** 4 Para, RE, age 28, 20 September 1944 [17.A.11.], Colonel Lionel Beaumont-Thomas, MC, General List, age 49, was lost in MV *Henry Stanley* on 7 December 1942. He was MP for Birmingham, Norton, and is commemorated on the Brookwood Memorial.

The twin brothers, **Privates Claude and Thomas Gronert** (qv), 2 Para, age 21, died in the same incident on 17 September and are buried side by side [18.A.17/18.]. Their graves both bear the same personal message: 'Winds of Heaven Blow softly here Where lie sleeping Those we loved so dear.' The brothers of the following also fell on service: **Lieutenant Alastair Clarkson,** 1 Para, age 22, 22 September [6.A.11.], Pilot Officer Bertrand Clarkson, RAF, age 19, 23 August 1940, buried in Edinburgh Piershill Cemetery; **Serjeant Roger Croft** 1st Wing Glider Pilot Regt, age 20, 18 September [3.A.16.], Trooper Godfrey Croft, 5th R Tanks, age 22, 29 May 1942, commemorated on the Alamein Memorial; **Private Arthur Evans**, 1st Hants, age 30, 2 October 1944 [9.C.8.], Private William Evans, Pioneer Corps, age 29, 11 January 1941, buried in Edmonton Cemetery, Middx; **Guardsman Eric Green,** 2nd Irish Guards, age 34, 2 October 1944 [11.A.8.], Gunner Leonard Green RA, age 35, 9 June 1944, buried in Kanchanaburi CWGC Cemetery, Thailand; **Lieutenant Leslie Kiaer,** 10 Para, age 25, 20 September [19.C.12.], Lieutenant Eric Kiaer RF & 3 Cdo, 6 June 1944, buried in Bayeux CWGC Cemetery; **Major David Madden,** RA/HQ 1st AB, age 25, 21 September, who was awarded the Benson Memorial Prize at the RMA, Woolwich in 1939, [2.B.14.], Lieutenant Keith Madden MC, RA, age 20, 3 March 1943, commemorated on the Medjez-el-Bab memorial, Tunis (their father, Major John Madden, had the DSO); **Private Norman Weaver,** 10 Para, age 25, 25 September [30.C.3.], Driver William Weaver, RE, age 29, 12 August 1944, buried in Douvres la Délivrande, Normandy; **Corporal Edward Wescott,** 7th Hants, age 27, 1 October 1944 [9.B.14.], Leading Motor Mechanic Robert Westcott, RN, age 19, 18 October 1944, commemorated on the Chatham Naval Memorial.

The Rev Bernard Benson, Chaplain 4th Class, attd 1st Airlanding Bde, age 30, died on 27 September [4.B.10.]. **The Rev Henry Irwin,** Chaplain 4th Class, attd 11 Para, age 28, died

20-25 September [26.A.2.].

The **Comte Jaques de Cordoue,** 190 Sqn RAF, age 29, son of the Marquis Hugues de Cordoue, died on 21 September [4.D.16.].

Lieutenant-Colonel John Fitch, Manchester Regt, **Commanding 3 Para,** age 32, 19-23 September [20.B.20.] was originally buried in Arnhem Communal Cemetery and reburied here on 27 August 1945. **Lieutenant-Colonel Kenneth Smyth,** OBE, SWB, **Commanding 10 Para,** age 38, 26 October 1944 [18.B.8.], was originally buried in Apeldoorn Municipal Cemetery and reburied here on 24 January 1946.

Private Walter Lewy-Lingen Schwartz, age 24, 20 September [6.B.9.], **served as** Landon. **Corporal Hans Rosenfeld,** age 29, 23 September [23.A.11.] **served as** John Peter Rodley (qv). They were both members of the 21 Indep Coy Para Company's German Jewish contingent (qv).

2nd Lieutenant Richard de Courcy Peele, 11 Para, age 20, 22 September [23.A.7.] was 'Head boy of Rugby School, 1941-42; Scholar of Trinity College, Oxford.'

Major Thomas Montgomery, 1st Airlanding Brigade, age 36, 21 November 1944 [Sp Mem], was originally buried in Lingen Cemetery, Germany but his grave is now lost. His headstone stands alone to the right as one enters the cemetery.

Graves IV.B.11 and **12** were originally marked as 'Unknown'. Grave 11 was later identified as '**Sergeant C.G. Lewis**'. On, 29 May 1946 Grave 12 was identified as **Flight Sergeant Gabriel Griffin,** RAF, age 23, crew of Mosquito 772 784 which crashed at Arnhem on 17 September, and then on 18 December 1946 further investigation on W/O Lewis (witness to the meticulous work of the Graves Registration Unit) found that the 'acceptance was obviously incorrect as it is understood that this W/O lost his life while serving in SEAC.' Eventually it was discovered that W/O Colin G. Lewis, RAF, who died on 27 May 1945, was commemorated on the Singapore Memorial and the grave inscription was changed to **W/O Pilot Alfred G. Lewis,** RAF who died on 17 September 1944.

In **Graves 4.B.13,14,15,16** lie the **crew of Dakota F2626** which crashed on 19 September in Bakenbergseweg (qv), **Pilot Officer J.L. Wilson,** age 32, **Flight Sergeants H. Osborne,** age 23 and **R. French,** age 24, and **Air Despatch Lance Corporal James Grace,** (originally marked as 'Unknown'). **Air Despatch Driver R. Newth,** age 35, also killed in the plane is in 6.D.2.

Amongst the many lads not long out of school lies the **46-year-old Private Walter Yates** of 3 Para, died 18-25 September [5.D.13.].

Three **Commonwealth War Graves Commission workers** are buried here in 23C: **Percy Henry Dawson, BEM,** 24 May 1987, age 71, **Herbert Alastair Denham,** 31 August 1993, age 49 and **William Gregory,** 20 October 1988, age 80. Percy Dawson worked in the cemetery with great devotion for 32 years, always refusing promotion so that he could stay with 'his men'. He was regarded with great admiration and affection by their relatives and by veterans.

There have been several interments in this cemetery since its inception, most recently:

12 April 1989: Private William Allen, found near the South Ginkel Restaurant in Ede in 1987. [23.C.16.], **Private Alfred Johnson,** S Staffs, found near the Old Church on Benedendorpsweg in 1987 [23.C.20.] and **2 Unknowns,** one found in Renkum in August 1984 and one at Bleijenbeek Castle in June 1985.

8 October 1993: Private Douglas Lowery, and **Private Ernest Ager,** both of the 1st AL Border Regt, the latter having previously been commemorated on the Groesbeek Memorial. Both bodies were found in a field grave in a private garden on Van Lennepweg (qv), Oosterbeek, 400m west of the Hartenstein [25.C.1]. Their funeral was attended by fourteen veterans of the battalion.

9 June 1994: Unknown RE, found in a field grave in the Bilderberg area [23.C.19.].

18 September 1998: After research carried out by the Dutch Army, the CWGC, the British Defence Attaché at the Hague and the MOD. As in 1945/6, records were made of all possible identification clues, photos were taken of the remains and the artefacts and next of kin were sought. **Serjeant Lawrence H. Howes,** [25.C.5.] and **Sergeant David Thompson,** both of the Glider Pilot Regt [25.C.7.] whose bodies were found on the Sonnenberg Estate in January 1994 and **Corporal George Froud,** Border Regt, found at Van Lennepweg (qv), Oosterbeek in July 1997 [25.C.9.] were duly re-interred.

11 July 2000: In 1995 during excavation work near Westerbouwing the body of an Unknown Airborne soldier was found. Despite extensive research no identification could be made and the soldier was reburied as 'Known Unto God'.

A detailed breakdown of the numbers of each unit buried here, and where they were originally buried, is given in the meticulously researched *ROLL OF HONOUR Battle of Arnhem 17-26 September 1944,* compiled by J.A. Hey MBE, published by the Society of the Friends of the Airborne Museum. This was updated in June 1999 with much new information and corrections and contains many poignant photos of original graves. In March 2001 Mr. Hey was awarded the MBE but sadly was too ill to be able to travel to accept it from the British Ambassador in the Hague, Dame Rosemary Spencer. At the same ceremony the Burgomasters of Arnhem, Mr P. Scholten and Mr Verlinden of Renkum were awarded the OBE for their dedicated work for veterans of the Operation.

Cross the road to the local cemetery.

• Oosterbeek Local Cemetery/Grave of Surgeon Lipmann Kessel/10 minutes/Map 3-24/25

The CWGC plot is signed by the entrance to the cemetery and then to the left after one enters. It is then up a path to the right. The nine RAF graves date from 1942 and 1943, six of them from 15 June 1943. Beside them (Grave No 762) is a large white stone, with a Star of David and the Pegasus insignia, to Lipmann Kessel (qv), MBE (Milty), MC, FRCS, Professor of Orthopaedics, Surgeon Teacher, Humanist, Fighter for Freedom, and the words, 'Lippy: remembered forever by all who loved you and those you served.' A.W. Lipmann Kessel was Surgeon to 16th Para Field Ambulance and a Captain in 1944. He died in 1986 and is buried in the civilian cemetery as it was his express wish to be buried as near as possible to his fallen comrades. However, as a Jew, he did not wish to be cremated and it is CWGC policy that only the cremated remains of those other than men and women who actually died during the two World Wars may be buried in the cemeteries under their control. In such cases a casket may be buried 'at the margins of the burial plots or by the boundary wall', but 'without ceremony or publicity'. Lippman Kessel decided that to be buried here, opposite his Airborne pals, was the solution.

Opposite the line of CWGC headstones is **a mass grave for Oosterbeek Civilians** killed during the war. Many were refugees from Western Holland who fled to Oosterbeek and were never registered. The Town Hall, where all relevant records were kept,

Grave of Surgeon
Lipmann Kessel

was destroyed during the battle and most of the registers were burnt. The refugees were sheltered by local families or in boarding houses. A **Plaque from the Rotary** records that this is a memorial to the 140 citizens of Oosterbeek who died during the war (some in Concentration Camps), two of whom died in the Battle of Arnhem. Some names are inscribed in the low brass rail that surrounds the plot and in it are some named headstones.

From the cemetery continue along the road to the memorial on the left, which is signed as one leaves the CWGC Cemetery.

• *Air Despatch Memorial/38.4 kms/ 24 miles/5 minutes/Map 3/23*

Inaugurated on 18 September 1994, this memorial gives overdue recognition to the vital Air Despatchers, known as 'The Forgotten Heroes of Arnhem'. Even in the 1914-1918 War primitive attempts had been made to provision military units from the air. Men of the RASC were trained to become 'Air Despatchers' as it was realised that this was specialised work that called for highly skilled men with custom-made equipment. By 1944, when it became apparent that there would be a high requirement because of the continuing war in Europe, the number of Air Despatchers was vastly increased. In June 1944 they provided 6th AB with supplies and also carried out drops near Falaise and Paris and to General Patton's forces.

MARKET-GARDEN offered the first opportunity to supply a large military unit from the air. Between 18-25 September 610 dropping missions were flown with Stirling and Dakota aircraft, manned by a pool of 800 Despatchers, flying in crews of four in the Dakotas, two in the Stirlings. Several flew more than one mission. Eighty-four planes were lost, in which seventy-nine Air Despatchers were killed. They had loaded 1,561 tons of supplies, of which 1,247 were actually dropped. Tragically, only 7.4% actually reached British troops. Because of the failing radio communication, word could not be sent back to the UK to warn that the designated LZ V to the west of Arnhem had fallen into German hands. When later drops were made in the terrain held by 1 AB it was into a much-decreased area around which the Germans increasingly deployed anti-aircraft guns.

In 2000 an exhibition was mounted in the Hartenstein Museum to show the work of these gallant and greatly unsung heroes.

The work of the Air Despatchers is continued to this day by 47 Air Despatch Squadron, Royal Logistic Corps, stationed in Lyneham.

The memorial was the inspiration of Mike Patey, conceived during the Nijmegen Marches in 1986 when he came with 10 Para and was aware, at a reunion of Air Despatchers, that the veterans were upset about being the forgotten people of Arnhem. Frank van den Berg, the historian at the Groesbeek Museum, was coopted as the Dutch Liaison Officer in the project. It was erected by the Comrades and Air Despatchers past and present with the help of the Burgomasters of Arnhem and Renkum and other Dutch friends.

Opposite the memorial is a Bench from the 'Basingstoke & Deane Borough Council to the Municipality of Renkum in memory of the RASC Air Despatchers who gave their lives in resupplying 1st (BR) AB Division between 17-25 September 1944. Cllr T. L. Garland, JP, Mayor. 5 May 1997.'

The Air Despatchers'
Memorial

Return to Utrechtseweg. Drive straight over The Crossroads.

You are now, to a first approximation, going to follow the route taken by 1st AB on the night of 25 September when they withdrew from The Perimeter down to the area of the Lonsdale Church and across the river.

Pass the Schoonoord and the Tafelberg on the left and continue down Pietersbergseweg. As the road bends to the right, on the right is

Huize de Pietersberg (Map 3/15). This was taken over as a dressing station by 133 Para Field Ambulance on 20 September to ease the overcrowding in other medical facilities, by which time there were over 2,000 casualties in the Oosterbeek area. Their CO was Lieutenant-Colonel W. C. Alford, OBE, MiD (in the Italian Campaign in 1943), who had been allowed to remain at the Schoonoord when it was overrun by the Germans. In the battered Pietersberg Alford calmly continued to give blood transfusions as the building came under fire from XXX Corps' 'friendly' box barrage. He was again MiD for his cool dedication.

Continue left down Kneppelhoutweg to Benedendorpsweg and turn left. Continue to the junction with Dr Breveestraat.

A short distance up Dr Breveestraat is the imposing yellow building of the **Concert Hall (Map 3/17).** (There is parking space there and if the traffic is heavy you may walk from here to the church.) When the remnants of the different battalions heading for the Bridge fell back on 19 September they were first stopped and rallied by Lieutenant Colonel 'Sheriff' Thompson of the Light Regiment RA. The group of 100 men of the 2nd S Staffs, 120 of 1st Para Battalion, 46 of 3rd Para and 150 of 11th Para were collectively known as 'Thompson Force'. All were grateful to receive firm orders again. Thompson made the Concert Hall his HQ until he was wounded and the rallying function fell to Major 'Dickie' Lonsdale of 11th Para Battalion.

Continue towards the church on the right and park where you can, preferably in Weverstraat to the left.

• Old ('Lonsdale') Church and Memorials/Airborne Commemorative Marker No 5/41.6 kms/26 miles/15 minutes/Map 3-19/20/OP

It was here that survivors from the 19 September savage fighting around St Elisabeth Hospital gathered and were reorganised by Major Lonsdale, 2i/c 11th Para. Enemy mortaring and shelling was increasing and ammunition was growing short, tired and dirty men coming into the church from all directions. General Urquhart described how they were rallied into an effective force:

The Old (Lonsdale Church): The ruined church after the battle

Airborne Memorial

'Lonsdale now appeared, his hands in bandages. He looked down at the strained and desperate faces as he climbed the steps to the pulpit. [Considerable local dispute centres around whether he did or did not use the pulpit!]) In the congregation were survivors from the 1st, 3rd and 11th Battalions, the South Staffords and some glider pilots... suddenly the place was hushed as Lonsdale, his hands gripping the edge of the pulpit began, 'You know as well as I do that there are a lot of bloody Germans coming at us...We must fight for our lives and stick together.... We've fought Germans before – in North Africa, Sicily, Italy. They weren't good enough for us then and they're bloody well not good enough for us now'.

The Church then became known as 'The Lonsdale Church'.

General Urquhart had returned from Zwarteweg (qv) to his HQ at the Hartenstein at 0730 that morning and decided to shorten his line (making it easier to defend with a decreasing number of effective troops) and bring his forces south of the Arhem-Ede railway with the idea of continuing the attack towards Arnhem along the Middle Route. German attacks intensified that day, particularly against the 7th KOSB and a force of glider pilots in the Heelsum area, the continuing pressure forcing the various elements of the Division into a tightening perimeter based around the Hartenstein Hotel. Despite the arrival of the Polish gliders at around 1600 hours that afternoon it was clear to Urquhart by the following day that there was no longer any chance of reinforcing Frost at The Bridge and that the Old Church was an essential foothold on the river bank.

The Church is open 'during the season' on Wednesday, Thursday and Sunday from 1400-1700 hours. It is reputedly the oldest church in the Netherlands and is built of volcanic tufa. Known locally as 'Old Oosterbeek Dutch Reformed Church', it was severely damaged by German shellfire during the battle. When the church was rebuilt, in 1947-49, it was to a much smaller, earlier design than the cruciform shape of that of 1944.

On the lawn in front of the church is **Airborne Commemorative Marker No 5,** stating 'A Last Stand was made at this church to cover the withdrawal across the Rhine'. (See entry at Engineers' Memorial OP, Driel.) Behind it on the lawn is an ancient lime tree which was so badly damaged during the battle that it was decided to cut it down. The tree surgeon was delayed in carrying out the task and the following spring new growth started to sprout around the apparently dead hollow centre of the tree. It seemed to symbolize the renewal of hope and life in the battle-torn town. Today the tree grows vigorously.

To the right of the door is a plaque with a summary of the history of the church, including the events of September 1944. The hole in the church wall to the left is not caused by war damage. It was originally made so that lepers could stand outside and listen to the service (and was only rediscovered during the restoration). To the left of the lawn, on the foundations of the area ruined in 1944 and not included in the rebuilding, is a splendid **Memorial with a golden Pegasus,** unveiled by General Hackett and Mrs Ter Horst in 1990. It records how

In September 1944 British Airborne soldiers and their Polish comrades with the support of brave Dutch men and women fought a grim battle around this ancient church in the struggle to liberate the Netherlands from Nazi tyranny. This stone commemorates all who took part in this action and above all those who died. NOT ONE SHALL BE FORGOTTEN.

Behind the church is a **Memorial Seat** donated by Margaret, the daughter of No 6404135 Private William Ronald Dodd, 3rd Battalion the Para Regiment, who died on 27.7.89. A second

Memorial Seat is 'In Loving Memory of Leslie Jack Plummer, 1st Para Squadron, RE, 1920-1997. Forever in our hearts. Forever close to Oosterbeek.' Two other seats were donated by the Dreyeroord Hotel, the KOSB HQ during the Battle, and often called The White House (qv).

In the field behind the church three guns of the 1st Light Regiment RA were sited in September 1944. Supply containers and panniers were lying behind the church and many attempts to reach them ended in tragedy. Stand facing the river. To the left the Railway Bridge can be seen. The withdrawal was made over the polder this side of it. Take the centre span of the bridge as 12 o'clock. At 2 o'clock across the river is the Engineers' Memorial OP and at 3 o'clock is the square tower with golden cockerel weather vane of Driel Church (the original of which is in the Hartenstein Museum). The edge of The Perimeter is marked by the line of poplar trees to the left.

As the Church meant so much to the men who gathered here in the last desperate days of the Battle, many of them wished to place a memorial in it. It could have become rather like St George's Church in Ypres, where practically every feature in it - pulpit, font, windows, chairs etc, is a memorial (First World War) to an Army, a Division, a Regiment – even an individual, with historical Standards hanging all around. The Council of Churchwardens, however, was determined to keep this simple building, which has been a place of worship for over 1,000 years, as a living Church for its congregation. The number of permitted battle-related memorials has, therefore, been strictly limited to the following:

1. The Pulpit. This was presented by Boston in Lincolnshire in 1949. On the pulpit is the ancient States Bible, printed in 1660 and bearing a bullet mark from the battle. When the church was renovated in 1972, three large **Light Regiment RA Memorial** Panels from the Pulpit were moved near the entrance on the south wall.

2. The Communion Table. This was presented during the first service in the restored church on 17 September 1950 by the British and Polish Airborne. On it is a **Bible in English and Welsh,** presented in September 1979.

3. Seat behind the table presented by the parents of LAC Eric A. Samwells, who died on 22 September 1944, age 21. He is buried in the Oosterbeek CWGC Cemetey [4.C.20.] **Kneeler and Desk** presented on 23 September 1973 by the Diocese of Lichfield.

4. Font. Made of Portland stone with a copper lid in the form of a parachute canopy. Presented by 1st (BR) AB Division on 17 September 1950.

5. Airborne Prayer. Presented by veteran R. Dixon, who painted the English text. His daughter painted the Dutch version.

6. Plaque to the men of 156th Para Battalion (although they did not form part of the 'Lonsdale Force'). It was unveiled on 20 September 1986 by Elizabeth, one of the three daughters of their CO, Lieutenant-Colonel Sir Richard des Voeux (qv) who was killed on 20 September 1944.

7. The Altar Cross. This was originally from the Bernulphus Roman Catholic Church in Oosterbeek. It was taken from the ruins of the church by Eric Collinge of the 1st Paras, sent from this church on a patrol to Oosterbeek. Eric kept the cross under his smock as he swam the Rhine during the Escape and on his return to the UK gave it to his devout Catholic mother. When she died he tried to contact the church with a view to returning the cross. His efforts were finally brought to the attention of Henk Duinhoven (qv) who, after consultation with other local friends, invited Eric to bring the cross back to Oosterbeek. This he did, and it found a place here in the Old Church.

The Lonsdale window
that never was

8. Lonsdale Force Memorial Seat. This large, handsome bench was specially made with the money that had originally been raised for the erection of a stained glass window to Lonsdale Force. This is a somewhat sad and controversial story. It dates back to 1974 when ex-Mechanic with 271 Squadron Alan Hartley (qv) was instrumental in raising an Arnhem stained glass window in Down Ampney, from which airfield many men flew during MARKET-GARDEN. When Colonel & Mrs Lonsdale saw the window, Mrs Lonsdale suggested that it would be a good idea to have a window in the Old Church. The Lonsdales started fund-raising with Alan Hartley and when the Colonel died (on 23 November 1988 at the age of 74) Hartley continued until he had raised £3,500, commissioned a design (which showed the then Major Lonsdale giving his address from the pulpit in the Church) and obtained permission from the Churchwardens and the Burgomaster for the erection of the window. Hartley was greatly supported by Henk Duinhoven (qv), a local Headmaster and English teacher who translated during all the negotiations. At this stage General Hackett expressed severe disapproval of the idea (ostensibly because he wished it to incorporate the badges of all the Airborne Units who had fought at Arnhem/Oosterbeek, privately because he considered it 'laughable and ludicrous' that 'an atheist like Dickie' should appear 'on a church window for posterity'). The project was vetoed. This was echoed by Generals Urquhart (who didn't like stained glass windows) and Frost (who considered that there were already too many memorials at Arnhem). The veterans who had subscribed had wished to commemorate 'Lonsdale Force' rather than its leader alone, and the idea that the money should be put to a substantial bench bearing the badges of all the Regiments that had comprised the Force was agreed. Kate ter Horst, who objected to 'the silly opposition' to the idea of the window, congratulated Hartley on his 'wonderful efforts' and thought the seat 'a wonderful idea'. The badges, of 1st, 3rd and 11th Para Battalions, 21st Independent, S Staffs', Glider Pilots Regiment, 1st Airborne Reconnaissance Squadron, Royal Artillery and the Royal Corps of Signals were carved in Srinigar, Kashmir by a wood carver called Gulam Hassan who had done some work for 48 Squadron RAF. The seat was unveiled by six veterans of Lonsdale Force in 1991, but on that day two veterans of the Border Regiment pointed out that their badge was missing. A design was rushed out to Gulam Hassan who carved the missing badge and the badges were then re-arranged to incorporate the Border badge. The bench was originally designed to stand outside the Church, but it was thought that the beautifully carved badges would prove an easy target for souvenir hunters. It now sits at the back of the Church awaiting a final, fitting site.

The famous door from the Church, now on show at the Hartenstein Museum, on which Major Lonsdale supposedly wrote his final instructions, was actually used by him as an *aide-mémoire* when filming *Theirs is the Glory* in August 1945 – but not in September 1944. For his leadership in the final days of the Arnhem battle 'Dickie' Lonsdale was awarded a second DSO, the first having been won in Sicily and having already won the MC in Jubbulpore in 1937. Lonsdale's obituaries claimed that he was the last man of his Force to withdraw, swimming the Rhine despite being hampered by his bandaged wounds.

MARKET-GARDEN **Battlefield Tours** for groups, especially of this area, are given by Henk Duinhoven, MBE (qv). Tel: + (0) 481 46509. Fax: + (0) 481 450837. E-mail: mefffert_duinhoven@wolmail.nl

• *Walking tour from the Old Church (approximate time 15 minutes)*

From facing the front of the Church walk down the short flight of steps on the right and onto the narrow brick path that runs parallel to the river.
This is the footpath, known as Kerkpad, that links the church to the Heveadorp ferry and it was across here and onto the polder that 1st AB made its withdrawal on the night of 25 September. In the 1915 disastrous Gallipoli campaign the one effective operation was the evacuation of the Allied forces from under the noses of the Turks without a single battle casualty. Oddly, Urquhart knew about it.

At the back of my mind was Gallipoli. As a young officer I had studied this classic withdrawal very thoroughly for a promotion examination. It all came back now: the extreme pains that were taken to thin out the forward positions... to keep up an appearance of opposition until the very last.... The elaborate care with which parties were organised for their move to the beaches.... I called Charles Mackenzie [the General's chief staff officer] over to help me with the evacuation plan. 'You know how they did it at Gallipoli, Charles? Well we've got to do something like that'.

They did, but unlike Gallipoli they came under fire. The night was dark, the rain pouring down which helped to deaden the sounds of the withdrawal, the men's boots covered in sacking as they moved slowly in single file, each holding onto the smock of the man in front. Tapes had been put out to lead parties down to the crossing points, guides waited to direct them, but some lost their way or were scattered by German fire. On the river bank, in the enveloping mud, were groups of men waiting for their turn to cross [a description of the crossing is given at the RE's memorial which is visited later in this itinerary]. Having crossed the river Urquhart's first thought was to report to General Browning. Near Driel he found General Thomas's (43rd Wessex Division) Tactical Headquarters and sent his ADC, Captain Graham Roberts, inside to get some transport. 'He was not received with any warmth.' Eventually they reached Browning's Headquarters.

Browning was a little time coming... I reported: 'The division is nearly out now. I'm sorry that we haven't been able to do what we set out to do.' Browning offered me a drink.... 'You did all you could,' he said. 'Now you had better get some rest.' It was a totally inadequate meeting.

One of the authors of this book was a professional soldier. If Urquhart's version of the meeting is correct then in our view Browning's behaviour is inexcusable, the action of a man displaying the classic signs of the 'Peter Principle' (Dr Laurence J. Peter), that of being promoted to their level of incompetence.
On the right is a large house

• Kate ter Horst House (Map 3/18)

This is the Old Rectory where in September 1944 so many wounded soldiers were treated by Army medics and the local

The Ter Horst House

doctor with the help of local Dutch ladies. On 18 September Captain Randall Martin, the RMO of the Light Regiment RA, asked if he could set up his Regimental Aid Post here. He was supported by a few medical orderlies under the indomitable 'Scan' Bolden. On the 25th The Perimeter was pierced by a German tank which fired a shot through the house. Bombardier Bolden, with the Padre, the Rev Thorne, ran out brandishing a piece of white cloth and let forth such a stream of furious Cockney that the tank withdrew. By the end the house, which was repeatedly hit by machine-gun and sniper fire, by shells from tanks and by mortar fire, had run out of food, fresh water and most medical supplies. For his tireless work, which finally became no more than 'patching up', Captain Martin was MiD.

Fifty-eight of the approximate 300 soldiers who were cared for in the house, the cellar and the garden died of their wounds and were originally buried in the garden until re-interred in the Airborne Cemetery (qv).

The scenes in and around the Old Rectory are depicted in *Theirs is the Glory* and *A Bridge Too Far*, in which Mrs Ter Horst, the owner of the house, was portrayed as the heroine and an Angel of Mercy, thus making her a legend for all post-war visitors, veterans and students of the battle. This modest lady always maintained that her role was glorified by the films and that her actions were being duplicated in many other houses in the area. Mrs Ter Horst, who kept a detailed diary, later published her memoirs under the title *Cloud Over Arnhem*.

After the withdrawal from The Perimeter the Germans forced all the local inhabitants to evacuate. Mrs Ter Horst was sent off with her children. Mr Jan ter Horst worked with the Resistance and early after the Landings offered his assistance to the Airborne who sent him to Heelsum on a recce. He was then sheltered in the house of Doctor Oorthuis on Utrechtseweg. He was therefore separated from his family during the Battle and they were not reunited until they were all evacuated to Friesland.

In the marshes in the polder the Germans left many mines, which were taken out by German PoWs. Inevitably some remained and in 1947 Mrs Ter Horst's son, Veldest, was killed with a friend when they jumped from a willow tree and landed on a mine.

In the garden of the house is a memorial in the shape of a Pegasus with drooping wings presented to Mrs Ter Horst by the veterans she sheltered and comforted. It is not visible from outside the garden.

Further tragedy hit the family when on 21 February 1992 Mrs Ter Horst, then aged 85, was killed by a fast-moving car driven by a policeman just outside her house as she was walking with her husband, both of whose legs were broken in the accident. Kate ter Horst was the daughter of a Dutch naval Officer. She married Mr Ter Horst, a lawyer, in 1930 and moved into this house in 1938. For her courage and help to the wounded in 1944 she was awarded the MBE, as was her husband.

N.B. Please remember that this historic house is a private dwelling place and respect the privacy of Mr Ter Horst who, at age 95, was still living in the house in 2001.

Continue along the brick path to the small junction to the right to Benedendorpsweg.
This is directly below the Hartenstein, and was the bottom of one of the escape routes.
Return to the church. Cross the road and turn left up Weverstraat. Walk past the pond on the right and turn right at the footpath marked by a blue sign with a parent and child. Cross over the road (Zuiderbeekweg), turn left and then right by the site of the old Lammegroep Textiel building, demolished in 2001 to make way for new houses. Walk to the bank at the back.

• **Site of Major Robert Henry Cain's VC (Map 3/16).** In 1944 this was the local Hofwegen Laundry, which drew water from the stream that runs into the pond over which you walked. Originally part of Thompson Force, Cain commanded a company of the 2nd S. Staffs which was virtually cut off from the main Battalion. He set up a position here below Ploegseweg, down which German tanks rumbled. Seizing a PIAT Cain knocked out six tanks and a number of self-propelled guns. His gallantry award was for his actions between 19-25 September when 'he was everywhere danger threatened, moving among his men and encouraging them to hold out. Although he had a perforated ear-drum and multiple wounds he refused medical attention.' By his dogged actions, Cain saved a vital sector from falling into enemy hands, as, after being repeatedly attacked by self-propelled guns and, finally, only a light 2" mortar, the enemy withdrew in disorder. This exceptional officer, born in Shanghai in 1909, became a member of the Nigerian House of Representatives in the 1950s and died in Crowborough in May 1974. He was the only Arnhem VC to survive the battle.

Return to your car and continue.

Shortly after passing the church a platoon of Major Victor Dover's C Company headed down a small lane, the Polderweg, towards the river in an attempt to capture the Railway Bridge, now seen ahead on the right. As the paratroopers gained the northern end of the bridge ramparts, the Germans blew the middle span. The Major then led his company back inland towards the Middle Route with the intention of following Lieutenant-Colonel Frost towards The Bridge, but came under murderous Schmeisser and 20mm fire in the gardens and houses near the St Elisabeth Hospital.

At the Doorgaand Verkeer sign to the left keep to the right. Follow the road round towards the junction with Acacialaan. Stop just before it in the layby to the right. Walk to Acacialaan.

• *Site of Lance-Sergeant Baskeyfield's VC/42.6 kms/26.6 miles/5 minutes/Map 3-26/27*

Just around the corner on the left Lance-Sergeant John Daniel Baskeyfield with his six-pounder anti-tank gun knocked out two Tiger tanks and a self-propelled gun on 20 September 1944. When all his other crew members were either killed or badly injured, Baskeyfield, himself badly wounded in the leg, continued to man his gun. When it was knocked out, he crawled under fire to another six-pounder which he operated single-handed, putting out another enemy self-propelled gun, until he himself was killed. His body was never identified but his name is recorded on the Groesbeek Memorial (qv) and his heroic feat is immortalised by several famous pictures – notably by Bryan de Grineau, the *Illustrated London News* artist at Oosterbeek in September 1944, and in 1970 by Terence Cuneo. There is also a bust of Baskeyfield in the Hartenstein (qv).

In the garden on the corner is a **Marker bearing the Staffs badge and 'Jack Baskeyfield. 20 September 1996.'**

Continue along Benedendorpsweg under the 3.8m high railway viaduct along Klingelbeekseweg (43.4 kms/27.1 miles).

This is the area (Map 2/33) where the **Gronert twins** (qv) were killed. Like the two sets of brothers killed on the Somme in July 1916 and buried in Flat Iron Copse Cemetery – the Tregaskis and Hardwidges – one man was killed as he went to the aid of his wounded brother. The tiny brothers, both in B Coy, 2nd Para Battalion, were moving with the

Site of Lance-Sergeant Baskeyfield's VC with detail of plaque

company towards the viaduct when a German armoured car swept round the corner, started firing with its heavy machine guns and then withdrew. 'A' Company came under machine-gun fire from the high ground at Den Brink and Colonel Frost then sent Douglas Crawley's 'B' Company left of the railway embankment 'to see what he could do'. Claude Gronert was then hit. Thomas moved up to tend to his wounded brother and they were both killed by a German machine gun firing from a railwayman's hut along the railway. Their Platoon Commander, Lieutenant Peter Cane, was also killed and is buried in the Oosterbeek Cemetery [Joint Grave 18.A.13-14.]. Their Company Commander, Major Doug Crawley, dealt with the Germans at Den Brink (part of SS Kampfgruppe Spindler (qv)) and then went on to reach The Bridge with Frost, where he was also wounded and taken prisoner. He was a frequent visitor to the Hartenstein Museum until his death on 12 May 1998.

There was a freight railway station here, Oosterbeek Laag, which was used by the Germans. Note the new bricks patched in to cover the 1944 damage.

N.B. In 2001 a new approach bridge was being constructed to the railway bridge which may alter the aspect of this historic site.

Continue uphill on Klingelbeekseweg and finally Hulkesteinseweg until it joins Utrechtseweg.
This junction, where the Lower and Middle Routes meet, is where the remnants of the forces trying to reach the bridge eventually came together. It looks very much the same today as it did in 1944. Frost passed this way with A Company but took the lower road at the fork ahead as you will in a moment, while Victor Dover's C Company of the battalion went uphill past the hospital (now apartments) and became bogged down in a stubborn conflict with Harzer's tanks and machine-guns.

Turn right on Utrechtseweg, signed Centrum.

• *Extra Visits to Plaque on 'Arnhem House' (Map 2/39); Women in War Memorial OP (Map 2/39); Plaque on Old German SD Building (Map 2/42); September 1944 Urquhart Memorial (Map 2/43); No 14 Zwarteweg (Map 4/1); Old St Elisabeth Hospital/Airborne Commemorative Marker No 6 (Map 4/4) Round trip: 2.4 kms/1.5 miles. Approximate time: 25 minutes*

Fork left at the 2nd traffic lights, past the old St Elisabeth Hospital on the left and continue along Utrechtseweg to the Museum of Modern Art on the right.

Extra visits continued

In the garden of the Museum (Map 2/40) is the sculpture by **Henry Moore called 'The Warrior',** which used to stand outside the Town Hall in Arnhem. It is one of five casts of the statue.

Park where you can and walk to the next three stops.

Immediately opposite is **House No 72** now beautifully restored and called'Airborne House'. Here Major Victor Dover and C Company of 2nd Para made their last stand and were finally forced to capitulate as their casualties were so high. A **Plaque** above the door recalls the efforts of thirty members of 1st AB Division who defended the building from 18-19 September. This was the closest point to The Bridge that 1st AB Division reached along this route and men of the 2nd Battalion, South Staffs got no further the following day. All attempts to reinforce 2nd Para at The Bridge along the Middle Route ceased after 19 September.

Some 200m past the Museum (in which Captain Brownscombe (qv) of the South Staffs established his RAP on 19 September until he was captured by the Germans and

Utrechtseweg Memorials: Plaque on old Sicherheitsdienst HQ. No 85

2nd Para Bn Plaque over doorway of No 72   Dutch Women in War Statue

Extra visits continued

taken to the Municipal Hospital) is a viewpoint on the right with some seats by the **Statue to Women in War.** The view depends on a clear day and minimum summer foliage! Immediately below is the Lower Route along which John Frost with A Company made his way to The Bridge, passing here about 2000 hours on Sunday 17 September. Beyond the road is the Neder Rijn. To the left, upstream, the Nelson Mandela Bridge should just be visible and, at water level, just this side of it, is the site of the old pontoon bridge and it was here that the final attempt by elements of 1st and 3rd Battalions to join Frost via the Lower Route failed. The Bridge is 950m beyond. In the distance the Groesbeek Heights above Nijmegen are visible on a clear day and sometimes the bulk of the Nijmegen power station where the 504th started their river crossing can be seen. To the right, downstream, is the Railway Bridge. Immediately to its right can be seen the blades of the wind generator (qv) on the opposite bank of the Rhine. Some 3kms behind the generator is the area of Driel where the Polish Brigade dropped on 21 September. A large modern sculpture representing 'Energy' crosses above the road at this point.

Beyond the open space of the viewpoint is No 85, PGEM Building, **the old SD (Sicherheitsdienst -German Security Police) HQ. A Plaque** bears witness to its 1944 use.

Turn round and return along Utrechtseweg, past the old St Elisabeth Hospital, over the traffic lights and immediately turn right up Oranjestraat. Turn right again at the first turning, Alexanderstraat, and park before the next junction (2kms/1.3 miles). Walk forward along the road to the second junction with Mauritsstraat. Immediately past that junction is house No 135 (Map 4/3).

On 17 September General Urquhart had arrived by glider and watched the main body of Lathbury's 1st Parachute Brigade land. It was, he said, 'a textbook drop'. However, his signaller was unable to make contact with his other main formation, Hicks's Airlanding Brigade, which had landed north of his position, so he set off in his jeep to visit them. Hicks was not there when he arrived and now, not able to contact anyone by radio, he set off again to see what was happening on the Lower Route where Lathbury's HQ was following Frost's 2nd Battalion. He made contact with the tail end of the 2nd Battalion but did not see Frost himself. He then decided to return to the Middle Route and talk to Gerald Lathbury who had joined 3rd Battalion, catching up with them at the Kussin crossroads. As the evening fell they came under heavy German fire and Urquhart decided to stay that night with Lathbury in a villa near the Koude Herberg Café (qv) west of the Hartenstein Hotel. At about 0400 hours the following morning the two set off together, making their way back to the Lower Route and reaching this area, following much the same path as you have done from the Old Church. Here they came under fire from self-propelled guns and took shelter in a nearby house. In the midst of intense German activity, Leo Heaps (qv) one of the most extraordinary figures of the MARKET-GARDEN story, appeared. In his memoirs Urquhart recalled,

> There suddenly appeared a Bren carrier, its engine roaring, its tracks clattering on the small setts. It was driven by a ubiquitous Canadian lieutenant called Heaps who was soon to develop a reputation for turning up in the most unlikely places... in fact I never really discovered to which unit he belonged [he was attached to 1st

Extra visits continued

Battalion]. In battle some men have a charmed existence: Heaps was such a man....
Heaps saluted and brought tidings from my own HQ, 'You were reported
missing', he told me, 'I was sent to try and find you.

Urquhart gave Heaps various messages to take back and then Heaps 'managed to set
off back along the road'. It seems strange that the General did not consider going with
him since Heaps was going back to Divisional HQ. As the fighting intensified further
the General decided that it was now vital to return to 1st AB Division HQ to retake
control. Various members of the Battalion who were in other houses in the vicinity had
called in from time to time and Lathbury had arranged to have paratroopers cover their
breakout with smoke bombs. 'Would you like to throw a bomb, sir?' he asked. The
General declined, but in their attempt to break out Brigadier Lathbury was wounded by
Spandau fire. The General, Captain Willie Taylor and Lieutenant Jimmy Cleminson
carried him to No 135 Alexanderstraat where he was taken in by the family and then
moved to the hospital.

*Turn up Mauritsstraat and immediately turn right up and across the road to the small
alleyway. This leads to the rear of No 14 Zwarteweg.*

After General Urquhart, Captain Taylor and Lieutenant Cleminson left Lathbury in
Alexanderstraat they turned the corner into this alleyway and then into the kitchen of
No 14 Zwarteweg, the home of Anton Derksen. Derksen directed them to the attic.
Outside the house in Zwarteweg itself was a German SP gun and crew and Urquhart
proposed that they should drop a grenade on it and make a dash for it. The others were
doubtful and, surprisingly, the General took a democratic vote on the matter which
went against him. Despite his urgent desire to return to his HQ, Urquhart did not
attempt to break out again until the early hours of the following day, Tuesday 19
September, when Derksen told them that the British were at the end of the road. The
three of them made a dash for it (watched by a surprised Surgeon Lipmann Kessel (qv)
from the hospital window), meeting some South Staffs where Zwarteweg joins the
Middle Route. They informed the General that his HQ was now at the Hartenstein. He
quickly drove there, arriving at 0725 hours. It may have been better had he stayed at
Zwarteweg as it was from this area that the last significant attempt was made to reach
2nd Para at The Bridge.

*Walk round the corner into Zwarteweg to the front of No 14 which may well have a
picture of General Urquhart in the window.*

Ahead is the site of the old **St Elisabeth** [called by English-speaking locals 'the St
Elisabeth's'] **Hospital** which was converted into apartments in 2000. The façade and the
Chapel (straight ahead) will be preserved and the **Memorial Plaques** it contained were
donated to the Hartenstein Museum (qv) in January 2001 by the last surviving Trustee
of the Hospital. There they safely await the time when they can be replaced in the
Hospital. The Plaque that was in the main hall bears Airborne and Medical insignia,
with the dates 17-25 September 1944, the other was donated to the Hospital by British
Airborne Veterans. Outside the main entrance is **Airborne Commemorative Marker No
6,** commemorating 16th Field Ambulance's stay in the Hospital.

'Remember September 1944' Memorial, Nassaustraat

The alleyway behind No 14 Zwartenweg

Façade of the old St Elisabeth Hospital with Airborne Commemorative Marker No 6

Plaques from the Hospital, at present in the Hartenstein

Extra visits continued

By 2200 hours on 17 September 16th Para Field Ambulance had established itself in the Hospital as planned and started to treat casualties. A large Red Cross flag was hung above the main entrance. Lieutenant-Colonel Townsend, the CO, and Captain Lipmann Kessel, Surgeon to 16th Para Field Ambulance (qv), who had already seen service in North Africa and Sicily, liaised with the Dutch doctors. During that night 1st Para, blocked on the Upper Route by infantry and armour of Colonel Harzer's 9th SS Panzer (Hohenstaufen) Division, swung down to this area and bitter house-to-house fighting by elements of 1st and 3rd Para took place in the small houses in the streets you have just walked through. By 0800 hours the following day the Germans had occupied the Hospital.

1st Para concentrated in the network of small streets while 3rd Para were some 400m further back along Utrechtseweg. That night, Monday, the 2nd South Staffs (1 Airlanding Brigade) and 11th Para Battalion (4th Para Brigade) arrived here and, at 0445 hours on Tuesday 19 September, a composite force set off towards what is now the PGEM building ahead with the aim of relieving 2nd Para at The Bridge. The attack was difficult. The force was spread out from the Lower Route, past here and uphill beyond the hospital, and was under heavy fire from all directions. Despite the fierce actions around the Hospital, the staff inside continued to care for German and British casualties. It was now under the command of Captain Skalka, the Divisionsarzt of the 9th SS, who ordered the entire medical unit to be ready to march off. Townsend protested vehemently and two surgical teams were permitted to stay at the Hospital under Major Longland and Captain Lipmann Kessel.

The British withdrew that night, reorganising around midnight at Oosterbeek first under Lieutenant-Colonel Thompson and then in the Church under Major Lonsdale.

CAPTAIN A.W. LIPMANN KESSEL AND BRIGADIER 'SHAN' HACKETT

On 24 September Brigadier Hackett (qv) arrived here by jeep and was soon seen by Lipmann Kessel who performed a brilliant operation on the serious wound in his lower abdomen and thereby saved his life. A German medical officer had advised that Hackett should be given a lethal injection of morphine as his case was hopeless. 'Lippy', whom Hackett described as 'a man with a dark ugly clever face and large intelligent eyes ... a South African Jew, inclined to Marxism, an intelligent and sensitive person who had settled into England in the thirties', eventually helped 'Piet van Arnhem' (Piet Kruijff), leader of the Dutch Resistance in Arnhem, to spring Hackett (who had originally been tagged as a Corporal Hayter, then as a major, to hide his high-ranking identity) from the hospital. Piet would later also have Brigadier Gerald Lathbury and Major Digby Tatham-Warter (qv) in his network of safe houses in and near Ede (qv). He disguised Hackett as a badly wounded Dutchman and drove him by car to the house of Tonny de Nooij where he was hiding Lathbury before moving him on to

Personal account continued

the house where he would spend so many weeks in Torenstraat (qv).

As the British wounded were moved on to POW camps, Kessel was the last remaining British surgeon. His dedication and bravery during this period, when operations were often interrupted by falling bombs, by running battles in and around the hospital and intrusive visits from SS Officers, and while he battled against the German determination to move patients he considered too ill to disturb, were legendary. On 13 October Lippy and his small team were eventually sent to the British Hospital that was created in the barracks at Apeldoorn to help deal with the over 2,000 Allied and over 1,500 German casualties from the Arnhem-Oosterbeek battle area. On 16 October he escaped with Padre McGowan, Lieutenant-Colonel Herford and Major Longland to a safe house in Ede (qv) as described above. On 20 September 1945, Captain A.W. Lipmann Kessel was awarded the MC and the MBE. His military service is described in his book *Surgeon at Arms* and his distinguished career continued after the war.

Extra visits continued

Continue along Zwarteweg and turn first left along Nassaustraat to the memorial on the small green ahead.

The **Memorial** bears the legend, 'Remember September 1944'. Erected by local residents, it was unveiled by General Urquhart in 1987, the year before he died and during the last visit he made to Zwarteweg. To the right at the top of Frederik Hendrikstraat runs the railway line.

Return down Frederik Hendrikstraat to your car, go back to the traffic lights on Utrechtseweg and pick up the main itinerary.

Continue over the next traffic light forking right downhill past the
4 Star Golden Tulip Rijnhotel with great views over the river on the right. Tel: + (0)26 4434642. You are effectively following the route taken by 2nd Para Battalion to the bridge.
Continue on Onderlangs past the grassed open space to the left with a modern sculpture group in the centre to

• Airborne Garden Sign and Memorial Seats (45.4 kms/28.4 miles) (Map 2/41)

By the sign is a traditional teak bench with the text,

> Donated in remembrance of their fallen comrades by the 3rd Parachute Battalion to the people of Arnhem in recognition of their courage and unflinching support during the Battle of Arnhem September 1944.

Another similar bench nearby had its plaque missing in 2001.
Continue towards Arnhem. At 45.9kms/28.7 miles, before the roundabout complex, take the

small slip road to the right on Boterdijk and park. Walk towards the grassy slope to the post on the wall to the right.

• Airborne Commemorative Marker No 7/45.9 kms/28.7 miles/10 minutes/Map 2/44

The plaque reads

> On the morning of Tuesday 19 September 1944 a final attempt by the 1st and 3rd Battalons the Para Regt to break through to the Rhine Bridge failed. After heavy losses the remaining British troops finally withdrew to Oosterbeek.

Continue (by car) to the 'blue' and white waves of Roermonds Plein. The ornamental 'waves' (originally blue and white but now faded to grey) on the ground mark the site of the old harbour and 'Ship Bridge' (pontoon bridge) which existed before the original road bridge was opened in 1935. RAF photographs show the centre of this floating bridge out of position as early as 6 September 1944 and on 17 September it was alongside the north bank of the river.

Continue under the Nelson Mandela Bridge following Centrum, Westervoort and Apeldoorn signs. Continue to the traffic lights and turn left signed P Markt. Follow the signs, passing the Eusebius Church on the left and park in the Market car park (47.5 kms/29.7 miles).

Airborne Commemorative Marker No 7, Mandela Bridge in background

Note that this is paid parking. It makes an ideal base for a walking tour of the area of The Bridge before climbing up onto it. The area close to The Bridge has changed so much (in 1944 the houses were next to it on both sides with their roofs level with the roadway) that the best way to understand what happened is to be clear exactly where the two main centres of action were - Colonel Frost's Headquarters and the school where Captain Eric Mackay fought. Both are visited on the walking tour.

• Walking tour of some of Arnhem's Monuments (approximate time: 40 minutes). See Sketch Map 6 for precise locations.

The Market Square, and most of the superb historic buildings surrounding it, was completely destroyed in September 1944. One exception is the medieval **Sabelspoort** which adjoins the modern **Provincial House (Map 5/5),** the first important building to be rebuilt after the war in 1954, the seat of the Gelderland Government. **Visitable during normal office hours only.**

Walk to the Provincial House, at the southern end of the square, go through the archway into the courtyard and look back.

To the right of the archway is a **Plaque to the Civil Servants** who lost their lives 1940-45. *Proceed into the building.*

To the left of the entrance is a glass cabinet containing the **Ceremonial Sword** presented by General Urquhart, on behalf of 1st (BR) AB and 1st Polish Para Brigade Group, to the people

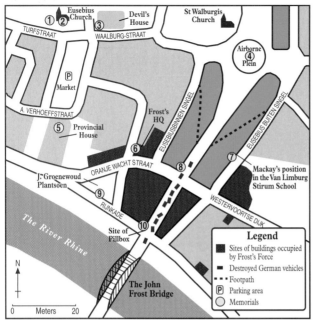

1. Arnhem War Memorial
2. Memorial Bells. SGW '1944'. Plaques 49th Div, 9th AB Fd Regt RE, Resistance Fighters
3. SGW 'Arnhem in Flames' Liberation Window
4. 1st AB Div Memorial
5. Ceremonial Sword & Civil Servants Plaque
6. 'John Frost HQ' Plaque
7. Airborne Commemorative Marker No.8
8. Plaque to John Frost and his men
9. 16th Para Fd Amb 25pr gun, propeller and Polish Memorial / Jacob Groenewould plaque
10. Plaque to the Soldiers who held The Bridge 17-21 Sept 1944

AB Ceremonial Sword, Provincial House

Stained glass window, Devil's House

Arnhem War Memorial

Descending parachutists, Eusebius Church

Site of John Frost HQ

Jacob Groenewoud Memorial Garden

Airborne Commemorative Marker No 8

Airborne Plein Memorial with twin spires of St Walburgis Church behind

of the Province of Gelderland to commemorate their courage and help during the Battle of Arnhem in September 1944 and after, when many risked their lives in assisting evaders to reach the Allied Forces operating south of the Rhine. The handsome Wilkinson Sword is engraved with all the badges of the participating Allies and has an enamelled Pegasus and Coat of Arms of the Province.

Also on the Market Square (in the top left hand corner) is the old **Weighhouse**, an 18th Century neo-classical building which was restored to its former style after the battle. Today it is a café/restaurant which makes a convenient lunch break: **De Waag**, 38 Markt. Tel: + (0)26 3705960.

• Just above the top right-hand corner of the Square on Walburgstraat is the **old Devil's House (Map 5/3),** another

Plaque on The Bridge

building which miraculously survived the battle. The residence of army commander Maarten van Rossum (whose statue stands atop the building) this 16th Century house was named for the satyrs which can be seen under the oriel window. Today it serves as the Burgomaster's ceremonial parlour and adjoins the modern city Hall. It contains a **Stained Glass Window (Map 5/3)** which shows Arnhem in flames with a Phoenix rising from the ashes and the coat of Arms of Arnhem - the double-headed eagle. It bears the dates 1945-1969 and *Labor vincit omnia* - work conquers all.

• To the left of the Devil's House is the **Eusebius Church/Memorials (Map 5-1/2)**
The original church was built between 1452 and 1650. During the German occupation most of the church bells were, as with many other Dutch churches, taken away to be melted down for the German war effort. In the 1944 battle, and by artillery fire during the following winter, the Eusebius Church was reduced to a shell by the fire bombs that rained on it and the decision was taken in the autumn of 1945 to rebuild it in the original style. Work began in 1947 and was not completed until 1964. German stone was used in the rebuilding of the tower. A second restoration of the church was undertaken in 1981-83 and the belfry was restored in 1992-4 when the carillon was enlarged with four heavy bells and a glass elevator was installed to take visitors 73 metres up to the panoramic platform on the tower. The view from the top gives a marvellous OP of the battlefield on a clear day and has identification markers and explanatory MARKET-GARDEN panels. From the lift the inscription on three of the new bells can be read and the top **bells commemorate the soldiers who took part in the battle: Irish, Scotch** [sic]**, Welsh, English, Polish, Canadians, Americans and Dutch.** The money was raised by the Arnhem Bell Appeal, founded in London in 1993 and supported by Sir John Hackett. On 17 September 1994, the 50th Anniversary, Prince Charles, Colonel-in-Chief of the Parachute Regiment, inaugurated the carillon by playing the bells.

From the vaulted arches of the Council Chapel to the right at the foot of the tower **nineteen bronze parachutists** appear to be descending. Designed by Simona Vergani, this dramatic and moving sculpture group was a gift of the Burgesses of Arnhem in 1994. In the Anna Chapel to the left is **a stained glass window** which commemorates all the citizens of Arnhem who lost their lives during the battle, a gift from a Committee of Inhabitants of Arnhem in 1994.

In the church itself is a **stained glass window** depicting the church in flames with dive bombing aeroplanes and the word '1944'. It is called the Battle of Arnhem or Liberation Window and was made by artist Joop Janssen. There are several memorial plaques throughout the church, one in memory of the **Soldiers of the 2nd Platoon, 9th AB Field Regiment, RE,** another commemorates the **Liberation of Arnhem by the British 49th West Riding ('Polar Bear') Division** and another the **Resistance Fighters of Arnhem.**

The historic but sophisticated Church Hall is a venue for social and business events. **Tower Open: Tuesday-Saturday 1000-1700 hours. Sunday 1200-1700. Tel: + (0) 26 4428844. Entrance fee payable.** There is a cafeteria and small souvenir stall by the entrance to the tower lift. A guide accompanies the visitor on the spectacular and speedy trip up.

In 2001 the need for further renovation work was discovered.

• In Kerk Plein outside the church is the **Arnhem War Memorial** which depicts a man defending himself against the might of the enemy. Entitled 'Man Against Power' the powerful bronze statue was sculpted by Gijs Jacobs van den Hof (1889-1965). It was unveiled by Queen Juliana in 1953. It is here that wreaths are laid and a 2-minute silence is kept at 0800 hours each year on 4 May, Commemoration Day.

From Broeren Straat at the top of the Square turn up Bakkerstraat.
• Halfway up Bakkerstraat on the left, on the shop at No 62, is a **Memorial Plaque to Five Civilians (Map 2/51)** shot in this building on 19 September 1944. Among them was Dr Zwolle who had treated Corporal Arthur Maybury of 89th Para Security Section in the Huishoudschool on the Rijnkade where he was being sheltered, and took from him the list of Dutch NSB (National Socialist Movement) Members he was carrying. This probably cost the Doctor his life as it was discovered by the Germans when he went to get food for refugees. Two days later he was shot here, the van Gend en Loos building, then being used by the Wehrmacht as an HQ. Maybury died of his wounds and his body, initially buried in the garden of the school, was removed by the Germans and re-interred in a garden along Utrechtseweg. He is now buried in the Arnhem-Oosterbeek Cemetery [25.A.4.].

The remnants of No 4 Platoon of 2nd Para under Lieutenant Hugh Levien, who were acting as rearguard as B Company approached The Bridge and ran into the side streets as they came under German fire. A member of the Dutch Resistance, Jan Brouwer, led them into the house of Miss Mieke Engelsman, also on Bakkerstraat, from where Levien was able to telephone his Company Commander, Doug Crawley (qv), at The Bridge. The house was soon surrounded by Germans and the group had to surrender after 24 hours when all their ammunition had been exhausted.

Return to the Market, walk down to the left of the Provincial House towards the river to the Oranje Wacht Straat.
• On the **Tax Office,** just past traffic lights, on the wall on the left is a black **Plaque commemorating the site of Frost's HQ (Map 5/6)** in September 1944.
• Opposite on the Rijn Kade is a small park. **Jacob Groenewoud Plantsoen/25-Pounder Gun/Polish Memorial/ Information Boards (Map 5-9/9a)**
The garden is named for Reserve Captain (Intelligence) **Jacob Groenewoud** and was opened on 8 September 1994. A sign board explains that Groenewoud, 'the only Dutch Serviceman killed in this area on 18 September 1944', was awarded the Military Order of William 4th Class, the Netherlands equivalent of the Victoria Cross or the Medal of Honour. Groenewoud, born in 1916, a Dutchman living in South Africa before the war, joined the Dutch Army in Britain. He then became a member of the Jedburgh Team Claude.

JEDBURGH TEAM CLAUDE

'Jedburghs' were teams of three (normally two officers and an NCO wireless operator) conceived by S.O.E. in 1942 to support Allied Operations with 'unconventional warfare requirements'. This included being dropped behind enemy lines, liaising with local Resistance groups to direct their attacks on rail and signal communications and to support an invasion. Their international personnel had to 'be experienced in handling men', to speak French and/or Dutch, to be experienced in small arms, all round physically fit and have completed para training. They were named after the district in Scotland where they trained. By the spring of 1944 over seventy teams had been trained, including American (100 US officers were allocated) Belgian, British, Dutch and French members.

Six Jedburgh teams supported MARKET-GARDEN, five of them deployed in Holland. The team which supported 1st (BR) AB Division was codenamed CLAUDE

Jedburgh Team Claude continued

and comprised Groenewoud and two Americans, Lieutenant Harvey Todd and T/Sergeant C.A. Scott. Its task was to advise the Divisional Commanders on using local Resistance groups and to maintain liaison between the AB Forces and Special Forces HQ in London. They dropped at 1400 hours on the 17th with the aim of advancing with the leading elements of 1st Brigade and contacting the ex-Burgomaster and Police Chief to help them re-establish government.

Todd, Groenewoud and Scott had a frenzied journey towards Arnhem, collecting transport, killing any Germans that crossed their path ['They might have surrendered,' wrote Todd, 'but no time for PWs here'], liaised with the German doctor in the St Elisabeth Hospital to take British wounded and moved on towards The Bridge. There they made contact with Brigade HQ and some local officials. It soon became apparent that vital communication between the Bridge party and Divisional HQ had been lost and the Jedburgh's wireless operator, Scott, had disappeared (he was actually with Divisional HQ). Despite initial successes, the situation had begun to worsen as heavy German tanks (a Tiger and a Mark IV) arrived and opened fire and Medics were overwhelmed with the number of wounded. Civilians reported a large column of vehicles heading towards Arnhem from the Amsterdam direction. Contact with HQ was vital. Groenewoud found out from civilians that there was still a working phone in the house of a doctor two blocks away. He persuaded Todd to accompany him and the two Jedburgh officers volunteered to make their way from the bridge area to the phone. Groenewoud was killed outright by a sniper's bullet to the head as he crossed the road. Todd's report stated that this was on 19 September. He later recommended his colleague for a gallantry award for 'action above and beyond the call of duty'.

The recommendation was endorsed by Major J. A. Hibbert, RA (Brigade Major at The Bridge) writing from 1 (BR) Air Corps HQ at Rickmansworth on 19 April 1945. He added that 'Captain Groenewoud was always in the forefront of the battle obtaining information from Dutch civilians and acting as interpreter when required. He led a section in the capture of the HQ of the German Area commander and seized some highly important documents dealing with the German plans for the destruction of docks and facilities in Rotterdam and Amsterdam.'

Todd fought through the whole of Frost's stand at The Bridge. On 18 September he took up a position on the roof of a building overlooking the road from which he killed ten Germans although he was hit on his helmet and was out of action until the next day. He then killed eight more Germans and, using a Bren gun, knocked out a 20mm gun before he and Groenewoud set off to use the telephone. On the 20th he destroyed a machine-gun post but was knocked out of his place in the rafters and fell through the building to the first floor. As the remnants of The Bridge force attempted to make their escape during the night he silenced another machine gun with a grenade and hid in a tree, hoping that XXX Corps would turn up. When they didn't he was captured on the 27th. After moves from camp to camp in Germany and in Poland, involving liberation by the Americans and recapture, he eventually escaped on 30 April 1945 and finally reported to OSS HQ in Paris with vital intelligence notes that he had managed to smuggle through repeated searches. When he was debriefed on 25 May his Report was classified as 'Secret'.

Beside Groenewoud's Board is a **Canadian 'Fickes'** [Vickers]-**Armstrong 25-pounder gun.** It is dedicated to 16th Para Field Ambulance and bears the legend, 'A stone with a badge, a name, a date buried here, brothers, friend and mate they fought their battles to free us all till the bugle sounded their last call.' The **aeroplane propeller** is a gift from the Arnhem '40-'45 War Museum (qv). There is a **Polish Memorial, Photographs** of the Battle and an **Information Board** with a sketch map of the action here.

In November 2000 the area was redecorated in Airborne colours and repaved.
Continue under The Bridge and turn left along Eusebiusbuitensingel to the concrete post on the left.

• *Airborne Commemorative Marker No 8, Site of the Van Limburg Stirum School (Map 5/8)*

This concrete marker, erected in 1999, with its bright golden-painted Pegasus, marks the site of the school which was held by a group of 1st Para Squadron RE under Captain Eric Mackay of A Troop from the evening of Sunday 17 September to midday Wednesday 20 September. Over the hours they sustained heavy casualties. When the upper storeys of the school were demolished by a Tiger tank on Wednesday, Mackay, down to about thirteen men, began to evacuate as many of his wounded as possible. Coming under fire again and sustaining more casualties, he was faced with a difficult decision – whether to surrender or to continue to fight. He decided that the safest thing for the wounded was to leave them, leading the remaining men north with the phrase 'Every man for himself', until only four remained. It was a decision that later brought him much criticism - doubtless he would also have been criticised had he surrendered.

On that Wednesday, the 20th, the only **VC** awarded at the John Frost Bridge was won by **Lieutenant John Hollington Grayburn** of No 2 Platoon, A Company, 2nd Para Battalion, known as 'Jack'. Grayburn had been in the thick of any action from the first day, when he was part of a tangle with a German machine gun near the beginning of the southern route, the successful outcome of which he signalled with a bugle call as taught by Digby Tatham-Warter (qv), his Company Commander. Grayburn's was the leading platoon and he reached The Bridge at about 2000 hours to take up a defensive position on the near side of the northern embankment. His first wound came when leading his platoon, with blackened faces and muffled boots, in an attempt to cross over the northern end of The Bridge. They were met with machine-gun fire at point blank range from the pill box on The Bridge and suffered heavy casualties. At the end of Tuesday, the 19th, Grayburn was put in charge of the remnants of A Company, as Tatham-Warter had been wounded for the second time and his 2i/c Captain Tony Frank was also wounded. During the morning of Wednesday the 20th the Germans placed explosive charges on the bridge. Grayburn accompanied a party of REs, led by Lieutenant Donald Hindley, in an attempt to remove the fuses. Grayburn was hit, but quickly had the wounds patched up and returned to the fray with a bandage round his head and his arm in a sling. A German tank then moved up in support and Jack Grayburn was killed.
Walk up Eusebiusbuitensingel and turn left under the tunnel into

• *Airborne Plein Memorial/Map 5/4*

In the centre of the circle is a Memorial to 1st AB Division in the form of a broken pillar –

debris from the destroyed Palace of Justice. It was unveiled on 17 September 1945 by the Governor of the Province of Gelderland in the presence of General Frost and 200 survivors of the Division. It is the focal point of the annual wreath-laying commemorations in Arnhem during the Anniversary weekend. [In 2000 it was at 1900 on Friday 15 September]. The benches and railings around the circular area are painted in Airborne magenta. At either side are stone bas reliefs, one with the Pegasus insignia the other with the words 'Battle of Arnhem '44', erected in 1945. The local nickname for the circle is 'the bear pit'!

The twin church spires to the left are on the St Walburgis Basilica. On 19 September 1944 a Focke-Wulf hit the towers whilst strafing the British soldiers on the bridge and crashed into a small lake which was on what is now Airborne Plein.

Walk through the tunnel on the left towards The Bridge.

The large complex of buildings to the right as you walk are the rebuilt Palais de Justice, State Archives and Tax and other administrative buildings.

Walk up the slope and onto The Bridge, being particularly aware of the fast-moving traffic on the cycle path.

• *John Frost Bridge/Memorials (Map 5-8/10)*

This is not the original bridge. The first one on this site was opened in 1935 and blown by the Dutch Army to stop the advancing Germans in the early hours of 10 May 1940. It was rebuilt by the Germans in early 1944 and was damaged by USAAF bombers on 6-7 October 1944. The Germans blew The Bridge at the end of October 1944. It was rebuilt by the Dutch and opened on 9 May 1950, the 5th Anniversary of the end of the War in Europe.

The Bridge was rebuilt to the original plans, so it looks much the same today as it did pre-war. This is **The Bridge Too Far**, the target of 1st AB Division which, curiously, was not even marked on most British-issued operational maps which had been printed earlier than 1944. The maps were American, based on Dutch originals, but there was no doubt as to the position of The Bridge. The fighting here was bloody and intense and is well-documented in the Hartenstein Museum and in many books. The film *A Bridge Too Far* used the bridge at Deventer. About 500 men of 2nd Para Battalion under Lieutenant-Colonel Frost reached The Bridge around 2000 hours on 17 September and received some reinforcement from C Coy of 3rd Para Battalion and some Royal Engineeers of 1 Para Squadron. They occupied the houses that abutted the bridge ramps, their top floors level with, or higher than, the roadway. Against armoured cars, half-tracks, tanks and SS (Colonel Heinz Harmel's 10th SS Panzer Division) the northern end (where you are standing) was held until around 0500 hours on Thursday 21 September when the remnants of the Battalion scattered, a final attempt to rally a force at what had been Frost's HQ being unsuccessful. A truce had been arranged for the wounded to be evacuated - including John Frost, wounded earlier in the day - on Wednesday evening, but from that point on, exhausted and surrounded, with little ammunition and being burned out of their positions, the stubborn defenders had little chance. The Germans helped to collect the wounded and, using the Airborne's jeeps, took them off to hospital. Although 1st AB Division did not capture the Arnhem Bridge, they did hold the northern end long enough to prevent German Panzers crossing it and influencing the battle for the Nijmegen Bridge.

• On the right at the top of the slope is a **Plaque to John Frost and his men.**

Stop here for a moment and locate Frost's Headquarters and the school.
The authors stood here with John Frost, at a position virtually opposite his old HQ, and asked him to describe what had happened. This is what he said: -

A PERSONAL MEMORY

By Major-General John Frost

We squeezed our way through [the Lower Route] and the leading company and headquarters actually began to run down the road until we saw the great big bridge looming up ahead of us. One thing we were terrified of was to see this go up like the other bridge and so we occupied it as quietly as we could in the gathering darkness. We got into all the buildings which were controlling the bridge from the north end and we continued to let the traffic use the bridge. And then when we thought it was the right moment the leading platoon of A Company tried to go across. But they very quickly got spotted - I think by a machine gun - we don't know if it was in some sort a pillbox [possibly on the site of the hut-like structure ahead that you will visit next] or much more likely in an armoured car. That produced sufficient fire, with the bullets ricocheting off the ground and off the spars of the bridge, so that almost half that platoon became casualties. So they came back. It was obvious that there was no future in trying to cross from this end of the bridge. To add to that, shortly afterwards three lorries came across and they were hit by machine-gun fire, caught fire and they began to blaze all through the rest of the night. Now the Germans began to attack, mostly from this side, but we were able to hold them off fairly successfully and then gradually as night grew on it became quieter. Now, unfortunately, the rest of the brigade was badly held up and they were given orders to stay where they were until the dawn and try again then. With me was the HQ of the Support Company and A Company and in the middle of the night along came C Company of the 3rd Battalion who had found a way up the railway line. Also there was the Brigade HQ, without the Brigadier, Freddy Gough's Recce Sqn HQ and some Sappers. So the total force was probably some 500-600 men, not a complete fighting battalion. Knowing of course that we wanted both ends of the bridge, we tried to find some craft at the side of the old pontoon bridge [on the site of the present Nelson Mandela Bridge]. We had the idea we might be able to get someone across the far side that way.

They were unable to do so as the centre section of the pontoon was moored on the northern bank. The pillbox was attacked with PIATs, a 6-pounder gun and a flamethrower, igniting ammunition in a nearby hut, the heat setting the paint of the bridge afire. Captain D. J. Simpson RE was then ordered to take his half-troop of men of B Troop 1 Para Squadron to occupy the school (whose marker you visited earlier) and was joined shortly after by Captain Eric Mackay RE and A Troop, making a total of about forty fit souls. There were no Germans in the vicinity and they began to prepare the school for defence, '...the men rushing about and smashing windows with great glee. They were in high spirits.' The night was relatively calm but at around 0930 hours the next day (18 September) a column of German half-tracks led by two scout cars came across the bridge. The scout cars got through but none of the half- tracks. In 1946 Captain Simpson wrote, 'The school was close to the ramp,

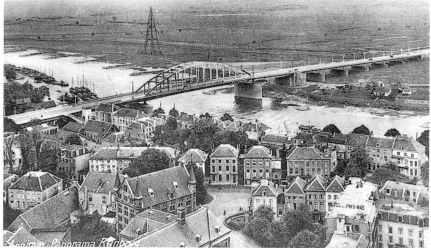

The Arnhem Road Bridge from the north bank 1. in 1938 2. in 2001

overlooking it and it was possible to throw grenades straight into the uncovered vehicles. Car after car was hit and stopped, some of them bursting into flames. Those of the crews who were still alive endeavoured to jump out and run for cover but so determined and accurate was our fire that not one man got away.' The school came under heavy mortar fire around midday and when Mackay discovered that it was 'friendly' and was coming from 2nd Para he stopped it 'with some very fruity words'. Also in the force at the school was Major 'Pongo' Lewis of 3rd Para Battalion and a dozen of his men. Airborne accounts often 'forget' to mention the Engineers and Engineer accounts 'forget' the Paras. John Frost, however, was complimentary. According to John Waddy (qv) he said, 'We of the Parachute Regiment always thought it a waste of time to use them as sappers when they were so good at killing the enemy.' Both Mackay and Simpson were captured, but, using Mackay's silk map, they escaped, together with two corporals, and were back in Nijmegen early on Saturday morning, 23 September. Mackay was awarded the DSC and Major Lewis was MiD.

• The Bridge was christened 'The John Frost Bridge' in September 1977 in the presence of the then Major-General Frost. A **Sign in Airborne colours names 'The John Frost Bridge'.**

After much controversy and debate in the local press, and following a test section and survey in November 2000, it was decided to paint parts of The Bridge in Airborne colours. Further protests were made and a compromise was then reached by agreeing to paint some of the railings, but to achieve the coloured effect at night with blue floodlights.

Walk carefully along the path on the right to the shelter.

Inside is another **Plaque, a Memorial to the soldiers who held The Bridge from 17-21 September 1944.** It stands where the pillbox stood.

Standing here, the authors asked Major-General John Frost to tell them what he would want visitors who came here to know. This is what he said –

A PERSONAL ACCOUNT

By Major-General John Frost

We were very proud to have been selected for this task and we were disappointed that we couldn't take both ends of this bridge, which was our aim. But we felt that that didn't really matter as long as we could hold on to the north end and to start with we were in a tremendous state of morale. We felt that we had captured the real prize of the whole war and as long as we could hold on to it then we were going to see Guards Armoured Division, XXX Corps, the whole thing, steaming by to finish the war. And then gradually, it began to dawn that if it was going to happen at all it was going to happen much later than we hoped or expected. The biggest blow I think was when my Intelligence Officer said, 'Oh sir, we are taking prisoners from the 9th SS Panzer Division and we have below an officer who speaks very good English. I think you ought to come and see him.' I went down and saw this officer and said, 'What are you doing here - I thought you were finished in the Falaise Gap.' He said, 'Well so did we, but we've got an awful lot of our drivers and gunners and radio operators and officers and we've been up the road refitting. We hope to get reinforcements and I hope and expect the whole of our Division to be around you before very long.' I think I offered him a whisky and soda. Anyway I wandered away rather sadly and knew then that the odds must be very much against us.

Frost was taken prisoner and was liberated from hospital in Obermassfeldt in March 1945 by General Patton's Sixth Army. Major-General John Dutton Frost, MC, DSO and Bar, CB, then a farmer, died on 23 May 1993, age 80. His last military appointment was as GOC Malta and Libya (1961-64).

A tower of strength to his Battalion CO and an inspiration to the beleagured men near The Bridge was the OC of A Company, Major Digby Tatham-Warter. He took command when Frost was wounded, because the 2i/c, Major David Wallis, was tragically killed on the 18th by an RE sentry. This tall and colourful character, described by Frost as 'a thruster if ever there was one' and, with other officers, 'tireless in directing men to new positions as and when they could. They kept control right to the end so that, when the wounded were evacuated and despite the resultant improvement in the enemy's position, our men could go on fighting till they were physically overwhelmed.' Tatham-Warter soon distinguished himself by his blasé brandishing of an umbrella which seemed to give him some sort of extraordinary protection until he, too, was twice hit. He continued, limping, with his arm in a sling, until he was forced to stay with the wounded, was taken prisoner and sent to hospital. He then crawled out of the hospital window with his 2/ic, Captain A. M. Frank. They were taken in by the Dutch Resistance and Tatham-Warter became the British co-ordinator of the great escape success of Pegasus 1 (qv) and was decorated with the DSO. After the war Tatham-Warter emigrated to Kenya. In 1991 he published his memoirs *Dutch Courage and Pegasus.* He died in March 1993, age 75.

Walk down the steps by the shelter and back to your car.

• Extra Visits to Evacuees Memorial, Arnhem Jewish & Moscowa Cemetery, Commemorative Cross, Dakota Crash site, Arnhem 1940-45 Museum, Diogenes German Command Bunker, Air Warfare Museum, Deelen Airport.
Round trip: 33 kms/20.6 miles. Approximate time: 90 minutes

Turn left out of the Market car park, past the Eusebius church and turn left following Doorgaand Verkeer [through traffic] signs and left again at the traffic lights under the bridge, direction Apeldoorn. Continue up Eusebiusbuitensingel, past Airborne Commemorative Marker No 8 on the left to the traffic lights. Go straight over, past the Musis Sacrum Concert Hall on the left to the junction with Apeldoornseweg to the right opposite the Rembrandt Cinema and Theatre Café.

NB. By continuing along Jansbuitensingel through to Willemsplein the **Arnhem VVV** is to be found on the right. Here you can obtain city plans, book accommodation, guided tours, walking and cycling tours, camping sites, find out about cultural or sporting events. Willemsplein 8, P.O.Box 552, 6800 AN Arnhem. Tel: 0900 2024075. Fax: + (0) 26 4426767. Beyond the VVV is the Arnhem Railway Station, with money-changing facilities and beyond it the Bus Station. Within easy walking distance of here there is a plethora of restaurants of all nationalities, supplying everything from a quick snack to an exotic Indonesian meal. A list of restaurants (and hotels, hostels, camping sites) may be obtained from the VVV, though much literature has to be paid for.

The 4 Star Best Western **Hotel Haarhuis** (qv) is opposite the Station.

Try to pull in just before the turning to Apeldoornseweg on the right.Walk round the corner.

Evacuees Plaque, Arnhem (Map 2/49) (2.2 kms/1.4 miles)
The bronze plaque is on the wall of the first building on the left along Apeldoornseweg. This is one of the main roads along which the evacuees from the fighting of September 1944 were swept. The *bas relief,* with the words which translate, 'Away, away, but where to...? 1944 Sept-April 1945', was sculpted by Mark Geels of Arnhem in 1995.

Extra visits continued

Return to your car and continue to the right up Apeldoornseweg,
under the railway, following signs to Moscowa.
On the left is Sonsbeek Park, designed in traditional English
garden style. It is a delightful leisure area with deer park,
lakes, a waterfall, a tea house and restaurants. Important
exhibitions of sculpture are held here, the 9th being in the
summer 2001.

N.B. At the end of the park there is a left turning along
Wagnerlaan (3.4 kms/2.1 miles). This is signed to the large
Rijnstate Hospital. During the war this was known as the
Municipal Hospital and British medics and their patients who
had been taken prisoner were brought here during the Battle. It
had been designated as the objective of 181st Airlanding Field
Ambulance in the MARKET plan (Map2/47).

Arnhem Evacuees
Memorial

THE SHOOTING OF CAPTAIN BRIAN BROWNSCOMBE

There on 24 September took place one of the most regrettable incidents of the
Battle. On 17 September Captain Brownscombe, RMO of the 2nd South Staffs,
landed on LZ S and set up an RAP at Reijers Camp Farm (qv). As the Staffords
moved on with the fighting , Brownscombe set up another RAP at the Muncipal
Museum. On the 19th the Germans overran the Museum and the medics and
their patients were taken prisoner. Brownscombe was then brought to the
Arnhem Municipal where he took care of both British and German casualties. On
Sunday 24 September he was invited for a chat and a drink with other doctors,
both British and German, and two British Chaplains and a Dane, Knud Flemming
Helweg-Larsen, who had joined the Waffen SS and was working with a
propaganda unit in the Arnhem area to fire off material to British troops.
Brownscombe was invited to the German billets. On his return he stood outside
the hospital talking when he suddenly fell, shot through the head. Helweg-
Larsen reported that the shooting had been committed by a drunken Karl
Gustave Lerche, another member of the SS propaganda unit. After a convoluted
story [told in detail in the booklet *For No Apparent Reason* by R. M. Gerritsen]
Lerche was finally arrested in 1952, brought to trial in 1955 and sentenced to ten
years' imprisonment (of which he served eight) for the war crime of murder.
Captain Brownscombe, 'a first-class doctor and ... possessed of all the soldierly
virtues', was originally buried in the grounds of the Municipal Hospital and later
reburied in the Oosterbeek CWGC Cemetery (qv).

Continue to the Synagogue in front of a walled cemetery to the left (4.5 kms/2.8 miles)

• Arnhem Jewish Cemetery (Map 2/48)

This adjoins the Moscowa cemetery and contains the grave of Sapper Gabriel Sion of the
Jewish Bde Group, RE, 9 April 1946. His grave is marked by a private memorial. To visit

Extra visits continued

the grave permission should be obtained from the Synagogue at the entrance.

Continue past the Jewish Cemetery. Take the next exit right signed Openluchtmuseum and turn back under Utrechtseweg signed to Moscowa Cemetery at the crossroads on to Schelmseweg. Continue to the Arnhem 50 kms sign on either side of the road. Turn left to Moscowa Cemetery and park by the gates to the right of which is a green CWGC sign.

• **Arnhem (Moscowa) General Cemetery (Map 2/46) (6.6 kms/4.1 miles)**

This wooded and landscaped cemetery covers many acres and in it are a Reception area, Chapel and Crematorium. It was named for Napoleon's campaign in Russia. The British plot lies on both sides of the avenue leading from the gate, S. H. Frederikslaan. It contains 37 graves, one of which is Unknown. There are 30 UK RAF, 3 RCAF (including WOII R.J. Lynn, 3 February 1943, age 29, whose personal message is 'An American citizen who gave all for his ideals') and 3 Polish Airmen. Dates of death range between 14 April 1940 and 10 September 1944. There are also two Dutch graves.

The touching custom of placing the floral tributes from cremations on these military graves is often observed.

Among other Resistance Workers buried in the cemetery are the brothers Bert and Hans Kuik, shot by the Germans on 3 November 1944. They were part of the 'Rolls Royce' group that helped with escapes from the St Elisabeth Hospital and also hid evading Paras and Jews in their house. Their story has been written up by Paul Vroeman (Paul.vfoemen@hetnet.nl).

The cemetery opens daily at 0830 and shuts at 1630 in the winter and 1900 in other months except May, June and July – 2100 hours.

Return to Schelmseweg, cross straight over at the NIBRA (Netherlands Fire Brigade Training Centre) sign. Turn off and park in the car park on the right. Walk up the cycle path to just short of the motorway. To the left is

CWGC Headstones, Moscowa Cemetery   Cross to 19 civilians

Extra visits continued

• **Cross in Memory of Nineteen Civilians (Map 2/45)**
They were shot on this spot in reprisal for the strike of May 1943. The nineteen victims came from many districts in the area and their names are listed on the granite panel below the wooden Celtic-shaped cross. Behind the cross is a steep bank into which errant bullets sank during the executions. The cross has been adopted by the local Pieter Breugel School.
   Return to your car and continue past the entrance to the right of
• **The Dutch Open Air [Openlucht] Museum (Map 2/50)**
This fascinating museum shows life in Holland as it used to be and as it is today. In the 'Hollandrama' a capsule takes the visitor past landscapes and townscapes from three centuries, incorporating changes in temperature, scents and sounds, with home videos and original artefacts. In the new entrance hall there are two exhibition rooms, an auditorium and a shop. In the car park is a coffee house.

In September 1944 600 of the evacuees who fled out of Arnhem along Apeldoornseweg sought refuge in the museum's listed ancient houses, brought from all parts of Holland, which were maintained with antique furniture and utensils. Because of the value of the historic contents of the houses, the evacuees were not allowed to light fires in them and had to rely for warmth and cooking facilities on stoves outside the buildings throughout the harsh winter of 1944/45. They stayed there for 100 days – until stray V1s fell on the museum from the nearby launching pads, when they were moved. In the museum today there are some photos from this period.
Open: 21 April – 29 October daily. Tel: + (0) 26 3576100.
   Continue past the entrance to the right to the
Burgers' Zoo. This was bombed during the Operation and many of the wild animals escaped and were seen roaming the area. Opened in 1913, today it shows wild life in different covered 'worlds' – the Bush, the Savannah, the Desert, the Ocean etc. – in natural-looking environments. There is a restaurant and other fast food outlets.
Open: Every day from 1 April-1 November 0930-1700 hours, June, July, August until 1800 hours. Tel: + (0) 26 4450373. Entrance fee payable.
   Take the third turning right after the traffic lights onto Bakenbergseweg. Continue some
   300m to a birch tree with broken branches on the right by house No. 264.
• **Dakota Crash Site (Map 2/32)** (10.7 kms/6.7 miles)
Dakota F2626 of 271 Squadron flown by Pilot Officer John Leonard (Len) Wilson had already made two sorties to Arnhem from Down Ampney on 17 and 18 September. Mechanic Alan Hartley begged to go on the third sortie. Wilson agreed, but at the last minute he was moved to a different aircraft and the replacement pilot refused to take Hartley. This saved his life as both Dakotas crashed, that flown by Len Wilson at this site. WO1 Les Gaydon (the navigator) parachuted to safety but Wilson, Flight Sergeants Herbert Osborne and Reginald French were all killed and are buried together at the Oosterbeek CWGC Cemetery [4.B.13/14/16.]. Visiting their graves in the early 1950s, Alan Hartley noticed an 'Unknown Airman' in their midst. Further research proved him to be Air Despatch Driver James Grace. The headstone has now been amended. Air Despatch Driver Richard Newth is buried in another plot [6.D.2.] (he died at the St

Extra visits continued

Elisabeth Hospital). Two other Air Despatchers, Jenkinson and Didworth, parachuted out and were taken prisoner.

Continue, following the road round to the right along Strolaan to the T-junction with Kemperbergerweg. Turn left. Continue under the motorway bridge and stop immediately on the right. Turn into the museum car park.

• **Museum 40-45 Arnhem (Map 2/31)** (13.9 kms/8.7 miles)

The Museum, as its name implies, covers more than the MARKET-GARDEN period and vividly pictures the life of the local people during the wartime years. Featuring largely is the Polar Bear insignia of the 49th West Riding Division which liberated Arnhem. It contains the collections of thirty local people, who jointly bought the building and brought their items together under one roof in 1994. It is manned by enthusiastic volunteers. As one approaches the entrance there is a plaque on the wall to the right which commemorates people shot by the Germans. The owners rescued it from the house on which it originally stood and placed it here.

The captions in the Museum are in Dutch, English and German. It contains many domestic and military artefacts and ephemera (such as an original photo album of wartime pictures that have never been published) which give a vivid picture of life in the '40s under Occupation and through the Allied invasion. In the MARKET-GARDEN section is an original parachute and an extremely accurate model of the John Frost Bridge. One of the prize exhibits is the rare *Kettenratt* – a tracked motorbike painted in desert colours, only two of which were used at Arnhem, mostly on the airfields. There is a re-creation of a radar outpost, codenamed *Teerose*, which was one of the outstations of the Diogenes Command Post Bunker (qv).

Note the original sign which proclaims 'SAFE LANE'. Had such a sign been placed on the main Corridor, or at the beginning of the Sand Road (qv), rather than a 'DANGER MINES' sign, XXX Corps might have reached John Frost in time.

There is a shop which sells militaria and a pleasant cafeteria. An annual Militaria Fair is held here. At the front of the museum is a German tank.

Open: Tuesday-Sunday 1000-1700. Closed Mondays, Christmas and New Year's Day. Entrance fee payable. Tel: + (0) 26 4420958.

Continue to the road junction. On the left is

• **Pannekoekhuis Den Strooper.** This is one of several traditional pancake houses in the area and is ideal for a fairly quick and simple lunch during a day's touring. The range of toppings for the hearty pancakes is staggering. Tel: + (0) 26 3516987.

Turn left on the N311 Koningsweg, signed Utrecht. Continue.

To the left, over the fence, is a campsite. In 1944 this was the site of the mess and dormitories for the Diogenes Command Bunker (qv).

Continue past the entrance on the right to the Kröller-Müller Museum

• **The Kröller-Müller National Museum** is set in Holland's largest nature reserve, 13,000 acres, 'De Hoge Veluwe', with red deer, wild boar and other species. In the centre is the world-famous collection of Van Gogh, Seurat, Picasso, Mondriaan etc, opened in 1938. **Museum Open daily,** except Mondays, 1000-1630 hours. Tel: + (0) 318 591041.

Extra visits continued

The Park is also **Open daily**, in the summer months from 0800 - at least 2000 hours. There is an entrance fee for the Park and a supplement for the Museum.

100m later turn up the small road to the right signed Rijks Archief.
• **German Command Bunker Diogenes (Map 2/30) (14.9 kms/9.3 miles)**
In early 2001 a new cycle path and entrance to the bunker were made, disclosing another smaller bunker nearby. Tel: + (0) 26 4455651. There is a set group Entrance fee - for one or more persons.

N.B. The interior of this vast edifice can only be visited by prior appointment during normal working hours. This extraordinary site is little-visited and rarely mentioned in accounts of the MARKET-GARDEN campaign and yet it had enormous importance. Well worth a visit if you can fit it into your schedule.

Today the vast building houses part of the State Archives (although they are due to move out in January 2002) and the overflow collections of some museums. On the exterior the traces of filled-in bullet holes can be seen.

In 1944 this was the Command Post for German Fighter Command covering all parts of Belgium and Holland. It was codenamed Diogenes, with its initial letter coming from the airport at Deelen, as all such facilities were named after philosophers. It had been built in 12 months in 1942/3 by slave labour with walls 3-3.5metres thick. A light railway line was constructed to bring up the tons of concrete required for the bunker from Wolfheze Station to here. Information about Allied air activity was phoned in from outlying radar posts (the remnants of many of which can be found in the area) and even directly from German pilots. A team of fifty German girls, known as *Luftnachrichtenhelferinnen* but nicknamed 'Grey Mouses' because of their field grey uniforms, then used a sophisticated system of plotting by triangulation and pinpointed the movements of aircraft on a huge glass screen by the use of little lights - green for German and red for Allied. The Luftwaffe was then despatched to attack the intruders. So advanced was its technology that the Command Post was featured - without, of course, divulging its location - in *Signal Magazine* No 10 in 1944. VIPs such as Göring visited it.

Security was extremely strict. The building was well camouflaged with earth on top in which disguising trees were planted. Only the personnel who worked on this system were allowed in the plotting room, although up to 400 people worked in the building at any one time in shifts. Few local people had any inkling of what took place here, although Dutch intelligence warned the Allies of a huge building with a railway leading to it. Their information was apparently ignored.

In one of those mystery stories which have become part of the MARKET-GARDEN mythology, it has recently been reported in Dutch articles that on 16 September, the day before MARKET-GARDEN, a lone B-17 flew over the area. The size of the B-17's escort varies from four to 400 planes! The story goes that a German working here reported the sighting to Hauptsturmführer Viktor Gräbner and the SS Panzer Divisions who were regrouping here. It was assumed that a very senior officer was on board - could it have been Montgomery himself? Something was obviously 'up'. Ground anti-aircraft were alerted and it was assumed that, in view of the extreme importance of the Command

Museum '40-'45

Diogenes Command Bunker

Extra visits continued

Post, any invasion force in the area would have as its prime target the destruction of the bunker. Further research, however, has established that while there were, in fact, two sorties by B-17s on that day they had nothing whatsoever to do with MARKET-GARDEN but were recconnaissance flights to discover information about the radio frequencies connected to the V-2 launching sites!

When the drops and landings were confirmed the following day the Germans attempted to blow up the bunker. Only a few minor holes were made in the thick walls, but all installations were destroyed and the building was abandoned. The personnel were transported by train to similar facilities in Germany and their work carried on seamlessly as these air tracking stations were designed to overlap. In 1948 a Dutch bomb disposal airman was defusing bombs in the area when one blew up and five people were killed. Little damage was sustained by the building itself.

In 1994 a German couple, who both worked here in 1944 and who later married, made a sentimental journey to the site of their courtship. Their visit was reported by the local paper.

Return to Koningsweg and turn left. Continue some 3kms, direction Apeldoorn, and continue to some imposing white buildings on the left.

Now the existing Deelen airport staff buildings, they were built by the Germans as administration buildings during the war.

Turn left on the small road Leipzigerweg signed to Deelen immediately after.

To the left in the large fenced area **Deelen Airport and assembly bunkers are clearly visible** after the trees. This is a military, not a commercial, airfield and is only otherwise used for VIP flights. During the war this was the Luftwaffe night fighter base. The runways are original and wartime hangars are currently used by the farmers who have permission to farm within the restricted area. The old Luftwaffe Cinema is now the mess for airfield staff. The airfield was heavily bombed in September 1944. After the war much military materiel - hundreds of vehicles, well-preserved in the sandy soil - was buried within the airfield perimeter.

Continue on Hoenderloseweg to a sharp bend left. Turn left into the car park of

• **The Luchtoorlog 1939-1945 Museum (Map 1N/58)** (20.6 kms/12.9 miles)

The Airwarfare Museum, opened in 1996, is in the old German Under-Officers' Mess/Squadron Admin HQ, erected in 1941/2 with the strong, thick walls of a bunker,

Extra visits continued

built to withstand a shot from a 500-pounder from 15 yards. The museum is manned by enthusiasts Robert Marcus and Piet Zeeman, whose personal collection forms the bulk of the exhibits. In 2000 the owners were worried that the museum was under threat in its present housing, – the natural place for it, but which is only on loan – so make sure you ring for the latest situation before you visit. A 3-year reprieve seemed likely in 2001.

On the wall by the car park is the propeller of an Unknown B17 Flying Fortress excavated from the IJsselmeer in 1995. Outside the entrance is the prize possession - a French 75mm gun used by the Germans, called 'Emil', which was dug out of the mud near Elden in 1996. On 17/18 September 1944 it shot down several planes and slowed down the Allied ground forces across the Rhine. It was ranged on the crossroads near the Airborne Garden on the lower road (qv). As the distance to the target was so small the gun could not depress sufficiently and it had to be placed in a pit. On 21 September, when German panic was at its highest as XXX Corps approached, the gun was blown up before the crew hurriedly departed. They have actually been traced and have visited their gun here.

The Museum illustrates many aspects of the activity in Dutch skies, with exhibits which include pilots'equipment, navigational instruments - even one of the light sticks used by a 'Grey Mouse' from Diogenes (qv) - and parts from excavated wrecks, and charts the history of Deelen Airfield at war, especially at night. It is very well maintained with clear captions in Dutch and English and has a good 'human' feeling with many personal stories.

It is the HQ of the Dutch Aircraft Examination Group, established in 1989 with the aim of studying the air war over Holland over the '39-'45 period when approximately 7,500 aircraft came down on Dutch soil. The DAEG works on the recovery of missing aircrew and the excavation of crash sites and is involved in historical research. Although some battlefield archaeologists have come under criticism for their excavation methods, the DAEG prides itself on its professionalism and meticulous liaison with the appropriate authorities whenever they discover an aircraft. One of their successes is illustrated in the Museum: the discovery of Spitfire Mk 9 Pilot, Richard Eric Chambers of 416 RCAF Squadron, listed as 'Missing with no Known Grave' on the Runnymede Memorial for 50 years. His aircraft was found 10kms to the east of Nijmegen. Pilot Officer Chambers, age 24, 29 September 1944, is now reburied in Groesbeek CWGC Cemetery (qv) [XXIV.D.14.]

Open: Saturday and Sunday 1000-1700. Tel: + (0) 26 4422881

Return to Koningsweg. Turn left signed Apeldoorn. Continue over the motorway, turn right immediately after and continue back into Arnhem Centrum, to the corner of Apeldoornseweg. Go straight over the traffic lights, with the Musis Sacrum on the left, to Airborne Plein and turn right signed Centrum and left following signs to Langstraat Parking and return to Markt Parking. Rejoin the main itinerary.

'Emil' gun, Deelen Airwarfare Museum

Leave the car park, return past the Eusebius church. Take the first left, signed Doorgaand Verkeer, to the traffic lights and turn left onto Eusebiusplein following Westervoort. Go under the John Frost Bridge and immediately turn left, following signs to Oosterbeek. Turn left at the second traffic lights, go round the roundabout and left to Nijmegen. Drive over the John Frost Bridge.

Note that the towers on The Bridge were for electrical equipment and, as is shown in contemporary photographs and drawings, that in 1944 the Germans had erected wooden structures on top of them. Also note that from the northern end one cannot see the southern end of The Bridge. Today trolley buses drive over The Bridge. The district at the southern end is the suburb of Arnhem to which the people of Rotterdam had been evacuated. They arrived only to be caught up in the fighting here.

Turn right at the traffic lights along Batavierenweg, signed Heteren/Geldredome past the entrance to the Nelson Mandela Bridge. Follow signs to the right to Heteren/Driel. Continue to the crossroads signed Elden to the left, Heteren/Driel to the right.

• *Extra Visits to Elden, Civilians' Memorial Column (Map 2/37)/Plaque on St Lucas Church (Map 2/37)/Original 1940s Roadway/Lancaster Bomber Memorial (Map 2/36). Round trip: 5.9 kms/3.7 miles. Approximate time: 15 minutes.*

Turn left over the bridge and immediately right signed Elden onto Klapstraat. Continue into the town and stop by the memorial column on the right.

The **Commemorative Column** in French Euville limestone is in the shape of a cross and crowned by the Dutch Lion holding the Dutch Coat of Arms on a shield, erected in 1954. It lists the thirty-nine citizens who lost their lives during the war - in May 1940, 22 February 1944 during an air raid on Arnhem, during raids on Huissen on 2 and 5 October and by landmines in June 1945.

Walk to St Lucas Church in the square, De Brink.

On the wall at the back of the Church is a Headstone Memorial to Johan van Hal, born in 1908 and his son, Theo, born in 1934. They were both killed in the bombardment of Arnhem 22 February 1944 and the stone was raised by both Catholics and Protestants of the district.

The white windmill behind the square is, like most restored mills in the Netherlands, open on Saturday for demonstrations of milling, sale of flour etc.

Turn right on Rijksweg West signed Elst. After some 300m you drive along
Original 1940s Roadway. The road ahead leads to Nijmegen along the line of the 1944 road. At the time it was barely wide enough for two vehicles to pass and had ditches on either side. High profile Sherman tanks were virtually sitting ducks to anti-tank weapons fired from the open flanks. As the houses (many of which are from pre-1944) end there is a small section of road which, although repaved, is still the same width and still has the characteristic deep ditches at either side. In the ditch on the left runs a small stream that used to flow all the way to Nijmegen

Continue to the traffic lights and turn right on Burgemeester Matsersingel signed Elst.
Continue over the traffic lights at Sporthal Elderveld, turn 1st right onto to

Extra visits continued

Rotterdamsingel and then 2nd right on Delftweg. Continue to the barrier and drive past the sign which says 'Uitgezonderd bestemmingsverkeer' (meaning 'residents only') and continue to the memorial on the left.

Lancaster Bomber Crash Monument

The memorial, which was unveiled in 1992, records that on this spot on 17 June 1944 a Lancaster of the RCAF came down with the entire crew. It then lists the names of seven men, although the normal crew of a Lancaster was ten. Locals rushed to try and help the men but sadly they all perished. Of the seven, Flying Officer A.F. Hupman, age 30, Pilot Officer, H. Fletcher, age 22, Pilot Officer C.S. Johnston, age 21, Pilot Officer P.J. McManus, age 27, Flying Officer D Morrison, and Pilot Officer E. Fahy, age 21, all of 419 Squadron RCAF, and Pilot Officer G.E. Quinn of 405 Squadron RCAF, age 26, are all buried in Groesbeek CWGC Cemetery (qv). Morrison, Fahy and McManus are misspelled on the memorial. Today the memorial is cared for by the local Scouts who hold an annual wreath-laying ceremony on the day of the crash.

Lancaster Bomber Crash Monument, Elden

Return to Burgemeester Matsersingel, turn left and left again at the traffic lights, signed Centrum following signs to Arnhem Noord. Filter right following signs to Driel to the left. Continue over the bridge to the junction and pick up the main itinerary.

Turn right along the small Drielsedijk signed Driel/Heteren.

The road runs along the top of the dyke and, when in flood, the river rises to within 1m of the road. The river has been considerably widened here since the war, but the panorama of the battlefield remains accurate. Ahead is the railway bridge and over to the right across the river is Oosterbeek.

Continue to the generator on the left.

• Windmill Generator/54.2 kms/33.9 miles/5 minutes/Map 2/35/OP

This is one of many pumps which drain water from the below-river-level Betuwe into the River Rhine. As an OP it gives a remarkable overall picture of the Arnhem battlefield and its salient points.

Face the radio/TV tower across the river.

That is Den Brink across the river at 12 o'clock. Immediately to its right is the round dome of the prison and the Eusebius Church spire and the twin spires of St Walburgis Church are at 2 o'clock. To their right is the span of the John Frost Bridge. Across the road to the right of the Water Authorities building (which is an original water station that was here in 1944) is a blue sign, erected by the Elden Historical Society, describing the **Battle of the Water in**

December 1944 (Map 2/34). On Saturday 2 December, in what they named OPERATION STORK, the Germans blew a great hole in the dyke here, thus flooding great tracts of The Island and forcing the Allies back south. So extensive was the flooding that it threatened the Germans' own defences and they were forced to try to build a caisson here, which was swept away by the strong current. In January 1945 the Over Betuwe was dry again but in February the Rhine came through once more with enormous force. In April 1945 the 225m hole was temporarily closed, but its traces can be seen by a careful examination of the dyke.

Continue under the railway bridge to the memorial on the left just before a bus stop.

• RE Memorial/55.8 kms/ 34.9 miles/10 minutes/Map 2/29

The main memorial of polished granite has the RE Badge and the Royal Canadian Engineers Badge and an image of the crossing of 25/26 September 1944 on black marble. In gold letters is the legend, '...they were just whispers and shadows in the night'. To the left is a marble frame with an orientation map of the North Bank sites and a description of the position on 25 September 1944 when the battle was still raging and the position of the troops on the northern bank had become untenable. [If foliage on the trees ahead obstructs the view in the summer, move slightly to the left.] The evacuation across the river, codenamed BERLIN, brought hundreds of soldiers in small parties following the marker tapes to the north-bank forelands below the Old [Lonsdale] Church, clearly visible from here. They waited to be rescued under heavy German fire from Westerbouwing. British and Canadian companies of Engineers made dozens of trips in their small boats from this bank, many boats being sunk by artillery and mortar fire. That one night, supported by other units, they managed to rescue 2,400 airborne troops [there is considerable variation in accounts as to the precise number - some say 2,720] between 2200 hours and 0545 hours on the 26th, landing them in this area. At the time the rescued hardly saw their savers, so they were never able to thank them. This monument was erected on 15 September 1989 to express their gratitude.

Many years later Horrocks reflected on the need for the operation in a fitting epitaph:

Royal Engineers Memorial and detail

25/26 SEPT. 1944

A PERSONAL MEMORY
By Lieutenant-General Sir Brian Horrocks, KCB, KBE, DSO, MC, LL.D.

I'm afraid things didn't go very well that night [24 September]. The 4th Dorsets were put across and they fought very gallantly but next morning all communication with them had ceased. We were getting desperately short of assault boats. Our road to the rear was cut again. The Germans got another armoured Division across it and it was cut this time for a further 48 hours. No transport could come up or down and the fresh assault boats - the ones we wanted - were the other side of the cut. We were also getting very short of ammunition. One regiment was down to 5 rounds per gun. So General Browning and I cleared our caravans and discussed the situation together and it was quite obvious it was impossible to go on now right up the Zuyder Zee - that was off. We were too stretched. The only thing to do was to bring back the 1st AB Division over the river into our lines and consolidate our gains which, after all, had been considerable - we had freed a large part of Holland and what was more important than anything else we were right up to the Rhine and that was to have a very important part in future operations. So that's what we did and that night of the 25th, under a Corps artillery barrage, 2,323 exhausted Airborne troops got back across the river into our lines. Some of them were naked, swimming across, some in rafts, some in boats. They had gone in 10,000 strong 9 days before. I shall never forget that night. It poured and it poured with rain and it seemed to me that even the Gods were weeping at this sorry end to a gallant enterprise.

It is ironic that from here, in the very centre of the area through which the survivors of 1st AB Division withdrew on the night of Monday 25 September, the exact point can be seen (face down the road behind you) where, just $7^1/_2$ miles (12kms) away, below the chimneys of the Nijmegen power station, 504st PIR of the 82nd AB Division made their heroic assault crossing of the River Waal at 1530 on Wednesday 20 September. So near, yet so far.

Continue along the dyke which becomes Rijndijk Oost.
To the right is a sign to Oosterbeek.

• *Driel-Heveadorp Ferry/56.6 kms/35.4 miles*

This is the site of the Driel-Heveadorp vehicle ferry, now only used for pedestrians and cyclists. **Sails:** February-November Mon-Fri 0700-1800. March-October Mon-Fri 0700-1800, Sat 0900-1800. Sun 1000-1800. Closed December-January. Tel: + (0) 26 3343083.

On the opposite bank the Westerbouwing tower (qv) can be seen, as well as the Old [Lonsdale] Church. It was to and from the north bank between the two that all crossings of the river came and went.

The task given to 1st AB Division was to capture all the bridges over the Lower Rhine at Arnhem. This was interpreted by General Urquhart to mean the railway bridge, the pontoon bridge (where the Nelson Mandela Bridge is today) and the road bridge (the John Frost Bridge). The Driel cable ferry, which in September 1944 was capable of carrying half a dozen cars, was not considered. As the situation of the troops within The Perimeter worsened and the position of 2nd Para at the northern end of The Bridge deteriorated, the drop of the Polish Brigade was shifted to Driel in the hope that the Brigade could be moved over the river using the ferry. The ferry was in full working order and Cora Baltussen, a Dutch girl working with the Resistance and who gave intelligence to the Poles (qv), travelled across it on Monday 18 September. As late as Tuesday 19 September civilians were still crossing on the ferry from Driel to Oosterbeek to buy bread.

It was still available on the night of 20 September and used by two sapper officers to cross en route from Oosterbeek to Nijmegen. By the time the Poles arrived on 21 September, the Germans controlled the northern ferry exit and the ferry had been sunk - the ferryman, Peter Hensen, claimed to have done this to prevent the Germans from crossing. Had elements of 1st AB Division been told to cross the river by the ferry on 17 September and to make their way to the southern end of The Bridge, the Arnhem story might have been quite different.

Continue to, and take, the turning to Driel. Continue to the T-junction by the church.

Heteren (Driel) Protestant Churchyard (Map 2/20). Just inside the gate of the small churchyard behind the church to the right is buried **WOII (CSM) Frederick Adams,** 5th DCLI, age 33, 24 September 1944, killed in the De Hucht Crossroads incident (qv).

Turn left and continue to the second church and park on the right by the memorial.

• *Polish Memorials, 5th DCLI Plaque, Driel/58.2 kms/36.4 miles/15 minutes/Map 2-21/22*

The dramatic monument symbolises the Polish Nation and bears the legend, 'Poland Arise!' It was sculpted by Jan Vlasblom of Rotterdam and was presented to the Polish Airborne forces by the inhabitants of Driel on 21 September 1959, the 15th Anniversary. It contains a casket filled with Polish soil and has the emblem of the Polish Brigade. On the 35th Anniversary in 1979 two short columns were erected, flanking the memorial. On the left is a black marble plaque with the roll of honour of the ninety-four Polish Airborne men killed in action. On the right are the coats of arms of Poland and Warsaw. There is also a stone plaque from the people of Driel to their Polish Liberators, the memorial tablet from the first, provisional, monument. This had been unveiled by Lieutenant-Colonel A. Szczerbo-Rawicz on 21 September 1946. The present monument is surmounted by a rising slab of concrete that symbolises Poland's spirit and intrepid courage. It was unveiled by Major-General Sosabowski on 16 September 1961. The figure of Youth steps forward from it, carrying the precious jewel of freedom in his hands.

Strong bonds were formed between the Polish Paratroopers and the residents of Driel and the surrounding area which remain to this day. The Driel-Polish Committee was formed in 1945 and the inhabitants adopted the graves of the Poles killed in action. When they were re-interred in the Oosterbeek CWGC Cemetery in 1946 the people of Driel continued to put flowers on the Polish graves. In December 1946 the schoolchildren sent Christmas greetings to all the Polish Parachutists who fought in Driel in 1944 and in February 1947 the Polish Paras donated a large sum of money for the rebuilding of the Boys' School which had served as a Military Hospital during the battle. In May 1949 this school (which no longer operates as a school) was named the St. Stanislaus Kostka School and the street in which it is situated was called Casimirstraat. The main square of Driel became Major-General S.

Sosabowskiplein. The Freedom of the Municipality of Heteren was bestowed on the General on 18 September 1954. A Standard was presented to the Polish Airborne Association by the inhabitants on 12 September 1959. In September 1969 a commemorative medal was presented to all Polish veterans who had fought at Driel. In September 1987 the children of the three schools in Driel adopted the Memorial and in 1991 the Square was reconstructed and became known as Plac Polski – Poland Square.

Opposite the Memorial is the **St Stanislav Church** whose tower was used as an OP by the Poles as well as by General Horrocks when planning the Dorsets' assault. To the right of the entrance is a **Plaque to Johan Kosman**, 8th R.I., who fell in May 1940 and to the left is a **Plaque to the 5th Battalion, DCLI,** erected by their Old Comrades to commemorate 'the Dash to Driel'. Inside the entrance porch to the right is a **Polish Memorial,** which mistakenly includes one more name than the tablet by the Memorial opposite the church, and other Polish badges. In the church is a **Stained Glass Light Box** with the Polish Airborne Badge which was presented by the Polish Paras to the Junior School for boys on 19 May 1947. After several moves it found its resting place here. If the Church is locked the key may be obtained from Huize Polska, Kerk Straat 17.

The original 1st AB Division plan called for the whole Division to be dropped over three consecutive days, beginning on 17 September. The Poles were to land on LZ L (qv) and immediately south of the Bridge on DZ K (qv) on Day 3 – Tuesday 19 September. On that day the Luftwaffe mustered more than 500 fighter aircraft which, together with bad weather in England, prevented the departure of the Polish parachutists. Thirty-four out of thirty-five Polish gliders did arrive at LZ L but ran into heavy opposition. The bad weather and poor radio communications caused most of the supplies, badly needed by the British airborne troops on the ground, to fall into German hands. On the morning of the following day, 20 September, General Stanislaw Sosabowski learned that his DZ had been changed to an area near Driel, but thick fog caused another postponement. Sosabowski insisted on being fully briefed on the military situation in the landing area, otherwise he would refuse to go. He had protested earlier about poor intelligence and over-confidence on the part of the British commanders. At 0700 hours on 21 September he was told that the Driel-Heveadorp ferry was in British hands.

Thus his new Driel DZ was ideally placed for his paratroops to move quickly across the river to help 1st AB. At 1415 hours the Poles took off in the American-piloted Dakotas and at 1715 hours began to drop south of Driel. Less than 3 hours later General Sosabowski learned from Cora Baltussen (qv) that the ferry had been destroyed and that the Germans dominated the far bank of the river. Attempts were made to ferry a few Poles across the river in rafts made from 10cwt jeep trailers, there being no boats, but no-one got across. So, that night of 21 September, the Polish Brigade took up defensive positions around this village and up to and including the river bank. Inside The Perimeter the next night, the 22nd, 4 Para Squadron RE gathered fifteen men, six recce boats and an RAF dingy and moved down to the river. Their plan was to tie signal cable to the back and front of the boats and pull two Polish paratroopers across at a time. The cables broke and two boats punctured. They found that they could only get one Pole across at a time, the round trip taking 20 minutes, but thanks to the extraordinary efforts of Lieutenant David Storrs who rowed across twenty-three times about sixty men got over. No more Polish re-inforcements were able to cross and after the withdrawal the Brigade was sent back to Nijmegen.

Driel Memorials: Polish Memorial, with church behind, 'Dash to Driel' Plaque on Church, Polish Memorials in Church

• **Extra Visit to Memorial to John James McNee and John Hyde, Fikkersdries Farm, Groenewoud (Map 2/19a).**

Round trip: 5.8 kms/3.6 miles. Approximate time: 15 minutes

Continue past the church.

N.B. Some 200m later on the left is Broekstraat and a further 200m up the street on the right was the farmhouse where General Sosabowski had his HQ.

Continue through Driel to the crossroads. Go straight over to the T-junction. Turn right and immediately left on Elstergrindweg. Turn right on Langstraat and first right on Groenewoudsestraat. Continue to the farm on the left by the gate to the Water Pumping Station (Waterbedrijf Gelderland). On the wall of the farm is a plaque.

The plaque is in remembrance J. I. Hyde, J. J. McNee. 4th Bn Lincs Regt. on 6 March 45 who lost their lives in a fight with the Germans who held this farm.

Their bodies were never recovered and the men are commemorated on the Groesbeek Memorial. A comrade, Harry Reeves, 18 years old at the time, recollected that a patrol of approximately twenty men of the 4th Lincolns were walking knee deep in

Plaque to McNee and Hyde, Fikkersdries Farm

> ## Extra visits continued
> flood water in the pitch dark. Harry was at the head of the patrol with Hyde and McNee just behind him. As they approached dry land the moon came came out from behind the clouds and the scene was illuminated by moonlight. A voice, sounding English, called 'Halt' and the Sergeant asked, 'Who is that? We are English.' Shots were then fired and Hyde was hit in the head and chest and died instantly. McNee was shot in the stomach and carried into the farm. Reeves was shot in the thigh and was taken to the farm (Fikkersdries Farm) in a wheelbarrow. McNee then died. The elderly, dirty and unshaven Germans showed sympathy to Reeves and took him to hospital the next day. Reeves later tried to contact McNee's next of kin, but was unsuccessful.
>
> John James McNee's widow (then remarried and called Mrs Britten) visited the war graves in Holland in 1976 and met Coby and Geurt de Hartog (qv) of Zetten. After extensive researches they contacted Harry Reeves and discovered the full story. Mrs Britten asked if a small plaque could be erected in memory of her first husband and John Hyde. She offered to pay for it but was told that the Water Company had paid for it.
>
> *Return to Driel church and pick up the main itinerary.*

Return to the dyke and turn left. Continue to the white weir and lock complex in the river (58.7 kms/36.7 miles).

The **Sluice Gate,** one of three along the stretch of the Rhine, acts as a 'tap'. When the gates are closed part of the Rhine is forced into the River IJssel. The foundations of the weir were laid in 1964 and the complex was completed in 1970. It is 260m long and each gate weighs 200 tons. They can be raised to an angle of 60 degrees in two and a half hours. There is a gangway along the top of the gates which can be used when the weir is closed and a tunnel which links the northern and southern banks. When the visor gates are closed the adjacent lock is used to allow large shipping to pass.

Continue to the memorial on the left behind the bus stop, opposite Castle Dorweth on the far bank.

• 7th Battalion Hants Memorial/59.8 kms/37.4 miles/5 minutes/ Map 2/19

The brick memorial commemorates those men of the 7th Battalion of the Regiment who gave their lives for the cause of freedom in this area 23 September-4 October 1944. It bears 42 names in gold on the roll of honour.

• End of Itinerary Five.

7th Hampshires
Memorial

ALLIED AND GERMAN WARGRAVES & COMMEMORATIVE ASSOCIATIONS

THE AMERICAN BATTLE MONUMENTS COMMISSION

The Commission was established by the United States Congress in March 1923 for the permanent maintenance of military cemeteries and memorials on foreign soil, their first task being the creation of cemeteries for the American dead of WW1.

After WW2 fourteen overseas military cemeteries were constructed. The US policy has always been to repatriate their dead if requested so to do by the relatives. The WW2 cemeteries contain approximately 39% of those originally buried. The ground on which each cemetery was built was granted by the host nation, free of rent or taxes.

A white marble stone (Star of David for the Jewish, Latin Cross for all others, whether they be Atheist, Buddhist, Christian or of any other belief) marks each burial. Memorials bearing the names of the Missing with no known grave, a non-denominational chapel and visitors' room containing the register and Visitors' Book and WCs are standard in all cemeteries.

Grave of Lt-Gen James Gavin, 23 February 1990, in West Point Cemetery. Strangely, on one of the sally ports at Westpoint, 'ARNHEM', not 'Market-Garden', is marked as a battle honour

To bury the American dead of MARKET-GARDEN two large cemeteries were constructed. One was in Molenhoek (qv) and contained 836 graves (including some British). The other was at Wolfswinkel (qv) and contained 450 graves. The setting up of the former and of the British Temporary Cemetery at Sophiaweg in Nijmegen (qv) and the details of all those buried in them are described in the minutely-researched book *Vanished (Temp) Cemeteries in the Nijmegen Area* by Father Thuring (qv) and J. Hey (qv).

Molenhoek and Wolfswinkel were both dismantled in 1948-9 and the burials were re-interred in the only American Military Cemetery now remaining in the Netherlands in which any casualties from MARKET-GARDEN not repatriated are buried. It is known as the Netherlands Cemetery and it is at Margraten, 6 miles to the east of Maastricht. In it is a tall Memorial Tower which dominates the 65.5-acre site. The entrance leads on to the Court of Honor with a pool in which the tower is reflected. To the right is the Visitors' building and to the left the Museum, containing three large engraved maps with texts depicting the military operations of the Armed Forces. Stretching along the sides of the court are the two walls of the Missing on which are recorded 1,722 names. Beyond the tower which contains the Chapel are the sixteen burial plots containing 8,301 graves, their headstones set in long curves. A wide tree-lined avenue leads to the flagstaff which crowns the crest. The light fitting in the Chapel, the altar candelabra and flowerbowl were gifts of the Government of the Netherlands and the local Provincial administration.

All American casualties of the Operation are recorded in the Roll of Honour at the National Liberation Museum, Groesbeek (qv).

The COMMISSION'S OFFICES are at: **UNITED STATES:** Room 2067, Tempo A and T Streets SW, Washington DC 20315. Tel: [001] 6936067

EUROPEAN: 68 Rue Janvier, 92 Garches, France. Tel: [0033] 1 9700173

BELGIAN MINISTRY OF INTERNAL AFFAIRS - GRAVES SERVICE

This Ministry is responsible for the care of Belgian Military Cemeteries. They were peviously maintained by the *Nos Tombes - Onze Graven* Association and the Red Cross. There are a total of 106 Military Cemeteries in Belgium, including CWGC, French and German as well as Belgian. Details of the Belgian Military Cemetery at Leopoldsburg, are described in Itinerary 1. There are Belgian burials in Jonkerbos (qv) and Groesbeek (qv) CWGC Cemeteries.

Contact: Mr Vermeiren, Ministerie van Binnenlandse Zaken, Wetgeving en Nationale Instelling der Militaire Begraafsplaatsen, Koningsstraat 66, 1000 Brussel. Tel: [00 32] 25002289.

CANADIAN CEMETERIES

The small Canadian Battle Cemeteries in the MARKET-GARDEN area were concentrated into the large CWGC cemetery at Groesbeek (qv). Other Canadians were buried in CWGC Cemeteries throughout the region.

COMMONWEALTH WAR GRAVES COMMISSION/
GRAVES REGISTRATION & ENQUIRY

The story of the foundation of the Imperial War Graves Commission in 1917 is told in *Major & Mrs Holt's Battlefield Guides* to *The Ypres Salient* and *The Somme*. Further details are in the Holts' Guide to *Gallipoli*. The post-WWII work of the Commission in Normandy is described in the Holts' *Battlefield Guide to the Normandy Landing Beaches*.

In France and Belgium there existed an organisation for the care of the WW1 graves that was quickly re-established (often with pre-War personnel) after WWII. The situation in Holland was quite different and it was not until November 1946 that a branch office was opened there. Within two years the work-load was such that the European command was split into two – the French District, based in Arras, and the District for Belgium, Germany, Holland, based in Brussels.

But before the Commission could start its traditional work of landscaping the cemeteries and erecting the familiar Portland stone grave markers, the Graves Registration & Enquiry (G.R. and E.), which had been incorporated into the Army as early as 1915, had to fulfil its terrible task of finding the bodies, recording as many details that would assist identification as possible and then re-interring them in the chosen cemetery sites. The Exhumation Report form was detailed, with spaces for Army No., Rank, Name, Cemetery or place of burial, plot, row and grave numbers, Height, Build, Colour of hair, fingers and hands, Nature of wound, Identity disc, Documents or other effects on body, Clothing, Boots, Equipment (including any arms) and finally General Remarks. Often a map reference of where the bodies were found was added, and the place of burial, e.g. '230E-89, nr. 693-775', 'isolated field, Elst', 'garden of large house, main road', 'in front of hotel', 'near hospital', 'beside burnt out glider', 'buried inside dropping container from Dakota', 'recovered from the Rhine','brought in by a civilian'. The form was signed and dated by the officer conducting the exhumation. The Arnhem-Oosterbeek exhumations did not start until almost a year after the original burial and in some cases over two years. By then bodies were in advanced state of decomposition and many of them had been badly burnt, yet the dedicated men conducting the exhumations examined them in meticulous detail, recording anything that could lead to an identification for the sake of the families and comrades. No wonder the forms were marked 'CONFIDENTIAL', much of their content would have been far too traumatic for the bereaved to bear. 'Other effects' included items such as '3rd class ticket for the 8A Putney to Charing X' [with a sketch of the ticket], 'one halfpenny', 'wallet bought in Cairo', 'NAAFI soap', 'escape map', '1 shell dressing', 'tin of choc', '50 cigs tin'. Laundry marks were noted, or the name of a tailor.

As well as in the Arnhem-Oosterbeek, in many other MARKET-GARDEN areas men had been buried by their crashed planes and gliders, beside hospitals, in local churchyards and (often by caring civilians) in local gardens. In some cases remains were so fragmented and intermingled that men had to be buried in 'Collective' or 'Joint' graves.

Work had begun three days after the liberation of Arnhem, on 20 April 1945, by a Graves Registration Unit led by Captain J. T. Long. In May a team of six O.R.s and an RC Padre, the Rev Father McGowan (ex 4th Para Bde Chaplain, who was awarded the MC), all of whom had been through the September 1944 operation, were sent to assist in locating the graves. G.R.Unit 37, which supervised the Arnhem-Oosterbeek area, had its HQ in Tilburg and there was a separate Canadian G.R.U., No. 2. Meanwhile, the Rev S. H. Chase, MC, Chaplain to the Forces of the 7th Duke of Wellington's Regiment, billetted in a Dutch Red Cross house in Ede, had been carrying out his own investigations, seemingly unaware of the G.R.U.'s work. He complained to the Deputy Assistant Director of the 1st Canadian Army G.R. & E. of the lack of a British Graves Registration Unit in the Oosterbeek area and detailed the work that he had personally carried out with 'endless journeys seeking for fuller information, and much time'. Dutch civilians, who had 'exposed themselves to considerable danger by performing these burials' informed him of mass graves (in Wolfheze, Oosterbeek Station, by a 'large house' and near the river) and many single graves. The Rev Chase was eventually placated by the energetic and capable Assistant Director of the G.R. and E., Lieutenant-Colonel A.C. Stott.

In July the Glider Pilot Regiments' Chaplains also arrived to help with identification but only succeeded in adding to the confusion. However, with the co-operation of the Airborne Section and from interviews with local civilians, by 20 July 1945 some 1,450 graves (at that time 80% of which were recorded as 'Unknown') had been located and firmly marked. The work had been hampered by the extensive minefields that remained in the district. Originally the graves had been 'twig-marked' – with a cross made of two twigs tied together. The Burgomasters of Arnhem and Renkum, anxious to expedite the proper reburial of the 1944 casualties as their citizens were returning to their homes after being evacuated to other parts of Holland, and they naturally feared a health hazard, co-operated in every possible way. Many of the returning civilians had made lists of the graves which they gave to the G.R. and E.

On 4-6 June Lieutenant-Colonel Stott had personally chosen the site for the cemetery which could accommodate up to 2,000 graves, all difficulties being overcome 'by the good offices of the Burgomaster of Oosterbeek'. At that time the acting Burgomaster of Renkum (which of course includes Oosterbeek) was none other than Mr Jan ter Horst (qv) who made a point of meeting General Urquhart, during what the latter hoped would be an incognito visit in September, as he and other military members of his party were nervous of the reception they would receive from civilians whose lives and homes they had destroyed in the battle. Mr Ter Horst was soon able to assure him otherwise.

By 25 June the site was levelled. Stott hoped that the concentration work could begin on 6 August, so that the bulk of the work could be completed before the bad winter weather set in. He applied for permission to erect a temporary Bailey Bridge over the railway at Oosterbeek Station which would 'reduce the distance to be travelled by about 12k' and would avoid having to transport the bodies through the town. Work went ahead apace with Stott's Arnhem-Oosterbeek Cemetery and as a result of the meeting with Mr Ter Horst and Urquhart it was consecrated on 25 September 1945 in the presence of British military representatives (including soldiers working on the filming of *Theirs is the Glory*) and Dutch personnel. The first pilgrimage of relatives, organised by the Airborne Forces Security Fund, with the support of the Dutch Government, was held in September 1946. The service was attended 'by almost the whole population' of Oosterbeek. [See also the entry on the Cemetery in Itinerary 5.]

In the Province of North Brabant alone there are fifty-two civilian cemeteries which contain Allied military burials.

Not included in any of the recommended Itineraries in this book is the **Reichswald Forest CWGC Cemetery**. The cemetery is 5kms south west of Kleve.

From Kleve take the Hoffmannallee from the town centre, which becomes Materbornerallee. This road enters Reichswald Forest and becomes Grunewaldstrasse. Follow the directions for Gennep and on entering Reichswald Forest the cemetery is 500m on the left.

This vast cemetery contains 7,495 Known and 162 Unknown burials, comprising 18 RN, 3,548 UK Army and 90 Unknown, 2,689 RAF and 68 Unknown, 327 RAAF and I Unknown, 704 RCAF and 1 Unknown, 127 RNAF, 1 South African, 13 non-Commonwealth Army and 65 airmen with 1 Unknown. The great majority of them are from the February-March 1945 Operations. They include **Private James Stokes,** KSLI, age 30, 1 March 1945 [62.E.14.] to whom the VC was awarded for his action during an attack on Kervenheim.

Illustrated here is the headstone of Private G. Gray, 2nd Gordon Highlanders, age 19, 25 September 1944. His headstone in Mierlo CWGC bears the personal message, 'O for the touch of a vanished hand, And the sound of a voice that is still!', a quotation from Tennyson's **Break, Break, Break**, a moving but oft-chosen inscription. Note that Private Gray has no religious symbol on his headstone. This is one of the advantages of the originally disputed headstone as opposed to a cross. The stone can bear the emblem of any religion - Jewish Star, Hindu symbols - or none - and has ample room for Name, Rank, Military Number, Regiment, Regimental Badge and, in many cases, a personal message from the family as described above.

Headstone of Private
G. Gray, Mierlo CWGC
Cemetery

This generous information, unique to British and Commonwealth headstones, gives a rounded picture of the person who lies beneath them.

CWGC HEADQUARTERS
UK: 2 Marlow Road, Maidenhead, Berks SL6 7DX.
Tel: 01628 632422. Fax: 01628 771208. E-mail (general): general.enq@cwgc.org (cemetery/casualties): casualty.enq@cwgc.org
Northern Europe Area (which covers Belgium and The Netherlands): Elverdingsestraat 82, B-8900 Ieper, Belgium. Tel: [00 32] (0)57 200118. Fax: [00 32] (0)57 218014. E-mail: neaoffice@cwgc.org

CWGC WEBSITE
In November 1995 the CWGC opened a website which includes the details of 1.7 million casualties. They are accessed on the Internet on www.cwgc.org, by the criteria of family name and regiment. This popular site has some 500,000 'hits' per week.

OORLOGSGRAVENSTICHTING
(Dutch Wargraves Association)
There are four Dutch Military Cemeteries in the Netherlands:
Loenen (Gelderland) 3,038 graves; **Overveen** (Noord Holland) 374 graves; **Rhenen** (Utrecht) 697 ;graves

Valkenburg (Zuid Holland) 36 graves.

There are also Dutch military graves in many local churchyards in the MARKET-GARDEN area and in CWGC Cemeteries. The presence of Dutch graves is indicated by a green Oorlogsgravenstichting sign at the cemetery entrance.

Contact: Area postbus 85981, 2508 CR Den Haag, Netherlands. Tel: + 70 3633434.

POLISH CEMETERY

The Polish Cemetery at Lommel in Belgium (see Itinerary One) is maintained by Mr Czeslaw Szkudlarski, M. Scheperlaan, 77, 3550 Heusden-Zolder, Belgium. Tel: [00 32] (01) 537480.

Other Polish graves for the MARKET-GARDEN Operation are in CWGC Cemeteries, e.g. Arnhem-Oosterbeek, Venray, Findhoven Woensel, Uden, Jonkerbos and Mook. The Polish headstones are easily distinguished from the straight-topped British and Commonwealth ones as they have a pointed top and bear the distinctive Polish Coat of Arms.

VOLKSBUND DEUTSCHE KRIEGSGRÄBERFÜRSORGE
(The German War Graves Welfare Organisation)

The organisation is similar in function to the CWGC and the American Battle Monuments Commission in that it maintains the graves of German war dead in military cemeteries from WW1 and WW2. It also organises subsidised pilgrimages for families to the graves of their loved ones. In 1994, the 75th Anniversary of the Founding of the organisation, a beautifully illustrated book, *Dienst am Menschen, Dienst am Frieden,* was published to commemorate their work after two World Wars.

German casualty figures for the Operation are almost impossible to verify with any reliable accuracy. In the Arnhem-Oosterbeek area some of the German dead were, like the Allied, buried where they fell. In the summer of 1945 many of these field burials were exhumed and the bodies concentrated in the German Cemetery at Zijpendaal, near the Burgers' Zoo, which had been in use since May 1940. There was also a provisional cemetery in Arnhem along Deelenseweg, used even during the battle. When the vast cemetery at Ysselsteyn was created, all the bodies from Arnhem and Renkum were re-interred there by the Grave Unit of the Dutch Army. A high proportion of the dead were unidentified. From Oosterbeek alone 150 of the 455 reburied there were Unknown.

Three German cemeteries are included in the itineraries - see Index for reference:

Lommel, Belgium, with 38,962 WW2 and 541 WW1 burials; **Ysselsteyn,** Holland, with 31,511 WW2 and 124 WW1 burials; **Donsbruggen,** Germany, with 2,381 WW2 burials.

Headquarters: Werner-Hilpert Strasse 2, 34112 Kassel, Germany. Tel: [00 49] (0) 5617009 221. E-mail: volksbund.kassel@t-online.de

COMMEMORATIVE ORGANISATIONS/EVENTS

MARKET-GARDEN and Arnhem Veterans' Associations and their links with Dutch supporting associations are extremely strong. There are a great many of them, in most towns and villages of any size along The Corridor and on The Island (many of them who also have active Historical Societies which specialise in MARKET-GARDEN research) and this list is representative but by no means comprehensive. It also contains details of annual Commemorative Events. There are also, of course, many Regimental Associations whose members are Arnhem Veterans.

AIRBORNE COMMEMORATION FOUNDATION *(Stichting Airborne Herdenkingen)*
This important foundation was formed in 1992 to co-ordinate commemorative events over the period of the Anniversary for veterans and pilgrims and to honour the Battle of Arnhem-Oosterbeek. Represented by it are the Municipalities of Arnhem, Ede, Heteren and Renkum, The Lest We Forget Foundation, the Arnhem 1944 Veterans' Club, the Driel-Poland Committee, the Society of Friends of the Airborne Museum, the RMP of Apeldoorn, the Airborne Forces Security Fund and the Arnhem Promotion Fund. **Contact:** Gemeentehuis, PO Box 9100, 6860 HA Oosterbeek, Netherlands. Tel: + (0) 26 3348322

AIRBORNE FIETSTOERTOCHT. This is a cycle event, starting in Doorwerth, which covers the main sites of the Arnhem-Oosterbeek 1944 battles. There are four different routes covering 25, 40, 80 and 150kms, each with a medal for those who complete the course. There is an entrance fee and the event takes place in the last week in August. **Contact:** + (0) 317 317436.

AIRBORNE WANDELTOCHT. These famous marches started in September 1947 and follow a circular route from and back to the Hartenstein around the battlefield. They now attract thousands of entrants (35,000 in 2000), singly or in groups. Part of the funds go to the Lest We Forget Foundation (see below). Distances of 10, 15 or 25kms. First Saturday in September. **Contact:** Police Sports Association Renkum. Tel: + (0) 26 3337960.

In recent years other marches have been organised in September that go from Wolfheze to the John Frost Bridge, giving the most realistic impression of just how far 1st AB landed from their objective. They are accompanied by re-enactment groups and 1940s military vehicles.

ARNHEM 1944 VETERANS' CLUB. The Club produces a Newsletter and provides free coach travel for members to the September Commemorations in Arnhem-Oosterbeek. The President is Major-General A.J. Deane-Drummond, CB, DSO, MC. **Contact:** Hon Sec. Austin Brearton, 56 Highfield Crescent, Heaton, Bradford, W Yorks BD9 6HP. Tel: 01274 495472.

'CREULLY CLUB' (Association of the 4th/7th RDG, NW Europe 1944-1945). The Association produces a regular Newsletter, es Pilgrimages to the Oostham and Elst Memorials and annual reunions. **Contact:** Secretary Cecil Newton Tel: 01672 540356. Fax: 01672 541221 E-mail: cnewton@freeuk.com

DEN DUNGEN MARKET-GARDEN COMITE (qv).
They have strong links with veterans (the village is twinned with Portishead and has its own website www.iae.nl/users/vandeven/portishead) and undertake considerable research.
Contacts: Jacq van Eekelen and Jos Korsten. Groot Grinsel 8, 5275 BZ Den Dungen. Tel: + (0) 73 5941687. E-mail joskorsten@netnet.nl

FIETSERSBOND enfb. The Cycling Club, founded in 1975, publishes an Airborne Route round the Son, St Oedenrode, Eerde, Heeswijk-Dinther, Veghel battlefields (35kms).
Contact: Postbus 2828, 3500 GV Utrecht.

FRIENDS OF THE 101st AIRBORNE: 'Remember September'. Like the Arnhem Lest We Forget Foundation they arrange commemorative events and battlefield tours for veterans of the 101st all along The Corridor. They have been hosting veterans since 1954 but were officially founded in 1966. They have 400 Dutch members, many of whom host veterans and their families, and have a newsletter *De Wanowan*. **Contact:** Thieu van Luyt, Postbus 25 – 5737 ZG Lieshout. Tel: + (0) 499 421711.

EINDHOVEN STICHTING 18 SEPTEMBER FESTIVAL. **Contact:** Secretary, Mrs M. Beeren, Pluisheuvel 5, 5685 Best NL. Tel/Fax: + (0) 49 9311101

EINDHOVEN CIRCUIT OF LIGHTS. **Contact:** Secretary H. Reijnen, Menelaos Laan 1, 5631 LM Eindhoven. Tel/Fax: + (0) 40 243186. e-mail: H. Reijnen@inter.NL.net. website: www.lichtjesroute.nl
Details of these organisations are described on page 39/40 above.

LEST WE FORGET FOUNDATION. This faithful foundation helps with travel arrangements and provides accommodation for Veterans and their immediate Next of Kin during the September Commemorations. Funds are partially raised by the annual Airborne March. The Founder and Chairman is Tanno Pieterse, MBE, of Oosterbeek. Tel: + (0) 31 84 16869. As a 16-year-old Tanno worked as a messenger boy for the Red Cross during the battle and remembers the first groups of pilgrims arriving in September '46-'47 by special train from the Hook of Holland. 1969 was considered to be 'The Last' commemorative gathering. In 1970 there were virtually no visitors. In 1974 Tanno helped a few veterans and was created an honorary member of the Luton Parachute Regiment Association (PRA), from where the first coach load of veterans arrived in 1975 with well-known veterans Dave Morris and Tex Banwell (who for many years took part in the annual jump.) In a couple of years the Committee was formed, an article in the local paper attracting host families and funds. The Arnhem Veterans Club (Tanno is Member No 41) was then formed to 'vet' applicants and the Foundation went from strength to strength. It now has branches in Poland, the USA, Canada, New Zealand and Australia. Sadly, of course, with the passage of time, the number of veterans is gradually decreasing. **Contact:** UK Co-ordinating Officer: Joe Roberts, 18 Dee Crescent, Farndon, Chester CH3 6QJ. Tel: 01892 270312.

NIJMEGEN FOUR-DAY MARCHES. The world-famous Marches had their origins in the 1907 Dutch Sports Days for the Field Army which in 1909 developed into a Four-Day March from Arnhem to Breda, Nijmegen being a staging post along the way. Gradually the marches became centred round the Prince Hendrik military barracks in Nijmegen, to which the participants return each day. In 1919 the first woman competitor finished the course and in 1928 the first foreigners (British, German, Norwegian and one French photographer) participated. In 1929 Spanish soldiers also joined in and the number of entrants then increased annually until in 1937 they totalled 3,900. A Four-Day Marches song was introduced and the event continued to grow in popularity until interrupted by the outbreak of WW2 in 1939.

In 1946 Nijmegen won the Marches back to its war-battered town and the tradition of accommodating civilian entrants in private homes began. Wearing discarded Canadian Army boots or borrowed shoes, 4,011 poorly trained entrants embarked on the gruelling course over the damaged roads. The British participation then grew apace and in 1955 more than 10,000 marchers reached the finish.

Over the period from the third Tuesday in July, marchers cover daily distances of 30, 40 or 50kms, which take them through forests, over hills and across rolling countryside. The weather at that time can be blisteringly hot or torrentially wet, often causing many dropouts. There are classes for groups, military, females, juniors and individuals and the prize for those who complete their four days is a 5-arm cross, in bronze, silver or gold-plated according to the number of marches completed. Many teams (especially from the British military) come back year after year and the camaraderie among participants is fantastic. The atmosphere is something like a cross between a carnival (many marching in bizarre costumes) and an Olympic Marathon. There are strict rules of conduct, however, as regards decency of clothing and the prohibition of expressing political views or unauthorised advertising.

In 2000 there were 41,093 Marchers and more are anticipated for the 85th Marches in 2001. **Contact:** KNLBO, PO Box 1020, 6501 BA Nijmegen. Tel: + (0) 24 3655500 Fax: + (0) 24 3655580 e-mail: 4daagse@knblo-nl.nl website: www.4daagse.nl

PEGASUS WANDELTOCHT. This march takes place every year on the fourth Saturday in October over distances of 8.5, 18.5 or 28.5 kms along the route taken by the escapers of 'Pegasus 1' (qv). It started in 1984 on the 40th anniversary. **Contact:** VVV Zuidwest Veluwe, Ede. Tel: + (0) 318 614444. E-mail: info@vvvede.nl

POLAR BEAR MARS (March). This 15kms march, which started in 1988, takes place in April (on the nearest Saturday to the anniversary of Arnhem's Liberation by the 49th West Riding Division), starting from the point where they crossed the Rhine and follows their route through Arnhem to the 1940-1944 Museum (qv). Finishers receive a commemorative book and a medal. **Contact:** + (0) 26 4428062

RAF DOWN AMPNEY ASSOCIATION. This was formed in 1971 on the initiative of Alan Hartley, who served as a Mechanic at the airfield. He organised reunions and instigated the erection of a commemorative stained glass window in the 13th Century Down Ampney Church. **Contact:** A. Hartley, 19 Staverton Close, Mount Nod, Coventry CV5 7LF. Tel: 02476 462659.

RE-ENACTMENT SOCIETY Victory in Europe. Founded in 1990 the group supports many major ceremonies with their authentic uniforms and vehicles. Founded in 1990. **Contact:** Steve Taylor (Chairman) on www.vera.org.vic

ROYAL BRITISH LEGION. ARNHEM-NIJMEGEN BRANCH. Meetings are generally held on the first and third Friday of the month at 2000 hours in the Wijkcentrum De Klokketoren, Slotemaker de Bruineweg 272, 6532 AD, Nijmegen. Although a dwindling band, the Branch organises Remembrance Services, helps Pilgrims on cemetery visits and is active during the Poppy Appeal period. **Contact:** Branch Secretary Mr E. Goldie. Tel: + (0) 24 3445605]. **VALKENSWAARD BRANCH: Contact:** + (0) 40 2013561

SOCIETY OF FRIENDS OF THE AIRBORNE MUSEUM (qv). This fosters interest in, gives assistance and support to the Museum, furthers knowledge about events during the Battle of Arnhem, including its own publications. **Contact:** Airborne Museum Hartenstein, Utrechtseweg 232, 6862 AZ Oosterbeek, Netherlands. Tel: + (0) 26 3337710. Fax: + (0) 26 3391785. e-mail: hartenstein@wxs.nl website: www.airbornemuseum.com

THANK YOU LIBERATORS COMMITTEE, EINDHOVEN. Object to promote and assist War Veterans on Pilgrimages. **Contact:** + (0) 70 5179775

40th Anniversary Poster for
the Arnhem Wandeltocht

Frank van den Bergh, Historian from
the Groesbeek National Liberation
Memorial with his Marchers' Cross

Marchers on the Nijmegen
Road Bridge

WELCOME VETERANS COMMITTEE, ZETTEN. They specialise in helping veterans who fought on 'The Island'. **Contact:** Geurt and Coby de Hartog, Wageningsestraat 110, 6671 DH Zetten. Tel: + (0) 488 451477.

TOURIST INFORMATION

Tourism in the Netherlands is organised on a Provincial basis through the nationwide network of tourist offices called VVVs. They are signed by a blue on white triangle of 'V's and the word *Informatie*. The Provinces covering the MARKET-GARDEN Corridor are Noord-Brabant - which contains the area from the Belgian Border to Grave - and Gelderland - the country's largest Province, which contains Groesbeek, Nijmegen, The Island, Arnhem and Oosterbeek. The border between the two is the River Maas and the bridge at Grave which crosses it gradually changes from the red of Brabant to the green of Gelderland.

The addresses and phone numbers of the relevant VVVs on the Itineraries are given as they occur in text. They provide lists of local hotels, restaurants, events and attractions, maps, souvenirs etc, although many leaflets have to be paid for.

Before travelling, the visitor is recommended to obtain the current *A Traveller's Guide to Holland*, which has useful general information, from their national Netherlands Tourist Board: website: www.holland.com.
London - PO Box 523 London SW1 6NT. Tel: 0906 8717777 E-mail: information@nbt.org.uk.
New York - 355 Lexington Avenue, New York, NY 10017. Tel: + 212 3389117. E-mail: info@goholland.com
Toronto - PO Box 1078, toronto, Ont. M5C2K5. Tel: + (0) 0416 3631577. E-mail: nbtor@aol.com
First and foremost the visitor to the Netherlands should be aware that **Credit Cards are not universally accepted throughout the country.** This applies to some petrol stations, cafés and photographic shops. So make sure that you have sufficient cash available or that credit cards are accepted before attempting to make a purchase.
Shops normally open later on Mondays (usually at 1100 hours). Tuesday-Saturday 0930-1800 (Thursday 0930-21/2200). **Banks** are open on Monday from 1300-1700 and Tuesday-Friday from 0800-1700.

How to Get There

By sea from the UK
P & O Stena. Dover - Calais. Frequent crossings: 75+ minutes.
Reservations: 087 0600 0600. Website: POSL.com
P & O North Sea. Hull - Rotterdam. Night crossing: 14 hours
Hull - Zeebrugge. Night crossing: 14 hours. Reservations: 01482 377177
Stena Line. Harwich - Hook of Holland. 3 hours 40 minutes. Reservations: 08705 707070
DFDS Seaways. Newcastle - Amsterdam. Day crossing: 14 hours. Reservations: 08705 333000

Hoverspeed. Seacat or the newer Super Seacat. Dover-Calais 50 minutes. Dover-Ostende 2 hours. Reservations: 08705 240241
Seafrance. Dover-Calais 90 minutes. Reservations: 08705 711711

By air from North America/UK. Flights into Amsterdam Schiphol. There are then frequent links with Eindhoven Airport. Tel: + (0) 40 291 818. KLM. Amsterdam - Tel: + (0) 20 474747. USA - Tel: 1-800 4474747 Northwest Airlines. USA Tel: 1 800 4474747.
Martinair nonstop from the USA and Canada. Tel: 1-800-MARTINAIR.

RentaCar. All major car rental car companies operate from Schiphol and other airports - Avis, Budget, Hertz etc and cars can be booked in advance more cheaply in your home country. There will probably be a minimum age requirement of 21-23 years. Valid national driving licences are required.

General Driving. Drive on the right, pass on the left. Seat belts compulsory. Speed limits are 30/50kms (25/30 mph) in built-up areas, 80kms (50mph) per hour out of town on normal roads, 100kms (62.5 mph) on A roads and 120kms (75mph) on motorways (with some sections clearly designated lower speed areas). Priority is normally from the right, but white signs like triangular sharks' teeth painted on the ground indicate that you do not have right of way as do inverted triangular red-bordered signs. There are many radar speed controls. Very few roads are numbered and navigation has to be done by road names or direction signs, an acquired technique.

Some useful road signs: *Afrit* Exit (from motorway); *Alle Richtingen* All Directions; *Doorgaand Verkeer* Through traffic; *Drempels* Sleeping policemen; *Fietsers* Cyclists; *Let op* Attention/watch out for...

By Rail. Eurostar. London (Waterloo) - Brussels and thence to Dutch destination by Intercity. Tel: 0990 186186
Eurotunnel. By car from Dover - Calais. 35 minutes crossing, plus waiting time to board. Tel: 0990 353535
Holland Rail. Rail card passes available for unlimited nationwide 3 or 5 days travel. Tel: 01962 773646.
Amsterdam Express. Direct service from London via Harwich . Tel: 08705 455455

Public Transport. This is reasonably priced and efficient. Buy an economical *Strippenkaart* (strip card) from newsagents, tobacconists, stations, VVVs, for nationwide travel valid on buses, trams and metros nationwide.

Cycling and Walking. The mostly car-bound visitor from the UK or North America will be astounded at the number of bikes on the road in the Netherlands. Mothers with a baby in front of them, a toddler behind them, a young child on a small bike beside them and large shopping panniers ride alongside businessmen in suits with their briefcases, carpenters balancing long planks of wood, postmen with heavy bundles of mail, senior citizens who still ride with confidence and panache and teachers leading their whole class on an outing. On weekends and holidays, hiking and rambling in the beautiful woods around Groesbeek and Arnhem-Oosterbeek, the most wooded areas of Holland, takes over. The foreign pedestrian must be alert at all times to the sheer volume of cylists and that what might be assumed to be a pavement is in actual fact a cycle (and moped) path. The colour of these ubiquitous paths is being standardized to RED throughout the country. Motorists should be aware of cyclists at all times and the fact that they have priority (a legal requirement since 1 May 2001).
    Cycles can be universally hired and all VVVs carry lists of outlets and supply special cycling and walking route maps. Additional road and traffic signs are placed at a low level for the benefit of cyclists and walkers. The small green ones give the distance every 100ms.
    'Airborne' Walking and Cycling route maps may be bought from the VVVs at Arnhem and Oosterbeek and Eindhoven.

WHERE TO STAY. There are three obvious bases for touring MARKET-GARDEN:
1. Eindhoven
Eindhoven is now the fifth largest city in the Netherlands with 2,000,000 inhabitants. Known as the 'City of Light' because of its long association with Philips (it is also the home of the DAF car, now owned by Volvo), the town was extensively damaged during WW2, hence the modern aspect of its rebuilt centre. Now it is a thriving conference centre with several interesting museums, such as the DAF Museum, the Prehistoric Open Air Museum and the Kempenland Museum (details from the VVV, Tel: + (0) 40 2979115).
There is a variety of **hotels** near the town centre:

Remember that it can
be very wet and muddy
in Holland

***** Dorint, Vestdijk 47. Newly refurbished. Leisure Centre. Own parking. Tel: + (0) 2326111.
**** Best Western Hotel Pierre, Leenderweg 80. Own Parking. Amrath Group (qv) Tel: [0031] (0) 2121012
**** Holiday Inn, Montgomerylaan 1. Swimming pool etc. Tel: + (0) 2433222
**** Mandarin Park Plaza, Geldropseweg 17. Swimming pool. Renowned oriental restaurant. Tel: + (0) 2125055
**** Novotel, Ant Fokkerweg 101.Swimming pool. Own Parking. Tel: + (0) 2526575
*** Tulip, Markt 35. Nearby Parking. Tel: [0031] (0) 2454545
*** Campanile, Noordbrabantlaan 309. Near A2. Own Parking. Tel: [0031] (0) 2545400
** Royal, Stratumsedijk 23F. Own Parking. Small and personal. Tel: [0031] (0) 2121330.
There are also some good value *Pensions and Guesthouses* in the area and Camping Sites (contact VVV).

There are plentiful **restaurants** to suit all tastes and pockets within easy walking distance of the VVV: typical hearty and tasty Dutch; the local favourite – Indonesian; French, café-style, often with live music; Italian; Greek; Japanese; Spanish - even Mongolian. There are restaurants for steak-lovers, fish-lovers and vegetarians.

Shopping is also a pleasure in Eindhoven, with large department stores like De Bijenkorf and the Heuvel Galerie which has more than 100 shops under one roof. There is a market in De Markt on Wednesdays and an antiques/collectors' market on Saturday. Supermarkets are open from 0800-2000 Monday to Friday and 0800-1800 on Saturday.

There is a **Currency Exchange** at the GWK office at the main railway station. The **Post Office** also adjoins the station

1. Nijmegen/Groesbeek

The University city of Nijmegen is the oldest in the Netherlands. It has many old areas where the ornate facades of the attractive and diverse-style houses, many with *art deco* and *art nouveau* features, survived the battering of the war. Remnants, too, of the ancient city walls and its Roman origins, many fine Gothic public buildings and churches and interesting themed museums can be visited on the recommended Nijmegen Town Walk (details from the VVV).

It is a bustling modern city, too, with large new shopping centres like the Dukenburg and the Molenpoort, a variety of small speciality boutiques and facilities like the Sanadome Health Spa, Tel: + (0) 24 3597200, based on natural thermal waters. Night life is lively, with the focal point being the Holland Casino, Tel: + (0) 24 3600000. Under the Casino are the remains of a Roman underfloor heating system. There are markets in the Grote Markt on Mondays and Saturdays.
Some hotel choices:
**** Belvoir. Stunning situation overlooking the Nijmegen Bridge. Swimming pool and sauna, parking. Part of Amrath Group (qv). Tel: + (0) 24 3232344.
**** Sanadome (qv). Adjoining the Spa. Weg door Jonkerbos 90. Tel: + (0) 24 3597200
**** Mercure. Near the Station. Sauna and sunbed. Parking. Tel: + (0) 24 3238888
*** Bastion, Neerbosscheweg 614. Tel + (0) 24 373 0100
** Atlanta, Grote Markt 38-40. Tel: + (0) 24 3603000
* City Parc, Hertogstraat 1. Tel: + (0) 24 3220498
Contact the VVV for details of Camping Sites and Hostels.
Groesbeek and Berg en Dal are attractive areas, with rolling wooded hills and delightful walks and cycle routes, making for a pleasant stay. Here is the famous Africa Museum + (0) 24 6842044 and the Holy Land Foundation, the Open Air Biblical Museum + (0) 24 3823110.
Some Hotel suggestions:
**** Hotel Erica. The authors' favourite, which they have been visiting with pleasure for   over20 years. Owned until 2001 by the Van Vliet family, with historic associations with MARKET-GARDEN, it is now owned by the Amrath Group. Set in delightful landscaped grounds, excellent food, swimming pool and sauna, ample parking. Molenbosweg 17, 6571 Berg en Dal. Tel: + (0) 24 6843514
**** Golden Tulip Val-Monte. High quality, pleasant setting, swimming pool and recreation room. Parking. Oude Holleweg 5, 6572 Berg en Dal. Tel: + (0) 24 68420000.
*** Hotel Sionshof. Historical associations with MARKET-GARDEN. Nijmeegsebaan 53. Tel: + (0) 24 3227727.
Contact the VVV + (0) 24 3297878 for more choices, Camping Sites and hostels.

2. Arnhem-Oosterbeek

Arnhem is the lively provincial capital of Gelderland. The centre was largely destroyed during the September 1944 battle, including many of the beautiful old houses of the wealthy. Today it is a modern city with only a few original architectural gems, such as the only remaining city gateway, the Sabelspoort (qv). Some of the

Euro 2000 football matches were played in the modern Gelredome with its moveable roof and extension pitch, and pop concerts are also held here. Like Eindhoven, Arnhem is a great shopping centre – the 5th most popular in Holland - with the famous De Bijenkorf department store, and many small fashion stores in the pedestrian precinct. Cultural events are staged in the imposing Musis Sacrum (qv) Tel: + (0) 26 4437343 and the Korenmarkt entertainment centre. Its surrounding wooded suburbs are extremely pleasant and boast some excellent museums (see Extra Visit, Itinerary Five).

A trolley bus system still operates in the area, unique in Holland. Note that there are extensive plans to redevelop the centre of Arnhem (including the Station and the waterfront) before 2015. The ambitious, modernistic designs aim to make the city the hub of the Eastern Netherlands when the high-speed train running from Amsterdam to Frankfurt will stop here, with vast shopping and leisure facilities. Huge new housing developments are also planned south of the River Rhine. In Arnhem the first Sunday of every month is a Shopping Sunday – open 1200-1700. On Friday there is a Fleamarket on Kerkplein from 0900-1700 and an Arts Market on the last Saturday of the month in Jannsplein from 1000-1700.

3. Oosterbeek in the district of Renkum, although the centre of the bitter fighting of 'The Cauldron' in September 1944, still retains an air of gentility with many fine houses restored to their former pre-WW2 glory. It is surrounded by lovely woods and heathland.
Some hotel choices:
**** Bilderberg Wolfheze. Lovely setting. Swimming pool, mini golf. On site of Krafft's 1944 HQ.
Tel: + (0) 26 3337852
**** Golden Tulip Rijnhotel. Superb situation overlooking the Rhine. Tel: + (0) 26 4434642
**** Hotel Haarhuis. Near Arnhem Central Railway Station. Fitness room, sauna. Tel: + (0) 26 4427441.
Papendal National Sports Centre. 3 hotels with 3 restaurants adjoining the well-equipped sports centre. Tel: + (0) 26 4837911
Hotel Dreyerood (qv), Oosterbeek. The September 1944 'White House'. Family run, welcoming, full of battle memorabilia. Tel: + (0) 26 3343169
Other hotels in the area appear in-text in Itinerary Five.
Contact the VVVs at Arnhem + (0) 26 4426767 and Oosterbeek + (0) 26 3338467 for more choices, Camping Sites and Hostels.

Golf Courses
Arnhem Rosendaelse Golfclub, Apeldoornseweg 450. Tel: + (0) 26 4421438
Est Golfbaan Welderen, Grote Molenstraat 173,. Tel: + (0) 48 1376591
Golf Baan Het Rijk van Nijmegen, Postweg 17, 6561 KJ Groesbeek, Tel: + (0) 24 3976644.

Restaurants/More Hotels. As described above, there is a wealth of variety available. Dutch portions are very generous and breakfast and lunch menus depend very largely on a delicious range of bread and rolls, eggs and ham or bacon. Substantial pancakes (the Dutch equivalent of the pizza as they come with up to forty different toppings) make a convenient lunch. Several Pannekoeken Houses are described as they occur en route. Chinese, Indonesian and Indian restaurants are highly popular and in traditional Dutch restaurants the range of fresh vegetables and salad garnishes is quite astounding as typified in the Van der Valk hotel restaurants. North American visitors may be reassured by the familiar golden arches which rear up in or near most towns of any size.
The good value Van der Valk hotels are in several convenient situations along the 5 Itineraries, e.g.
Motel Eindhoven, Aalsterweg 322. Recreation Centre. Tel: + (0) 40 2116033
Hotel Vught, Bosscheweg 2, Vught. Swimming pool. Tel: + (0) 73 6587777
Motel de Molenhoek, Rijksweg 1, Mook. Tel: + (0) 24 3582175
Hotel Cuijk, Raamweg 10, Cuijk. Tel: + (0) 485 335124
Hotel West-End, Amsterdamseweg 505, Arnhem. Tel: + (0) 26 4821614.
There are also several around Ghent and Beveren on the Approach Route in Belgium.
Head Office enquiries: + (0) 76 5221240.

River Cruises.
A novel way to view the MARKET-GARDEN battlefields is from a boat on the Waal or the Lower Rhine.
Waal. Stoomboot Brandaris-Rederij Tonissen. Boat trips from the Waalkade,
Nijmegen, opposite the Holland Casino in the summer months. Tel: + (0) 24 3233285.
Lower Rhine. Rederij Eureka. Trips from Arnhem. Tel: + (0) 57 0615914.

ACKNOWLEDGEMENTS AND SOURCES

Our thanks go, once again, to that most praiseworthy of organisations, the **Commonwealth War Graves Commission.** At their Head Office in Maidenhead, David Parker, Peter Francis, Derek Butler, Shirley Hitchcock and Maureen Annetts in our researches for this book. Thanks, too, go to the staff at the Parachute Regiment and Airborne Forces Museum at Browning Barracks, **Aldershot** – the energetic Director, Mrs Belinda Brinton, and her staff, especially Alan Brown and Tina Pittock; to the Curator, Captain (Retd) P.H. Starling and his staff at the superb R.A.M.C. Historical Museum at Keogh Barracks, Aldershot, and to Colonel John Richardson, Defence Medical Services Professor of General Practice for his introduction. To Lord Carrington for permission to quote from his letter to us; to Colonel Robert Kershaw (author of *It Never Snows in September*); to Alan Hartley of the RAF Down Ampney Association for providing us with much information about the abortive 'Lonsdale Force' stained glass window; Captain Vivian Taylor MC, Adjutant of the Irish Guards at Joe's Bridge, for information about his Regiment; Cecil Newton, Secretary of the 'Creully Club' (qv) for information about the 4th/7th RDG memorials; Johnny Peters for information about the Arnhem 1944 Veterans' Club; Joe Roberts (author of *With Spanners Descending*, the story of REME with the Airborne 1942-45) for details of the Lest We Forget Foundation; Graham Day of the Air Historical Branch, RAF for details of 83 Group Air Support; Niall Cherry, author *Red Berets and Red Crosses*; Sam Holt, our hysterical researcher, for dedicated and rewarding work at the PRO.

In the Netherlands our old friends Jetse Bos, Promotions Manager of the **Gelderland and Overijssel** Tourist Board, and Wilm van Vliet, ex-proprietor of the excellent Erica Hotel in **Berg en Dal**, have been as helpful as ever. At the principal museums and historical centres at **Oosterbeek and Groesbeek**, the support has been outstanding. At the former, the fount of so much knowledge, the delightful Anglophile, Drs Adrian Groeneweg, OBE, Vice-Chairman of the Board of Trustees of the Hartenstein Airborne Museum, has been extraordinarily generous with his time, advice and practical assistance and the Director, W. Boersma, has been whole-hearted in his support. Our friend for many years, the dedicated and knowledgeable Curator Berry de Reus, with his boyhood friend, Drs Robert Voskuil - owner of a unique collection of Arnhem documentation and information gained at first hand from his parents – have been as helpful as they were when we wrote our first small book on MARKET-GARDEN nearly 20 years ago. At the newly-enlarged National Liberation Museum at **Groesbeek**, the Director, Drs W. P.H. Lenders, was equally supportive and gave us into the enthusiastic hands of their historian, the 'Para manqué' Frank van den Bergh, who has shared his encyclopaedic knowledge and time with us, and the inimitable Father Thuring, whose publications we acknowledge throughout the book. Henk Duinhoven, MBE, of **Bemmel** has been more than generous with his time and information.

Frans Ammerlaan, amateur historian from **Elden** and colleague of researcher Andries Hoekstra, who has created a unique, extraordinarily detailed and constantly up-dated **website on MARKET-GARDEN** www.marketgarden.com has provided us with many offers of help, useful maps, information and contacts, accompanied us on many exciting expeditions and put in long hours of persistent investigation on our behalf. During the last twelve months he and his family have become good friends indeed.

In **Eindhoven**, we thank Corine de Hart, Marketing Director of the of the VVV, Rosemary van Mierlo, Front Office Manager, Ilse de Groot and Mr. Michel Besnard, Chairman of the 18 September Festival Foundation, and H. Reijnen, Secretary of the Light Tour and Dr J. M. W. Paulussen, Philips' company Archivist, We are grateful to Dr Stephen Temming, Managing Director of the Dutch National War Resistance Museum at **Overloon**; Dr Jeroen van den Eijnde of the National Monument, Kamp **Vught**. In **Best** our thanks go to the extraordinarily energetic and enthusiastic Chairman of the Bevrijdende Museum, Jan Driessen; in **Hoogeloon** to Mr G. H. Fonteyn for information about the Hei-end Memorial; in **Son** to R. J. van den Hoef for literature about the town in 1944 and to the faithful Van Overveld family at the Paulushoeve – Liza who remembers with clarity September 1944, her brother, Wan, who built the parachute memorial in his garden, and her niece, Clara, who keeps remembrance alive. In **Uden** our gratitude goes to Mr M. M. Verstegen who has voluntarily, for more than half a century, given unstinted assistance to pilgrims to the CWGC Cemetery and made a unique record of the men who lie in it. In **Zetten** we pay tribute to the dedicated couple, Geurt and Coby de Hartog, who both lived through the battles as children and who have made it their lives' work to research the campaign and do their utmost to help veterans and relatives trace graves and sites of actions

In **Leopoldsburg**, Belgium, following help from the Belgian Defence Attaché in London, Captain A. Kockx, we had tremendous support from Colonel Cuylets, Commandant of Camp Beverlo, and his knowledgeable and helpful PR Officer, Bob Vranken, who has provided us with some unique information and diligent research.

In **the USA** Alan Denman Jr has been an indefatigable and determined self-appointed researcher, travelling miles and writing reams of letters to provide us with many rare personal accounts and fascinating information, as well as direct contact with many official sources, such as the US Army Military History Institute. T. Mofatt Burriss, author of *Strike and Hold, a Memoir of the 82d Airborne in WW2*, a veteran of the Waal Crossing, has given us permission to quote from his extraordinary book.

Uniquely in the writing of this series of *Major & Mrs Holt's Battlefield Guides* we have received an enormous amount of help from previous publications that describe some of the local memorials. Their authors have been most generous in allowing us to use their works as a reference and in providing us with additional information and photographs. They are:

1. *Ter Nagedachtenis en Ter Bezinning* [Remember and Reflect]: War and Resistance Monuments in Nijmegen and Environs by Margreet Janssen Reinen. This was first published in 1989 and was presented to veterans and pilgrims on the 45th Anniversary of Nijmegen's Liberation and up-dated in 1994.

2. *In Het Spoor van MARKET GARDEN*: Monuments and Memorials in Noord Brabant by Jacq van Eekelen and Jos Korsten of The MARKET-GARDEN Committee of Den Dungen (qv). Published 1998. Jacq and Jos have spared no effort in giving us information and providing us with illustrations and hospitality.

3. *Sta Eens Even Stil Ter Nagedachtenis En Ter Bezinning* [Stay Awhile and Ponder on Those Deeds Which Here Befell]: War and Freedom Monuments in the Over-Betuwe [The Island] by Dr Jan Brouwer. Published in 1990, this was produced for local schoolchildren. Dr Brouwer, a distinguished author and Alderman of the new Municipality of Overbetuwe, has put in some formidable research on our behalf, particularly with regard to the 'Sand Road', and provided us with the illustrations from his book.

Our thanks go to all others who contributed to our first Holts' Battlefield Guide: MARKET-GARDEN CORRIDOR and whose memories we have quoted from, e.g: Peter Robinson, Bill Croft, General Tony Jones, General John Frost.

And finally, as always, our thanks to our editor, Tom Hartman, for his wisdom and his entertainment, to Leo Cooper for starting it all, and to our resourceful book designer, Paul Wilkinson.

Frans Ammerlaan, with
a bottle of fund-raising
'Airborne beer'

INDEX

FORCES

These are listed in descending order of size, i.e. Armies, Corps, Divisions, Brigades, Regiments... then numerically and then alphabetically. Many more units are mentioned in the Cemetery descriptions throughout the book.

GENERAL INDEX

MEMORIALS

In addition to those listed below, many streets, roads and squares are named as memorials to individuals and units who took part in the Operation. Most Dutch memorials are listed by town/village

MUSEUMS

WAR CEMETERIES/GRAVES/MEMORIALS